# A DICTIONARY OF ULSTER PLACE-NAMES

*Do Cholette agus Dheirbhile*

**The Place-Names of Northern Ireland series**

**Vol 1, Co Down I: Newry and South-West Down**
Gregory Toner and Mícheál B Ó Mainnín

**Vol 2, Co Down II: The Ards**
AJ Hughes and RJ Hannan

**Vol 3, Co Down III: The Mournes**
Mícheál B Ó Mainnín

**Vol 4, Co Antrim I: The Baronies of Toome**
Patrick McKay

**Vol 5, Co Derry I: The Moyola Valley**
Gregory Toner

**Vol 6, Co Down IV: North-West Down/Iveagh**
Kay Muhr

**Vol 7, Co Antrim II: Ballycastle and North-East Antrim**
Fiachra MacGabhann

The price for each volume is £8.50 paperback (sterling), £20.00 hardback (sterling).

The authors are members or former members of the Northern Ireland Place-Name Project at The Queen's University of Belfast, c/o Celtic Studies, School of Modern Languages, 7 University Square, Belfast BT7 1NN. E-mail: townlands@qub.ac.uk

# A DICTIONARY OF ULSTER PLACE-NAMES

Patrick McKay

The Institute of Irish Studies
The Queen's University of Belfast

First published in 1999
The Institute of Irish Studies
The Queen's University of Belfast

This book has received support from the Cultural Diversity Programme of the Community Relations Council, which aims to encourage acceptance and understanding of cultural diversity. The views expressed do not necessarily reflect those of the NI Community Relations Council.





British Library Cataloguing-In-Publication Data.
A catalogue record for this book is available from the British Library.

ISBN 0 85389 742 5

Set in Times
Printed by W. & G. Baird, Ltd, Antrim

*Front cover*: Mixed media collage by Anne M. Anderson

# CONTENTS

# ACKNOWLEDGEMENTS

I wish to express my sincere gratitude to the following individuals and organisations:

The Cultural Traditions Group (now the Cultural Diversity Programme) of the Community Relations Council who awarded me the Deirdre Flanagan Fellowship in Irish Place-Names; *Iontaobhas Ultach* (The Ultach Trust) who contributed to the funding of the research; my extremely helpful supervisor, Aodán Mac Póilín of *Iontaobhas Ultach*; Dr Nollaig Ó Muraíle, Senior Lecturer in Celtic Studies, The Queen's University of Belfast and Dr Kay Muhr of the Northern Ireland Place-Name Project, The Queen's University of Belfast, both of whom provided invaluable specialised knowledge as well as unflagging guidance and advice; Dónall Mac Giolla Easpaig, Chief Place-Names Officer of the Place-Names Branch of the Ordnance Survey of Ireland, Phoenix Park, Dublin who allowed me to have access to the archives of the Survey and who generously contributed specialised knowledge and advice. Pádraig Ó Cearbhaill and the other Dublin place-names officers who were extremely helpful and supportive; the staff and research fellows of the Institute of Irish Studies, The Queen's University of Belfast, with whom I had many stimulating discussions. As regards publication, a special word of appreciation to Margaret McNulty not only for her matchless expertise and efficiency but also for her enthusiasm for the subject matter of the book. Thanks are also due to Margaret's excellent colleague, Catherine McColgan, to Cormac Bourke of the Ulster Museum and to Jim Blaney.


# ILLUSTRATIONS

The line drawings and lino cuts on pages 3, 43, 46, 47, 54, 55, 76, 78, 83, 92, 102, 120, 129, 142 and 143 are by Anne E. Anderson; the line drawings on pages 5, 67, 133 and 144 are by EE Evans and are reproduced by kind permission of Mrs Gwyneth Evans; the line drawings on pages 18, 21 (lower), 24, 30, 34, 37, 53, 72, 94, 103, 117 and 147 by Lawson Burch were first published in *Discover Northern Ireland* by Ernest Sandford, (Belfast, 1976) and are reproduced courtesy of the Northern Ireland Tourist Board; the line drawings on pages 6, 12, 19, 21 (upper), 27, 28, 56, 65 and 80 are reproduced by permission of the Environment and Heritage Service (DOENI); and the line drawings on pages 35, 58, 86 and 109 are from *Irish Castles* by Harold Leask, (Dundalk, 1986) and are reproduced by permission of the Dundalgan Press (W. Tempest Ltd). The maps are from the following sources; the 17th century county maps on pages 39 and 99 are from *A geographical description of the Kingdom of Ireland …*, 1689 by Lamb after Petty; the Escheated Counties maps pages 7 and 118 (PRONI T1652/ 30/A (Armagh) and T1652/15 (Omagh) are reproduced by kind permission of the Deputy Keeper of the Public Record Office of Northern Ireland; the drawing on page 66 is from *Speed's Ulster*, by John Speed, 1610; and the map on page 131 is from *Hibernia from State Papers of Henry VIII, 1567*, John Gough.

# INTRODUCTION

This book has been written to remedy a long-standing need for a reliable and up-to-date dictionary of Ulster place-names which, as well as supplying the derivations and meanings of the names, will also provide the kind of background information which it is felt will be of interest to the general reader and to the serious scholar alike.

Ulster has a rich and diverse cultural heritage and nowhere is this more apparent than in the place-names which are so much part-and-parcel of our everyday lives. For instance, a resident of Belfast will find within a small radius of his home place-names which have their origin in Irish (Belfast itself, Shankill, Falls), Scots (Sandy Knowes), English (Fortwilliam, Black Mountain), Old French (Belvoir), Old Norse (Copeland Islands), as well as a number of names which show Norman influence (Gransha, Jordanstown) and some imported place-names of various linguistic origins, including Sydenham and Mossley (Old English) and Balmoral which is a combination of Scottish Gaelic and Brittonic. The dictionary reflects the diversity of Ulster's cultural heritage and the place-names are dealt with without prejudice to their linguistic origins.

The area covered is the nine counties of Ulster. Of course, in a work of this kind it is impossible to include all the place-names and a fairly rigorous selection procedure has had to be adopted. For the most part the names chosen are those which appear in the *Gasaitéar na hÉireann / Gazetteer of Ireland* (Dublin, 1989). The reason for choosing the *Gazetteer* list is that it includes all places (irrespective of linguistic origin) which have a post-office and are therefore of some importance in the life of the community, though the settlements themselves are sometimes small. The *Gazetteer* also includes the names of prominent physical features such as mountains, rivers and headlands.

A number of place-names which are not in the *Gazetteer* are included in the dictionary. Some of these were chosen because they appear on the Ordnance Survey *Éire Thuaidh / Ireland North* map of 1988 which is to a large extent based on the *Gazetteer* but includes a small number of additional names. Other place-names were included because, although they may not be particularly well-known, they were deemed to be of some interest or significance. In terms of status the places included in the dictionary therefore cover a very wide range. At one end of the scale a place may be simply a townland or hill, at the other end a city or diocese or high mountain.

Ultimately, any choice of lesser-known place-names must involve a certain element of subjectivity and the author can only apologise to those who are disappointed if the name of their own beloved place does not appear!

**The Northern-Ireland Place-Name Project Database**

In 1987 the Northern Ireland Place-Name Project was set up with the aim of researching the origin of all the place-names appearing on the Ordnance Survey 1:50,000 (*Discoverer Series*) maps. This involved the establishment of a database of the historical forms of the place-names, work on which is ongoing and is now nearing completion. In 1990 the remit of the Project was widened to include the names of all the townlands of Northern Ireland and a programme of publication was embarked upon which has so far produced seven volumes in the *Place-Names of Northern Ireland* series (see list on p ii).

In this dictionary the *Northern Ireland Place-Name Project* database is the source of many of the historical spellings which accompany the Northern Ireland entries, while the author has added more in the course of his research. For place-names in the Republic of Ireland, the author is indebted to the Chief Place-Names Officer of the Ordnance Survey of Ireland for permission to use the extensive archive of historical forms (see *Acknowledgements*).

# HOW TO USE THIS BOOK

The layout of a typical entry:

| | | *status* | *county* | *grid reference* |
|---|---|---|---|---|
| *headword(s)* | **Bellanamallard** | tl, vill., | Fermanagh | 2235 |
| *variant spelling* | (usually *Ballinamallard*) | | | |
| *location* | *9km NNE of Enniskillen* | | | |
| *parish and barony* | par: *Magheracross* bar: *Tirkennedy* | | | |
| *derivation and pronunciation guide* | Ir. *Béal Átha na Mallacht* [bell aha na **mal**aght] | | | |
| *meaning* | 'ford-mouth of the curses'. | | | |
| *discussion* | According to a legend, St Columcille placed a curse on the roosters here in the sixth century. | | | |
| *earlier spelling and date*: | [*Béal Átha na Mallacht* 1645]. | | | |

**Notes**

The spellings of the headwords are as they appear in the *General Alphabetical Index to the Census of Ireland, 1851* and, in the case of minor place-names, on the Ordnance Survey 1:50,000 *(Discoverer Series)* maps. In some cases, an alternative spelling is in common use and this is given in italics below the official spelling, e.g. **Bellanamallard**, the example shown above, is commonly spelt *Ballinamallard.* The headwords are arranged in alphabetical order, which is strictly adhered to whether the place-name is made up of one word or two or more, e.g. **Castlecaulfield** appears before **Castle Coole, Glentogher** before **Glen Ullin**.

The status of the place is defined in terms of whether it is a townland, village, town or parish or, in the case of natural features, a mountain, river, etc. Quite frequently, the headword will belong to more than one category, e.g. Connor in Co. Antrim is at the same time a townland, a village, a parish and a diocese. The distinction between a hamlet and a village and also between a village and a town is sometimes a fine one and the author can only hope that not too many people will be offended by having their place of residence wrongly assigned to one category or the other!

In some cases the headword refers to two townlands, usually adjacent and often distinguished by the qualifiers NORTH and SOUTH, UPPER and LOWER or EAST and WEST, e.g. the townlands of Carnlough North and South in Co. Antrim, Ballysillan Upper and Lower in Belfast, Belcoo East and West in Fermanagh. In these cases, the status of the place referred to is 'townlands' rather than 'townland'. This approach also applies to a small number of towns or villages where the headword covers two or more parishes or baronies, e.g. the status of Moville in Co. Donegal is defined as 'parishes' rather than 'parish', referring to the parishes of Moville Upper and Lower, the status of Omagh in Co. Tyrone is defined as 'baronies' rather than 'barony', referring to the baronies of Omagh East and West.

The name of the county in which the place is situated is followed by the Irish Grid reference as found on the Ordnance Survey 1:250,000 maps such as *Éire Thuaidh/Ireland North.*

The location of each place is normally defined by distance in kilometres from the nearest substantial settlement. The distance is as the crow flies and to the nearest half kilometre and the intention is to provide a good rough guide as to the location rather than an accurate measurement by road.

Each place-name is assigned to its appropriate civil parish and barony. Civil parishes were chosen because, for the most part, they more accurately reflect the original medieval parishes than do either the modern Catholic or Church of Ireland parishes.

In the case of a place-name which is of Irish-language origin, the derivation is followed in square brackets by a rough guide to its pronunciation in Irish, notes on the use of which are provided on p xii. In cases where the linguistic origin of a place-name is in doubt, the line is prefixed by the word *perhaps*. In cases where the derivation of a place-name is clear but there is doubt about its meaning, the word *perhaps* is included before any tentatively proposed meaning.

In the short discussion of the origin of each place-name, names which appear as headwords elsewhere in the book are given in bold type for the purpose of cross-reference. Other place-names which occur in the text normally appear in small capitals. In the case of a parish name, the discussion will as far as possible give the location of the medieval parish church. This, of course, is not possible if the parish is a later creation and the fact that it does not date back to the medieval period is noted.

Where possible each place-name is provided with a dated earlier spelling in square brackets at the end of the entry. The spelling chosen will usually be among the earliest recorded and in many cases will throw light on the derivation of the place-name as well as giving a rough indication of its age.

**A note on dates with AM suffixes**

A small number of dates carry the suffix AM which stands for *Anno Mundi* or 'in the year of the world'. These accompany some early spellings of place-names extracted from the *Annals of the Four Masters* and they represent a system of measuring time in the period from the creation of the world to the birth of Christ. A very rough method of converting AM dates to conventional BC dates is to subtract the AM date from 5200 though it cannot be emphasised too strongly that dates in this period can by no means be regarded as reliable and the events referred to are often legendary or semi-legendary in nature.

# ABBREVIATIONS

| | | | |
|---|---|---|---|
| A.F. | Anglo-French | M.E. | Medieval English |
| AM *Anno Mundi* | 'in the year of the world' (see note on p x) | Mod. Ir. | Modern Irish |
| anc. mon. | ancient monument | MP | Member of Parliament |
| bar(s) | barony/baronies | mtn | mountain |
| ch. | church | N | North |
| c. *circa* | 'about' | N.E. | Northern English |
| cf. | compare | N.F. | Norman French |
| co. | county | O.E. | Old English |
| dioc. | diocese | O.F. | Old French |
| distr. | district | O.Ir. | Old Irish |
| dmsne | demesne | O.N. | Old Norse |
| E | east | par(s) | parish(es) |
| E. | English | pen. | peninsula |
| F. | French | prom. | promontory |
| gen. | genitive | RC par. | Roman Catholic parish |
| ham. | hamlet | S | South |
| H.E. | Hiberno English | Sc. | Scottish |
| h.est. | housing estate | Sc.G. | Scottish Gaelic |
| hist. mon. | historic monument | SS | Saints |
| hl | headland | Stand. Ir. | Standard Irish |
| Ir. | Irish | tl | townland |
| inl. | inlet | tls | townlands |
| isld | island | tn | town |
| km | kilometres | U.E. | Ulster English |
| L. | Latin | var. | variant |
| m | metres | vill. | village |
| | | W | West |
| | | W. | Welsh |

# NOTES ON THE PRONUNCIATION GUIDES

A rough guide to pronunciation appears in square brackets after Irish language derivations. In most cases the reader may simply read the guide as if it were in English. However, a number of sounds call for special comment:

**au** as in *cow, plough*
**ch** as in *chip, church*
**ġ** does not occur in English. In Irish it can be written as initial *Dh-* or *Gh-* and occurs in names like *Baile Uí Dhálaigh* 'Ballygawley' or *Ard Ghlas* 'Ardglass'. To approximate this sound try gargling without water. If you cannot manage the sound just pronounce it like *g* in *go*
**fy** as in *fuse, fury*
**hy** as in *Hugh, Hugenot*
**kh** represents initial *ch* in Irish, as occurs in e.g. *Baile* ***Ch****óplainn* 'Ballycopeland'. It is sounded the same as final *-gh* in *lough*
**ky** as in *cure, McKeown*
**ny** as in *new, neutral*

Stressed syllables are shown in bold type, e.g. *Ard Mhacha* [ard **wagh**a] (Armagh); *Clochar* [**clogh**er] (Clogher); *Béal Átha Seanaidh* [bell aha **shan**ee] (Ballyshannon).

# GLOSSARY OF TECHNICAL TERMS

In this dictionary every effort has been made to avoid the use of technical terms. However, the inclusion of the following terms could not be avoided:

**ballybetagh** Ir. *baile biataigh* 'land of a food-provider'. A native land-unit, the holder of which had a duty to maintain his lord and retinue when travelling in the area.

**bawn** Ir. bábhún. A fortified enclosure, usually around or in front of a tower-house, sometimes used loosely for the house itself.

**booley** Ir. *buaile*. A cattle-enclosure, often in an upland pasture and connected with the practice of *booleying*, i.e. the practice of moving cattle to higher grazings during the summer months.

**crannog** Ir. *crannóg* 'wooden structure'. An artificial lake-island on which a house was constructed.

**cromlech**
**dolmen** now almost-obsolete terms for a megalithic burial chamber formed of a horizontal capstone supported on two or more upright stones.

**erenagh** Ir. *airchinneach* 'stewart'. A hereditary officer in charge of church lands, later a tenant to the bishop.

**glebe** (the house) and land (and its revenue) provided for the clergyman of a parish.

**motte** a steep, flat-topped mound, forming the main feature of a late 12th or 13th-century (usually Anglo-Norman) earthwork castle, and often associated with a bailey which was the courtyard attached to the motte.

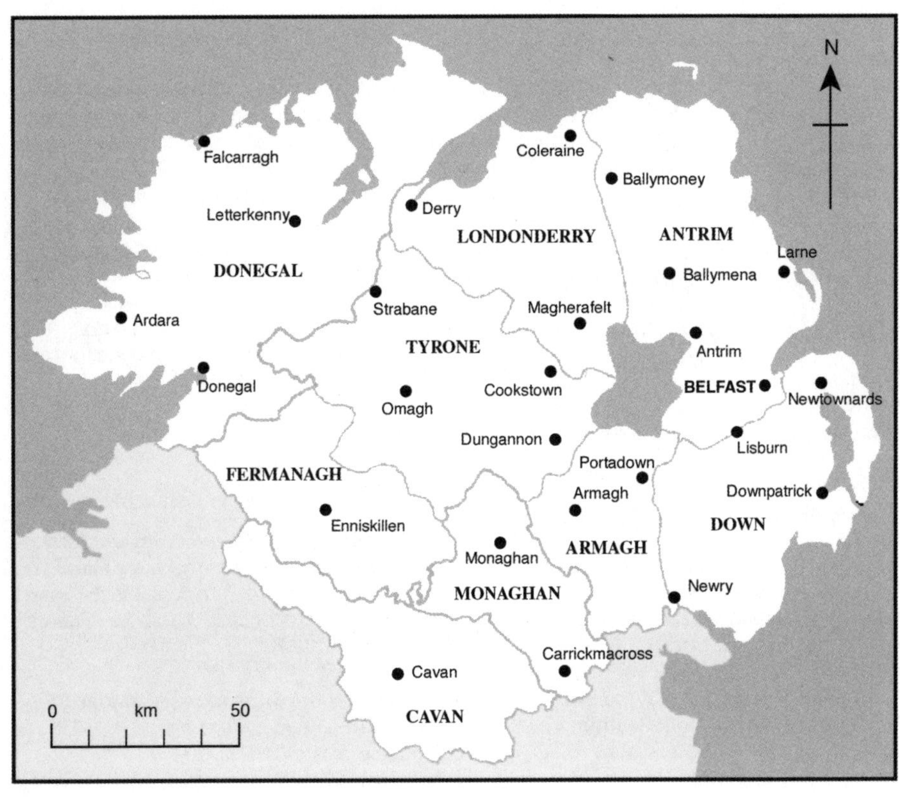


*Map of Ulster*

# A

**Acton** tl, vill., Armagh 3034
*Close to Co. Down border, 5.5km SSE of Tandragee*
par: *Ballymore* bar: *Orior Lower*
In 1600 Lieutenant Charles Poyntz who successfully defended the pass of **Poyntz Pass** against Hugh O'Neill Earl of Tyrone (*see below*) was granted land here on which he built a house and *bawn* and it was around this residence that the village of Acton grew up. It was named from Lieutenant Poyntz's native village of IRON ACTON (O.E. *Actun* 'oak-tree farmstead') in Gloucestershire. The old name for the townland of Acton was *Curryotragh* which appears to derive from Ir. *An Chora Uachtarach* 'the upper weir' and may have referred to a weir or rocky ford on a nearby river, the course of which is marked by the now-disused NEWRY CANAL. ACTON GLEBE and ACTON HOUSE are in the neighbouring townland of BRANNOCK [(*the manor of*) *Acton* 1619].

**Agangarrive Hill** Antrim 3143
*8.5km WNW of Cushendall*
par: *Culfeighrin* bar: *Cary*
Ir. *Aigeán Garbh* [agan **gar**oo] 'rough hill' + E. *hill*. This is the name of a prominent summit (376m) to the west of **Glendun**. The first element appears to be a variant of *aigéan* 'ocean, abyss' or, simply, 'hollow' but it could clearly also apply to hills. The E. element *hill* has been added at a later stage.

**Aganlane** tl, Antrim 3142
(*see* ***Parkmore or Aganlane***)

**Aghabog** tl, par., Monaghan 2532
*Townland is 3km E of New Bliss*
bar: *Dartree*
Ir. *Achadh Bog* [aghoo **bog**] 'soft field'. There is now no trace of the original parish church or graveyard [*Aghabog* 1665].

**Aghacommon** tl, ham., Armagh 3935
*3km W of Lurgan*
par: *Seagoe* bar: *Oneilland East*
Ir. *Achadh Camán* [aghoo **cam**an] 'field of the little bends' [*Aghcamon* 1617].

**Aghadowey** tl, vill., par., Derry 2842
*Village is 11km S of Coleraine*
bar: *Coleraine*
Ir. *Achadh Dubhthaigh* [aghoo **doo**ee] '*Dubhthach*'s field'.
*Dubhthach* (Stand. Ir. *Dufach*), which derives from *dubh* 'black', was a common forename in early Ireland and from it is formed the modern surname *Ó Dufaigh* '(O')Duffy'. The present Church of Ireland church in the village appears to occupy the site of an early monastery and also of the medieval parish church. The name of the patron saint of the parish, i.e. *Guaire* is commemorated in SEYGORRY (Ir. *Suí Guaire* '*Guaire*'s seat'), the name of a townland 1km to the south-west [*Achad Dubthaig* c.1170].

**Aghafatten** tl, ham., Antrim 3241
(often *Aughafatten*)
*12km NW of Ballymena*
par: *Skerry* bar: *Antrim Lower*
*perhaps* Ir. *Achadh Pheatáin* [aghoo **fat**ine] '*Peatán*'s field'. The personal name *Peatán* is a diminutive form of Patrick and is the basis of the Donegal surname *Ó Peatáin* 'Patton' [*Aghafatten* 1780].

**Aghagallon** tl, vill., distr., par., Antrim 3136
(sometimes *Aughagallon*)
*Village is 5.5km NNE of Lurgan*
bar: *Massereene Upper*
Ir. *Achadh Gallán* [aghoo **gal**an]. The Mod. Ir. form of the place-name means 'field of (standing) stones'. However, it appears to be a development from an earlier form *Eanach Gallánach* 'marsh/moor of (standing) stones'. There are no standing-stones in the area but 'a large ancient cairn of stones' is recorded in the townland in 1835. There are remains of an ancient church in a circular graveyard in the north of the townland. The village of Aghagallon is partly in the neighbouring townland of DERRYNASEER [(*Capella de*) *Enacha* c.1306].

**Aghalane** tl, ham., Fermanagh 2331
*On border with Cavan, 5km SW of Newtownbutler*
par: *Kinawley* bar: *Knockninny*
Ir. *Achadh Leathan* [aghoo **la**han] 'broad field' [*Aghalane* 1622].

**Aghalee** tl, vill., par., Antrim 3136
*Village is 7.5km NNE of Lurgan*
bar: *Massereene Upper*
Ir. *Achadh Lí* [aghoo **lee**]. The first element of the place-name is Ir. *achadh* 'field', but the meaning of the final element is obscure. The ruins of the medieval parish church are in a graveyard a short distance north-east of the village [*Acheli* 1306].

**Aghalurcher** ch., par., Fermanagh 2333
*Church ruins are 2km S of Lisnaskea*
bar: *Magherastephana*
Ir. *Achadh Urchair* [aghoo **urr**igher] 'field of the shot or cast'. The ruins of the former parish church of Aghalurcher are in the townland of AGHALURCHER GLEBE. A local tradition explains the final element of the place-name by the common motif of the casting of a stone to decide where to build the church [*Achadh Urchair* 1258].

**Aghanloo** ham., par., Derry 2642
*Hamlet is 4km N of Limavady*
bar: *Keenaght*
Ir. *Áth Lú* [ah **loo**] '*Lú*'s ford'. *Lú* (earlier *Lug*) is the name of a Celtic god (usually described as *Lú Lámhfhada* '*Lú* of the long arm') and is also an early Irish personal name. The hamlet of Aghanloo is in the townland of BALLYCASTLE while the remains of the former parish church are 1km to the north in the townland of RATHFAD near the present Church of Ireland parish church [*Athlouge* 1397].

**Aghintain** tl, Tyrone 2435
(often *Aughintain*)
*4km W of Clogher*
par/bar, *Clogher*
Ir. *Achadh an tSéin* [aghoo an **chey**in] 'field of the good luck/prosperity' [*Aghityan* 1613].

**Aghla** mtn, Donegal 1839
*450m high, 7km NE of Glenties*
par: *Inishkeel* bar: *Boylagh*
Ir: *An Eachla* [an **agh**la]. The modern form of the place-name suggests that it derives from Ir. *each* [agh] 'horse'. However, it appears to be a reinterpretation of the original name *Achla*, a form of *Aichill* which seems to mean 'look-out point/prospect' and is found (in the variant form *Acaill*) in the name of ACHILL ISLAND in Co. Mayo.

**Aghla More** mtn, Donegal 1942
*7.5km SE of Gortahork*
par: *Tullaghobegly* bar: *Kilmacrenan*
Ir. *An Eachla Mhór* [an aghla **wore**] 'great Aghla'. As in the case of the previous entry, *Eachla* appears to be a reinterpretation of *Achla* 'lookout point/prospect'. Aghla More (584m) stands to the north-east of **Errigal** and slopes down to the shores of **Lough Altan**. AGHLA BEG (564m) stands a short distance farther to the north-east.

**Aghnamullen** tl, vill., par., Monaghan 2631
(often *Aughnamullen*)
*Village is 7.5km ENE of Cootehill*
bar: *Cremorne*
Ir. *Achadh na Muileann* [aghoo na **mwill**an] 'field of the mills'. The site of a corn mill is marked by MILL POND a short distance north of the village. The parish of Aghnamullen was created in 1530 out of the now obsolete parish of Cremorne. 11km ESE, in the townland of LATTONFASKY, the ruins of a Franciscan friary (known as TEMPLEMOYLE CHURCH) stand on the north shore of LOUGH EGISH [*Aughamullen* 1530].

**Aghory** tl, ham., Armagh 2934
(often *Ahorey*)
*8km SSW of Portadown*
par: *Kilmore* bar: *Oneilland West*
Ir. *Áth Oirir* [ah **urr**ir] 'ford of the boundary'. The ford in question appears to have been over the BALLYBAY RIVER which borders the townland on the east. Aghory marks the southern boundary of the the parish of KILMORE and also the boundary between the baronies of ONEILLAND WEST and ORIOR LOWER [*Aghoorier* 1610].

**Aghyaran** tl, Tyrone 2138
*9km SW of Castlederg*
par: *Termonamongan* bar:*Omagh West*
Ir. *Achadh Uí Áráin* [aghoo ee **aar**ine] '(O')Haran's field'. The surname *Ó hÁráin* '(O')Haran/(O')Haren' is normally associated with Co. Fermanagh [*Aghagaran* 1666].

**Agivey** ham., par., Derry 2842
*Hamlet is 10.5km SSE of Coleraine*
bar: *Coleraine*
Ir. *Áth Géibhe* [ah **gey**va] *perhaps* 'ford of the fetter'. The significance of the name may be something like 'ford of the impasse/difficult ford'. The ford appears to have been over the

AGIVEY RIVER which flows into the **Lower Bann** a short distance to the east. The last remnants of AGIVEY OLD CHURCH are in a graveyard in the townland of MULLAGHMORE, on the north bank of the AGIVEY RIVER, close to its intersection with the AGHADOWEY RIVER. Mullaghmore is adjoined on the south by the townland of LANDAGIVEY which derives from Ir. *Lann Átha Géibhe* 'the church of Agivey' [*Athgeybi* 1492].

**Agnew's Hill** Antrim 3340
*7.5km W of Larne*
par: *Kilwaughter* bar: *Glenarm Upper*
This is a prominent hill of 474m on the boundary between the townlands of OLD FREEHOLD and HIGHTOWN. The family of Agnew (Ir. *Ó Gnímh* [o **greeve**]) were formerly bardic poets to the O'Neill rulers of Clandeboy and are credited with building KILWAUGHTER CASTLE which is now in ruins.

**Ahoghill** vill., par., Antrim 3040
*Village is 6km WSW of Ballymena*
bar: *Toome Lower*
Ir. *Achadh Eochaille* [aghoo **awgh**ilya] 'field of the yew wood'. The village has portions in each of the four townlands of CARMACMOIN, LISMURNAGHAN, KILLANE and GLOONAN. The parish, a portion of which is in the barony of TOOME UPPER, formerly also included the neighbouring parishes of **Craigs** and **Portglenone** and was the largest parish in Co. Antrim. The site of the medieval parish church is marked by the modern Church of Ireland church in the townland of CARMACMOIN [*Achochill* 1306].

**Aldergrove** ham., Antrim 3137
*8km S of Antrim town*
par: *Killead* bar: *Massereene Lower*
In 1832 we find a reference to 'a place called Aldergrove' in the townland of BALLYQUILLIN. Aldergrove is well-known as the site of Belfast International Airport.

**Allistragh** tl, vill., Armagh 2834
*4km NNW of Armagh city*
par: *Grange* bar: *Armagh*
Ir. *An tAileastrach* [an **tal**istragh] 'the place of wild irises' [*Tallastagh* 1609].

**Altachullion** tls, Cavan 2132
*6km SW of Swanlinbar*
par: *Templeport* bar: *Tullyhaw*
Ir. *Allt an Chuilinn* [alt a **khull**in] 'glen of the holly'. Altachullion is named from a deep valley with plenty of holly-trees which forms the north boundary of the townland of ALTACHULLION LOWER, on the eastern edge of the **Cuilcagh Mountains** [*Altaughullen* 1795].

**Altahullion Hill** Derry 2641
*7.5km NW of Dungiven*
par: *Bovevagh* bar: *Keenaght*
Ir. *Allt an Chuilinn* [alt a **khull**in] 'glen of the holly' + E. *hill*. Altahullion Hill (276m) is in the townland of DRUM. ALTAHULLION BURN is a stream which rises on the south-east side of the hill and flows into the BOVEVAGH RIVER close to the ruins of the ancient parish church of **Bovevagh**.

**Altamooskan** tl, Tyrone 2536
(often *Altamuskin*)
*16km SE of Omagh*
par: *Errigal Keerogue* bar: *Clogher*
Ir. *Allt an Mhúscáin* [alt a **woos**kine] 'glen of the spongy ground' [*Altmuskan* 1611].

**Altan** tl, Donegal 1942
(*see **Lough Altan***)

**Altinure** tl, Cavan 2132
*5km SW of Swanlinbar*
par: *Templeport* bar: *Tullyhaw*
Ir. *Allt an Iúir* [alt an **yure**] 'glen of the yew tree'. The valley which gave name to the townland lies a short distance to the east of **Altachullion** [*Altanure* 1836].

**Altishahane** tl, ham., Tyrone 2439
*7km NNW of Plumbridge*
par: *Donaghedy* bar: *Strabane Lower*

*Allistragh, the place of wild irises*

Ir. *Allt Inse Uí Chatháin* [alt insha ee **kha**hine] 'glen of O'Kane's island'. The island in question appears to have been in a small lake known as WHITE LOUGH in the middle of the townland. The family of *Ó Catháin* 'O'Kane/ O'Cahan' originated in East Donegal but they spread across Ulster and became rulers of the barony of KENNAGHT with their headquarters at **Dungiven** [*Altonisechan* c.1655].

**Altmover Glen** glen 2641
*3.5km W of Dungiven*
par: *Bovevagh* bar: *Keenaght*
Ir. *Allt Mómhar* [alt **mo**war] 'pleasant glen' + E. *glen*. The E. element *glen*, which means the same as Ir. *allt*, has been added at a later date. Altmover Glen is the valley of the WOOD BURN which forms the south and east boundaries of the townland of BALLYHARIGAN.

**Altnahinch** tl, Antrim 3142
*16km ESE of Ballymoney*
par: *Loughguile* bar: *Kilconway*
Ir. *Allt na hUinse* [alt na **hinsh**a] 'glen of the ash tree'. Altnahinch has given name to the ALTNAHINCH BURN which flows into ALTNAHINCH DAM, a small lake which is traversed by the head waters of the river **Bush** and lies to the south-east of the village of **Loughguile**.

**Andersonstown** tn, Antrim 3337
*Now a suburb, 4km SW of Belfast city centre*
par: *Shankill* bar: *Belfast Upper*
Andersonstown in the townland of BALLYDOWNFINE is described in 1832 as 'a village consisting of eleven families'. The identity of the Anderson referred to in the place-name is unknown. However, he is likely to have been of Lowland Scots origin as are the majority of the Andersons of Ulster [*Anderson's Town Village* 1832].

**Annaclone** vill., par., Down 3134
*Village is 7km SE of Banbridge*
bar: *Iveagh Upper, Upper Half*
Ir. *Eanach Luain* [anagh **loo**in] 'marsh of the haunch-like hill'. The site of the former parish church of Annaclone is marked by a graveyard in the townland of ARDBRIN. The village of Annaclone is partly in the latter townland and partly in TULLINTANVALLY [*Enaghluan* 1422].

**Annacloy** tl, vill., Down 3434
*5km NW of Downpatrick*
par: *Inch* bar: *Lecale Lower*
Ir. *Áth na Cloiche* [ah na **cloy**ha] 'ford of the stone'. The ford was over the ANNACLOY RIVER on which the village stands, straddling the townlands of ANNACLOY and ROSSCONOR in the parish of KILMORE. Ir. *cloch* 'stone' can sometimes refer to a stone castle and in this case it could possibly refer to a castle which formerly stood in the townland of ANNACLOY but no trace of which now remains. The final portion of the ANNACLOY RIVER is known as the **Quoile** [*Annacloy* 1621].

**Annadorn** tl, vill., Down 3434
*5.5km W of Downpatrick*
par: *Loughinisland* bar: *Kinelarty*
Ir. *Áth na nDorn* [anagh **dorn**] 'ford of the fists'. There is some uncertainty as to the exact significance of the element *dorn* (literally 'fist') and there are several possible explanations. First, it may refer to a people who are referred to as *lucht na nDornand* 'people of the *Dornanns*' i.e. 'fist people'(?) in an early genealogy. From them are descended the family of *Ó Dornáin* '(O')Dornan', a surname which is peculiar to East Ulster. Second, in some parts of Co. Down the word *dorn* is applied to a rocky causeway or shallow stretch of water and in this case it could refer to such a feature in LOUGHINISLAND LAKE which is partly in this townland. Finally, it is possible that the word *dorn* is used metaphorically in the sense of 'boulder' and that it refers to the *dolmen* or prehistoric chambered grave which stands in the northern corner of the townland at BUCK'S HEAD CORNER, close to the shore of the lake. The ford referred to in the first element of the place-name may have been over the BLACKSTAFF RIVER, close to where it rises in the southern end of LOUGHINISLAND LAKE [*Annaghdorney* 1627].

**Annagary** tl, vill., Donegal 1741
(sometimes *Annagry*)
*On NW Donegal coast, 8km NNE of Dunglow*
par: *Templecrone* bar: *Boylagh*
Ir. *Anagaire* [**an**agara]. This may be a compound place-name with *doire* 'oak-wood' as its final element. However, the meaning of the first element is obscure [*Angory* 1641].

**Annaghmore** tl, Armagh 2935
*9.5km WNW of Portadown*
par: *Loughgall* bar: *Oneilland West*
Ir. *Eanach Mór* [anagh **more**] 'great marsh or bog'. There is a large area of bog in the vicinity [*Annaghmore* 1629].

**Annahilt** vill., par., Down 3235
*Village is 8km NW of Ballynahinch*
bar: *Iveagh Lower, Lower Half*
Ir. *Eanach Eilte* [anagh **eltch**a] 'marsh of the doe'. The village of Annahilt is in the townland of BALLYCRUNE. The ruined church in the graveyard in the townland of GLEBE a short distance to the north-east appears to mark the site of the ancient parish church [(*Molibae*) *Enaig Elti* c.830].

**Annalong** vill., Down 3331
*8.5km NE of Kilkeel*
par: *Kilkeel* bar: *Mourne*
Ir. *Áth na Long* [ah na **lung**] 'ford of the ships'. Annalong is an important fishing village situated at the mouth of the ANNALONG RIVER, partly in the townland of MONEYDORRAGH MORE and partly in MULLARTOWN [*Analong* c.1655].

**Annayalla** tl, ham., Monaghan 2732
(sometimes *Anyalla*)
*6km NW of Castleblayney*
par: *Clontibret* bar: *Cremorne*
Ir: *Eanaigh Gheala* [annee **yal**a] 'white marshes'. There is a marshy area in the west of the townland [*Anyalle* 1591].

**Annsborough** vill., Down 3333
*1.5km NE of Castlewellan*
par: *Kilmegan* bar: *Lecale Upper*
The name Annsborough has its origin in ANNSBOROUGH HOUSE in the townland of CLARKILL, a former residence of Mr James Murland who founded linen mills here in the early 19th century and appears to have named the house in honour of the Annesley family of nearby **Castlewellan**. The village is partly in the townland of BALLYBANNAN and partly in BALLYLOUGH [*Anne-borough* 1823].

**Antrim** tn, par., bars., co. 3138
*Town is 16.5km SSE of Ballymena*
bar: *Antrim Upper*
The original name of Antrim was Ir. *Aontreibh* [**ain** trev] 'single house/habitation', referring to an early monastery, the site of which is a little to the north of the modern town and is marked by a round tower locally known as THE STEEPLE. The name was later reinterpreted as *Aontroim* [**ain**trim] 'single ridge' and this is now the accepted Ir. form of the name. Antrim has given name to the county in which it is situated. The town of Antrim is mainly in the barony of ANTRIM UPPER which is bounded on the north by the barony of ANTRIM LOWER [(*Fiontan*) *Oentreibh* 612AD].

**Aran Island** isld, Donegal 1641
(*see **Arranmore***)

**Arboe** vill., distr., par., Tyrone 2937
(sometimes *Ardboe*)
*Village is on W shore of Lough Neagh, 15km E of Cookstown*
bar: *Dungannon Upper*
Ir. *Ard Bó* [ard **bo**] 'height of the cow(s)'. The site of a sixth-century monastery founded by St Colman is marked by a tenth-century high cross which stands on a small rise in the townland of SESSIA on the shore of **Lough Neagh** [(*Colman*) *Airdi Bó* c.830].

**Ardara** tl, tn, Donegal 1739
*8km WSW of Glenties*
par: *Killybegs Lower* bar: *Banagh*
Ir. *Ard an Rátha* [ard a **ra**ha] 'height of the fort'. The remains of the fort are on a low ridge to the east of the town, in the townland of ARDARA. Most of the town is in the neighbouring townland of DRUMBARAN [*Árd an Rátha* c.1854].

**Ardarragh** tl, Down 3133
*5km W of Rathfriland*
par: *Newry* bar: *Lordship of Newry*

*The old lighthouse at Annalong*

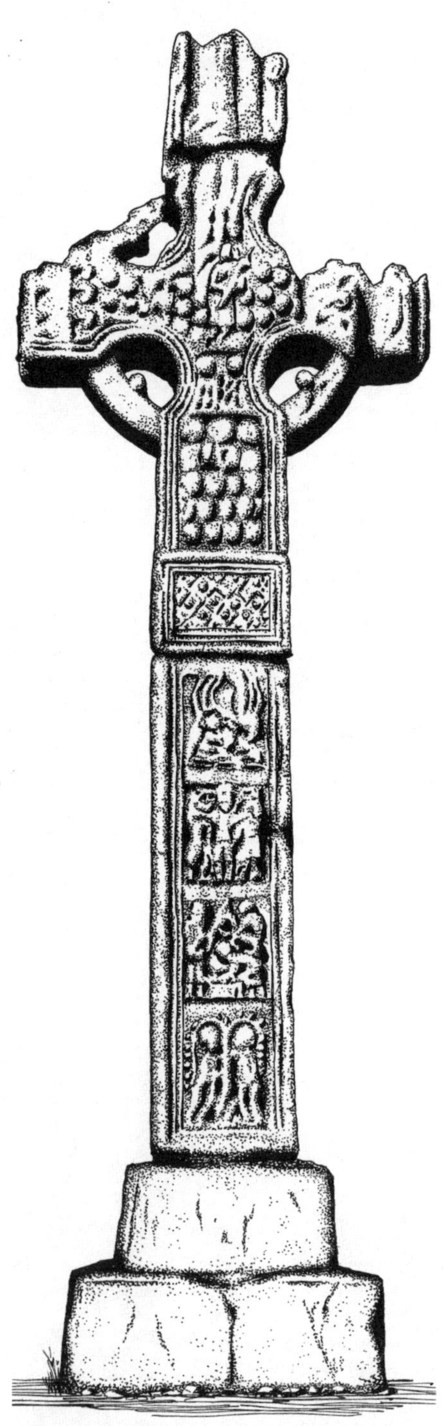

*High cross at Arboe*

Ir. *Ard Darach* [ard **dar**agh] 'height of the oak tree'. There is a hill of 120m in the townland [*Ardarre* 1549].

**Ardgarvan** tl, ham., Derry 2642
*3km SE of Limavady*
par: *Drumachose* bar: *Keenaght*
Ir. *Ard an Gharbháin* [ard a **ghar**awine] 'height of the gravel' [*Ardagarnen* 1616].

**Ardglass** tl, vill., par., Down 3533
*Village is 9.5km SE of Downpatrick*
bar: *Lecale Lower*
Ir. *Ard Ghlas* [ard **ġlas**] 'green height'. *Ard* 'height' in this case appears to be feminine rather than masculine as is normally the case. The place-name seems to refer to the hill known as THE WARD which overlooks the harbour. The present Church of Ireland church marks the site of an earlier church, though the original parish church of St Nicholas was about 1km north-east of the village, in the townland of ARDTOLE where the ruins of a church still stand [(*go*) *hAird Glais* 1433].

**Ardkeen** tl, vill., par., Down 3635
*Village is 5.5km N of Portaferry*
Ir. *Ard Caoin* [ard **keen**] 'fair/pleasant height'.
bar: *Ards Upper*
The ruins of a Church of Ireland church a short distance west of the village mark the site of the medieval parish church of St Mary's of Ardkeen [(*Ecclesia de*) *Ardkene* 1306].

**Ardlougher** tl, ham., Cavan 2231
(sometimes *Ardlogher*)
*6km S of Ballyconnell*
par: *Killinagh* bar: *Tullyhaw*
Ir. *Ard Luachra* [ard **loo**aghra] 'height of (the) rushes/rushy place'. A large area of 'uncultivated rough and boggy pasture' is recorded in the townland in 1835 [*Ardloagher* 1611].

**Ardmillan** vill., Down 3536
*On W shore of Strangford Lough, 7.5km SE of Comber*
par: *Tullynakill* bar: *Castlereagh Lower*
*perhaps* Ir. *Ard Millín* [ard **mill**een] 'height of little knoll'. Ardmillan is in the townland of BALLYMARTIN, at the point where the river BLACKWATER enters STRANGFORD LOUGH. There are a number of low hills in the vicinity.

**Ardmore** tl, Derry 2441
*5km E of Londonderry*
par: *Clondermot* bar: *Tirkeeran*

Ir. *An tArd Mór* [an tard **more**] 'the big height'. There is a hill of 299m in the south of the townland. The river **Faughan**, which forms the eastern boundary of the townland, is spanned by ARDMORE BRIDGE [*Tardmore* 1613].

**Ardmore** tl, Armagh 3036
*On S shore of Lough Neagh, 8km NW of Lurgan*
par: *Montiaghs* bar: *Oneilland East*
Ir. *An Aird Mhór* [an ardge **wore**] 'the large point of land'. Ardmore takes its name from ARDMORE POINT which projects into **Lough Neagh** in the north of the townland. [*Anardvore* 1609].

**Ardress** tls, vill., Armagh 2935
*9.5km W of Portadown*
par: *Loughgall* bar: *Oneilland West*
Ir. *An tArdriasc* [an tard **ree**ask] 'the high moor/bog.' There was formerly an area of bog in this vicinity. The village of Ardress straddles the townlands of ARDRESS EAST and ARDRESS WEST which lie on the north bank of the TALL RIVER [*Tardresk* 1609].

**Ards Peninsula** Down
*On Co. Down coast, stretching from Newtownards in the N to Ballyquintin Point in the S*
bar: *Ards Lower/Ards Upper*
Ir. *Aird Uladh* [*ardge* **ull**oo] 'peninsula of the Ulstermen'. In the seventh and eighth centuries the Ards peninsula was known as *Aird Ua nEchach* 'peninsula of the *Uí Echach* (tribe)'. After the *Uí Echach* were conquered by the Vikings in the ninth century their name disappeared from the place-name and was replaced by *Uladh*, i.e. 'of the Ulstermen'. The northern portion of the peninsula forms the barony of ARDS LOWER while the southern portion forms the barony ARDS UPPER. The name of the peninsula forms the final element of the name of the town of **Newtownards** (*see below*) [(*i*) *nAird Ulad* c.830].

**Ardstraw** tl, vill., par., Tyrone 2338
*Village is 10km S of Strabane*
bar: *Strabane Lower*
Ir. *Ard Sratha* [ard **sra**ha] 'height of the river holm'. The village of Ardstraw which straddles the townlands of ARDSTRAW and CARNKENNY across the river **Derg** contains an old graveyard marking the site of an early monastery founded by St *Eoghan* or Eugenius who is said to have died in 617 AD [(*muintir*) *Aird Sratha* c.900].

*Armagh, 1609*

**Armagh** city, par/bar, co. 2834
*City is 22.5km NE of Monaghan town*
Ir. *Ard Mhacha* [ard **wagh**a] 'height of *Macha*'. *Macha*, which signifies 'pasture', was formerly the name of the district and originally the name of a land-goddess who represents sovereignty in the myths of the ancient Ulstermen where she figures prominently. The name of the district of *Macha* (sometimes known as *Maigh Mhacha* 'plain of *Macha*') is also found in *Eamhain Mhacha* or **Navan**, the name of the ancient capital of Ulster [*Ard Macha* 444].

**Armoy** vill., par., Antrim 3043
*Village is 9km SW of Ballycastle*
bar: *Cary*
Ir. *Oirthear Maí* [urrher **mwee**] 'the east of the plain'. The present Church of Ireland church in the townland of GLEBE marks the site of an earlier church traditionally associated with St Olcan. The latter is said to have been baptised by St Patrick who placed him as bishop over the church. A portion of Armoy parish is in the barony of **Dunluce Upper** [*Airther Maigi* c.900].

**Arranmore** isld, Donegal 1641
(sometimes *Aran Island*)
*Off NW coast of Donegal, 7.5km NW of Dunglow*
par: *Templecrone* bar: *Boylagh*
Ir. *Árainn Mhór* [aarin **wore**] 'great back or ridge'. The name *Árainn* is derived from *ára* which signifies 'kidney' but which at an earlier period could mean 'back' and, hence,

'ridge'. The adjective *mór* 'great' in the place-name is comparatively recent and is presumably to distinguish the island from ARAN ISLAND in Galway Bay [(*go*) *hAruinn Uí Dhomhnuill* c.1600].

**Articlave** tls, vill., Derry 2743
*6.5km WNW of Coleraine*
par: *Dunboe* bar: *Coleraine*
Ir. *Ard an Chléibh* [ard a **khleyv**] 'height of the basket'. Ir. *cliabh*, literally 'basket', can refer to a wickerwork frame, and also to the framework of the ribs (hence also signifying 'breast/bosom'). In this case it is possible that 'breast/bosom' is used metaphorically to refer to a hill brow. The village of Articlave is in the townland of ARTICLAVE LOWER and there is high ground to the south-west, in the townland of ARTICLAVE UPPER. The ARTICLAVE RIVER forms the east boundary of both townlands [*Ard Cleibh* c.1680].

**Artigarvan** tl, vill., Tyrone 2340
*5.5km NE of Strabane*
par: *Leckpatrick* bar: *Strabane Lower*
Ir. *Ard Tí Garbháin* [ard tee **gar**awine] 'height of *Garbhán*'s house'. The personal name *Garbhán* is derived from Ir. *garbh* 'rough' and is the basis of the surname *Ó Garbháin* '(O') Garvin' which is generally regarded as being of Munster origin. The townland of Artigarvan lies on the west side of the GLENMORNAN RIVER while a large portion of the village lies east of the river in the townland of GLEBE [*Ordogarvan* c.1655].

**Artnagross** tl, ham., Antrim 2941
*10km SSW of Ballymoney*
par: *Finvoy* bar: *Kilconway*
Ir. *Ard na gCros* [ard na **gross**] 'height of the crosses'. Artnagross appears to be named from an old graveyard known as FINVOY GRAVEYARD a short distance to the north-west, on the east bank of the **Lower Bann** (*see **Finvoy***) [*Artnagross* 1780].

**Artrea** ham., par., Tyrone 2837
(usually *Ardtrea*)
*Hamlet is 4.5km ESE of Cookstown*
bar: *Dungannon Upper*
Ir. *Ard Tré* [ard **trey**] '*Tré*'s height'.
Artrea takes its name from the virgin saint *Tré* who is referred to as *Trea ingen Chairthind* '*Tré* daughter of *Cáirtheann*' in c.830AD and whose feast day was celebrated on August 3rd. A large portion of the parish of Artrea lies in the neighbouring barony of LOUGHINSHOLIN in Co. Derry [(*airchindeach*) *Arda Trea* 1127].

**Arvagh** vill., Cavan 2229
(sometimes *Arva* )
*15km SW of Cavan town*
par: *Killashandra* bar: *Tullyhunco*
Ir. *Ármhach* [**ar**awagh] 'place of slaughter'. The place-name suggests the site of a battle which is otherwise unattested. Arvagh is at the south-west corner of GARTY LOUGH, in the townland of DRUMALT [*Arvaghbeg, Arvaghmore* 1630].

**Attical** tl, vill., Down 3231
*5.5km NNW of Kilkeel*
par: *Kilkeel* bar: *Mourne*
Ir. *Áit Tí Chathail* [aitch tee **kha**hil] 'place of Cathal's house'. The identity of the Cathal referred to is unknown [*Atty Caell* c.1659].

**Aughamullan** tl, ham.,Tyrone 2836
(sometimes *Aughamullen*)
*On W shore of Lough Neagh, 5km E of Coalisland*
par: *Clonoe* bar: *Dungannon Middle*
Ir. *Achadh Uí Mhaoláin* [aghoo ee **weel**ine] '(O')Mullan's field'. *Ó Maoláin* '(O')Mullan' is among the five most common surnames in Co. Tyrone [*Aghmoylan* 1609].

**Augher** vill., Tyrone 2535
*25km WSW of Dungannon*
par/bar, *Clogher*
Ir. *Eochair* [**ogh**er] 'edge/border'. The village of Augher is in the townland of AUGHER TENEMENTS, close to the river **Blackwater** and beside a small lake [*Ogher* c.1655].

**Aughnacleagh** tl, Antrim 2940
*3.5km N of Portglenone*
par: *Portglenone* bar: *Toome Lower*
Ir. *Achadh na Cléithe* [aghoo na **cley**ha] 'field of the wattle or hurdle' [*Aghcleagh* 1662].

**Aughnacloy** tn, Tyrone 2635
*16.5km SW of Dungannon*
par: *Carnteel* bar: *Dungannon Lower*
Ir. *Achadh na Cloiche* [aghoo na **cloy**ha] 'field of the stone'. In c.1655 we find a reference to the *stone house of Aghenecloy* but it is uncertain if this is the feature referred to in the final element of the place-name. Aughnacloy is in the townland of RAVELLEA [*Aghenecloy* c.1655].

**Aughrim** tl, ham., Derry 2939
*3km E of Magherafelt*
par: *Artrea* bar: *Loughinsholin*
Ir. *Eachroim* [**agh**rim] 'horse ridge'. The name may signify either 'horse-like ridge' or, perhaps more likely, 'ridge of horses' [*Aghram* 1613].

# B

**Baileysmill** vill., Down 3335
(sometimes *Baillie's Mills*)
*7.5km SE of Lisburn*
par: *Annahilt/Drumbo*
bar: *Kinelarty/Castlereagh Upper*
The village of Baileysmill grew up in the late 18th century around a flax and corn mill owned by a gentleman named Bailey, in the townland of DRENNAN, parish of **Drumbo**. Most of the modern village, however, is on the other side of the RAVERNET RIVER, in the townland of CARGACREEVY, parish of **Annahilt**. The Bailie family from Scotland were granted lands in the nearby parish of **Killyleagh** in the 17th century [*Bailey's Mill* 1814].

**Bailieborough** tn., par., Cavan 2629
*Town is 25km ESE of Cavan town*
bar: *Clankee*
Bailieborough in the townland of TANDERAGEE is named from William Bailie of Renfrewshire in Scotland who was granted 1000 acres here in 1610 and who built BAILIEBOROUGH CASTLE around which the town grew up. The site of the castle is marked by a 19th-century mansion of the same name. The parish of Bailieborough was created in 1778 out of the former medieval parish of *Killan* which also included the modern civil parish of **Shercock**. A portion of the parish is in the neighbouring barony of CASTLERAHAN. The Ir. name of Bailieborough is *Coill an Chollaigh* [kill a **khull**ee] 'wood of the boar' [*Kilcothie al. Bailie-Borrow* 1629].

**Ballee** tl, ham., Antrim 3040
*2km S of Ballymena*
par: *Connor* bar: *Antrim Lower*
Ir. *Baile Aodha* [bala **ee**] 'Hugh's townland' [*Balee* 1669].

**Ballee** par., Down 3534
*5.5km SE of Downpatrick*
bar: *Lecale Lower*
Ir. *Béal Ia* [bell **ee**a] *perhaps* '(ford-)mouth of the deer'. The ford is said to have been on a stream which separates CHURCH BALLEE from the neighbouring townland of BALLYBRANNAGH. The present Church of Ireland church (built c.1749) may mark the site of the ancient parish church. The townland of CHURCH BALLEE is bordered on the west by the townland of SPITTLE BALLEE [(*capella de*) *Baliath* 1306].

**Ballerin** tl, ham., Derry 2842
(*see* ***Boleran***)

**Balliggan** tl, ham., Down 3636
*On Ards Peninsula, 5km SE of Greyabbey*
par: *Inishargy* bar: *Ards Upper*
Ir. *Baile Uí Uiginn* [bala ee **igg**in] '(O') Higgins's townland'. *Ó hUiginn* '(O') Higgins' is the name of a famous literary family and the surname is widely scattered in Ireland [*Ballyhiggin* 1623].

**Ballinamallard** tl, vill., Fermanagh 2235
(*see* ***Bellanamallard***)

**Ballindarragh** distr., Fermanagh 2333
*4km NW of Lisnaskea*
par: *Aghalurcher* bar: *Magherastephana*
Ir. *Baile na Dara* [bala na **dar**a] 'farmstead of the oak-tree'. Ballindarragh is in the townland of DRUMMACK. It has given name to BALLINDARRAGH CROSSROADS and to BALLINDARRAGH BRIDGE which crosses the COLEBROOK RIVER.

**Ballinderry** tl, par., Antrim 3136
*Townland is 9.5km NE of Lurgan*
bar: *Massereene Upper*
Ir. *Baile an Doire* [bala an **dirr**a] 'townland of the oak-wood'. The townland of Ballinderry lies on the east shore of **Lough Neagh** and has given name to the hamlets of LOWER BALLINDERRY and UPPER BALLINDERRY. The latter was formerly known as *Largy's Lane Ends* and lies 3km to the east, in the townland of BALLYSCOLLY. The remains of the former parish church are in a graveyard on the shore of **Portmore Lough** [*Ballynderry* 1661].

**Ballinderry** tl, par., Derry 2938
*Townland is 12km ENE of Cookstown*
bar: *Loughisholin*
Ir. *Baile an Doire* [bala an **dirr**a] 'townland of the oak wood'. The site of the former parish church is marked by an old graveyard on CHURCH HILL. A portion of the parish of Ballinderry is in the barony of DUNGANNON UPPER in Co. Tyrone, the two portions being linked across the BALLINDERRY RIVER by BALLINDERRY BRIDGE [*B:Derry* 1609].

**Ballindrait** tl, vill., Donegal 2339
*2.5km WNW of Lifford*
par: *Clonleigh* bar: *Raphoe*
Ir. *Baile an Droichid* [bala an **dry**hidge] 'townland of the bridge'. Ballindrait is named from a bridge across the river **Deele** (sometimes known as the *Dale Burn*). In c.1655 we find a reference to 'a wooden bridge and pass' [*Ballendraite* c.1655].

**Ballinran** tls, ham., Down 3331
*4km N of Kilkeel*
par: *Kilkeel* bar: *Mourne*
Ir. *Baile an Raithin* [bala an **ra**hin] 'townland of the ferns'. Ballinran has given name to the adjacent townland of BALLINRAN UPPER which is on the slopes of SLIEVENAGORE MOUNTAIN [*Ballynynranny* 1540].

**Ballintoy** tl, vill., par., Antrim 3044
*Village is on N Antrim coast, 7.5 km NW of Ballycastle*
bar: *Cary*
*perhaps* Ir. *Baile an Tuathaigh* [bala an **too**hee] 'townland of the ruler of the *tuath*'. The word *tuath* signifies a petty Irish kingdom. The parish of Ballintoy formed part of the neighbouring parish of BILLY until the late 17th or early 18th century. The townland of Ballintoy is bordered on the west by the townland of BALLINTOY DEMESNE [*Ballenatoy* 1603].

**Ballintra** tl, vill., Donegal 1936
*11km S of Donegal town*
par: *Drumhome* bar: *Tirhugh*
Ir. *Baile an tSratha* [bala an **tra**ha] 'townland of the river holm'. The village of Ballintra is on the north bank of the BALLINTRA RIVER [*Baile an tSrátha* 1934].

**Balloo** tl, vill., Down 3536
*1km W of Killinchy*
par: *Killinchy* bar: *Dufferin*
Ir. *Baile Aodha* [bala **ee**] 'Hugh's townland'. Balloo has the same derivation as two other townlands of the same name which lie some 15km to the north, in the parish of **Bangor** [*Ballow* 1605].

**Balloughry** tl, ham., Derry 2441
*On W bank of the Foyle, 4.5km SW of Derry*
par: *Templemore*
bar: *NW Liberties of Londonderry*
Ir. *Baile Dhúdhoire* [bala **ġoo**girra] 'townland of the black oak-wood'. BALLOUGHRY HILL (100m) stands in the middle of the townland [*Ballidowgry* 1637].

**Ballsmill** vill., Armagh 2931
*Close to Louth border, 7km E of Crossmaglen*
par: *Creggan* bar: *Fews Upper*
Thomas Ball was granted lands in this area in the middle of the 17th century and flax and corn mills are recorded in the village in 1888. The Ir. name of the village is *Baile na gCléireach* [bala na **gler**agh] 'town of the clerics'. There is now no trace or record of a religious foundation but a Franciscan friar was still residing here in 1743. Ballsmill is partly in the townland of BALLYNACLOSHA and partly in GLASDRUMMAN [*Ballinaglera* 1838].

**Ballyaghlis** tl, ham., Down 3336
(sometimes *Ballyaughlis*)
*4km ENE of Lisburn*
par: *Drumbeg* bar: *Castlereagh Upper*
Ir. *Baile na hEachlaisce* [bala na **hagh**liska] 'townland of the horse enclosure' [*Ballyhaghliske* 1625].

**Ballyalton** tl, vill., Down 3534
*3km E of Downpatrick*
par: *Ballee* bar: *Lecale Lower*
Ir. *Baile Altúin* [bala **alt**ooin] 'Alton's townland'. *Altún* is a gaelicised form of the Anglo-Norman surname *Alton* which derives from a number of places so-named in England [*Ballyawlton* 1547].

**Ballyardel** tl, ham., Down 3231
(sometimes *Ballyardle*)
*2km W of Kilkeel*
par: *Kilkeel* bar: *Mourne*
Ir. *Baile Ardail* [bala **ard**il] '*Ardal*'s townland'. The personal name *Ardal* (earlier *Ardghal* 'high valour') is the basis of the surname *Mac Ardail* which can be anglicised 'MacArdle' and is found in this area [*Bally Ardell* 1661].

**Ballybay** tn., par., Monaghan 2732
*10.5km W of Castleblayney*
bar: *Cremorne*
Ir. *Béal Átha Beithe* [bell aha **bey**ha] 'ford-mouth of the birch tree'. The site of the ford is marked by a bridge over a stream which flows out of LOUGH MAJOR close to the southern end of the town. The parish of Ballybay was formed in 1796 from portions of the neighbouring parishes of **Aghnamullen** and TULLYCORBET. A small portion of the parish is in the barony of **Monaghan** [*Balloghnebegh* 1591].

**Ballybeen** tl, h.est., Down 3437
*Part of Dundonald, 7.5km E of Belfast city centre*
par: *Dundonald* bar: *Castlereagh Lower*
*perhaps* Ir. *Baile Bín* [bala **been**] 'townland of Bean'. The final element of the place-name appears to be a gaelicised form of the Anglo-Norman surname 'Bean' [*Ballibeine* 1605].

**Ballybofey** tl, tn., Donegal 2139
*17km S of Letterkenny*
par: *Stranorlar* bar: *Raphoe*
Ir. *Bealach Féich* [balagh **fay**igh] '*Fiach*'s way/pass'. The personal name *Fiach* (literally 'raven') is the basis of the surname *Ó Féich/Ó Fiaich* which can be anglicised *Fay*, *Foy* or *Fee*. An earlier Ir. name for the townland of Ballybofey was *Srath Bó Fiaich* [sra bo **fee**igh] 'river-holm of the cows of *Fiach*', the first element referring to the flat land along the river **Finn**. Ballybofey is twin town to **Stranorlar** which stands on the opposite side of the river [*(ar) Srath Bó Fiaich* 1548].

**Ballybogy** tl, ham., Antrim 2943
(sometimes *Ballybogey*)
*7km NNW of Ballymoney*
par: *Dunluce* bar: *Dunluce Lower*
Ir. *Baile an Bhogaigh* [bala an **wugg**ee] 'townland of the boggy ground'
[*Ballyboggy* 1669].

**Ballyboley** tl, Antrim 3339
*10km SW of Larne*
par: *Ballycor* bar: *Antrim Upper*
Ir. *Baile na Buaile* [bala na **boo**la] 'townland of the *booley*'. The word *booley* is from Ir. *buaile* and commonly refers to a cattle-enclosure in a summer grazing pasture. There is another townland named BALLYBOLEY on the western outskirts of **Larne** [*Ballineboyley* 1605].

**Ballyboylands** tls, Antrim 2942
(sometimes *Ballyboyland*)
*4km E of Ballymoney*
par: *Ballymoney* bar: *Dunluce Upper*
Ir. *Baile Uí Bhaolláin* [bala ee **weel**ine] '(O')Boylan's townland'. The surname *Ó Baolláin* '(O')Boylan' originated in Co. Monaghan but is now fairly widespread in Ulster and also in Co. Meath. The townlands of BALLYBOYLANDS UPPER and BALLYBOYLAND LOWER lie on the east bank of the GREENSHIELDS RIVER [*Bellebolan* c.1659].

**Ballycarry** tls, vill., Antrim 3439
*7km NE of Carrickfergus*
par: *Templecorran* bar: *Belfast Lower*
Ir. *Baile Cora* [bala **kor**a] 'townland of the causeway or ford'. The site of the ford is marked by the present bridge across the shallow head waters of LARNE LOUGH, between Ballycarry and **Island Magee** peninsula. The village of Ballycarry is at the intersection of the four townlands of BALLYCARRY NORTH-WEST, BALLYCARRY SOUTH-WEST, REDHALL and FORTHILL [*Ballycarry* 1669].

**Ballycassidy** tl, ham., Fermanagh 2235
*6.5km N of Enniskillen*
par: *Trory* bar: *Tirkennedy*
Ir. *Baile Uí Chaiside* [bala ee **khashi**dya] '(O')Cassidy's townland'. The family of *Ó Caiside* '(O')Cassidy' were formerly hereditary poets and physicians to the Maguire rulers of Fermanagh. The BALLYCASSIDY RIVER flows into **Lower Lough Erne** a short distance to the west [*Ballicashedy* 1659].

**Ballycastle** tl, Antrim 3144
*22km NE of Ballymoney*
par: *Ramoan* bar: *Cary*
Ir. *Baile Chaisleáin* [bala **khash**line] 'townland of the castle'. The former townland of Ballycastle is represented by the modern TOWN PARKS. The townland was named from a medieval castle in the middle of Ballycastle, on the site of which another castle was erected in 1609 by Randal Mac Donnell, 1st Earl of Antrim. No trace of either castle now remains [*Baile Caislein* 1565].

**Ballyclare** tl, tn, Antrim 3239
*17.5km NNW of Belfast*
par: *Ballynure/Grange of Doagh*
bar: *Antrim Upper/Belfast Lower*
Ir. *Bealach Cláir* [balagh **klar**] 'way/pass of the plain' [*Balleclare* 1620].

*Ballycopeland windmill*

**Ballyconnell** tn, Cavan 2231
*10km W of Belturbet*
par: *Tomregan* bar: *Tullyhaw*
Ir. *Béal Átha Conaill* [bell aha **kon**ell] '*Conall*'s ford-mouth'. A local legend has it that the *Conall* referred to was *Conall Cearnach* a mythical warrior in the Ulster Cycle of tales who was slain here by the soldiers of Queen Maeve of Connaught and is buried nearby. Ballyconnell straddles the WOODFORD RIVER [*Beallaconnell* 1630].

**Ballycopeland** tl, ham., Down 3537
*On east coast of Ards Peninsula, adjoining village of Millisle on the N*
par: *Donaghadee* bar: *Ards Lower*
Ir. *Baile Chóplainn* [bala **khoap**lin] 'Copeland's townland'. The final element of the place-name is a gaelicised form of the Norman surname *de Coupland*. There is an island named **Copeland Island** 7km to the north [*Ballicoppland* 1605].

**Ballyculter** tls, ham., par., Down 3534
*Hamlet is 9km ENE of Downpatrick*
bar: *Lecale Lower*
Ir. *Baile Uí Choltair* [bala ee **khol**tir] 'Coulter's townland'. The Irish surname *Ó Coltair* 'Coulter' is peculiar to Co. Down where it is very numerous. However, Coulter can also be Scottish in origin, from the manor of COULTER in Lanarkshire. The surname is also common in Antrim and Fermanagh. The site of the former parish church of Ballyculter may be at CHURCHTOWN in the townland of BALLYCULTER UPPER [*Balinculter* 1183].

**Ballydugan** tl, ham., Down 3434
*3km SW of Downpatrick*
par: *Down* bar: *Lecale Upper*
Ir. *Baile Uí Dhúgáin* [bala ee **ġoo**gine] '(O')Dugan's townland'. The surname *Ó Dúgáin* '(O')Dugan/(O')Dougan/ (O')Doogan' is very widespread in Ireland [*Boile Í Dhubhagán* 1646].

**Ballyeaston** tl, vill., Antrim 3239
*2km N of Ballyclare*
par: *Ballycor* bar: *Antrim Upper*
Ir. *Baile Uistín* [bala **us**teen] 'Austin's townland'. The final element of the place-name is a gaelicised form of the Anglo-Norman surname *Austin*. The foundations of the former parish church of BALLYCOR lie a short distance to the east [*Austin's town* 1306].

**Ballygalley** tl, vill., Antrim. 3340
(sometimes *Ballygally*)
*On Antrim coast road, 5.5km NNW of Larne*
par: *Carncastle* bar: *Glenarm Upper*
Ir. *Baile Geithligh* [bala **geh**lee] *perhaps* '*Geithleach*'s townland'. The personal name *Geithleach* appears to be of rare occurrence [*Ballegelly* 1635].

**Ballygawley** tl, vill., Tyrone 2635
*17.5km WSW of Dungannon*
par: *Errigal Keerogue* bar: *Clogher*
Ir. *Baile Uí Dhálaigh* [bala ee **ġaal**ee] '(O')Daly's townland'. A branch of the famous literary family of *Ó Dálaigh* '(O')Daly' were hereditary poets to the O'Neills of Ulster. Ballygawley stands on the north bank of the BALLYGAWLEY WATER, a tributary of the **Blackwater** [*Ballygally* 1608].

**Ballygorman** tl, vill., Donegal 2445
*10km NNW of Malin village*
par: *Clonca* bar: *Inishowen East*
Ir. *Baile Uí Ghormáin* [bala ee **ġor**imine] '(O')Gorman's townland'. The element *Mac* in the widely-distributed surname *Mac Gormáin* has often, as in this case, been replaced by *Ó*. Part of the village is in the neighbouring townland of ARDMALIN [*Balligorman* c.1660].

**Ballygowan** tl, vill., Down 3436
*6km SW of Comber*
par: *Comber/Killinchy*
bar: *Castlereagh Lower*
Ir. *Baile Mhic Gabhann* [bala vick **go**an] 'MacGowan's townland'. The surname *Mac Gabhann* [mack **go**an] 'son of the smith' can be anglicised as *MacGowan, Magowan* or *Smith* and is largely confined to Ulster, along with Cos Leitrim and Sligo [*Balle-McGowen* 1623].

**Ballygrainey** tl, Down 3537
*6km NE of Newtownards*
par: *Bangor* bar: *Ards Lower*
Ir. *Baile na Gréine* [bala na **grey**na] 'townland of the sun'. Ballygrainey was clearly regarded as occupying a sunny situation. It appears to have the same derivation as the other townland of the same name which lies 3km northeast of **Holywood** [*Ballinegrene* 1630].

**Ballyhackamore** tl, distr., Down 3337
*Suburb on the E side of Belfast*
par: *Holywood* bar: *Castlereagh Lower*
*perhaps* Ir. *Baile an Chacamair* [bala an **khack**amir] 'townland of the slob land or mud flat'. The townland of Ballyhackmore is now inland but may have bordered on **Belfast Lough** before modern land-reclamation schemes [*Ballcakamer* 1620].

**Ballyhaise** vill., Cavan 2431
*6km NNE of Cavan town*
par: *Castleterra* bar: *Loughtee Upper*
Ir. *Béal Átha hÉis* [bell aha **hesh**]. *Béal Átha* signifies 'ford-mouth' and refers to a ford on the ANNALEE RIVER, the site of which is marked by the present bridge. The final element of the place-name can signify either 'track/path' or 'band/troop'. Otherwise, one might consider that it could represent a shortened form of *éise* 'reins/harness' and that it could possibly apply to some restriction or obstacle on the ford (*cf.* **Agivey** *above*). Ballyhaise is in the townland of TOWN PARKS [(*go*) *Béal Átha Haeis* 1644].

**Ballyhalbert** tl, vill., par., Down 3636
*Village is on E coast of Ards Peninsula, 4km N of Portavogie*
bar: *Ards Upper*
Ir. *Baile Thalbóid* [bala **hal**bodge] 'Talbot's townland'. The Talbot family settled in Cos Down and Antrim after the Anglo-Norman invasion. The parish goes by the *alias* name of ST ANDREWS, from a Benedictine priory founded in 1204 and named after St Andrews priory of Stogursy in Somerset, England. The priory, no trace of which now remains, was also known as BLACK ABBEY [(*Ecclesia de*) *Talbetona* 1306].

**Ballyheelan** tl, vill., Cavan 2428
*16km S of Cavan town*
par: *Ballymachugh* bar: *Clanmahon*
Ir. *Bealach an Chaoláin* [balagh an **kheel**ine] 'way/pass of the marshy stream'. The final element of the place-name refers to the stream which flows through the village and formerly powered a mill [*Ballagheelan + Mill* 1734].

**Ballyheerin** tl., Donegal 2143
*On Mulroy Bay 12km N of Millford*
par: *Clondavaddog* bar: *Kilmacrenan*
Ir. *Baile Uí Shírín* [bala ee **heer**een] '(O')Sheeran's townland'. The family of *Ó Sírín* '(O')Sheeran/Sheerin' is indigenous to Donegal and Fermanagh (cf. ***Bolleran***) [*Ballyherrinmore, Ballyherrinbegg* c.1660].

**Ballyholme** tl, vill., Down 3538
*2.5km E of Bangor*
par: *Bangor* bar: *Ards Lower*
*perhaps* Ir. *Baile Hóm* [bala **home**] '*Hóm*'s townland'. The final element may be a gaelicised form of the English surname *Holm(es)* which derives from O.N. *holmr* 'river meadow' and signifies 'one who dwells on flat land in a fen or beside a river' [*Ballehum* 1603].

**Ballyhornan** tl, vill., Down 3534
*On Down coast, 10.5km ESE of Downpatrick*
par: *Dunsfort* bar: *Lecale Lower*
Ir. *Baile Uí Chornáin* [bala ee **khorn**ine] '(O')Cornan's townland'. *Ó Cornáin* appears to be a variant of the Cavan/Leitrim surname *Ó Cuirnín* 'Curneen' [*Ballyhornan* 1636].

**Ballyhugh** tl, Cavan 2331
*6km WSW of Belturbet*
par: *Drumlane* bar: *Loughtee Lower*
Ir. *Bealach Aodha* [balagh **ee**] 'Hugh's pass/way' [*Bellaghea* 1610].

**Ballyjamesduff** vill., Cavan 2529
*15km SE of Cavan town*
par/bar, *Castlerahan*
Ir: *Baile Shéamais Dhuibh* [bala haymish **ġiv**]

'James Duff's town'. Ballyjamesduff in the townland of CORNAKILLY is named from James Duff, Earl of Fife in Scotland, who appears to have been granted lands here in the early 17th century. His descendant, Sir James Duff, commanded English troops in the Rebellion of 1798 [*Bally James Doough or Black James' town* c.1744].

**Ballykeel** tl, distr., Antrim 3140
*Suburb on the E. side of Ballymena*
par: *Ballyclug* bar: *Antrim Lower*
Ir. *An Baile Caol* [an bala **keel**] 'the narrow townland/farmstead' [*Ballykeele* 1669].

**Ballykeel** tl, ham., Down 3235
*7km E of Dromore*
par: *Dromore* bar: *Iveagh Lower, Lower Half*
Ir. *An Baile Caol* [an bala **keel**] 'the narrow townland/farmstead'. In the early 17th century the name of the townland was qualified by the name of the lough it borders, i.e. LOUGH AGHERY. This was no doubt to distinguish it from other townlands of the same name in the vicinity, including BALLYKEEL west of **Banbridge**, BALLYKEEL in the parish of **Donaghmore** and BALLYKEEL EDENAGONELL and BALLYKEEL ARTIFINNY in the neighbouring parish of BLARIS [*Ballikeeleloghaghery* 1632].

**Ballykelly** tl, vill., Derry 2642
*4km W of Limavady*
par: *Tamlaght Finlagan* bar: *Keenaght*
Ir. *Baile Uí Cheallaigh* [bala ee **khal**ee] '(O')Kelly's townland'. *Ó Ceallaigh* '(O')Kelly' is the second most numerous surname in Ireland and the third most numerous in Co. Derry [*Ballykellye* 1613].

**Ballykilbeg** tl, Down 3434
*5km SW of Downpatrick*
par: *Down* bar: *Lecale Upper*
Ir. *Baile na gCeall Beag* [bala na gal **beg**] 'townland of the little churches'. There was previously a burial ground near an earthen fort close to the present Catholic church and this may mark the site of an earlier church which is referred to as *the chapel of Wytiketona* in 1306 [*Ballenagallbee*, 1512].

**Ballykinler** tl, vill., par., Down 3433
*On Co. Down coast, 9km SW of Downpatrick*
bar: *Lecale Upper*
Ir. *Baile Coinnleora* [bala **kin**lora] 'townland of the candlestick'. The name has its origin in a grant of c.1200 by John de Courcy of the lands of Ballykinler to Christchurch Cathedral, Dublin for the upkeep of a perpetual light before the crucifix there. The three townlands of BALLYKINLER LOWER, BALLYKINLER MIDDLE and BALLYKINLER UPPER make up the entire parish of Ballykinler which lies on the east shore of **Dundrum Bay**. In BALLYKINLER MIDDLE there is an ancient graveyard and holy well which mark the site of the former parish church [*Ballicanlor* 1542].

**Ballyleny** tl, ham., Armagh 2934
*1.5km N of Rich Hill*
par: *Kilmore* bar: *Oneilland West*
Ir. *Baile Léana* [bala **ley**na] 'townland of the wet meadow' [*Ballylaney* 1661].

**Ballylesson** tl, vill., Down 3336
*8km S of Belfast*
par: *Drumbo* bar: *Castlereagh Upper*
Ir. *Baile na Leasán* [bala na **lass**an] 'townland of the little forts'. In the south of the townland there is a very prominent fort, known as FARRELL'S FORT [*Ballenelassan* 1623].

**Ballyliffin** tl, vill., Donegal 2344
*8km WNW of Carndonagh*
par: *Clonmany* bar: *Inishowen East*
Ir. *Baile Lifín* [bala **lif**een] 'farmstead of the halfpenny'. The final element of the place-name is an alternative spelling of Ir. *leathphingin* 'halfpenny'. The term 'halfpenny' appears to refer to a land division but its exact significance is obscure [*Ballylaffin* 1608].

**Ballylintagh** tl, ham., Derry 2842
*7km S of Coleraine*
par: *Aghadowey* bar: *Coleraine*
Ir. *An Baile Linnteach* [an bala **lin**chagh] 'the townland of pools'. The townland of Ballylintagh is partly in the neighbouring parish of **Macosquin**. The pools in question may be in the MACOSQUIN RIVER which borders the townland on the west [*Bellylintach* 1663].

**Ballylumford** tl, Antrim 3440
*On Island Magee, facing the port of Larne*
par: *Island Magee* bar: *Belfast Lower*
Ir. *Baile an Longfoirt* [bala an **lung**furtch] 'townland of the stronghold/fortress'. The site of the feature referred to in the final element of the place-name is uncertain [*Ballylemford* 1669].

**Ballymacarret** tl, distr., Down 3337
*Suburb of Belfast on E bank of Lagan*
par: *Knockbreda* bar: *Castlereagh Upper*
Ir. *Baile Mhic Gearóid* [bala vick **gar**odge] 'MacGarrett's townland'. The fairly rare surname *Mac Gearóid* 'MacGarrett' derives from the personal name *Gearóid* 'Gerald/Garrett'. Ballymacarret has given name to the neighbouring townland of BALLYMACARRET INTAKE which consists of land reclaimed from **Belfast Lough** [*Bally McCarritt* 1623].

**Ballymaconnelly** tl, Antrim 2941
*3.5km NW of Rasharkin*
par: *Rasharkin* bar: *Kilconway*
Ir. *Baile Mhic Conaíle* [bala vick **kon**eela] 'Connolly's townland'. *Mac Conaíle* appears to be a variant of the more common *Ó Conaíle* '(O')Connolly', a surname which is widely distributed in Ireland [*Ballymaconnally* 1635].

**Ballymagan** tl, ham., Donegal 2343
*2.5km NE of Buncrana*
par: *Fahan Lower* bar: *Inishowen West*
Ir. *Baile Mhic Cionaoith* [bala vick **kyin**ee] 'MacCanny's townland'. The surnames MacCanny and MacKeany which derive from Ir. *Mac Cionaoith* are common in **Inishowen**. *Mac Cionaith* is also the name of a prominent family of Monaghan where it is anglicised MacKenna. The official title of the townland of Ballymagan is BALLYMAGAN UPPER & LOWER AND CLONBLOSK [*Ballimcganny* c.1655].

**Ballymagorry** tl, vill., Tyrone 2340
*5km N of Strabane*
par: *Leckpatrick* bar: *Strabane Lower*
Ir. *Baile Mhic Gofraidh* [bala vick **goff**ree] 'MacGorry's townland'. The surname *Mac Gofraidh* signifies 'son of Godfrey' and is sometimes anglicised *MacCaffrey*. It is the name of a branch of the Maguires of Fermanagh [*Ballemagorie* 1616].

**Ballymagrorty** tl, vill., Derry 2441
(sometimes *Ballymagroarty*)
*On NW outskirts of Derry city*
par: *Templemore*
bar: *NW Liberties of Londonderry*
Ir. *Baile Mhic Robhartaigh* [bala vick **roar**tee] 'MacGroarty's townland'. The family of MacGroarty originate from BALLYMAGRORTY near Donegal town, where they were anciently keepers of St Columcille's bell. A large townland adjoining Ballymagrorty is known as WHITE HOUSE OR BALLYMAGRORTY [*Ballym'roartie* 1604].

**Ballymaguigan** tl, ham., Derry 2938
*On NW shore of Lough Neagh, 4.5km SW of Toome*
par: *Artrea* bar: *Loughinsholin*
Ir. *Baile Mhic Guaigín* [bala vick **goog**een] 'MacQuiggin's townland'. The surname *Mac Guaigín* can also be anglicised 'MacGuigan' and it can sometimes represent a corrupt form of *Mac Eochaín* 'MacGuckin', a surname which is common in this area [*Ballymccuggin* c.1659].

**Ballymaleel** tl, Donegal 2241
*7.5km NE of Letterkenny*
par: *Aghanunshin* bar: *Kilmacrenan*
Ir. *Baile Uí Mhaolaíola* [bala ee wail**eel**a] 'townland of *Ó Maolaíola*'. *Ó Maolaíola* may be a variant of *Ó Maolalaidh*, a Galway surname which is normally anglicised *Mullally* [*Ballymaleley* 1622].

**Ballymartin** tl, vill., Down 3331
*4km NE of Kilkeel*
par: *Kilkeel* bar: *Mourne*
Ir. *Baile Mhic Giolla Mhártain* [bala vick gilla **war**tin] 'Martin's townland'. The literal meaning of the surname represented in this place-name (*Mac Giolla Mhártain*) is 'son of the devotee of (St) Martin' which can be anglicised *Gilmartin* or *Martin*. Martin is a common surname in Co. Down [*Ballymicgyll Mertyn* 1552].

**Ballymena** tn, Antrim 3140
*16.5km NNW of Antrim town*
par: *Kirkinriola*
bar: *Toome Lower/Antrim Lower*
Ir. *An Baile Meánach* [an bala **man**agh] 'the middle townland/farmstead'. The old townland of Ballymena which gave name to the town has been renamed TOWN PARKS. The townland was originally named 'middle townland' from its 'middle' position between two other local features or possibly it took its name from a farmstead within it which was seen as occupying a 'middle' situation between two other features. The common idea that Ballymena owes its name to its central situation in Co. Antrim is therefore a mistaken one. The modern town was founded by William Adair,

a Scot from Kinhilt in Galloway, who was granted a large tract of land here in 1624 [*Ballymeanagh* 1626].

**Ballymoney** tn, par., Antrim 2942
*Town is 11.5km SE of Coleraine*
bar: *Dunluce Upper*
Ir. *Baile Monaidh* [bala **mun**ee] 'townland of the moor'. The old townland of Ballymoney, which gave name to the town and the parish, has been renamed TOWN PARKS. There are several large bogs in the vicinity of the town. The site of the original parish church appears to have been in the townland of KILMOYLE UPPER or KIRKMOYLE a short distance to the north-west [*Bali Monaid* 1412].

**Ballynabragget** tl, ham., Down 3135
*6km N of Banbridge*
par: *Donaghcloney*
bar: *Iveagh Upper, Lower Half*
Ir. *Baile na Brád* [bala na **braad**] 'townland of the neck/gorge/valley'. It is difficult to identify the exact feature referred to by the final element of the place-name [*Ballynebrade* 1612].

**Ballynacor** tl, Armagh 3035
(sometimes *Ballynacorr*)
*5km N of Portadown*
par: *Seagoe* bar: *Oneilland East*
Ir. *Baile na Cora* [bala na **kor**a] 'townland of the weir or causeway'. Ballynacor lies close to the east bank of the **Upper Bann** [*Ballinecorrowe* 1610].

**Ballynafeigh** distr., Down 3337
*Suburb on the SE side of Belfast*
par: *Knockbreda* bar: *Castlereagh Upper*
Ir. *Baile na Faiche* [bala na **fai**ha] 'townland of the green'. Ballynafeigh is in fact a variant spelling of BALLYNAFOY, the name of the townland in which it is situated [*Ballinefeigh* 1605].

**Ballynagarrick** tl, Down 3035
*On Armagh border, 9km NW of Banbridge*
par: *Tullylish* bar: *Iveagh Lower, Upper Half*
Ir. *Baile na gCarraig* [bala na **garr**ick] 'townland of the rocks'. There are quarries in the south of the townland [*Ballynegaricke* 1611].

**Ballynahinch** tl, tn, Down 3335
*15km SE of Lisburn*
par: *Magheradrool* bar: *Kinelarty*
Ir. *Baile na hInse* [bala na **hinch**a] 'townland of the river meadow'. The western boundary of the townland of Ballynahinch is formed by the BALLYNAHINCH RIVER, the lower course of which is known as the ANNACLOY RIVER and the final portion of which is known as the **Quoile** [*Ballynehinchy* 1634].

**Ballynamallaght** tl, ham., Tyrone 2439
*13.5km E of Strabane*
par: *Donaghedy* bar: *Strabane Lower*
Ir. *Béal Átha na Mallacht* [bell aha na **mal**aght] 'ford-mouth of the curses'. Ballynamallaght is on the north bank of the **Burn Dennet** river. The derivation of the place-name is the same as that of **Bellinamallard** in Fermanagh.

**Ballynascreen** par., Derry
(*see* ***Draperstown, Moyola***)

**Ballynashannagh** tl, Donegal 2243
*10km NNE of Milford*
par: *Clondavaddog* bar: *Kilmacrenan*
Ir. *Baile na Seanach* [bala na **shan**agh]. The first element of the place-name is *baile* 'townland' but the meaning of the final element is obscure [*Ballysheany* 1623].

**Ballynaskeagh** tl, ham., Down 3133
*8km SSE of Banbridge*
par: *Aghaderg* bar: *Iveagh Upper, Upper Half*
Ir. *Baile na Sceach* [bala na **skagh**] 'townland of the thorn-bushes' [*Ballyneskeagh* 1609].

**Ballyneaner** tl, Tyrone 2540
*18km NE of Strabane*
par: *Donaghedy* bar: *Strabane Lower*
Ir. *Baile an Aonfhir* [bala an **ain**ir] 'townland of the lone man'. 'The lone man' may perhaps refer to a standing stone in the east of the townland [*Baile an Aoin-fhir* c.1675].

**Ballynease** tls, Derry 2940
*3.5km NE of Bellaghy*
par: *Ballyscullion* bar: *Loughinsholin*
Ir. *Baile Naosa* [bala **nees**a] '*Naos*'s townland'. *Naos* is a contracted form of *Aonghus*, a personal name which in Scotland is anglicised as *Angus*. Ballynease lies on the west bank of the **Lower Bann** and consists of the townlands of BALLYNEASE-HELTON, BALLYNEASE-MACPEAKE and BALLYNEASE-STRAIN. The surname MacPeake (Ir. *Mac*

*Péice*) is native to the area and still common [*Bellinees, two townes* 1654].

**Ballynure** vill, par., Antrim 3339
*Village is 3.5km NE of Ballyclare*
bar: *Belfast Lower*
Ir. *Baile an Iúir* [bala an **yure**] 'farmstead of the yew tree'. The village of Ballynure straddles the townlands of TOBERDOWNEY and DUNTURKY. The ruins of the former parish church are in a graveyard opposite the present Church of Ireland church in the townland of TOBERDOWNEY [*Ballinower* 1605].

**Ballyoran** tl, h.est., Armagh 3035
*On NW outskirts of Portadown*
par: *Drumcree* bar: *Oneilland West*
Ir. *Baile Uaráin* [bala **oor**ine] 'townland of the spring or fountain'. The location of the spring or fountain is now unknown [*B:uoran* 1609].

**Ballyquintin** tl, Down 3634
*Forms the southernmost tip of the Ards Peninsula*
par: *Witter* bar: *Ards Upper*
Ir. *Baile Chuintín* [bala **khin**teen] 'Quintin's townland'. *Cuintín* appears to be a gaelicisation of the Anglo-Norman surname or forename *Quintin*. Ballyquintin has given name to BALLYQUINTIN POINT in the south of the townland [*Ballyconton* 1588].

**Ballyrashane** vill., par., Derry 2843
*Village is 4km E of Coleraine*
bar: *NE Liberties of Coleraine*
Ir. *Baile Ráth Singean* [bala ra **shing**an] 'farmstead of St John's fort'. The element *ráth* 'fort' may refer to the site of the former parish church which was close to the present Church of Ireland church in the townland of GLEBE. The church was anciently a possession of the Order of St John of Jerusalem and in the 15th century the site is referred to as *Singintone or St John's town*. The parish of Ballyrashane is partly in the barony of DUNLUCE LOWER in Co. Antrim [*Singaynton al. Rathsyne* 1542].

**Ballyreagh** vill., Tyrone 2635
*3km NE of Ballygawley*
par: *Carnteel* bar: *Dungannon Lower*
Ir. *An Baile Riabhach* [an bala **ree**wagh] 'the grey or speckled farmstead'. Ballyreagh is in the townland of INISHMAGH.

**Ballyrobert** vill., Antrim 3238
*14km NW of Belfast*
par: *Templepatrick* bar: *Belfast Lower*
Ir. *Baile Roibeaird* [bala **rob**irdge] 'Robert's farmstead'. Ballyrobert is situated in the townland (formerly parish) of GRANGE OF BALLYROBERT. It contains the site of a medieval chapel which was a possession of the Abbey of **Muckamore** near the town of **Antrim** [*Ballyrobert* c.1659].

**Ballyronan** tl, vill., Derry 2938
*On W shore of Lough Neagh, 9km ENE of Moneymore*
par: *Artrea* bar: *Loughinsholin*
Ir. *Baile Uí Rónáin* [bala ee **roan**ine] '(O')Ronan's townland'. The surname (O')Ronan, while well attested in the south of Ireland, is rare in the north. The village of Ballyronan was founded in 1788 in the townland of BALLYRONAN MORE in the parish of **Artrea** while the neighbouring townland of BALLYRONAN BEG is in the parish of **Ballinderry** [*Two Ballioronans* 1654].

**Ballyroney** tl, vill., Down 3233
*4.5km NE of Rathfriland*
par: *Drumballyroney*
bar: *Iveagh Upper, Lower Half*
Ir. *Baile Uí Ruanaí* [bala ee **roon**ee] '(O')Rooney's holding'. At an earlier period the name Ballyroney seems to have referred not to a single townland but to a number of townlands held by the family of (O')Rooney (sometimes *Roney*), chief tenants to the Magennis chieftains. What is now the townland of Ballyroney was known as *Ballycastleglass* which derives from Ir. *Baile an Chaisleáin Ghlais* 'townland of the green castle', the castle in question being a Norman *motte-and-bailey*, the remains of which stand on the north bank of the **Upper Bann**, in the north of the townland. The village of Ballyroney is not in the townland of that name but in the neighbouring townland of LACKAN. The place-name has given rise to the parish name DRUMBALLYRONEY, from Ir. *Droim Bhaile Uí Ruanaí* 'ridge of (O')Rooney's holding' [*Ballyronowe* 1611].

**Ballysallagh** tl, Down 3235
(sometimes *Ballysallough*)
*2.5km SE of Dromore*
par: *Dromore* bar: *Iveagh Lower, Lower Half*
Ir. *Baile Sealbhach* [bala **shal**awagh]

*Ballyskeagh, townland of thorn-bushes*

'townland of herds'. An alternative earlier name for the townland appears to have been *Baile na mBó* [bala na **mo**] 'townland of the cows' [*Ballyshallagh al. Ballinaboshalagh* 1614].

**Ballysally** tl, h.est., Derry 2843
*Suburb, 1km N of Coleraine town centre*
par: *Coleraine* bar: *NE Liberties of Coleraine*
Ir. *Baile Uí Shalaigh* [bala ee **hal**ee] '(O')Sally's townland'. The surname *Ó Salaigh* is rare and appears to be a variant of *Mac Salaigh* 'Sally'. A small portion of the large townland of Ballysally is in the neighbouring parish of BALLYAGHRAN. The townland includes the campus of the University of Ulster at Coleraine [*Ballyosallye* 1543].

**Ballyscullion** tls, par., Derry 2939
*Parish is 5km NE of Magherafelt*
bar: *Loughinsholin*
Ir. *Baile Uí Scoillín* [bala ee **skull**yeen] '(O')Scullion's townland'. The Scullions were medieval *erenagh*s or lay custodians of the parish's church lands. The ruins of the medieval parish church lie in an overgrown graveyard on CHURCH ISLAND in **Lough Beg**, a widening of the **Lower Bann** a short distance north of **Toome**. A small portion of the parish, i.e. the townland of BALLYSCULLION EAST, lies opposite the townland of Ballyscullion West, east of the Bann in the barony of TOOME UPPER in Co. Antrim [*Balle Oskullyn* 1397].

**Ballyshannon** tn., Donegal 1836
*17.5km SSW of Donegal town*
par: *Inishmacsaint/Kilbarron* bar: *Tirhugh*
Ir. *Béal Átha Seanaidh* [bell aha **shan**ee]. This is the official Ir. name of the town but it seems to be a development from the original form *Béal Átha Seanaigh* 'ford-mouth of *Seanach*'. The significance of the element *Seanach* is uncertain but it may represent a personal name which was very common in early Ireland. There was a St *Seanach* of **Lough Erne** whose feast day is 11 May. Ballyshannon stands on the river **Erne**, close to its mouth, and adjoining ASSAROE LAKE on the west [*(far) Bhel Atha Senaigh* 1398].

**Ballysillan** tls, distr., Antrim 3337
*District forms a suburb on the NW side of Belfast*
par: *Shankill* bar: *Belfast Upper*
Ir. *Baile na Saileán* [bala na **sal**an] 'townland of the willow groves/sally groves'. The townland of BALLYSILLAN UPPER contains SQUIRE'S HILL (374m) [*Ballynysillan* 1604].

**Ballyskeagh** tl, ham., Down 3336
*3.5km NE of Lisburn*
par: *Lambeg* bar: *Castlereagh Upper*
Ir. *Baile Sceach* [bala **skagh**] 'townland of thorn-bushes'. Ballyskeagh is on the south bank of the river **Lagan**, in the Co. Down portion of the parish of **Lambeg**.

**Ballystrudder** tl, vill., Antrim 3439
*At head of Larne Lough, 9km NE of Carrickfergus*
par: *Island Magee* bar: *Belfast Lower*
Ir. *Baile Strudair* [bala **strudd**ir] '*Strudar*'s townland'. The final element of the place-name is a gaelicised form of the Norse surname *Trodder* [*Ballytredder* 1669].

**Ballyvoy** tl, vill., Antrim 3144
*3.5km E of Ballycastle*
par: *Culfeightrin* bar: *Cary*
Ir. *Baile Bhuí* [bala **wee**] 'yellow townland'. The adjective *buí* [bwee] 'yellow' could refer either to the colour of the vegetation or to the colour of the soil [*Ballyvoy* c.1657].

**Ballywalter** tl, vill., par., Down 3636
*Village is on E coast of Ards Peninsula, 5km E of Greyabbey*
bar: *Ards Upper*
Ir. *Baile Bháltair* [bala **waalt**ir] 'Walter's townland'. *Walter* was a common personal name among the Anglo-Normans. An *alias* name for the parish of Ballywalter is WHITECHURCH which is the name of the townland containing the ruins of the former parish

church a short distance north-west of the village [*Whitechurch al. Ballywalter* 1661].

**Ballyward** tl, vill., Down 3233
*6.5km WNW of Castlewellan*
par: *Drumgooland*
bar: *Iveagh Upper, Lower Half*
Ir. *Baile Mhic an Bhaird* [bala vick a **wardge**] 'Ward's townland'. The literary family of *Mac an Bhaird* 'son of the bard' held lands from the Magennis chieftains in this area (*cf.* ***Lettermacaward*** in Donegal) [*Ballymc-Ewarde* 1611].

**Ballywildrick** tls, ham., Derry 2743
*7km W of Coleraine*
par: *Dunboe* bar: *Coleraine*
Ir. *Baile Ualraic* [bala **oo**alrick] '*Ualrac*'s townland'. The personal name *Ualrac* was popular among the MacQuillans of Co. Antrim and may be a gaelicisation of the O.E. name *Wulfric* 'wolf-powerful'. The hamlet of Ballywildrick is in the townland of BALLYWILDRICK LOWER which is bounded on the south by BALLYWILDRICK UPPER [*Ba:Wolrick* 1613].

**Balmoral** distr., Antrim 3337
*Suburb, 4km SW of Belfast city centre*
par: *Shankill* bar: *Belfast Upper*
The name Balmoral has been imported from Scotland where it is the name of a residence of the royal family in Aberdeenshire and signifies 'farm of the big clearing', deriving from Sc.G. *baile, mór* in combination with Brittonic *ial* 'open space'. The term *Brittonic* relates to the P-Celtic language which was spoken in Scotland before the arrival of Gaelic. Balmoral is in the townland of MALONE LOWER.

**Balnamore** vill., Antrim 2942
*3km SW of Ballymoney*
par: *Ballymoney* bar: *Dunluce Upper*
Ir. *Béal an Átha Móir* [bell an aha **more**] 'mouth of the big ford'. The site of the ford may be marked by BALNAMORE BRIDGE which crosses the BALLYMONEY RIVER at the east side of the village. Balnamore is in the townland of BALLYNACREE SKEIN.

**Banagher** distr., par., Derry 2640
*District is 3.5km SSW of Dungiven*
bar: *Keenaght*
Ir. *Beannchar* [**ban**agher] 'place of peaks'. This is the traditional interpretation of the

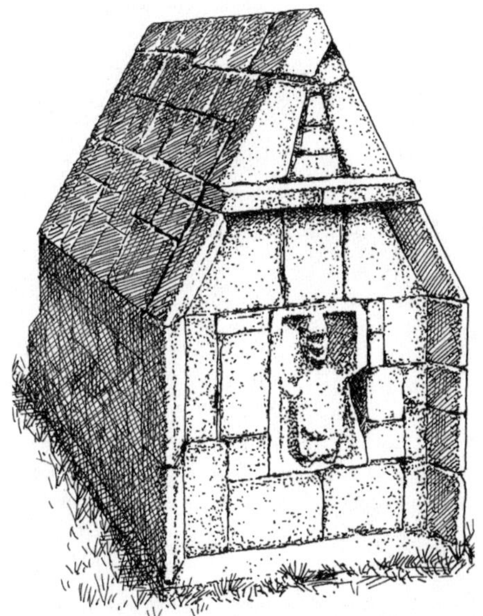

*O'Heney tomb, mortuary house at Banagher*

place-name. However, it is possible that the name could refer to a palisaded enclosure around a monastic settlement (*see* ***Bangor***). The ruins of the 12th-century BANAGHER OLD CHURCH are in a graveyard in the townland of MAGHERAMORE and may mark the site of an early church. A portion of the parish of Banagher is in the neighbouring barony of TIRKEERAN [*Benchor* 1397].

**Banbridge** tn, Down 3134
*20km NNE of Newry*
par: *Seapatrick* bar: *Iveagh Upper, Upper Half*
The town was laid out c.1767 and named from the first bridge built over the **Upper Bann** in 1712. At the beginning of this century it was known to native Irish speakers in Omeath and Monaghan as *Droichead na Banna* [dryhid na **bana**] 'bridge of the Bann', a direct translation of its English name. Banbridge is in the townland of BALLYVALLY which signifies 'townland of the way or pass' [*Bann Br.* 1743].

**Bangor** tn, par., Down 3538
*17km NE of Belfast*
bar: *Ards Lower*
Ir. *Beannchar* [**ban**agher]. The place-name goes back to the Ir. root *beann* 'point/peak' but its exact significance is uncertain. The name could refer to pointed rocks on the shore or to a pointed wattled enclosure around the

monastic settlement. The monastery of Bangor was founded by St Comgall in 555 or 559 and the site is marked by the present Church of Ireland church (the ABBEY CHURCH) at the head of the town, in the modern townland of CORPORATION. Most of the parish of Bangor is in the barony of ARDS LOWER while a small portion is in CASTLEREAGH LOWER [*ecclesia Bennchuir* 555].

**Bann** river Down/Armagh/Antrim/Derry
*Rises at Deer's Meadow in the Mournes and enters Lough Neagh at Bannfoot 9km NW of Portadown. Leaves Lough Neagh at Toome and enters the sea 2.5km W of Portstewart*
Ir. *An Bhanna* [an **wan**a] 'the goddess'. The river south of **Lough Neagh** is known as the UPPER BANN while the portion north of the lough is known as the LOWER BANN [*Banda* c.800].

**Bannfoot** vill., Armagh 2936
(*see* ***Charlestown or Bannfoot***)

**Barnes Gap** pass, Tyrone 2538
*7km NE of Gortin*
par: *Bodoney Upper* bar: *Strabane Upper*
Ir. *Bearnas* [**barn**as] 'gap' + E. *gap*. The E. element *gap*, which means the same as Ir. *bearnas*, has clearly been added at a later date. The gap in question is a pass in the **Sperrin Mountains** between **Glenelly Valley** and the valley of the **Owenkillew River**. The northern portion of the gap divides the townlands of BARNES LOWER and BARNES UPPER [*Barniss* c.1655].

**Barnesmore Gap** pass, Donegal 2038
*11km NE of Donegal town*
par: *Donegal* bar: *Tirhugh*
Ir. *An Bearnas Mór* [an barnas **more**] 'the great gap' + E. *gap*. Barnesmore Gap has CROGHCONNELLAGH (523m) to the west and BARNESMORE MOUNTAIN (451m) to the east. The hamlet of Barnesmore is 3km to the south-west, in the townland of KEADEW UPPER [(*tar*) *Bernus* 1522].

**Barnmeen** tl, ham., Down 3133
*2.5km WSW of Rathfriland*
par: *Drumgath* bar: *Iveagh Upper, Upper Half*
Ir. *Bearn Mhín* [barn **veen**] 'smooth or level gap'. Barnmeen is situated on low ground with hills to the north and south [*Ballybarnemyne* 1612].

**Barons Court** mansion, tl, Tyrone 2338
(sometimes *Baronscourt*)
*4.5km SW of Newtownstewart*
par: *Ardstraw* bar: *Strabane Lower*
Barons Court is named from the Georgian mansion which stands in the middle of the townland. It was originally built between 1779 and 1781 by James Hamilton, 8th Earl of Abercorn, whose ancestor, the 1st Earl (also named James Hamilton) from Renfrewshire in Scotland was granted land around **Strabane** during the Plantation of Ulster. The Hamiltons named the lakes in their estate LOUGH CATHERINE, LOUGH FANNY and LOUGH MARY and the nearby mountains **Bessy Bell** and MARY GRAY. The original name of the townland of Barons Court was *Derrywoone*, from Ir. *Doire Eoghain* [dirra **ow**en] 'Owen's oak-wood' [*Baronscourt demesne* 1831].

**Battery, The** ham., Tyrone 2937
*On W shore of Lough Neagh,16km E of Cookstown*
par: *Arboe* bar: *Dungannon Upper*
The name originally referred to a military embankment which formerly stood close to the shore of **Lough Neagh**. An *alias* name for the Battery is NEWPORT TRENCH, the element *trench* referring to the defensive wall and *Newport* to an adjacent fishing harbour. The Battery is in the townland of ARDEAN [*Battery Stone House recte Newport Trench* c.1835].

**Bawnboy** tl, vill., Cavan 2231
*6km W of Ballyconnell*
par: *Templeport* bar: *Tullyhaw*
Ir. *An Bábhún Buí* [an ba-woon **bwee**] 'the yellow *bawn* or fortified enclosure'. Bawnboy was a former stronghold of the family of *Mag Shamhráin* 'MacGovern/Magauran', medieval rulers of this area of north-west Cavan. There are castle ruins a short distance east of the village [*Bawnboy* 1664].

**Beagh-more** tls, Tyrone 2638
*14.5km NW of Cookstown*
par: *Kildress* bar: *Dungannon Upper*
Ir. *An Bheitheach Mhór* [an veyhagh **wore**] 'the place of birches (large)'. The very large townland of BEAGH-MORE is adjoined on the south by the townland of BEAGHBEG the name of which is from Ir. *An Bheitheach Bheag* 'the place of birches (small)' [*Beagh-more* 1621].

*Stone circles at Beagh-more*

**Beglieve** tl, Cavan 2630
*7km NW of Bailieborough*
par: *Knockbride* bar: *Clankee*
Ir. *Beagshliabh* [**beg**leeoo] 'little mountain'. The land in the townland rises to 200m [*Begleive* 1586].

**Belcoo** tls, vill., Fermanagh 2033
*14.5km WSW of Enniskillen*
par: *Cleenish* bar: *Clanawley*
Ir. *Béal Cú* [bell **koo**] '(ford-) mouth of the narrow'. The final element of the place-name is a shortened form of *cúnga*, the genitive of *cúng* 'a narrow'. In this case it appears to refer to the stretch of river which connects **Upper** and **Lower Lough Macnean** across a narrow neck of land and forms the southern boundary of the townlands of BELCOO EAST and BELCOO WEST. The village of Belcoo is in the townland of BELCOO EAST and the site of the ford is marked by the bridge over the river, at the bottom of the village street [*Beallacoungamore, Beallacoungabegg* 1607].

**Belfast** city, bars, Antrim/Down 3337
par: *Shankill/Knockbreda/Holywood*
bar: *Belfast Upper/Castlereagh Lower/Castlereagh Upper*
Ir. *Béal Feirste* [bell **ferst**ya] 'mouth of the sand-bank ford'. The 'sand-bank ford' was across the mouth of the river **Lagan**. The little river FARSET which flows below HIGH STREET and enters the Lagan near this point has also been named from the ford (*fearsaid* genitive *feirste*). The greater part of Belfast is west of the **Lagan** in the barony of BELFAST UPPER in Co. Antrim. The portion which lies east of the **Lagan** in Co. Down is shared between the baronies of CASTLEREAGH UPPER and CASTLEREAGH LOWER [(*bellum*) *Fertsi* 668].

**Belfast Lough** estuary, Antrim/Down 3337
Ir. *Loch Lao* [lough **lee**] 'estuary of the *Lao* or Lagan'. Ir. *loch* which commonly means 'lake' can also mean 'sea inlet/estuary'. The river **Lagan** which flows into Belfast Lough was at an early period known as *Lao* 'calf',

*Belfast Castle and Cave Hill*

from the bovine goddess which was believed to inhabit it [*Logia* 150AD].

**Bellaghy** vill., Derry 2939
*7km NW of Toome*
par: *Ballyscullion* bar: *Loughinsholin*
Ir. *Baile Eachaidh* [bala **agh**ee] '*Eochaidh*'s townland'. The personal name *Eochaidh* [**awgh**ee] which forms the final element of the surname *Ó hEachaidh* '(O')Ha(u)ghey', was once extremely common in Ireland. The former townland of Bellaghy has been renamed OLD TOWN and is divided into OLD TOWN DEER-PARK and OLD TOWN DOWNING. The village of Bellaghy was founded by the Londoners' Guild of Vintners in the early 17th century and was sometimes referred to as *Vinters Town* at that period [*Boile Eachaidh* c.1645].

**Bellanaleck** tl, vill., Fermanagh 2233
*On W bank of Upper Lough Erne, 7km S of Enniskillen*
par: *Cleenish* bar: *Clanawley*
Ir. *Bealach na Leice* [balagh na **leck**a] 'way/pass of the (flag)stone/flat rock'. The reference of the final element may be to a former ford across the narrow channel of **Upper Lough Erne** (*cf.* ***Belleek***) [*Ballanaleck* 1837].

**Bellanamallard** tl, vill., Fermanagh 2235
(usually *Ballinamallard*)
*9km NNE of Enniskillen*
par: *Magheracross* bar: *Tirkennedy*
Ir. *Béal Átha na Mallacht* [bell aha na **mal**aght] 'ford-mouth of the curses'. According to a legend St Columcille placed a curse on the roosters here in the sixth century. The village of Bellanamallard was founded in the early 17th century and stands on the north side of the BALLINAMALLARD RIVER [*Béal Átha na Mallacht* 1645].

**Bellanamore** tl, Donegal 1940
(sometimes *Ballinamore*)
*21km WNW of Ballybofey*
par: *Inishkeel* bar: *Boylagh*
Ir. *Béal an Átha Móir* [bell an aha **mo**-ir] 'mouth of the big ford'. The ford was across the river **Finn** which bounds the townland on the south [*Beallanaymore* 1621].

**Bellananagh** tl, vill., Cavan 2329
(usually *Ballinagh*)
*7km SSW of Cavan town*
par: *Kilmore* bar: *Clanmahon*
Ir. *Béal Átha na nEach* [bell aha na **nyagh**] 'ford-mouth of the horses'. The site of the ford may be marked by a bridge over the little river which flows into a lake at the south end of the village [*Ballinenagh* c.1657].

**Bellanode** vill., Monaghan 2633
(sometimes *Ballinode*)
*5km WNW of Monaghan town*
par: *Tedavnet* bar: *Monaghan*
Ir. *Béal Átha an Fhóid* [bell aha an **oy**idge] 'ford-mouth of the sod/mass/heap'. The site of the ford may be marked by the bridge which crosses the river **Blackwater** in the village, linking the townlands of MULLAGHMORE WEST and CLONTOE [*Ballynode* 1835].

**Bellarena** mansion, tl, Derry 2643
par: *Magilligan* bar: *Keenaght*
*At W foot of Binevenagh, 6.5km NNW of Limavady*
*perhaps* F. *belle* 'beautiful' + L. *arena* 'sandy place/strand'. The name Bellarena was coined in the late 18th century to refer to a house and demesne. The mansion, which still stands on the north bank of the **Roe**, was built in 1797 by Conolly Gage, on land settled in the mid 17th century by his ancestor William Gage from Northamptonshire in England. It incorporates parts of an earlier house built in 1690. The original Ir. name of the townland of Bellarena was *Baile an Mhargaidh* [bala an **war**agee] 'townland of the market' [*Bellarena* 1835].

**Belleek** tl, vill., Armagh 2932
(often *Belleeks*)
*12km W of Newry*
par: *Loughgilly* bar: *Orior Upper*
Ir. *Béal Leice* [bell **leck**a] '(ford-)mouth of the flat rock'. The site of the ford, which clearly consisted of a flat submerged rock, appears to be marked by BELLEEK BRIDGE which crosses a stream a short distance north of the village [*Bellick* 1657].

**Belleek** vill., par., Fermanagh 1935
*Village is on the border with Donegal, close to the W end of Lower Lough Erne*
bar: *Lurg*
Ir. *Béal Leice* [bell **leck**a] '(ford-)mouth of the flat rock'. As in the case of the previous entry, the ford was a flat submerged rock and its site is marked by the present bridge over the river **Erne**. The village is on the north bank

of the river, partly in the townland of RATHMORE and partly in FINNER. The parish of Belleek was created in 1792 out of the neighbouring parish of TEMPLECARN [*Bel-leice* 1409].

**Belmont** distr., Down 3337
*Suburb on the E side of Belfast*
par: *Holywood* bar: *Castlereagh Lower*
O.F. *Belmont* 'beautiful hill'. *Belmont* or *Belmount* was popular as a name for landlords' residences from the 18th century onwards. In this case the house was the residence of Mr Will Bateson in 1776 but it was demolished in 1894 and replaced by CAMPBELL COLLEGE. Belmont is in the townland of BALLYCLOGHAN [*Bellmount* 1834].

**Beltoy** tl, ham., Antrim 3439
*6.5km N of Carrickfergus*
par: *Glynn/Raloo* bar: *Belfast Lower*
*perhaps* Ir. *Béal tSóidh* [bell **to**ee] '(ford-) mouth of the turning'. The townland of Beltoy is divided into two adjacent portions, one in the parish of **Glynn** and the other in the parish of RALOO. The final element of the place-name may refer to a bend in the BELTOY WATERCOURSE which divides the two portions of the townland [*Beltid* 1608].

**Belturbet** tn., Cavan 2331
*On the E bank of the Erne, 13km NW of Cavan town*
par: *Annagh* bar: *Loughtee Lower*
Ir. *Béal Tairbirt* [bell **tar**abirch] '(ford-) mouth of the isthmus/neck of land'. The ford appears to have been between the east bank of the river **Erne** and the river-island known as TARBERT ISLAND. On the island are ruins of a 16th-century castle of the O'Reillys, built to defend the ford. In 1610 a large tract of land in the area was granted to Sir Stephen Butler of Huntington in England and erected into the Manor of *Castle Butler al. Belturbet* (*see* ***Butlers Bridge***, ***Newtownbutler***) [*Bél Tarbert* 1621].

**Belvoir** distr., Down 3336
*Forms a suburb on E bank of the Lagan, 5km S of Belfast city centre*
par: *Knockbreda* bar: *Castlereagh Upper*
O.F. *Belvoir* 'fine view'. Belvoir was originally the name of a house and demesne. The house was completed c.1758 and occupied by Arthur Hill who assumed the name of Trevor and was created Viscount Dungannon in 1765. By 1832 it had come into the possession of Sir Robert Bateson, MP for Co. Down. The house was demolished in 1961. The extensive BELVOIR PARK FOREST is partly in the townland of **Breda** which contains an old graveyard, the site of the former parish church of that name (*see* ***Knockbreda***). Belvoir Castle in Leicestershire in England was the ancestral home of the Duke of Rutland who became Lord Lieutenant of Ireland in 1784 (*see* ***Rutland Island***) [*Belvoir* 1744].

**Benbane Head** hl, Antrim 2944
*On N Antrim coast, 5.5km NE of Bushmills*
par: *Billy* bar: *Cary*
Ir. *An Bhinn Bhán* [an vinn **waan**] 'the white headland' + E. *head*. The E. element *head* has clearly been added at a later date. Benbane Head is in the townland of TONDUFF MOUNTAIN, a short distance east of the **Giant's Causeway**.

**Benbradagh** mtn, Derry 2741
*4km NE of Dungiven*
par: *Dungiven* bar: *Keenaght*
Ir. *An Bhinn Bhradach* [an vinn **vrad**agh] 'the treacherous/dangerous peak'. Benbradagh is a conspicuous peak of 465m in the townland of DERRYDUFF. A local tradition suggests that Benbradagh is named from a woman of depraved character named *Maevebradagh* (Ir. *Méabh Bhradach* 'treacherous/dishonest Maeve'). An alternative Ir. name for Benbradagh was *Gealbhinn* [**gal**avin] 'white/bright peak', a name which occurs in GELVIN RIVER, a stream which rises on the west side of Benbradagh and flows into the river **Roe** 4.5km north of **Dungiven**. [*Binn Bhradach* 1680].

**Benburb** tl, vill., Tyrone 2835
*On Co. Armagh border, 9km NW of Armagh city*
par: *Clonfeacle* bar: *Dungannon Middle*
Ir. *An Bhinn Bhorb* [an vinn **wurr**ib] 'the bold/prominent cliff'. The cliff in question overlooks the river **Blackwater** a short distance south of the village [*Beunn Bhoruib, Pinna Superba* 1621].

**Bendooragh** tl, vill., Antrim 2942
*3.5km SW of Ballymoney*
(sometime *Bundooragh*)
par: *Ballymoney* bar: *Dunluce Upper*
Ir. *Bun Dúraí* [bun **door**ee] 'bottom-land of

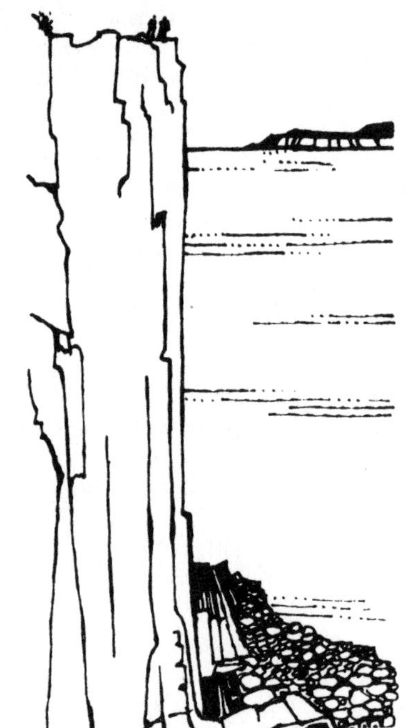

*Benmore/Fair Head with Rathlin Island beyond*

black soil'. Bendooragh has given name to a stream known as the BENDOORAGH BURN [*Bun Dubhroighe* c.1645].

**Benmore or Fair Head** hl, Antrim 3144
*On N Antrim coast, 6.5km ENE of Ballycastle*
par: *Culfeightrin* bar: *Cary*
Ir. *An Bhinn Mhór* [an vin **wore**] 'the great cliff'. Benmore or Fair Head is a conspicuous promontory in the townland of CROSS. 'Fair Head' is not an accurate translation of Ir. *An Bhinn Mhór* and it is possible that Fair Head and *An Bhinn Mhór* originally referred to two different parts of the promontory [*Fayre forland* 1567].

**Benone** tl, ham., Derry 2743
*On N Derry coast, 14km WNW of Coleraine*
par: *Magilligan* bar: *Keenaght*
Ir. *Bun Abhann* [bun **ow**en] 'foot of the river'. The 'river' in question may be the stream which flows into the sea at DOWNHILL STRAND, a short distance to the east [*Bunowne* 1654].

**Beragh** tl, vill., Tyrone 2536
*11km SE of Omagh*
par: *Clogherny* bar: *Omagh East*
Ir. *Bearach* [**bar**agh] 'place of points/peaks'. The place-name may refer to the numerous hills in the area or possibly to standing stones on BERAGH HILL [*Berhagh* 1631].

**Bessbrook** vill., Armagh 3032
*4km NW of Newry*
par: *Killevy* bar: *Orior Upper*
The village of Bessbrook is named from Elizabeth or Bess Nicholson, wife of Mr Joseph Nicholson whose family had carried on a linen business in the district from 1806 until 1845, the first mill having been originally established by William Pollock at the end of the 18th century. The present 'model village' of Bessbrook was founded in 1846 by John Grubb Richardson, son of James Nicolson Richardson and a relation by marriage of the Nicolson family. The Richardsons were descended from John Richardson from Gloucestershire in England who had settled in **Loughgall** at the end of the 16th century. The brook in question is the BESSBROOK RIVER, the upper portion of which is known as the CAMLOUGH RIVER. The village of Bessbrook straddles the three townlands of MAGHERNAHELY, CLOGHAREVAN and MAYTOWN [*Bessbrook* 1888].

**Bessy Bell** mtn, Tyrone 2338
*3km SSW of Newtownstewart*
par: *Ardstraw* bar: *Strabane Lower*
Bessy Bell (420m) in the townland of BALLYRENAN is in the estate of **Barons Court**, home of the Duke of Abercorn (*see above*), and both Bessy Bell and the nearby MARY GRAY (230m) were named after heroines in an old Scottish ballad which begins 'Bessie Bell and Mary Gray they were two bonnie lassies'. The original Ir. name of Bessy Bell was *Sliabh Troim* [sleeoo **trim**] 'mountain of elder' [(*ucht*) *Slebhe Truim* 1275].

**Big Collin** mtn, Antrim 3239
*18km SW of Larne*
par: *Rashee* bar: *Antrim Upper*
E. *big* + Ir. *collann, perhaps* 'height/high ground'. The form *collann* appears to be derived from O.Ir. *coll*, literally 'neck/jaw/head'. Big Collin (353m) in the townland of TILDARG, is 4.5km south-west of **Wee Collin** (306m) [*Collin Mt.* 1780].

**Big Dog/Little Dog** hills, Fermanagh 2035
(*see* ***Dog Big/Dog Little***)

**Binevenagh** mtn, Derry 2643
(sometimes *Benevenagh*)
*7km N of Limavady*
par: *Magilligan* bar: *Keenaght*
Ir. *Binn Fhoibhne* [bin **ev**ena] '*Foibhne*'s peak'. A legend has it that *Foibhne* son of *Taircheltar* was slain here in pre-Christian times. *Aibhne* [**ev**ena], of which *Foibhne* is a variant spelling, was a common forename in the area until recent times. Binevenagh (385m) is in the townland of BALLYLEIGHERY UPPER [*Bend Foibne* c.1397].

**Birches, The** vill., Armagh 2936
*9km NW of Portadown*
par: *Tartaraghan* bar: *Oneilland West*
The village is named from an area of birch trees which in 1837 is referred to as 'a small grove of birch trees in the townland of BALLYNARRY on the main road from Dungannon to Portadown' [*the Birches* 1835].

**Bishops Court** tl, ham., Down 3534
*7.5km ESE of Downpatrick*
par: *Dunsfort* bar: *Lecale Lower*
Bishop's Court was so-named because the land formerly belonged to the bishop of Down. In 1833 we find a reference to a castle but no trace now remains. The original Ir. name of the townland, which contains the site of an ancient chapel, was *Lios Mhaoláin* [liss **wee**line] '*Maolán*'s fort' [*Lismolyn* 1306].

**Black Head** hl, Antrim 3439
*On E Antrim coast, 9.5km NE of Carrickfergus*
par: *Island Magee* bar: *Belfast Lower*
The promontory of Black Head is made of black basalt and the name contrasts with **White Head**, a limestone promontory a short distance to the south-west (*see below*).

**Black Hill** hill, Derry 2842
(sometimes *Blackhill*)
*10.5km S of Coleraine*
par: *Aghadowey* bar: *Coleraine*
Black Hill (90m) is in the townland of MULLAN, the name of which derives from Ir. *An Mullán* 'the hillock'. It is possible, therefore, that both place-names refer to the same feature [*Mullan* 1654].

**Blacklion** vill., Cavan 2033
*16km WSW of Enniskillen*
par: *Killinagh* bar: *Tullyhaw*
Blacklion, in the townland of TUAM, is named from a sign over the door of a public house which formerly stood in the village. The village was known in Ir. as *An Leargaidh* [an **lar**agee] 'the slope', from the district in which it is situated. There was formerly a hamlet named RED LION a short distance to the south-west [*Largay or Black Lion Inn* 1778].

**Black Mountain** mtn, tl, Antrim 3337
par: *Shankill* bar: *Belfast Upper*
*4.5km W of Belfast city centre*
Black Mountain (390m) has given name to the townland of that name, even though its summit stands a short distance to the north, in the neighbouring townland of **Divis** (Ir. *Dubhais* 'black ridge, peak'). It is possible that the E. name Black Mountain is in fact a translation of Ir. *Dubhais* [**doo**ish] (*see **Divis***).

**Blackskull** vill., Down 3135
*6km N of Banbridge*
par: *Donaghcloney*
bar: *Iveagh Lower, Upper Half*
Blackskull in the townland of BALLYGUNAGHAN was named from an inn with a negro-head sign which from the end of the last century until recently was a post office. A macabre local story tells how a black man was beheaded and his skull mounted above the door of the inn [*Blackskull* 1898].

**Blackstaff** river, Antrim
*Rises on the slopes of Black Mountain west of Belfast. Enters the Lagan a short distance E of Belfast city centre*
par: *Shankill* bar: *Belfast Upper*
Ir. *Abhainn Bheara* [owen **var**a] 'river of the staff'. The E. element *staff* is a translation of the original Ir. element *bior* (gen. *beara*) which is likely to have referred to a primitive crossing-place, formed from beams of oak. The element *black* presumably referred to the colour of the beams.

**Blackwater** river, Tyrone/Armagh/Monaghan
*Rises N of Fivemiletown in Co. Tyrone. Enters Lough Neagh at Maghery in Co. Armagh*
The Ir. name of the river was *An Abhainn Mhór* [an owen **wore**] 'the great river', which, curiously enough, is also the Ir. name of the river BLACKWATER in Cork. An earlier Ir. name for the Blackwater was *An Dabhall* [an **dau**al] 'the water'. Part of its course forms the bound-

ary between Cos Tyrone and Monaghan and later between Tyrone and Armagh. Another **Blackwater** rises in Co. Monaghan close to **Slieve Beagh** and (under the name COR RIVER) joins this Blackwater 2km south of **Caledon** in Co Armagh [*for brú Abhann Móire* 1483].

**Blackwatertown** tl, vill., Armagh 2835
*8km NNW of Armagh city*
par: *Clonfeacle* bar: *Armagh*
The village of Blackwatertown is named from its situation on the east bank of the river **Blackwater**. The Ir. name for the village is *An Port Mór* [an port **more**] 'the great fort', referring to a fort built in 1575 by the Earl of Essex. The townland of Blackwatertown goes by the *alias*-name LISBOFIN which is from Ir. *Lios Bó Finne* [liss bo **fin**ya] 'fort of the white cow' [(*ex*) *Portu Magno* 1578].

**Blagh** tl, ham., Derry 2843
*4km NE of Coleraine*
par: *Coleraine*
bar: *NE Liberties of Coleraine*
Ir. *Lios na Bláiche* [liss na **blai**ha] 'fort of the buttermilk'. The first element of the place-name may refer to a *motte-and-bailey* which formerly stood in the townland [*Lisnablagh* 1780].

**Blaney** tls, Fermanagh 2135
*11km NW of Enniskillen*
par: *Inishmacsaint* bar: *Magheraboy*
Ir. *Bléinigh* [**bley**nee] '(place of the) inlet/bay'. Ir. *bléin* literally means 'groin' but in place-names it can mean 'inlet/bay/creek'. The townlands of BLANEY EAST and MILLTOWN BLANEY border on BLANEY BAY on the south shore of **Lower Lough Erne**. The townland of BLANEY WEST adjoins MILLTOWN BLANEY on the south [*Bleny* 1659].

**Bleary** tl, vill., Down 3035
*4km S of Lurgan*
par: *Tullylish* bar: *Iveagh Lower, Upper Half*
*perhaps* Ir. *Bladhraigh* [**bler**ee] '(place of the) portion'. Bleary was originally a subdivision of a larger townland in a now-obsolete district named *Clanconnell* and this may account for its name [*Blyery in Clanconnell* 1611].

**Bloody Bridge** bridge, Down 3332
*On Co Down coast, 4km S of Newcastle*
par: *Kilkeel* bar: *Mourne*
Bloody Bridge which spans the BLOODY BRIDGE RIVER in the townland of BALLAGHANERY UPPER is named from an infamous murder of Protestants in the rebellion of 1641 [*Bloody bridge* 1836].

**Bloody Foreland** hl, mtn., Donegal 1843
*10km WNW of Gortahork*
par: *Tullaghobegly* bar: *Kilmacrenan*
Ir. *Cnoc Fola* [kruck **fol**a] 'hill of blood'. According to one tradition the blood was that of the Fomorian giant *Balar Bailcbhéimneach* 'Balor of the Great Blows' who was killed here by his grandson in revenge for the beheading of his son-in-law *Cionnaola*, ruler of the nearby district of **Cloganeely** (*see below*). *Balar* was also known as *Balar Birug-derc* 'Balor of the Evil Eye' and had his base on nearby **Tory Island**. The E. name Bloody Foreland is a loose translation of the Ir. *Cnoc Fola* and is used for both the headland and the mountain (314m) which stands a short distance to the south-east. However, the Ir. name is used strictly for the mountain, while the headland is known as *Rinn Aird Dealbha* [rinn ard **jal**awa] 'point of the bleak height' or *An Reannach Rua* [an ranagh **roo**a] 'the red promontory'. Both mountain and headland are situated in the townland of KNOCKFOLA which is an anglicisation of Ir. *Cnoc Fola* 'hill of blood' [*Knockfalla* 1613].

**Bloomfield** distr., Down 3337
*Suburb on the E side of Belfast*
par: *Holywood* bar: *Castlereagh Lower*
Bloomfield is named from a former mansion in the townland of **Ballyhackamore**, the residence of Arthur Crawford in 1819 [*Bloomfield* 1837].

**Bluestack Mountains** Donegal 1938
(*see* ***Croaghgorm or Blue Stack Mountains***)

**Boa Island** Fermanagh 2136
*Off N shore of Lower Lough Erne*
par: *Drumkeeran/Templecarn*
bar: *Lurg/Tirhugh*
Ir. *Inis Badhbha* [inish **boa**] '*Badhbh*'s island'. In Irish mythology, *Badhbh* is the name of a war goddess, though the original meaning of *badhbh* was 'carrion crow' (*see* ***Knockavoe*** *below*). Boa is a long, narrow island, now connected to the mainland by a road-bridge at each end [*Badhba* 1369].

**Boardmills** vill., Down 3335
*7km N of Ballynahinch*
par: *Killaney/Saintfield*
bar: *Castlereagh Upper*
Boardmills is named from wooden corn mills which formerly stood in the townland of CARRICKMADDYROE. There is also the stump of a windmill a short distance north of the village, a portion of which is in the townland of BRESAGH [*Boardmills* 1904].

**Bodoney** tl, ham., Tyrone 2336
*3km NW of Dromore*
par: *Dromore* bar: *Omagh East*
Ir. *Both Dhomhnaigh* [boh **ġoan**ee] 'hut/monastic cell of the (early) church'. There is now no trace or record of an ecclesiastical site in the townland. There is another townland named BODONEY 10km to the south in the parish of KILSKEERY and there are parishes named BODONEY UPPER and BODONEY LOWER some 35 km to the north, all sharing the same derivation [*Bodony* 1613].

**Boho** vill., par., Fermanagh 2134
*Village is 11km W of Enniskillen*
bar: *Clanawley*
Ir. *Botha* [**boh**a] 'huts/monastic cells'. There is now no trace of the features referred to in the place-name, though the site of an early monastery is marked by the remnants of a ninth-century high cross in the graveyard of the present Catholic church, in the townland of TONEEL NORTH. Boho is in the townland of TULLYHOLVIN LOWER [*Botha* 1432].

**Bolea** tl, vill., Derry 2742
*4.5km NE of Limavady*
par: *Drumachose* bar: *Keenaght*
Ir. *Both Liath* [boh **lee**a] 'grey hut/monastic cell'. There is now no trace or record of the feature referred to in the place-name [*Boleah* 1613].

**Boleran** tl, vill., Derry 2842
(often *Ballerin*)
*5km NW of Garvagh*
par: *Errigal* bar: *Coleraine*
Ir. *Baile Uí Shírín* [bala ee **heer**een] '(O')Sheeran's townland'. The surname *Ó Sírín* '(O')Sheeran/Sheerain' is also prominent in Donegal and Fermanagh (cf. ***Ballyheerin***). A subdivision of the townland is called SCOTCH BOLERAN OR GOLDS TOWN [*Ballyirin* 1613].

*A celtic cow*

**Bonamargy** tl, Antrim 3144
*On E bank of the Margy river, adjacent to the town of Ballycastle*
par: *Culfeightrin* bar: *Cary*
Ir. *Bun na Margaí* [bun na **mar**agee] 'foot of the river Margy'. The little Margy river which flows into the sea east of **Ballycastle** is formed by the confluence of the GLENSHESK RIVER with the CAREY RIVER. The name Margy is from Ir. *An Mhargaigh* [an **war**agee] 'the boundary river'. Bonamargy is well-known as the site of BONAMARGY FRIARY, a Franciscan establishment founded c.1500, the ruins of which stand close to the east bank of the river [*Bunanmargaidh* c.1617].

**Bottlehill** tl, ham., Armagh 2935
(often *Battlehill*)
*3km SW of Portadown*
par: *Kilmore* bar: *Oneilland West*
H.E./Sc. *bottle* 'bundle of straw' + E. *hill*. There is a conspicuous hill of 50m in the west of the townland which clearly produced a good harvest of hay. The original Ir. name of the townland was *An Céide Mór* [an kedga **more**] 'the big flat-topped hill' [*Keadymore als. Botle hill* c.1657].

**Bovedy** tl, ham., Derry 2841
*3km W of Kilrea*
par: *Tamlaght O'Crilly* bar: *Coleraine*
Ir. *Both Mhíde* [boh **veedg**a] '*Míde*'s hut/monastic cell'. *Míde* is a pet form of the female personal name *Íde* 'Ita' and in this case is likely to be the name of an early saint. There

*Mortuary house at Bovevagh*

is now no trace or record of a monastic building [*Bovidie* 1654].

**Bovevagh** tl, par., Derry 2641
(sometimes *Boveva*)
*Townland is 5km NW of Dungiven*
bar: *Keenaght*
Ir. *Boith Mhéabha* [boy **vey**va] 'Maeve's hut/monastic cell'. In this case the 'hut' or 'monastic cell' seems to have been on the site of the former parish church of Bovevagh, the ruins of which are close to the confluence of the BOVEVAGH RIVER with the ALTAHULLION BURN. In Irish mythology *Medb* (Mod. Ir. *Méabh*) was a goddess of sovereignty but in this case she has clearly been 'christianised'. The name was formerly very common and has latterly become popular in the anglicised form *Maeve* [(*derteach*) *Bothe Medba* 1100].

**Braid** river, Antrim 3140
*Rises near Berry Hill, W of Carnlough. Flows into the Main at Galgorm, 2.5km W of Ballymena*
Ir. *Abhainn na Brád* [owen na **braad**] 'river of the throat or gorge'. The Braid is named from the long valley through which it flows, dividing the parishes of RACAVAN and SKERRY east of **Ballymena** [*Owenbrade* 1606].

**Branch, The** ham., Derry 2441
*On NW outskirts of Londonderry*
par: *Templemore*
bar: *NW Liberties of Londonderry*
The place-name has its origin in THE BRANCH ROAD, a short stretch of road which connects the old road from Derry to **Buncrana** with the new road between the two places. The Branch is in the townland of **Ballymagrorty** [*The Branch Road* 1909].

**Braniel** tl, distr., Down 3337
*Suburb, 5km SE of Belfast city centre*
par: *Knockbreda* bar: *Castlereagh Upper*
The origin of this place-name is obscure. The root may be Ir. *broinn* 'breast/bosom; brink/verge' possibly referring to the conspicuous BRANIEL HILL (176m) [*Ballybronill* 1632].

**Brantry** distr., Tyrone 2735
*10km SSW of Dungannon*
par: *Aghaloo* bar: *Dungannon Lower*
Ir. *An Bréantar* [an **breyn**tar] 'the place of odours'. The place-name may refer to a swamp or bog. There was formerly a Franciscan friary in the townland of GORT. Brantry has given name to BRANTRY LOUGH and BRANTRY WOOD [(*imlibh*) *a'Bhrentair* 1642].

**Bready** ham.,Tyrone 2340
*11.5km N of Strabane*
par: *Donaghedy* bar: *Strabane Lower*
Ir. *An Bhréadaigh* [an **vrey**dee] 'the (place of) broken land', (*literally* 'place of fragments, remnants'). Bready is in the townland of TAMNABRADY which derives from Ir. *Tamhnach na Bréadaí* [taunagh na **brey**dee] 'field of the broken land'.

**Breda** tl, Down 3335
(*see* ***Knockbreda, Newtownbreda***)

**Bridge End** vill., Donegal 2342
(sometimes *Bridgend*)
par: *Burt* bar: *Inishowen West*
Bridge End is named from a bridge over the SKEOGE RIVER on which the village stands.

**Bridge End** distr., Tyrone 2339
(sometimes *Bridgend*)
*Forms portion of town of Strabane adjoining Strabane Bridge on the W*
par: *Urney* bar: *Strabane Lower*
Bridge End is in the townland of MAGIRR, on the west bank of the river **Mourne**.

**Brigh** tl, ham., Tyrone 2837
*2km NNE of Stewartstown*
par: *Ballyclog* bar: *Dungannon Upper*
Ir. *Bríoch* [**bree**agh] 'hilly place' [*Breigh* 1633].

**Bright** tl, par., Down 3533
*Townland is 6.5km SSE of Downpatrick*
bar: *Lecale Upper*
Ir. *Breachtán* [**braght**an] 'speckled place'. The present Church of Ireland church occupies the site of the medieval parish church and also of an early church [*Mrechtan* c.900].

**Brockagh** tl, Derry 2741
*4.5km SW of Garvagh*
par: *Errigal* bar: *Coleraine*
Ir. *An Bhreacach* [an **vrack**agh] 'the speckled or rocky place'. The townland of Brockagh contains the hamlets of LOWER BROCKAGH and MIDDLE BROCKAGH. It is is adjoined on the south by the townland of BROCKAGHBOY (Ir. *An Bhreacach Bhuí* [an vrackagh **wee**] 'the yellow speckled place') and a stream named BROCKAGH WATER flows through the townland [*Brackagh* 1610].

**Brookeborough** vill., Fermanagh 2334
*15km ESE of Enniskillen*
par: *Aghavea* bar: *Magherastephana*
The village of Brookeborough grew up in the 19th century on land which originally belonged to Conor Maguire but which was granted in 1666 to Sir Henry Brooke, a descendant of Sir Basil Brooke from Cheshire in England, governor of Donegal in the early 17th century. Sir Basil's namesake, Viscount Brookeborough, was Prime Minister of Northern Ireland from 1943 to 1963. The ancestral home is the nearby mansion of **Colebrooke** (*see below*). Brookeborough is situated in the townland of AGHALUN (Ir. *Achadh Lon* [aghoo **lun**] 'field of blackbirds') [*Brookeborough* 1835].

**Broughderg** tl, Tyrone 2638
*16km NW of Cookstown*
par: *Lissan* bar: *Dungannon Upper*
Ir. *Bruach Dearg* [brooagh **jar**ig] 'red bank/margin' [*Brugh Derge* 1666].

**Brougher** tl, Fermanagh 2335
*13km NE of Enniskillen*
par: *Enniskillen* bar: *Tirkennedy*
Ir. *Bruachar* [**broo**agher] 'brink/edge'. The townland takes its name from BROUGHER MOUNTAIN (316m) which stands on the Fermanagh/Tyrone border [*Brochar* 1610].

**Broughshane** tls, vill., Antrim 3140
*5km NE of Ballymena*
par: *Racavan* bar: *Antrim Lower*
Ir. *Bruach Sheáin* [brooagh **hyine**] 'Shane's dwelling'. In this case, the element *bruach* 'bank/brink' appears to be a corruption of *brugh* 'dwelling/mansion', apparently referring to a castle of Shane mac Brian O'Neill, ruler of LOWER CLANDEBOY from 1595 to 1617 (*see* ***Shane's Castle***) which formerly stood on the north side of the village street. The previous name for the townland of Broughshane was *Aghnaclare* (*perhaps* Ir. *Achadh an Chláir* 'field of the plank, plain'). The village of Broughshane is mainly in the townland of BROUGHSHANE UPPER which is bounded on the south-west by BROUGHSHANE LOWER, the latter stretching westwards to the eastern outskirts of **Ballymena** [*Bruaghshane* c.1655].

**Browndod** hill, tl., Antrim 3139
*7km NE of Antrim town*
par: *Donegore* bar: *Antrim Upper*
The element *dod* signifies 'a bare round hill' and is derived from either O.E. *dodden* 'to pollard or cut' or O.N. *toddi* 'a foothill'. It is found in the English Lake District and also in the Scottish eastern Borders. Browndod (262m) stands in the middle of the townland. There is another hill and townland of the same name 3km west-south-west of **Larne**.

**Brown's Bay** ham., Antrim 3440
*At N end of Island Magee, 3km E of Larne*
par: *Island Magee* bar: *Belfast Lower*
Brown's Bay in the townland of BALLYCRONAN BEG is said to be named from a James Brown, farmer, who is recorded as living beside the bay in 1683. In 1840 the surnames Brown and Wilson were the most prevalent surnames on the tombstones in the new Brown's Bay churchyard. In Ulster, Brown is generally of English or Scottish origin, but in this area it is most likely to be Scottish [*Brown's Bay* 1780].

**Bruce's Cave** Antrim 3145
*At NE tip of Rathlin Island*
par: *Rathlin* bar: *Cary*
The cave, which is in the townland of BALLYCARRY, is said to have been frequented by Robert Bruce when he fled to **Rathlin** from Scotland in the early 14th century. A short distance to the south are the last remnants of BRUCE'S CASTLE where it is said that Bruce was inspired to gain the Scottish crown at the BATTLE OF BANNOCKBURN by watching the relentless efforts of a spider to spin its web.

*A folly at Bryansford*

**Bruckless** tl, ham., Donegal 1737
*On Donegal Bay, 16km W of Donegal town*
par: *Killaghtee* bar: *Banagh*
Ir. *An Bhroclais* [an **vruck**lish] 'the den, cave or hollow' [*Brucklis* 1802].

**Bryansford** vill., Down 3343
*3km NW of Newcastle*
par: *Kilcoo* bar: *Iveagh Upper, Lower Half*
Ir. *Áth Bhriain* [ah **vree**in] 'Brian's ford'. The E. name appears to be a translation of the original Ir. The Brian referred to is said to have been Brian son of Brian mac Hugh Magennis who held lands here in 1640 and was descended from the dominant ruling family in the barony of IVEAGH from medieval times. The ford appears to have been at the south-west end of the village, across the stream which divides the townlands of AGHACULLION and BALLYHAFRY and flows through TULLYMORE PARK before entering the river **Shimna** [*Bryansford* 1743].

**Buckna** tl, vill., Antrim 3240
*11km NE of Ballymena*
par: *Racavan* bar: *Antrim Lower*
Ir. *Bocshnámh* [**buck**nau] 'stag ford'. The ford appears to have been over the GLEN BURN which flows through the townland. While the hamlet of BUCKNA UPPER is in the townland of Buckna, the village of Buckna is divided between the townlands of BALLYNACAIRD and TAMYBUCK [*Boughna* 1669].

**Bunbeg** tl, vill., Donegal 1842
*12.5km NNE of Dunglow*
par: *Tullaghobegly* bar: *Kilmacrenan*
Ir. *An Bun Beag* [an bun **beg**] 'the little (river-) foot'. The river referred to is the **Clady River**. The adjective 'little' is to distinguish this river foot from the foot of the larger GWEEDORE RIVER a short distance to the south. The village of Bunbeg is not in the townland of that name but in the neighbouring townland of MAGHERACLOGHER.

**Buncrana** tn., Donegal 2343
*On E shore of Lough Swilly, 15.5km NW of Derry city*
par: *Fahan Lower* bar: *Inishowen West*
Ir. *Bun Cranncha* [bun **cran**agha] 'foot of the (river) Crana'. The CRANA RIVER rises near **Slieve Snaght** 10km to the north-east and flows into **Lough Swilly** to the north of the town. The name of the river is derived from Ir. *An Chrannach* 'the wooded one' [*Boncranagh* 1601].

**Bundoran** tn., Donegal 1835
*On Donegal Bay, 6km WSW of Ballyshannon*
par: *Inishmacsaint* bar: *Tirhugh*
Ir. *Bun Dobhráin* [bun **doar**ine] 'foot of the (river) *Dobhrán*'. The *Dobhrán* appears to be an older name for the BRADOGE RIVER which flows into the sea here. The name *Dobhrán* signifies 'little water' [*Bundorin* 1802].

**Bunkers Hill** Antrim 3140
*4.5km S of Ballymena*
par: *Connor* bar: *Antrim Lower*
Bunkers Hill is a small hill in the townland of SLAGHT. The name commemorates the battle of Bunker Hill in Boston during the American War of Independence (1776). A number of other places in Ulster have been named from the same battle.

**Burn Dennet** river, Tyrone
*Rises in the Sperrins, 8km NE of Plumbridge. Enters the Foyle 7km N of Strabane*
Sc./N.E. *burn* 'stream' + Ir. *Dianaid* [**jain**idge] 'swift one'. The Sc./N.E. element

*burn* has clearly been added at a later date [(*go*) *Dianait* 1600].

**Burnfoot** vill., Donegal 2342
*8km NW of Londonderry*
par: *Burt* bar: *Inishowen West*
Sc./N.E. *burn* 'stream' + E. *foot*. Burnfoot is so-named because it stands at the point where the BURNFOOT RIVER formerly entered **Lough Swilly**. Due to land-reclamation schemes, the village is now 2.5km east of the foot of the river. The village is in the townland of BALLYEDEROWEN, the name of which derives from Ir. *Baile Idirabhainn* 'between-river townland', the rivers in question being the BURNFOOT RIVER and the SKEOGE RIVER which flows a short distance to the south. The hamlet of BURNFOOT UPPER lies a short distance to the south-east [*Burnfoot Bridge* 1762].

**Burntollet River** Derry
*Rises at Altahullion Hill, 7.5km NW of Dungiven. Enters the river Faughan 5.5km NW of Claudy.*
Sc./N.E. *burn* 'stream' + Ir. *tolaid* [**toll**idge] 'flooding one/abundant one' + E. *river*. The E. element *river* and the Sc./N.E. element *burn* which are roughly the same in meaning have clearly been added at a later date [*Taluide* c.1680].

**Burren** tl, vill., Down 3132
*3.5km N of Warrenpoint*
par: *Clonallan* bar: *Iveagh Upper, Upper Half*
Ir. *An Bhoirinn* [an **wurr**in] 'the rocky district/large stone'. It is possible that Burren is named from a *dolmen* or prehistoric chambered grave which stands a short distance north west of the village [*Ballibowrne al Bowryn* 1570].

**Burt** vill., par., Donegal 2342
*Village is 7.5km WNW of Derry city*
bar: *Inishowen West*
Ir. *An Beart* [an **bart**]. The modern Irish name is a shortened form of *Droim Beartach* 'heaped/piled(?) ridge'. The name may refer to a very conspicuous knoll on the shore of **Lough Swilly**, on top of which there are the remains of a 16th-century O'Doherty castle. The parish of Burt was created in 1809 out of the neighbouring parish of TEMPLEMORE. Burt is in the townland of BURT LEVEL (*INTAKE*) which consists mainly of land reclaimed from **Lough Swilly** [(*espoc*) *Droma Bertach* c.830].

**Burtonport** tl, vill., Donegal 1741
*7km NW of Dunglow*
par: *Templecrone* bar: *Boylagh*
The village of Burtonport grew up beside a fishing port which was established in1785 by William Burton, later William Burton Conyngham (1733–96) (*see also* ***Rutland Island, Mount Charles***). The village was further developed by Burton's grand-nephew, the 2nd Marquis Conyngham. The original Ir. name of the townland of Burtonport was *Aillt an Chorráin* [altch a **khorr**ine] 'glen/gully of the crescent or curve'. The Conyngham family were descended from Charles Conyngham who gave name to **Mount Charles** in the south of the county [*Burton Port* 1835].

**Bush** river, Antrim
*Rises at Bush Head, 6.5km SE of Loughguile. Enters the sea at Bushfoot, 2km N of Bushmills*
Ir. *An Bhuais* [an **woo**ish] 'the cow-like one'. The river name appears to be that of the goddess who was believed to dwell therein [(*per*) *Buás* c.670].

**Bushmills** tl, vill., Antrim 2944
*12km NE of Coleraine*
par: *Billy/Dunluce* bar: *Cary/Dunluce Lower*
The town of Bushmills is named from a 17th-century corn mill which stood on the river **Bush** and which in the 19th century was adapted to generate power for the electric tramway between **Portrush** and the **Giant's Causeway**. The town straddles the townlands of BUSHMILLS OR MAGHERABOY and BUSHMILLS OR BALLAGHMORE, on the east and west banks of the **Bush** respectively. Bushmills is famous for its whiskey distillery which was founded in 1608 [*Bushmills* 1636].

**Butlers Bridge** vill., Cavan 2431
(sometimes *Butler's Bridge*)
*7.5km SE of Belturbet*
par: *Castleterra* bar: *Loughtee Upper*
Butlers Bridge which stands on the ANNALEA RIVER is named from the Butler family whose ancestor Sir Stephen Butler was granted lands in this area in 1610 (*see* ***Belturbet, Newtownbutler***) [*Butlers Br.* 1728].

# C

**Cabragh** tl, Down 3233
(sometimes *Cabra*)
*6km SW of Rathfriland*
par: *Clonduff* bar: *Iveagh Upper, Lower Half*
Ir. *An Chabrach* [an **khab**ragh] 'the poor land' [*Ballinecabre* 1605].

**Cabragh** tl, ham., Tyrone 2736
*9.5km W of Dungannon*
par: *Killeeshil* bar: *Dungannon Lower*
Ir. *An Chabrach* [an **khab**ragh] 'the poor land' [*Cabragh* 1614].

**Caddy** tl, ham., Antrim 3039
*On W bank of the river Main, 4km N of Randalstown* (often *The Caddy*)
par: *Drummaul* bar: *Toome Upper*
*perhaps* Ir. *Cadaigh* [**kad**ee] 'land held by treaty' [*Cady* c.1657].

**Caheny** tl, vill., Derry 2841
*6.5km NNW of Kilrea*
par: *Aghadowey* bar: *Coleraine*
*perhaps* Ir. *Cáitheanaigh* [**ca**hanee] 'place of chaff/winnowing place'. The root word may be cáithleach 'chaff/husks' [*Cakenagh* 1657].

**Caledon** tl, vill.,Tyrone 2734
*On Co. Armagh border, 12km W of Armagh city*
par: *Aghaloo* bar: *Dungannon Lower*
The village of Caledon was originally named *Kinaird* and was founded in the Plantation period. Its name was changed to Caledon with the building of CALEDON HOUSE which was commenced in 1779 by James Alexander of Londonderry who bought the Caledon estate in 1778 and was created Earl of Caledon in 1800. The name Caledon appears to be from *Caledonia*, an archaic Roman name for Scotland. The name *Kinaird* is from Ir. *Cionn Aird* [kyun **ardge**] 'head/top of the hill' and originally referred to a castle of the O'Neills, the site of which is a short distance west of the village [(*i ndoras caisléin*) *Chind Aird* 1500].

**Calheme** tl, Antrim 2942
*3.5km E of Ballymoney*
par: *Ballymoney* bar: *Dunluce Upper*
The name represents Sc. 'cold home' and refers to a homestead or settlement on poor or marshy ground. There are five townlands named CALHAME in east Donegal. Calheme lies on the west bank of the GLENLOUGH RIVER.

**Callan** river, Armagh 2835
*Rises in Tullynawood Lake, 4km SSE of Keady. Enters the Blackwater a short distance N of Charlemont*
Ir. *An Challainn* [an **khal**in] 'the noisy one'. According to legend, the Callan is one of the three 'black rivers of Ireland' which burst forth in prehistoric times [*Callann* 3656AM].

**Calone** tl, ham., Armagh 2934
*5km SE of Armagh city* (sometimes *Collone*)
par: *Lisnadill* bar: *Fews Lower*
*perhaps* Ir. *Call Luain* [kal **loo**in] 'hazel-tree of the haunch-like hill' [*Culloine* 1609].

**Camlough** vill., Armagh 3032
*5km W of Newry*
par: *Killevy* bar: *Orior Upper*
Ir. *Camloch* [**kam**lough] 'crooked lough'. The village of Camlough which is mainly in the townland of CROSS takes its name from the nearby CAMLOUGH LAKE which is the source of the CAMLOUGH RIVER. CAMLOUGH MOUNTAIN (423m) stands on the east side of the lake [*Loch Chamloch* c.1840].

**Camowen River** Tyrone
*Rises near Cregganconroe, 4km NW of Pomeroy. Merges with the Drumragh River at Omagh to form the Strule*
Ir. *Camabhainn* [**kam**owen] 'crooked river' + E. *river*. The E. element *river* has been added later. The river has given name to the townland of CAMOWEN which is situated at a conspicuous bend in its course, 4km south-east of **Omagh**.

**Campsey** tls, vill., Derry 2442
(sometimes *Campsie*)
*7km NE of Londonderry*
par: *Faughanvale* bar: *Tirkeeran*
Ir. *Camsán* [**kam**san] 'river bends'. The bends are in the river **Faughan** which forms the western boundary of the townland of CAMPSEY LOWER before entering **Lough Foyle**. The village of Campsey is shared between the townlands of CAMPSEY UPPER and CLOGHOLE [*Camsan* 1613].

**Campsie** tl, distr.,Tyrone 2437
*Suburb on the E side of Omagh*
par: *Cappagh* bar: *Omagh East*
Ir. *Camsán* [**kam**san] 'river bends'. The bends are in the **Camowen River** which forms the northern boundary of the townland [*Campsie* 1661].

**Camus** tl, Derry 2842
*4.5km S of Coleraine*
par: *Macosquin* bar: *Coleraine*
Ir. *Camas* [**kam**as] 'river bend'. Camus is named from a bend in the **Lower Bann** which forms the eastern boundary of the townland [*Camus iuxta Bann* 1669].

**Cape Castle** tl, ham., Antrim 3043
*5km SW of Ballycastle*
par: *Ramoan* bar: *Cary*
Ir. *Ceap Caistéil* [kap **kash**chel] 'tillage plot of the castle'. The final element of the place-name appears to refer a castle which stood in the neighbouring townland of CLOGHANMURRY and is said to have been a stronghold of the MacQuillans who formerly ruled the area [*Capecastle* c.1657].

**Cappagh** tl, vill., Tyrone 2636
*5.5km S of Pomeroy*
par: *Pomeroy* bar: *Dungannon Middle*
Ir. *An Cheapóg* [an **khap**og] 'the little tillage plot'. Cappagh has given name to the nearby CAPPAGH MOUNTAIN (286m) [*Cappoge* 1614].

**Cappagh** par., Tyrone
*Borders on the town of Omagh on the north*
bar: *Omagh East/Strabane Upper*
Ir. *Ceapach Mhic Cuarta* [kapagh vick **koort**a] 'McCourt's tillage-plot'. The McCourts were the ancient *erenaghs* of the parish. The ruins of the former parish church are in a graveyard on the south bank of the CAPPAGH BURN in the townland of DUNMULLAN, 7km north of the town of **Omagh**, the northern portion of which is included in the parish [(*sagurt*) *Cheapaigh Mhec Cuarta* c.1645].

**Cargan** tl, vill., Antrim 3141
*15km NNE of Ballymena*
par: *Dunaghy* bar: *Kilconway*
Ir. *An Carraigín* [an **kar**ageen] 'the little rock'. Cargan takes its name from CARGAN ROCK, a hill of 290m which stands a short distance east of the village and has a cairn on its summit [*Carrigan* c.1655].

**Carland** vill., Tyrone 2736
*4km N of Dungannon*
par: *Donaghmore* bar: *Dungannon Middle*
Ir. *Domhnach Carr* [doanagh **kar**] 'church of the *Carra*'. *Na Carra* 'the rocky patches' was originally the name of one of ten territories which made up the parish of **Donaghmore** and the modern name Carland may represent Ir. *Carrlann* 'place of rocky patches'. There is now no trace or record of a church in the territory. The village of Carland is in the townland of CREEVAGH LOWER [*Donaghcarr* 1609].

**Carlingford Lough** inl., Down/Louth 3131
*9km SE of Newry*
par: *Clonallan/Carlingford*
bar: *Upper Iveagh, Upper Half/Dundalk Lower*
O.N. *Kerlingfjörthr* 'narrow sea-inlet of the hag' + E. *lough*. The E. element *lough* which is a borrowing from Ir. *loch* 'lake/estuary' has clearly been added later. The Ir. name of Carlingford Lough is *Loch Cairlinn*, a gaelicisation of the O.N. *Kerlingfjörthr*. The element *kerling* 'hag' seems to be used figuratively to refer to a hag-shaped rock; it could possibly refer to the three mountain tops which are locally known as THE THREE NUNS and are important navigational landmarks. Carlingford Lough has given name to the village and parish of CARLINGFORD on the south shore of the lough in Co. Louth. Early Ir. names for Carlingford Lough were *Snám Aignech* 'swift sea-channel or ford' and *Cuan Snáma Ech* 'bay of the sea-channel of horses' [*an Carrlongphort* 1213].

**Carn** tl, ham., Derry 2740
*6km SE of Dungiven*
par: *Dungiven* bar: *Keenaght*
Ir. *An Carn* [an **karn**] 'the cairn/heap of rocks'. There are a number of cairns in this townland, including one known as SLAUGHTY CAHAL (Ir. *Sleacht Chathail* [slaght **ka**hil] '*Cathal*'s memorial cairn'). The *Cathal* in question is said to be one Charles McCloskey who was murdered here. Curiously, there is no trace of a cairn on CARN HILL (448m) which stands in the middle of the townland [*Carne* 1613].

**Carnagh** ham., Armagh 2832
*5km SSW of Keady*
par: *Keady* bar: *Tiranny*
Ir. *Carranach* [**kar**anagh] 'rocky place'. Carnagh is in the townland of CROSSNENAGH.

**Carnalbanagh** tl, ham., Antrim 3240
*13km ENE of Ballymena*
par: *Tickmacrevan* bar: *Glenarm Lower*
Ir. *Carn Albanach* [karn **al**aban-agh] 'cairn of the Scotsmen'. There are still remains of a cairn in the townland which contains a hamlet named CARNALBANAGH SHEDDINGS to distinguish it from **The Sheddings**, a nearby hamlet in the townland of TAMYBUCK. Both hamlets are named from crossroads and contain the Sc. element *shedding* 'a place where roads separate; a crossroads' [*Carnalbanagh* 1780].

**Carnanelly** mtn, Tyrone 2639
*11km WSW of Draperstown*
(*see* **Glenelly**)

**Carnanreagh** tl, Derry 2540
*On Tyrone border, 7km S of Claudy*
par: *Learmount* bar: *Tirkeeran*
Ir. *An Carnán Riabhach* [an karnan **ree**wagh] 'the (little) grey cairn'. There is both a mound and a standing stone in this townland [*Carnanreagh* 1654].

**Carncastle** vill., par., Antrim 3340
*Village is 6km NW of Larne*
bar: *Glenarm Upper*
Ir. *Carn an Chaistéil* [karn an **khash**chel] 'cairn of the castle'. Carncastle is named from a small castellated rock in the sea on the north side of BALLYGALLEY HEAD, said to be a former stronghold of the Agnews (*see **Agnew's Hill** above*). The remnants of the former parish church are in the graveyard of the present Church of Ireland church, also in the townland of **Ballygalley**. The village of Carncastle is partly in the townland of BALLYGALLEY and partly in CORKERMAIN [*Carlcastel* 1279].

*Limestone bridge at Carnlough*

**Carncormick** hill, Antrim 3141
*8km NE of Broughshane*
par: *Skerry* bar: *Antrim Lower*
Ir. *Carn Chormaic* [karn **khor**mick] 'Cormac's cairn'. Carncormick (436m) is a named from a cairn which marks its summit, in the townland of CROOKNAHAYA. Cormac was one of the most popular names in early Ireland.

**Carndonagh** tn., Donegal 2444
*Town is 17.5km NE of Buncrana*
par: *Donagh* bar: *Inishowen East*
Ir. *Carn Domhnach* [karn **doan**agh] 'the cairn of (the parish of) Donagh'. The parish name Donagh is derived from Ir. *Domhnach*, a shortened form of *Domhnach Glinne Tóchair* '(early) church of Glentogher', the site of which is marked by the 7th-century DONAGH CROSS which stands near the present Church of Ireland church, a short distance west of the town. **Glentogher** is the name of a valley which lies a short distance to the south (*see below*) [*Donagh-Clantagh al. Carnedony* 1620].

**Carnearny** mtn, tl, Antrim 3139
*6km N of Antrim town*
par: *Connor* bar: *Antrim Lower*
*Carn Éireann* [karn **er**in] '*Ériu*'s cairn'. *Ériu* (Mod. Ir. *Éire*) was the usual O. Ir. name for Ireland but also a goddess name and a woman's name. There is a cairn on top of CARNEARNY MOUNTAIN (319m) [(*go*) *Cárn Ereann* 912].

**Carnlough** tls, vill., Antrim 3241
*On East Antrim coast, 3.5km NW of Glenarm*
par: *Ardclinis* bar: *Glenarm Lower*
Ir. *Carnlach* [**karn**lagh] 'place of cairns'. There is a cairn on the summit of LITTLE TROSK (385m) in the neighbouring townland of CREGGAN. The CARNLOUGH RIVER marks the southern boundary of the townland of CARNLOUGH SOUTH and also the boundary between the parishes of ARDCLINIS and TICKMACREVAN. The village of Carnlough straddles the townlands of CARNLOUGH SOUTH and CARNLOUGH NORTH [*Carnalloch* 1780].

**Carnmoney** tls, vill., par., Antrim 3338
*Forms a district of Newtownabbey, 9km N of Belfast city centre*
bar: *Belfast Lower*

Ir. *Carn Monaidh* [karn **munn**ee] 'cairn of the hill'. There is a cairn on the summit of CARNMONEY HILL (232m). Carnmoney has given name to the neighbouring townlands of CARNMONEY BOG and CARNMONEY GLEBE. In the latter, the present Church of Ireland church is close to the site of the medieval parish church which was earlier known as *Coole*, from Ir. *Cúil* 'corner/recess' ( *see* ***Rathcoole***) [(*Ecclesia de*) *Coole of Carnmonie* 1615].

**Carnteel** tl, vill., par., Tyrone 2635
*Village is 3.5km NE of Aughnacloy*
bar: *Dungannon Lower*
Ir. *Carn tSiail* [karn **chee**il] '*Sial*'s cairn'. The forename *Sial* [**shee**il] is the basis of the surname *Ó Siail* '(O')Shiel/Shields' which is found mainly in the north-west of Ireland. The site of the medieval parish church is the graveyard adjoining the village [(*cath*) *Cairn tSiadhail* 1239].

**Carntogher** mtn, Derry 2740
*8km NW of Maghera*
par: *Killelagh* bar: *Loughinsholin*
Ir. *Carn Tóchair* [karn **togh**er] 'cairn of the causeway'. Carntogher (464m) is the highest point in the parish of KILLELAGH and appears to have been named from a cairn a short distance to the south of its peak which is in the townland of TIRKANE. The old road from **Maghera** to **Dungiven** passed over Carntogher, close to the cairn [(*mullach*) *an Cháirn* c.1740].

**Carrick** vill., tls Donegal 1537
*12.5km W of Killybegs*
par: *Glencolumbkille* bar: *Banagh*
Ir. *An Charraig* [an **kharr**ick] 'the rock'. Carrick is on the west bank of the GLEN RIVER, in the townland of CARRICK UPPER which is bordered on the north-west by CARRICK LOWER [*An Charraig* 1835].

**Carrickaboy** vill., Cavan 2429
*5.5km SSE of Cavan town*
par: *Denn* bar: *Loughtee Upper*
Ir. *Carraigigh Bhuí* [karrigee **wee**] 'yellow rocky place'. Carrickaboy is in the townland of CARRICKABOY GLEBE. The townland is quite hilly with some rocky portions [*Careghaboy* 1629].

**Carrickarade Island** Antrim 3044
(often *Carrickarede*)
*On N Antrim coast, 7km NW of Ballycastle*
par: *Ballintoy* bar: *Cary*
*perhaps* Ir. *Carraig an Raid* [carrick an **radge**] 'rock of the throwing or casting' + E. *island*. Carrickarade Island is a large rock which forms a tiny island off the coast, in the townland of KNOCKSOGHEY. It is famous for its rope bridge which connects the island with the mainland and was traditionally 'thrown' across to the island each year to enable fishermen to fish from the island [*Carrickarede* 1780].

**Carrickart** tl, vill., Donegal 2143
(often *Carrigart*)
*25km NNW of Letterkenny*
par: *Mevagh* bar: *Kilmacrenan*
Ir. *Carraig Airt* [karrick **artch**]. The literal meaning of the modern form of the place-name is 'Art's rock'. However, this form is likely to represent a development from the original Ir. form *Ceathrú Fhiodhghoirt* [karoo **igg**urtch] 'the quarter(land) of the field of the wood'. The townland appears to have been originally named *Fiodhghort* [**figg**art] 'wood field', the element *ceathrú* 'quarter(land)' being added at a later date. The name *Fiodhghort* survives as FIGART but is now applied only to a peninsula in the extreme north of the townland [*Carrowfiggart* 1609].

**Carrickfergus** tl, tn, par/bar, Antrim 3438
*Town is on N shore of Belfast Lough, 15km NE of Belfast*
Ir. *Carraig Fhearghasa* [karrick **ar** agasa] 'Fergus's rock'. The rock referred to is that on which the famous late 12th-century Norman castle now stands. The place-name may well predate this period, even though there must be considerable doubt about the reliability of the tradition that Carrickfergus is named from Fergus son of *Erc*, the sixth-century founder of the joint Irish/Scottish kingdom of *Dál Riada* who is reputed to have been drowned here. The present Church of Ireland church of St Nicholas dates back to pre-Norman times,

*Carrickfergus Castle*

though none of the original building now survives. Carrickfergus enjoyed the status of a county prior to the establishment of the county of Antrim in 1584 [(go) *Carraic* Ferghusa 1204].

**Carrickmacross** tn, Monaghan 2830
*20km W of Dundalk*
par: *Magheross* bar: *Farney*
Ir. *Carraig Mhachaire Rois* [karrick waghera **rush**] 'rock of Magheross'. The first element of the place-name reflects the fact that the town is built on a rock while MAGHEROSS is the name of the townland and parish and is derived from Ir. *Machaire Rois* [maghera **rush**] 'plain of the (wooded) height'. The ruins of the medieval parish church stand close to the town [*Rosse als. Machair Roysse* 1541].

**Carrickmore** tl, vill., Tyrone 2637
*16km E of Omagh*
par: *Termonmaguirk* bar: *Omagh East*
Ir. *An Charraig Mhór* [an kharrick **wore**] 'the large rock'. An *alias* name for Carrickmore village is TERMON ROCK, *Termon* being the first element of the parish name TERMONMAGUIRK (Ir. *Tearmann Mhig Oirc* 'McGurk's monastic sanctuary') and *rock* referring to the rocky hill on which the village is situated. The McGurks were *erenaghs* or hereditary lay custodians of the parish's church lands. The site of the former parish church is adjacent to the village of Carrickmore [*Termon* 1633].

**Carrigan** tl, vill., Cavan 2329
*On N bank of the river Erne, 12km S of Cavan town*
par: *Ballintemple* bar: *Clanmahon*
Ir. *An Carraigín* [an **karr**igeen] 'the little rock/rocky hill' [*Carrigin* 1699].

**Carrigan Head** hl, Donegal 1537
*On SW Donegal coast, 15km W of Killybegs*
par: *Glencolumbkille* bar: *Banagh*
Ir. *Ceann an Charraigín* [kyun a **kharr**igeen] 'headland of the little rock/rocky hill'. The E. name appears to be a translation of the original Ir. Carrigan Head is in the townland of CROAGHLIN and commands a fine view across **Donegal Bay**.

**Carrigans** tl, vill., Donegal 2341
*On inlet of river Foyle, 7.5km SW of Derry city*
par: *Killea* bar: *Raphoe*
Ir. *An Carraigín* [an **karr**igeen] 'the little rock/rocky hill'. The final *-s* of the E. name has no basis in the original Ir. form [(*isin*) *cCairrcćín* 1490].

**Carrigart** tl, vill., Donegal 2143
(*see* ***Carrickart***)

**Carrigatuke** hill, Armagh 2933
*6km SE of Keady*
par: *Lisnadill* bar: *Fews Upper*
Ir. *Carraig an tSeabhaic* [carrick a **cho**-ick] 'rock/rocky hill of the hawk'. Carrigatuke (364m) is in the townland of ARMAGHBRAGUE. It commands a fine view over the surrounding countryside.

**Carrowdore** vill., Down 3537
*8.5km ESE of Newtownards*
par: *Donaghadee* bar: *Ards Lower*
Ir. *Ceathrú Dobhair* [karoo **dore**] 'water quarter'. The place-name suggests that the land was formerly of a wet and marshy character. Carrowdore is in the townland of BALLYRAWER [*Kerrowe Dorne* 1627].

**Carrowkeel** tl, vill., Donegal 2243
(usually *Kerrykeel*)
*On E shore of Mulroy Bay, 6km N of Millford*
par: *Tullyfern* bar: *Kilmacrenan*
Ir. *An Cheathrú Chaol* [an karroo **keel**] 'the narrow quarter'. There is another townland and village named CARROWKEEL adjacent to **Quigley's Point** on the west shore of **Lough Foyle** [*Carrowkeele* 1639].

**Carry Bridge** ham., Fermanagh 2233
*11km SE of Enniskillen*
par: *Derrybrusk* bar: *Magherastephana*
Ir. *Cora* [**kor**a] 'causeway' + E. *bridge*.
The hamlet of Carry Bridge is named from a bridge which connects the island of INISHMORE in **Upper Lough Erne** with the mainland. The bridge is named from the townland of CARRY on the island which derives from Ir. *Cora* 'causeway/rocky ford' and no doubt refers to a feature which was replaced by the bridge. The hamlet of Carry Bridge on the mainland is in the townland of AGHNACARRA which is from Ir. *Achadh na Cora* [aghoo na **kor**a] 'field of the causeway'.

**Carryduff** tl, tn, Down 3336
*9km S of Belfast*
par: *Drumbo* bar: *Castlereagh Upper*
Ir. *Ceathrú Aodha Dhuibh* [karoo ee **ġiv**]

'black-haired Hugh's quarter' [*Carow-Eduffe al. Carow-Hugh-Duffe al. Tyduffe* 1623].

**Castle Archdale** country park, Fermanagh 2135
*On E shore of Lower Lough Erne 5km WNW of Irvinestown*
par: *Derryvullan* bar: *Lurg*
Castle Archdale is named from a castle (now in ruins) which was built in 1617 on CASTLE HILL in the townland of BUNANINVER by John Archdale of Norfolk in England. The modern Castle Archdale (now a youth hostel) was built by Colonel Mervyn Archdale in 1778 and is 1.5km to the south-west, in the townland of ROSSMORE [*Archedale* 1612].

**Castleblayney** tn, Monaghan 2931
*20km SE of Monaghan town*
par: *Muckno* bar: *Cremorne*
Castleblayney takes its name from Sir Edward Blayney, governor of Monaghan, who was granted land here by James I in the early 17th century. Sir Edward built a small castle, no trace of which now remains but the site of which is close to the 18th-century mansion originally known as BLAYNEY CASTLE, close to the shore of **Muckno Lake**, in the townland of ONOMY. Blayney Castle is now known as HOPE CASTLE and has become the guest house of a Franciscan convent. The Ir. name of Castleblayney is *Baile na Lorgan* 'town of the long low ridge' [*Castleblayney* 1663].

**Castlecat** tl, ham., Antrim 2943
(sometimes *Castlecatt*)
*3.5km SSE of Bushmills*
par: *Billy* bar: *Dunluce Lower*
Ir. *Caiseal Cait* [kashel **kitch**] 'stone ring-fort of the (wild) cat'. Castlecat was named from a fort which formerly stood in the townland [*Castlecat* 1780].

**Castlecaulfield** vill., Tyrone 2736
*4km W of Dungannon*
par: *Donaghmore* bar: *Dungannon Middle*
Castlecaulfield is named after Sir Toby Caulfield, ancestor of the Earls of Charlemont, who erected the now-ruined CASTLE CAULFIELD c.1612, on the site of a fortress of the Donnellys, in the townland of LISNAMONAGHAN. The entire district was formerly known as *Baile Uí Dhonnaíle* [bala ee **ġon**eelya] 'territory of (O')Donnelly' and this name was also applied to the aforementioned fortress [*Castle-Caufield* 1618].

*Castle Coole*

**Castle Coole** tl, demesne, Fermanagh 2234
*2km SE of Enniskillen*
par: *Derryvullan* bar: *Tirkennedy*
The original castle was built in the early 17th century by an Englishman named Captain Roger Atkinson who was granted an estate of 1000 acres named Coole (Ir. *Cúil* 'corner/recess'). The castle was destroyed in the 1641 rebellion. The present classical mansion of CASTLE COOLE was built between 1790 and 1796 close to the site of the original castle by Armar Lowry-Corry, first EARL OF BELMORE, a descendant of John Corry from Dumfriesshire in Scotland who had purchased the estate in 1655. The name of the estate or district of *Coole* occurs in LOUGH COOLE (Ir. *Loch Chúile* 'lake of *Coole*'), a lake which is partly in this townland and partly in the neighbouring townland of KILLYNURE [*Coole* 1610].

**Castledawson** vill., Derry 2939
*3.5km NE of Magherafelt*
par: *Magherafelt* bar: *Loughinsholin*
The village of Castledawson is named from Joshua Dawson, chief secretary for Ireland, who founded it in 1710 and whose family, the Dawsons of Westmoreland, held land here since 1622. The site of the castle is in the townland of TAMNIARAN which adjoins the village on the north. The village was formerly known as *Dawson's Bridge* from its stone arch over the river **Moyola**. The Ir. name for Castledawson is *An Seanmhullach* [an **shan**wullagh] 'the old hilltop', a name which originally applied to the townland of SHANEMULLAGH in which it is situated [*Castledawson al. Dawson's Bridge* 1677].

**Castlederg** tn, Tyrone 2238
*15km SW of Strabane*
par: *Urney* bar: *Omagh West*

Ir. *Caisleán na Deirge* [kashlan na **jer**iga] 'castle of the (river) Derg'. The ruins of the castle, built c.1610 by Sir John Davies, Attorney General for Ireland, on the site of an earlier castle, are on the north bank of the **Derg**, in the townland of CASTLESESSAGH. Davies was granted 2,000 acres in this area in 1609 [*Caislén na Deircce* 1497].

**Castle Espie** tl, Down 3436
*On W shore of Strangford Lough, 3km SE of Comber*
par: *Tullynakill* bar: *Castlereagh Lower*
Ir. *Caisleán an Easpaig* [kashlan an **as**pick] 'the bishop's castle'. The townland contains the site of a castle, though it is not clear if this was a stone building. Historically the townland was church property, hence the designation of the castle as belonging to the bishop [*Castell Nespeg* c.1625].

**Castlefinn** tl, vill., Donegal 2239
(sometimes *Castlefin*)
*On the river Finn, 7.5km SW of Lifford*
par: *Donaghmore* bar: *Raphoe*
Ir. *Caisleán na Finne* [kashlan na **fin**ya] 'castle of the (river) Finn'. Castlefinn is situated on the north bank of the river. The castle in question was a stronghold of (Sir) *Niall Garbh* (i.e. 'rough') *Ó Dónaill* at the beginning of the 17th century and stood adjacent to the bridge, but no trace of it now remains [*Castleffynne* 1617].

**Castlereagh** tl, distr., bars, Down 3337
*District forms a suburb, 4km SE of Belfast city centre*
Ir. *An Caisleán Riabhach* [an kashlan **ree**wagh] 'the grey castle'. Castlereagh is named from a stone house or castle (sometimes called *Castle Clannaboy*) which was the stronghold of the Clandeboye O'Neills in the 16th century and was sold by Conn O'Neill (*see* ***Connswater***) to Sir Moses Hill in 1616. There is now no trace of the building but the site is marked by the Orange Hall close to Castlereagh Presbyterian chuurch on CHURCH ROAD. The townland of Castlereagh is in the barony of CASTLEREAGH UPPER which is adjoined on the north-east by CASTLEREAGH LOWER [*Castell Rewe* 1574].

**Castle Robin** hist. mon., Antrim 3236
*4.5km NNW of Lisburn*
par: *Derryaghy* bar: *Belfast Upper*
The 'castle' was in fact a three-storied house built in the townland of MULLAGHGLASS by Robert 'Robin' Norton, a lieutenant of Sir Arthur Chichester in the early 17th-century. The ruins are still visible, close to the remains of an Anglo-Norman *motte-and-bailey* [*Castle Robin* 1641].

**Castlerock** vill., Derry 2743
*8km NW of Coleraine*
par: *Dunboe* bar: *Coleraine*
The village of Castlerock is named from a rock on the seashore a short distance to the west of the mouth of the **Lower Bann**, where Robert Castles and his crew of seven perished in the brig *Trader of Greenock* in 1826. The village straddles the three townlands of BOGTOWN, FREEHALL WATSON and FREEHALL DUNLOP.

**Castle Upton** castle, Antrim 3238
*14km NW of Belfast*
par: *Templepatrick* bar: *Belfast Upper*
In 1619 Sir Humphrey Norton, brother of Robert Norton of **Castle Robin** built a castle here, adjacent to the present village of **Templepatrick**, on the site of a monastery of the Order of St John of Jerusalem. Sir Humphrey sold off the property to Henry Upton, a captain in the army of the Earl of Essex. In the early 19th century, a descendant of Henry Upton who had acquired the title Viscount Templeton changed the name of the castle to CASTLE UPTON [*Upton Castle* 1838].

**Castleward** tl, hist. mon., Down 3534
*9.5km NE of Downpatrick*
par: *Ballyculter* bar: *Lecale Lower*
The townland of Castleward is named from a late 16th-century tower-house, apparently built by Nicholas Ward of Cheshire, ancestor of the present Viscount Bangor. The remains of the tower-house stand on the shore of STRANGFORD BAY, an inlet of **Strangford Lough**, a short distance north-east of CASTLEWARD HOUSE, a great mansion built by Lord and Lady Bangor in 1764 to replace an earlier mansion built c. 1715.

**Castlewellan** tl, tn, Down 3333
*6km NW of Newcastle*
par: *Kilmegan* bar: *Iveagh Upper, Lower Half*
Ir. *Caisleán Uidhilín* [kashlan **eel**een] '*Uidhilín*'s castle'. The final element is a gaelicised form of the Anglo-Norman forename *Hugelin*

(a double diminutive of Hugh) which is the basis of the surname *Mac Uidhilín* 'MacQuillan'. The site of the castle may be in the townland of CLARKILL on the north shore of CASTLEWELLAN LAKE where there are remnants of the farm buildings of the Annesley family who resided here since 1741, on land previously held by the Magennis chieftains of IVEAGH. The present castle was built by the 5th Earl Annesley and dates from only the 1850s [*Ballycaslanwilliam* 1605].

**Cavan** tn, co. 2430
*County town of Cavan, 13km SE of Belturbet*
par: *Urney* bar: *Loughtee Upper*
Ir. *An Cabhán* [an **kaa**wan] 'the hollow'. The original settlement at Cavan grew up around a medieval castle and friary of the O'Reillys, lords of the territory of EAST BREIFNE. No trace of either building now remains [(*i mainistir*) *in Cabhain* 1330].

**Cave Hill** mtn, Antrim 3337
(sometimes *Cavehill*)
*368m high, 5.5km NNW of Belfast city centre*
par: *Shankill* bar: *Belfast Upper*
Ir. *Binn Uamha* [bin **oo**va] 'peak/cliff of the cave'. The E. name appears to be a translation of the original Ir. There are in fact three caves on the face of the cliff which stands in the townland of BALLYAGHAGAN. An earlier Ir. name for Cave Hill was *Beann Mhadagáin* [ban **wad**agine] '*Madagán*'s peak', *Madagán* being a king of Ulster who died in 856AD [(*hi*) *mBind Uamha* 1468].

**Caw** tl, distr., Derry 2441
*Suburb, 3km NE of Derry city centre*
par: *Clondermot* bar: *Tirkeeran*
Ir. *Caoth* [**keeh**] 'bog-hole/swamp' [*Kae* 1637].

**Chanterhill** tl, Fermanagh 2234
(*see* ***Moneynoe Glebe or Chanterhill***)

**Chapeltown** vill., Down 3534
*9km SE of Downpatrick*
par: *Dunsfort* bar: *Lecale Lower*
Chapeltown is named from the present Roman Catholic chapel of the parish of DUNSFORT, erected in 1791 in the townland of BALLYEDOCK UPPER [*Chapeltown* 1886].

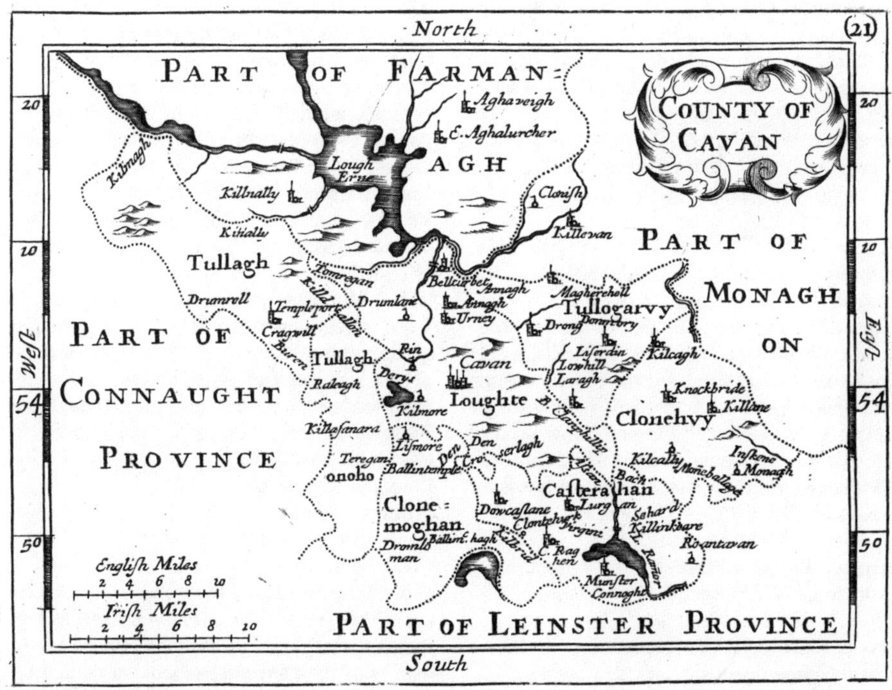

*Cavan in the 17th century*

**Charlemont** vill., Armagh 2835
*On border with Tyrone, 8.5km SE of Dungannon*
par: *Loughgall* bar: *Armagh*
Charlemont takes its name from Charles Blount, 8th baron Mountjoy (commonly called 'Lord Mountjoy'), Lord Deputy of Ireland and later Earl of Devonshire, for whom Sir Toby Caulfield erected a fort here in 1602 (*see* ***Castlecaulfield***). The name Charlemont is a combination of *Charles* and the *mount-* element of *Mountjoy*. Sir Toby Caulfield, who died in 1627, became the first Lord Charlemont. Charlemont is in the townland of BOROUGH OF CHARLEMONT, the original Ir. name of which was *Achadh an Dá Chora* [aghoo an da **khor**a] 'field of the two weirs', the latter having presumably been on the river **Blackwater**. Charlemont is twin village to **Moy** which lies opposite it on the west bank of the river, in Co. Tyrone [*Achadh in dá Charad* c.1645].

**Charlestown or Bannfoot** vill., Armagh 2936
*On S shore of Lough Neagh, 9km NW of Portadown*
par: *Montiaghs* bar: *Oneilland East*
The village of Charlestown in the townland of DERRYINVER is named from Charles Brownlow, a landlord who built roughly twenty houses here c.1830. The *alias* name BANNFOOT refers to the position of the village at the point where the **Upper Bann** enters **Lough Neagh** and where a ferry used to cross the river [*Charlestown* 1837].

**Cherryvalley** tl, Down 3436
*On E outskirts of town of Comber*
par: *Comber* bar: *Castlereagh Lower*
The valley appears to be that of the COMBER RIVER which bounds the townland on the south. An earlier name for the townland was *Carrowcrossnemuckley* which seems to represent Ir. *Ceathrú Chros na Muclaí* [caroo khross na **muck**lee] 'quarter(land) of the cross of the piggery' [*Chirrivally al. Carrowcrossnemuckley* 1679].

**Church Hill** tl, vill., Donegal 2041
(sometimes *Churchhill*)
*10km WNW of Letterkenny*
par: *Gartan* bar: *Kilmacrenan*
The original Ir. name of the townland of Church Hill was *Mín an Lábáin* [meen a **laab**ine] 'mountain-pasture of the mud' and this is also the current Ir. name of the village. Church Hill is close to the east shore of **Gartan Lough**, with its many associations with St Columcille. However, the church referred to (no trace of which remains) appears to have been built as late as the 18th century when the village was founded. The hill referred to may be BROWN MOUNTAIN (224m) which stands a short distance south-west of the village [*the Church of Minnylobban* 1770].

**Church Hill** vill., Fermanagh 2135
*3.5km N of Derrygonnelly*
par: *Inishmacsaint* bar: *Magheraboy*
The village of Church Hill was founded in the early 17th century by Sir John Hume of nearby TULLY CASTLE and named from a Church of Ireland church which was rebuilt in 1688 and served as the parish church of **Inishmacsaint** from 1714 until its use was discontinued in 1831. The site is marked by a disused graveyard in the townland of DRUMMENAGH BEG [*Church-Hill* 1837].

**Church Island** Derry 2939
*In Lough Beg, 3km SE of Bellaghy*
par: *Ballyscullion* bar: *Loughinsholin*
The Ir. name for Church Island is *Inis Taoide* [inish **teedg**a] '(St) *Taoide*'s island', so-called because the island contained an early monastery founded by St *Taoide*, the site of which is marked by the ruins of the medieval church of **Ballyscullion**. The E. name Church Island was not coined until after 1788 when Frederick Hervey, Earl of Bristol and bishop of Derry, constructed a square tower with a steeple beside the ruins of the medieval church, to improve his view from his residence which formerly stood on the western shore of **Lough Beg**. Due to the lowering of the level of **Lough Beg**, Church Island has ceased to be an island proper and is now joined to the western shore of the lough. The name *Taoide* is still found in the area, in the anglicised form *Teady* [(*Inse*) *Toitae* c.830].

**Churchtown** ham., Derry 2838
par: *Lissan* bar: *Loughinsholin*
*4km N of Cookstown*
Churchtown is named after the present Church of Ireland parish church, now known as LISSAN CHURCH, in the townland of TULLYNURE. However, the medieval parish church of **Lissan** may have been in the neighbouring

townland of CLAGGAN. There is also a Catholic church in TULLYNURE.

**Churchtown** ham., Down 3534
(*see* ***Ballyculter***)

**Clabby** vill., Fermanagh 2435
*4km NW of Fivemiletown*
par: *Enniskillen* bar: *Tirkennedy*
Ir. *Clabaigh* [**clab**ee] *perhaps* 'place of rough/pock-marked land'. Ir. *clab* literally means 'mouth/opening' and the place-name may refer to land which is rough or indented. There are areas of boggy land in the vicinity. Clabby is in the townland of RAMALEY which is bordered by the townland of LURGAN-CLABBY (Ir. *Lorgain Chlabaí* [lurragin **khlab**ee] 'long low ridge of the pock-marked land') and in which there is a small lake named CLABBY LOUGH [*Clabby* 1611].

**Clady** ham., Antrim 3237
*3km SW of Templepatrick*
par: *Templepatrick/Grange of Muckamore* bar: *Belfast Upper/Massereene Lower*
Ir. *Cláidigh* [**kladg**ee] 'the one who washes/stong-flowing one'. The hamlet of Clady is named from the CLADY WATER on which it stands, straddling the townlands of STRAIDBALLYMORRIS and SHANEOGUESTOWN. Ir. *Cláidigh* is a common name for streams and rivers and goes back to an Indo-European root signifying 'the one who washes' or 'the strong-flowing one'.

**Clady** vill., Derry 2940
*2km W of Portglenone*
par: *Tamlaght O'Crilly* bar: *Loughinsholin*
Ir. *Cláidigh* [**kladg**ee] 'the one who washes/strong-flowing one'. The village of Clady takes its name from the CLADY RIVER on the south bank of which it stands. Clady is in the townland of GLENONE which adjoins the town of **Portglenone** on the west.

**Clady** tl, vill., Tyrone 2239
*6km SW of Strabane*
par: *Urney* bar: *Strabane Lower*
Ir. *Cláidigh* [**kladg**ee] 'the one who washes/strong-flowing one'. The townland and village are named from a stream formerly known as *Clady* which flows into the river **Finn** a short distance west of the village [*(Dún) Cloitighe* 972] .

**Clady More** tl, ham., Armagh 2833
*5km SW of Markethill*
par: *Kilclooney* bar: *Fews Lower*
Ir. *Cláidigh Mhór* [kladgee **wore**] 'great Clady'. The townland of Clady More is named from the CLADY WATER which divides it from the townland of CLADY BEG (Ir. *Cláidigh Bheag* 'little Clady') on the east. The name of the stream signifies 'the one who washes/strong-flowing one'. There is a village named CLADY MILLTOWN on the north-east boundary of CLADY MORE [*Cladiach* 1322].

**Clady River** Donegal
*Rises in Lough Nacung in Gweedore. Flows into the Atlantic at Bunbeg*
Ir. *An Chláidigh* [an **khladg**ee] 'the one who washes/strong-flowing one'.

**Clanabogan** tls, Tyrone 2436
*5km SW of Omagh*
par: *Drumragh* bar: *Omagh East*
Ir. *Cluain Uí Bhogáin* [klooin ee **wugg**ine] '(O')Bogan's meadow'. The surname *Ó Bogáin* '(O')Bogan' is normally associated with Wexford and Donegal. The townland of CLANABOGAN LOWER is bordered on the north by CLANABOGAN UPPER [*Clonyboggan* c.1655].

**Clandeboy** distr., Down 3437
*3km SW of Bangor town centre*
par: *Bangor* bar: *Ards Lower*
Ir. *Clann Aodha Buí* [klan ee **bwee**] 'family of Yellow-Haired Hugh'. The name Clandeboy originally applied to a sept descended from Yellow-Haired Hugh of Tyrone who died in 1283. It was later applied to a large territory in south Antrim and north Down which was settled by this sept in the 14th century. In the last century, Lord Dufferin of Bangor used the name CLANDEBOY for his house and estate. Today, the name Clandeboy refers to only a small portion of the former estate, lying to the south-west of the town of **Bangor** [*Cloinn Aedha buidhe* 1319].

**Clanrye River** Down
*The upper portion of the Newry River which rises near Rathfriland and flows into Carlingford Lough 9km SE of Newry.*
The original Ir. name of the Clanrye River was simply *Rí*, a name which is of uncertain meaning but which may signify 'river'. The modern name Clanrye is from Ir. *Gleann Rí* 'glen

of the river *Rí* and originally applied to the glen through which the river flows. The E. element 'river' has clearly been added later [(*hi*) *Rig* c.850].

**Clare** tl, vill., Armagh 3034
*On W bank of the Cusher river, 4km SW of Tandragee*
par: *Ballymore* bar: *Orior Lower*
Ir. *An Clár* [an **klar**] *perhaps* 'the plank bridge'. The name may have originally referred to a wooden bridge over the CUSHER RIVER [(*don*) *Chlár* c.1645].

**Clare** distr., Tyrone 2235
*5.5km S of Castlederg*
par: *Ardstraw* bar: *Omagh West*
Ir. *An Clár* [an **klar**] 'the plain'. Ir. *clár* literally 'board/plank' can be used to signify 'level land/plain'. In this case it may refer to level land along the FAIRY WATER. The district of Clare includes the townlands of CLARE UPPER and CLAREMORE.

**Claudy** tl, vill., Derry 2540
*14km SE of Londonderry*
par: *Cumber Upper* bar: *Tirkeeran*
Ir. *Clóidigh* [**klodg**ee] 'the one who washes/strong-flowing one'. *Clóidigh* represents a variant form of *Cláidigh*, a common name for streams and rivers (*see* ***Clady*** *above*). In this case it may represent a former local name for this section of the river **Faughan** which borders the townland on the south. There is also a stream which enters the Faughan close to the east end of the village and a stream named GLENRANDAL WATER which flows into the Faughan a short distance to the south-west [*Cládech* c.1680].

**Clogh** vill., Antrim 3041
(sometimes *Clough*)
*11km N of Ballymena*
par: *Dunaghy* bar: *Kilconway*
Ir. *An Chloch* [an **khlogh**] 'the stone (castle)'. Of the former CLOGH CASTLE, which was originally a stronghold of the MacQuillans and later of the MacDonnells, only the gateway now survives, at the north end of the village. Clogh is in the townland of CLOGHGALDANAGH [*Cloghmagher-Dunaghy* 1606].

**Clogh River** Antrim
(*see* ***Glenravel River***)

**Cloghan** tls, ham., Donegal 2039
*11km WNW of Ballybofey*
par: *Kilteevoge* bar: *Raphoe*
Ir. *An Clochán* [an **klogh**an] 'the stepping stones'. The place-name refers to a rocky ford which was formerly the only crossing over the river **Finn** between **Stranorlar** and **Bellanamore**. The hamlet of Cloghan is in the townland of CLOGHAN BEG which is bordered by the townland of CLOGHAN MORE [*Cloghan* 1610].

**Cloghaneely** distr., Donegal
*The portion of N Donegal which lies between Errigal mountain and the north coast*
par: *Raymunterdoney/Tullaghobegly* bar: *Kilmacrenan*
Ir. *Cloich Chionnaola* [kloygh khin**eel**a] '*Cionnaola*'s stone'. Legend has it that it was on this stone that *Cionnaola*, the prehistoric ruler of the district, was beheaded by his father-in-law 'Balor of the evil eye' (*see also* ***Bloody Foreland***). The stone is still pointed out in the townland of DRUMNATINNY which lies on the coast a short distance north of **Falcarragh**. The personal name *Cionnaola* (earlier *Ceann Faoladh* 'wolf-head') was very common in the early period and is also found in **Dunkineely**, the name of a townland and village in the south of the county [(*taoiseach*) *Cloiche Chinnfhaoladh* 1284].

**Cloghastucan or White Lady** rock, Antrim 3342
*On E Antrim coast, 6km N of Carnlough*
par: *Ardclinis* bar: *Glenarm Lower*
The place-name refers to a conspicuous pillar of limestone rock which stands by the roadside in the townland of GALBOLY LOWER. Cloghastucan is from Ir. *Cloch an Stuacáin* [klogh a **stook**ine] 'stone of the stack or pile'. The length of Ireland is traditionally defined as being from *Carn Uí Néid*, i.e. MIZEN HEAD in Co. Cork, to *Cloch an Stuacáin* in Co. Antrim [(*go*) *Cloich an Stocáin* c.1633]. *See White Lady for illustration.*

**Cloghcor** tl, ham., Tyrone 2340
*7km N of Strabane*
par: *Leckpatrick* bar: *Strabane Lower*
Ir. *An Chloch Chorr* [an khlogh **khorr**] 'the odd/pointed stone'. The reference may be to a prehistoric monument such as a standing-stone or a stone circle, no trace of which now remains [*Cloghcor* 1837].

**Clogher** vill., par/bar, dioc. Tyrone 2535
*Village is 22.5km SSE of Omagh*
Ir. *Clochar* [**klogh**er] 'stony place'.
The place-name appears to have originally referred to the ruins of a Later Bronze Age stone ring-ditch which appears to have been reconstructed in the sixth century and was known as '*Clochar mac nDaimhíne* 'stony place (fort?) of the sons of *Daimhíne*', the latter being a king of *Airghialla*, an early Irish kingdom of which Clogher was the capital. Clogher is also the site of an early monastery which appears to be marked by the present Church of Ireland cathedral, the head-church of the diocese of Clogher. The village of Clogher is partly in the townland of CLOGHER DEMESNE and partly in CLOGHER TENEMENTS [(*abb*) *Clochair mic nDaimhine* 765].

**Cloghfin** tl, Tyrone 2636
*18km ESE of Omagh*
par: *Termonmaguirk* bar: *Omagh East*
Ir. *An Chloch Fhionn* [an khlogh **inn**] 'the white stone'. The place-name may refer to a group of three standing stones which appear to form the remains of a larger megalithic structure. Cloghfin is a long townland, stretching 8km south-eastwards from **Sixmilecross** along the CLOGHFIN RIVER [*Cloghfin* 1640].

**Clogh Mills** tl, vill., Antrim 3041
(sometimes *Cloughmills*)
*14km NNW of Ballymena*
par: *Killagan* bar: *Kilconway*
The element *mills* refers to former flax and corn mills in the village, while the element *Clogh* is derived from the name of the nearby village of **Clogh** (*see above*).

**Cloghoge** tl, ham., Armagh 3032
(sometimes *Cloughoge*)
*2.5km S of Newry*
par: *Killevy* bar: *Orior Upper*
Ir. *Clochóg* [**klogh**og] 'stony place'. There are rocky outcrops in this townland. There is also a mountain named CLOGHOGE MOUNTAIN (190m) in the neighbouring townland of ELLISHOLDING [*Claghoge* 1661].

**Cloghy** tl, vill., Down 3635
(sometimes *Cloughey*)
*On E shore of Ards Peninsula, 3.5km NE of Portaferry*
par: *Castleboy* bar: *Ards Upper*
Ir. *Clochaigh* [**klogh**ee] 'stony place'. There is another village with the same name and derivation 2km south of **Strangford** [*Cloghie* 1623].

*Round tower at Clones*

**Clones** tn, par., Monaghan 2532
*Town is 19km WSW of Monaghan town*
bar: *Dartree*
Ir. *Cluain Eois* [klooin **o**ish] '*Eos*'s meadow'. The site of a sixth-century monastery of St *Tighearnach* is marked by the remains of a round tower in a graveyard on the south side of the town. However, *Eos* appears to be the name of a pagan chieftain, suggesting that there was an earlier, pre-Christian, settlement. A small portion of the parish of Clones is in the barony of **Monaghan**. However, the greater part is in the barony of CLANKELLY in Fermanagh [(*abb*) *Cluana hEois* 701].

**Clonmany** vill., par., Donegal 2344
*Village is 13km N of Buncrana*
bar: *Inishowen East*
Ir. *Cluain Maine* [klooin **man**a] 'meadow of *Maine*'. *Maine* was a very popular name in early Ireland. The *Maine* referred to here appears to have been *Maine Caol* [mana **keel**] 'slender *Maine*' who was the father of Conall,

the patron saint of the West Donegal parish of INISHKEEL. The village of Clonmany is in the townland of GADDYDUFF while the present Church of Ireland church a short distance to the west in the townland of STRAID marks the site of an early church reputed to have been founded by St Colmcille [*Clonmane* 1397].

**Clonoe** par., Tyrone 2836
*Stretches eastwards from Coalisland to the W shore of Lough Neagh.*
bar: *Dungannon Middle*
Ir. *Cluain Eo* [klooin **o**] 'meadow of the yew tree(s)'. The site of the medieval parish church is marked by St Michael's Church of Ireland church 4km east-north-east of **Coalisland** in the townland of KILLARY GLEBE [*Clondeo* c.1306].

**Clontibret** vill., par., Monaghan 2732
*Village is 8km SE of Monaghan town*
bar: *Cremorne*
Ir. *Cluain Tiobrad* [clooin **tib**rad] 'meadow of the well'. The site of an early monastery (and holy well?) and also of the medieval parish church appears to be marked by the old graveyard beside the present Church of Ireland church in the townland of GALLAGH. However, most of the village of Clontibret is in the townland of CARRICKADERRY. There is a townland named CLONTIBRET a short distance south of **Clones** [(*Mocumae cruimthir*) *Clúana Tiprat* c.830].

**Clontivrin** tl, ham., Fermanagh 2432
*On border with Monaghan, 1.5km SW of Clones*
par: *Clones* bar: *Clankelly*
Ir. *Cluain Tibhrinne* [klooin **tiv**rinya] *perhaps* '*Tibhreann*'s meadow'. The meaning of the final element of the place-name is uncertain, but it may represent a female personal name. The remains of an old church, apparently marking the site of an early monastery, were removed in the 19th century [(*ancoire*) *Cluana Tibhrinne* 740].

**Clontygora** tl, ham., Armagh 3032
(sometimes *Clontigora*)
*7km S of Newry*
par: *Killevy* bar: *Orior Upper*
Ir. *Cluainte Ó gCorra* [klooncha o **gorr**a] 'the meadows of the Corrs or descendants of *Corra*'. The personal name *Corra* is the basis of the surname *Ó Corra* '(O')Corr' which is of Tyrone/Fermanagh origin but is now widespread in Ulster [*Clontegora* 1609].

**Clough** tl, vill., Down 3434
*9km SW of Downpatrick*
par: *Loughinisland* bar: *Kinelarty*
Ir. *An Chloch* [an **khlogh**] 'the stone (castle)'. The castle at Clough was originally a Norman *motte-and-bailey* to which a succession of stone buildings was later added, a portion of one of which still survives from the 13th century. An earlier Ir. name for Clough was *Cloch Mhachaire Cat* [klogh waghera **kat**] 'stone (castle) of the plain of the cats' [*Cloghmagherechat* 1634].

**Cloyfin** tls, Derry 2943
*4km NE of Coleraine*
par: *Ballywillin/Ballyrashane* bar: *NE Liberties of Coleraine*
Ir. *An Chloich Fhionn* [an khlygh **inn**] 'the white stone'. The townland of CLOYFIN NORTH is in the parish of BALLYWILLIN while CLOYFIN SOUTH is in the parish of of **Ballyrashane**. There is a rocky outcrop in the townland of KILLYGREEN LOWER near its boundary with CLOYFIN NORTH [*Illanneclogh fynny* 1637].

**Cluntoe** tls, Tyrone 2937
*15km E of Cookstown*
par: *Arboe* bar: *Dungannon Upper*
*perhaps* Ir. *Cluain Tó* [klooin **to**] '*Tó*'s meadow'. The townland of CLUNTOE (*Richardson*) lies on the west shore of **Lough Neagh** and is bordered on the north-west by CLUNTOE (*Quin*) [*Clonto* 1615].

**Coa** tl, Fermanagh 2235
*8km NE of Enniskillen*
par: *Magheracross* bar: *Tirkennedy*
Ir. *An Cuach* [an **koo**agh] 'the hollow' [*Coagh* 1609].

**Coagh** tl, vill., Tyrone 2837
*9km E of Cookstown*
par: *Tamlaght* bar: *Dungannon Upper*
Ir. *An Cuach* [an **koo**agh] 'the hollow'. The village and townland of Coagh stand on the east bank of the BALLINDERRY RIVER [*Coagh* 1639].

**Coalisland** tn, Tyrone 2836
*5.5km NE of Dungannon*
par: *Tullyniskan/Donaghenry/Clonoe*
bar: *Dungannon Middle*

Coalisland was the inland port for Ulster's only sizeable coal field. The town grew up with the construction of the Tyrone Canal to **Lough Neagh**, commenced in 1744. However, while it is estimated that over 30 million tons of coal is available in the area the resource has never really been successfully exploited [*Coal Island* 1837].

**Colebrook Demesne** tl, Fermanagh 2434
*18km E of Enniskillen*
par: *Aghalurcher* bar: *Magherastephena*
The name Colebrook is a combination of the surnames *Cole* and *Brooke*, the latter referring to Major Thomas Brooke whose father Sir Henry Brooke had come into possession of an estate here in 1666 (*see* ***Brookeborough*** *above*) and *Cole* being the surname of Major Thomas's wife Catherine, daughter of Sir John Cole of Dublin, whom he had married in 1652. Major Thomas and Catherine were the first of the Brooke family to make their permanent residence in Fermanagh. The present large classical house was built in 1820 by Sir Thomas Brooke, a descendant of Major Thomas. Colebrook has given name to the COLEBROOK RIVER (formerly known as *Maguire's River*) which flows through the demesne and the original Ir. name of which was *Abha Dhubh* 'black river'. The mansion of ASHBROOKE in the neighbouring townland of LURGANBANE was also built by Sir Henry Brooke, in 1830 [*Colebrook* 1817].

**Coleraine** tn, par., bars., Derry 2843
*Town is on the Lower Bann, 12km NW of Ballymoney*
Ir. *Cúil Raithin* [kool **ra**hin] 'corner/nook of ferns'. The town of Coleraine which is mainly east of the **Lower Bann** in the townland of COLERAINE AND SUBURBS contains the site of an early monastery which may be marked by the present Church of Ireland parish church. The latter dates from 1614, though much altered since then.

The portion of the town which is west of the river is divided between the townlands of WATERSIDE and CHURCHLAND in the parish of KILLOWEN. Coleraine was the original name of the county of **Londonderry** and has also given name to the baronies of COLERAINE and NORTH-EAST LIBERTIES OF COLERAINE [(*cellola*) *Cuile Raithin* c.630].

**Collin** mtn, Antrim 3237
*8.5km SW of Belfast*
par: *Derryaghy* bar: *Belfast Upper*
Ir. *Collann* [**koll**in] *perhaps* 'height/high ground'. Collin (328m), in the townland of BALLYCOLLIN, has given name to COLLIN RIVER and COLIN GLEN on the north-east slopes of the mountain [*Collin* 1837].

**Collin Top** mtn, Antrim 3241
*7km W of Carnlough*
par: *Skerry* bar: *Antrim Lower*
Ir. *Collann perhaps* 'height/high ground' + E. 'top'. Collin Top (429m) is in the townland of QUOLIE and has given name to the stream known as COLLIN BURN [*Collin* 1835].

**Collon, The** distr., Derry 2441
*Suburb on the NW side of Derry city*
par: *Templemore*
bar: *NW Liberties of Londonderry*
Ir. *Cuilleann* [**kull**yin] 'slope'. The Collon is in the townland of **Shantallow**.

**Comber** tn, par., Down 3436
*Town is 5.5km SW of Newtownards*
bar: *Castlereagh Lower*
Ir. *An Comar* [an **kumm**er] 'the confluence'. Comber is so named because of its situation close to where the ENLER RIVER (in its tidal course known as the COMBER RIVER) flows into **Strangford Lough**. The Church of Ireland parish church in the townland of TOWN PARKS appears to occupy the site of a 12th-century Cistercian abbey. There was also an early monastery in the townland [(*ab*) *Comair* 1221].

**Commeen** tl, ham., Donegal 2039
*12km W of Ballybofey*
par: *Kilteevoge* bar: *Raphoe*
Ir. *An Coimín* [an **kim**een] 'the common land'. Commeen is on the north bank of the REELAN RIVER [*Cuimin* 1835].

**Coney Island** isld, Armagh 2936
par: *Tartaraghan* bar: *Oneilland West*
*In SW corner of Lough Neagh, 12km NW of Portadown*
*Coney* or *Cony* is a M.E. word meaning 'rabbit' deriving from A.F. *coning*. The original Irish name for the island was *Inis Dabhaill* 'island of the Blackwater', referring to the location of the island opposite where the river **Blackwater** enters **Lough Neagh** [*Enish Douel or Sidney* c.1605].

**Coney Island** tl, vill., Down 3533
*On the coast, 1km SW of Ardglass*
par: *Ardglass* bar: *Lecale Lower*
The 'island' is in fact a narrow peninsula which may have at one time been cut off by the sea. The first element of the place-name appears to represent the Anglo-Norman surname *Conning* which derives from A.F. *coning* 'rabbit' (*see previous entry*) [*Conningsiland* 1636].

**Conlig** tl, vill., Down 3537
*3km S of Bangor*
par: *Bangor* bar: *Ards Lower*
Ir. *An Choinleac* [an **khin**lack] 'the hound-stone'. The place-name is likely to refer to the standing-stone in the townland, though the significance of the prefix 'hound-' is not clear [*(feall) na Coinnleice* 1744].

**Connor** tl, vill., par., dioc., Antrim 3139
*Village is 10km N of Antrim town*
bar: *Antrim Lower*
Ir. *Coinnire* [**kon**yira] '(wild-)dog oak-wood'. The present Church of Ireland church occupies the site of the pre-Norman monastery and medieval cathedral. Connor is twin village to **Kells** which adjoins in on the west bank of the CONNOR BURN [*(espoc) Condere* 514].

**Connswater** distr., Down 3337
*Suburb 2.5km E of Belfast city centre*
par: *Holywood* bar: *Castlereagh Lower*
Connswater is named from the stream CONN'S WATER which flows into **Belfast Lough** at VICTORIA PARK a short distance to the north. The stream, in turn takes its name from Conn O'Neill, the chief landholder in north Down at the beginning of the 17th century (*see* **Castlereagh**) [*Conn's Water* 1775].

*Connor*

**Convoy** vill., par., Donegal 2240
*Village is 12.5km WNW of Lifford*
bar: *Raphoe*
Ir. *Conmhaigh* [**kon**wy] '(wild-)dog plain'. The parish was formed in 1832 out of the neighbouring parish of **Raphoe**. The village of Convoy is on flat land in the townland of CONVOY TOWNPARKS which is adjoined by CONVOY DEMESNE and is bordered by the river **Deele** [*Convoigh* 1610].

**Cookstown** tl, tn, Tyrone 2837
*16km N of Dungannon*
par: *Derryloran* bar: *Dungannon Upper*
The town of Cookstown is named after the planter Allan Cook who founded a settlement here in 1609 on land leased from the Archbishop of Armagh and obtained a patent for fairs and markets in 1628. The present town, which has portions in the four townlands of COOKSTOWN, LOY, GORTALOWRY and COOLNAFRANKY, was laid out c.1750 by William Stewart of nearby KILLYMOON. The Ir. name for Cookstown is *An Chorr Chríochach* [an khorr **khreegh**agh ] 'the boundary hill' [*a' Corr Críochach* c.1645].

**Coolessan** tl, distr., Derry 2642
*On S side of town of Limavady*
par: *Drumachose* bar: *Keenaght*
Ir. *Cúil Leasáin* [kool **lass**ine] 'corner of the little fort'. There is no record of a fort in the townland. However, at DAISY HILL in the townland of MULLAGH on the west bank of the **Roe** directly opposite Coolessan there is a mound or raised *rath* which marks the site of the famous convention of DRUMCEATT where in 574AD St Columcille pleaded the cause of the poets of Ireland with *Aodh mac Ainmhireach*, high king of Ireland [*Coulasson* 1615].

**Coolkeeragh** tl, ham., Derry 2442
*6.5km NE of Londonderry*
par: *Clondermot* bar: *Tirkeeran*
Ir. *Cúil Chaorach* [kool **kheer**agh] 'corner/angle of the sheep'. Coolkeeragh lies on the south side of the river **Faughan** at the point where it enters **Lough Foyle** [*Cool Keerah* 1613].

**Coolmaghry** tl, Tyrone 2736
*8km NW of Dungannon*
par: *Pomeroy* bar: *Dungannon Middle*
Ir. *Cúil Mhachaire* [kool **wagh**ara] 'corner/angle of the plain' [*Coolemagheri* 1690].

**Cooneen** tl, ham., Fermanagh 2434
*4.5km SSE of Fivemiletown*
par: *Aghalurcher* bar: *Magherastephana*
Ir. *An Cúinnín* [an **koon**yeen] 'the little corner'. The 'little corner' may be that formed by the junction of the COONEEN WATER with the COLEBROOK RIVER [*Cunen* 1659].

**Cootehill** tn, Cavan 2631
*20km NE of Cavan town*
par: *Drumgoon* bar: *Tullygarvey*
The place-name Cootehill is a combination of the surnames *Coote* and *Hill,* the former referring to Thomas Coote whose predecessor Sir Charles Coote acquired lands confiscated from the O'Reillys in the early 17th century and the latter referring to Frances Hill of **Hillsborough** in Co. Down whom Thomas Coote married c.1650. Cootehill has portions in the townlands of MUNNILLY and MAGHERANURE, the former being an anglicisation of the original Ir. name *Muinchille* [**mwin**khillya] 'sleeve' which in this case may signify 'ridge' and is also the current Ir. name of the town [*Coote Hill* 1725].

**Copeland Island** isld, tl, Down 3638
*Off N Down coast, 8km ENE of Bangor*
par: *Bangor* bar: *Ards Lower*
The name of the group of islands in which Copeland Island is located is referred to in a Norse source of 1230 AD as *Kaupmanneyjar* 'merchant islands' which has led to the suggestion that the islands were used as a Viking merchant store. However, it is also possible that *Kaupmann* represents a Norse surname (anglicised *Copman/Copeman*). The development to the modern form *Copeland* may be by analogy with the name of the Anglo-Norman family of *de Coupland* who arrived in the area in Norman times (*see* ***Ballycopeland***). The other two islands in the Copeland Island group are MEW ISLAND and LIGHT HOUSE ISLAND. The original Ir. name of the group of islands appears to have been *Oileáin Árann* [illine **aar**an'] 'islands of the back or ridge' (*see* ***Arranmore***) [*Kaupmanneyjar* 1230].

**Corbet** tl, Down 3134
*5km E of Banbridge*
par: *Magherally*
bar: *Iveagh Lower, Lower Half*
Ir. *An Carbad* [an **kar**abad] 'the jaw/boulder'. The exact feature referred to in the name of this townland has not been identified. Corbet has given name to CORBET LOUGH and to the village of CORBET MILLTOWN which is in in the neighbouring townland of TULLYCONNAUGHT [*Corbudd* 1609].

*Cootehill*

**Corboe** tl, Tyrone 2535
*6.5km NW of Clogher*
par/bar, *Clogher*
Ir. *Corr Bhó* [corr **wo**] 'round hill of the cow(s)' [*Corbo* 1655c].

**Corkey** tls, ham., distr., Antrim 3042
*2.5km S of Loughguile*
par: *Loughguile* bar: *Dunluce Upper*
Ir. *Corcaigh* [**kork**ee] 'moor'. The district of Corkey is made up of the townlands of CORKEY NORTH, LOVE'S CORKEY, CORKEY MIDDLE and CORKEY SOUTH OR LITTLE, all of which form long strips on the western slopes of **Slieveanorra** mountain [*Corcach* 1333].

**Cornafannoge** tl, ham., Fermanagh 2334
(sometimes *Cornafanog*)
*On E bank of Tempo river, 9.5km E of Enniskillen*
par: *Aghavea* bar: *Magherastephana*
Ir. *Corr na bhFeannóg* [korr na **van**og] 'round hill of the grey/scald crows'. Cornafannoge has given name to CORNAFANNOGE LOUGH which is partly in this townland and partly in the neighbouring townland of DRUMLONE [*Cornafenoge* 1751].

**Corranny** tl, Fermanagh 2433
*8km NNW of Clones*
par: *Clones* bar: *Clankelly*

Ir. *Corr Eanaigh* [korr **an**ee] 'round hill of the marsh'. The townland is bounded on the south by CORRANNY LOUGH [*Corroney* 1659].

**Correen** tl, ham., Antrim 3140
*7km NE of Ballymena*
par: *Skerry* bar: *Antrim Lower*
Ir. *An Curraín* [an **kurr**een] 'the moor'. There is rough hilly pasture in the north of the townland [*Curreen* 1780].

**Crabtreelane** ham., Armagh 2935
(sometimes *Crabtree Lane*)
*5km NW of Portadown*
par: *Drumcree* bar: *Oneilland West*
Crabtreelane in the townland of DERRYALL is named from crab-apple trees, sometimes called 'crabtrees', which formerly grew along the road (previously a lane) [*Crabtree Lane* 1888].

**Craig** vill, Tyrone 2539
*17.5km E of Strabane*
par: *Donaghedy* bar: *Strabane Lower*
Ir. *An Chreig* [an **khreg**] 'the rock'. Craig is on the north bank of the **Burn Dennet**, in the townland of CARRICKAYNE. There is a rocky outcrop south-west of the village.

**Craigantlet** tl, vill., Down 3437
(*see* ***Craigogantlet***)

**Craigavad** tl, vill., Down 3438
*On S shore of Belfast Lough, 3km NE of Holywood*
par: *Holywood* bar: *Castlereagh Lower*
*perhaps* Ir. *Creig an Bháda* [kreg a **waad**a] 'rock of the boat'. The place-name could refer to a boat-like rock in the sea. It has also been suggested that the name goes back to Ir. *Creig an Mhada* 'rock of the dog' and that the final element in fact refers to seals who were heard 'barking' on the rocky shore [*Cregevada* 1623].

**Craigavole** tl, ham., Derry 2841
*9.5km N of Maghera*
par: *Desertoghill* bar: *Coleraine*
Ir. *Creig an Ghuail* [creg an **ġooi**l] 'rock of the coal' [*Cregogola* 1613].

**Craigavon** tn, Armagh 3035
*Halfway between Lurgan and Portadown*
par: *Shankill/Seagoe* bar: *Oneilland East*
Craigavon was designated a new town in 1965 and named after James Craig (1871–1940), first prime minister of Northern Ireland, whose title was Viscount Craigavon.

**Craignamaddy** hill, Tyrone 2538
*4.5km NE of Gortin*
par: *Bodoney Lower* bar: *Strabane Upper*
Ir. *Creig na Madaí* [kreg na **mad**ee] 'rock/rocky hill of the (wild) dogs'. Craignamaddy (366m) is in the townland of GARVAGH.

**Craigogantlet** tl, vill., Down 3437
(usually *Craigantlet*)
*6km NW of Newtownards*
par: *Newtownards* bar: *Castlereagh Lower*
Ir. *Carraig Ó gCaoindealbháin* [karrick o **geen**jalawine] '*Ó Caoindealbháin*'s rock'. The surname *Ó Caoindealbháin* is normally anglicised *Quinlan* or *Kindelan/Kennellan* and is generally regarded as being of Leinster origin. There is a rocky outcrop a short distance west of the village [*Ballicarigogandolane* 1605].

**Craigs** tl, ham., par., Antrim 3040
*Hamlet is 2.5km NW of Cullybackey*
bar: *Kilconway*
Ir. *Na Creaga* [na **krag**a] 'the rocks'. The site of the medieval parish church is in a graveyard in the subdenomination of the townland of Craigs known as AGHNAKILLA (Ir. *Achadh na Cille* 'field of the church') [*the Creggs* 1604].

**Craigyhill** distr., Antrim 3340
(sometimes *Craigy Hill*)
*Suburb on the NW side of Larne*
par: *Larne* bar: *Glenarm Upper*
Craigyhill takes its name from the townland of BALLYCRAIGY (Ir. *Baile Creige* 'townland of the rock/rocky hill') in which it is partially situated and in which there are rocky outcrops.

**Cranagh** vill., Tyrone 2539
*In Glenelly Valley, 10.5km E of Plumbridge*
par: *Bodoney Upper* bar: *Strabane Upper*
Ir. *An Chrannóg* [an **khran**og] 'the wooden structure'. The wooden structure may have marked a halting place for travellers in **Glenelly Valley**, as Cranagh was earlier known as *Crannóg na Cónaí* [kranog na **koan**ee], i.e. 'Cranagh of the dwelling or resting'. The word *cónaí* may also have connotations of watching or keeping vigil so that the place-name may have religious associations, perhaps suggesting a place of prayer or a

resting-place for funerals. Cranagh is in the townland of OUGHTDOORISH [*Cranoc na Comhnaigh* c.1680].

**Cranagill** tl, ham., Armagh 2935
*8km W of Portadown*
par: *Tartaraghan* bar: *Oneilland West*
Ir. *Crannaigh Ghil* [kranee **yil**] 'white woodland'. The townland of Cranagill contains the hamlet of CRANNAGAEL whose name appears to have the same origin [*Cranagill* 1608].

**Crana River** Donegal
(*see **Buncrana***)

**Cranfield** tl, par., Antrim 3038
*Townland is on N shore of Lough Neagh, 5km SW of Randalstown*
bar: *Toome Upper*
Ir. *Creamhchoill* [**krau**khil] 'wild-garlic wood'. The ruins of the medieval parish church are in a graveyard on the shore of **Lough Neagh**. Nearby is a holy well dedicated to St Olcan and it is likely that there was an early monastery on the same site [*Cremc[h]aill* c.830].

**Cranfield** tl, Down 3231
*On the coast, 5.5km SW of Kilkeel*
par: *Kilkeel* bar: *Mourne*
Ir. *Creamhchoill* [**krau**khil] 'wild-garlic wood'. CRANFIELD POINT at the entrance to **Carlingford Lough** forms the southernmost tip of Co. Down [*Creamchoill* c.1200].

**Cranford** tl, vill., Donegal 2143
*On W shore of Mulroy Bay, 6.5km N of Millford*
par/bar, *Kilmacrenan*
Ir. *Creamhghort* [**crau**ghort] 'wild-garlic field' [*Crawarte* 1603].

**Cranny** tl, Derry 2838
*4km SW of Magherafelt*
par: *Desertmartin* bar: *Loughinsolin*
Ir. *Crannaigh* [**kran**ee] 'wooded place'. CRANNY HILL (160m) is in the south-west of the townland [*Crannagh* 1609].

**Crawfordsburn** vill., Down 3438
*4km W of Bangor*
par: *Bangor* bar: *Castlereagh Lower*
Crawfordsburn in the townland of BALLYMULLAN is named from CRAWFORD'S BURN, a stream which flows through the village and enters **Belfast Lough** a short distance to the north. The place-name is made up of the Scottish surname *Crawford* plus Sc./N.E. *burn* 'stream'. The branch of the Crawford family who settled in this area as tenants of James Hamilton in the early 17th century appear to be of Ayrshire origin. There is a place named CRAWFORDSBURN near Greenock in Ayrshire. However, the surname Crawford derives from the name of the barony of CRAWFORD in Lanarkshire [*Crawford's Burn* 1744].

**Creagh** tl, Fermanagh 2334
*5.5km W of Fivemiletown*
par: *Aghavea* bar: *Magherastephana*
Ir. *Créach* [**krey**agh] 'coarse pasture'. The townland contains a well-known road junction known as CREAGH CROSS ROADS [*Creagh* 1752].

**Creagh, The** tl, Derry 2939
*Adjoining Toome, on the W side of the Lower Bann*
par: *Artrea* bar: *Loughinsholin*
Ir. *An Créach* [an **krey**agh] 'the coarse pasture'. The extremely large townland of The Creagh was originally known as *Moyola* which is now the name of the river which bounds it on the west (*see **Moyola***). It is a remarkably flat townland, stretching from the Moyola to **Lough Beg** and was formerly divided into *Etre* (Ir. *Íochtarach* 'lower') and *Otre* (Ir. *Uachtarach* 'upper') portions [*Creagh* 1813].

**Creeslough** tl, vill., Donegal 2043
*22km NW of Letterkenny*
par: *Clondahorky* bar: *Kilmacrenan*
Ir. *An Craoslach* [an **krees**lagh] 'the gullet/gorge'. The name may have originally applied to the little lake named Creeslough which lies to the south-west of the village [*Creslagh* 1610].

**Cregagh** tl, distr., Down 3337
*Suburb 3km SE of Belfast city centre*
par: *Knockbreda* bar: *Castlereagh Upper*
Ir. *An Chreagaigh* [an **khrag**ee] 'the rocky place' [*Craigogh* c.1659].

**Creggan** tl, distr., Derry 2441
*Part of townland forms a suburb on W side of Derry city*
par: *Templemore*
bar: *NW Liberties of Londonderry*

Ir. *An Creagán* [an **krag**an] 'the rocky place'. There is a rocky outcrop in the west of the townland [*Craigan* 1663].

**Creggan** tl, distr., Tyrone 2637
*18km ENE of Omagh*
par: *Termonmaguirk* bar: *Omagh East*
Ir. *An Creagán* [an **krag**an] 'the rocky place'. There is a rocky area known as CREGGAN ROCKS in the west of this very large townland [*Creggan* 1633].

**Creggan** vill., par., Armagh 2931
*Village is 2.5km NE of Crossmaglen*
bar: *Fews Upper*
Ir. *An Creagán* [an **krag**an] 'the rocky place'. The present Church of Ireland church occupies the site of the medieval parish church, in the townland of CREGGAN BANE GLEBE. The neighbouring townland is known as CREGGAN DUFF (Ir. *An Creagán Dubh*) which signifies 'black Creggan' and is said to be so-named because it is more rocky and less cultivable than CREGGAN BANE (Ir. *An Creagán Bán*) which signifies 'White Creggan'. Creggan has given name to the CREGGAN RIVER which flows through the parish, a small portion of which is in the barony of DUNDALK UPPER in Co. Louth. The portion of Creggan parish which is in Co. Armagh is often known as LOWER CREGGAN [*(paróiste) an Chreagáin* c.1735].

**Crilly** tl, ham., Tyrone 2635
*3km SE of Aughnacloy*
par: *Aghaloo* bar: *Dungannon Lower*
Ir. *Crithligh* [**kreeh**lee] 'quaking bog' [*Crelly* 1608].

**Crindle** tl, ham., Derry 2642
*4km NNW of Limavady*
par: *Tamlaght Finlagan* bar: *Keenaght*
*perhaps* Ir. *Cruinneall* [**krin**yal] 'rounded or smooth place'. The land is flat, close to the west bank of the river **Roe** [*Crinnell* 1613].

**Croaghgorm or Blue Stack Mountains**
Donegal 1938
*9km N of Donegal town*
Croaghgorm is an anglicisation of *An Chruach Ghorm* [an khrooagh **ġor**im] 'the blue stack', a peak of 674m which is the highest in the range. The name of this peak has been translated as BLUE STACK and this is the basis of the E. name BLUE STACK MOUNTAINS. In local usage, the Ir. name of the mountains is simply *Na Cruacha* 'the stacks', anglicised *The Crows*, reflecting the fact that so many of the peaks have Ir. *Cruach* as the first element of their names [*Blue Stack* 1837].

**Crockaneel** mtn, Antrim 3143
*5.5km W of Cushendun*
par: *Grange of Layd* bar: *Glenarm Lower*
Ir. *Cnoc an Aoil* [kruck an **eel**] 'hill of the lime'. Crockaneel (403m) is on the boundary of the three townlands of KINURE, CARNAMADDY and GLENMAKEERAN [*Crockaneel* 1855].

**Crolly** tl, ham., Donegal 1841
*9km NE of Dunglow*
par: *Tullaghobegly* bar: *Kilmacrenan*
Ir. *Croithlí* [**krih**lee] 'shaking bog'. Crolly stands on the east bank of the *Abhainn Chroithlí* (literally 'Crolly River') which is known in English as the GWEEDORE RIVER and which enters the sea a short distance to the north-west.

**Cross, The** ham., Derry 2441
(sometimes *Cross*)
*On E bank of the Faughan, 5.5km SE of Derry city*
par: *Cumber Lower* bar: *Tirkeeran*
The Cross is named from the townland of CROSSBALLYCORMICK in which it is situated (Ir. *Crosbhaile Chormaic* [kross wala **khor**mick] 'the cross- or transverse townland of Cormac'). The townland seems to have been so-named because it occupies a diagonal position on the east bank of the river **Faughan**. The shortened form *The Cross* appears to have been first used to apply to a house which was the residence of James Smith Esq. in the early 19th century [*Crosballe Cormak* 1622].

**Crossdoney** tl, vill., Cavan 2330
*6km SW of Cavan town*
par: *Kilmore* bar: *Clanmahon*
Ir. *Cros Domhnaigh* [kross **doan**ee] 'cross of the (early) church'. There is no record of either a cross or a church here [*Crossdony* c.1660].

**Crosserlough** tl, vill., par., Cavan 2429
*Village is 11km SSE of Cavan town*
bar: *Castlerahan*
Ir. *Crois ar Loch* [crush ar **lough**] 'cross on a lake'. There is a tradition that there was a stone cross on the gable of the ancient parish church before it was replaced by the present Church of Ireland church in the village in 1812.

Presumably the cross was formerly on an island on the little lake which lies a short distance to the south. The parish of Crosserlough has small portions in the neighbouring baronies of CLANMAHON and LOUGHTEE UPPER. It formerly went by the *alias* name of *Kildrumferton* [*Croserlagh* 1601].

**Crossgar** tl, vill., Down 3435
*8km NW of Downpatrick*
par: *Kilmore* bar: *Castlereagh Upper*
Ir. *An Chrois Ghearr* [an khrush **yarr**] 'the short cross'. There is a holy well known as *St Mary's Well* in the townland which suggests that in this case *crois* 'cross' is likely to refer to an ecclesiastical cross, no trace of which now remains. The adjective 'short' in the place-name may suggest that the cross was damaged or in some way defective.

**Crossgare** tl, ham., Derry 2842
*6km S of Coleraine*
par: *Macosquin* bar: *Coleraine*
Ir. *An Chros Ghearr* [an khrus **yarr**] 'the short cross'. As in the case of **Crossgar** in Co. Down, *crois* in this place-name appears to refer to an early cross of which is there is no trace in the townland, though there was formerly a graveyard in the neighbouring townland of KILLURE [*Crosgarre* 1613].

**Crosskeys, The** distr., Antrim 3039
*6km NNE of Toome*
par: *Grange of Ballyscullion*
bar: *Toome Upper*
The Crosskeys is named from a well-known thatched public house (formerly a post office) in the townland of ARDNAGLASS. The crossed keys of the inn sign are the insignia of St Peter. 6km north-east of **Maghera** there is another CROSSKEYS which appears to have been named from a public house which no longer survives [*Crosskeys* c.1858].

**Cross Keys** vill., Cavan 2429
(sometimes *Crosskeys*)
*8km SE of Cavan town*
par: *Denn* bar: *Loughtee Upper*
The village of Cross Keys was named from an inn, no trace of which remains, but which in 1744 is referred to as 'a convenient good inn'. The Ir. name of Cross Keys is *Carraig an Tobair* [karrick an **tubb**er] 'rock of the well', the original Ir. name of the townland of CARRICKATOBER in which the village is situated [*Crosskeys* 1728]

**Crossmaglen** tl, tn, Armagh 2931
*22km SW of Newry*
par: *Creggan* bar: *Fews Upper*
Ir. *Crois Mhic Lionnáin* [krush vik **linn**ine] '*Mac Lionnáin*'s cross'. The surname *Mac Lionnáin* may be a variant of *Ó Lionnáin* 'Lennon' or, possibly, of *Mag Leannáin* 'MacGlennan'. The first element of the place-name may refer to the intersection of roads in the middle of the town [*Crosmoyglan* 1609].

**Cross Roads** vill., Donegal 2139
(sometimes *The Cross*)
*5km ESE of Stranorlar*
par: *Donaghmore* bar: *Raphoe*
The village takes its name from a crossroads 1.5km south of **Killygordon**, in the townland of DROMORE [*Crossroads* 1835].

**Cruit** tls, isld, Donegal 1742
*Off NW Donegal coast, 7.5km NW of Dunglow*
par: *Templecrone* bar: *Boylagh*
Ir. *An Chruit* [an **khritch**] 'the hump'. An earlier name for the island of Cruit, which is now joined by a bridge to the mainland, appears to have been *Inis Tuath Ros* 'island of the district of the Rosses'. The island is divided into two townlands, CRUIT UPPER and CRUIT LOWER [(*occ*) *Insi tuath Rass* 1247].

**Crumlin** vill., Antrim 3137
*10km S of Antrim town*
par: *Camlin* bar: *Massereene Upper*
Ir. *Cromghlinn* [**krumm**lin] 'crooked glen'. The place-name seems to refer to the winding valley of the CRUMLIN RIVER. The village of Crumlin is in the townland of BALLYTROMERY [*Crumlin* 1780].

**Cuilcagh** mtn., Fermanagh/Cavan 2132
*On Fermanagh/Cavan border, 18km SW of Enniskillen*
Ir. *Binn Chuilceach* [bin **khilk**agh] 'chalky peak'. Cuilcagh (665m) is named from the whiteness of its face, *cuilceach* being a variant of *cailceach* 'chalky'. Cuilcagh is the highest peak in a long ridge known as the CUILCAGH MOUNTAINS [*Quilkagh* 1613].

**Culcavy** tl, vill., Down 3235
*1.5km NW of Hillsborough*
par: *Blaris* bar: *Iveagh Lower, Upper Half*
Ir. *Cúil Chéibhe* [kool **khey**va] 'corner/nook of the long grass' [*Cowlecavy* 1632].

**Culcrow** tl, Derry 2842
*10km SSE of Coleraine*
par: *Agivey* bar: *Coleraine*
Ir. *Cúil Chnó* [kool **khro**] 'corner/nook of nuts'. Culcrow is close to the west bank of the river **Bann** [*Coolecroe* 1612].

**Culcrum** tl, Antrim 3042
*2.5km NW of Clogh Mills*
par: *Killagan* bar: *Kilconway*
Ir. *Cúil Chrom* [kool **khrum**] 'crooked or sloping corner/nook'.

**Culdaff** tl, vill., par., Donegal 2544
*Village is at head of Culdaff Bay, 7.5km NE of Carndonagh*
bar: *Inishowen East*
Ir. *Cúil Dabhcha* [kool **dau**gha] 'corner/recess of the vat or large vessel'. The final element of the place-name refers to a rock in the CULDAFF RIVER, near the site of an early church. The rock has a large hollow in it and was formerly known as '*Baodán*'s boat', the tradition being that St *Baodán*, the patron saint of the parish, sailed from Scotland to Ireland in this 'boat'. Culdaff has given name to the neighbouring townland of CULDAFF GLEBE [*Culldavcha* 1429].

**Culky** tl, Fermanagh 2234
(sometimes *Culkey*)
*On W bank of Upper Lough Erne, 3km S of Enniskillen*
Ir. *Cuilcigh* [**kil**kee] *perhaps* 'place of reeds'. Given the similarity of its E. name to that of **Cuilcagh** mountain one might propose a similar derivation, i.e. 'chalky place' (*see above*). However, considering the situation of Culky between UPPER LOUGH ERNE and the SILLEES RIVER, 'place of reeds' appears more appropriate [*Colkie* 1609].

**Cullaville** tl, vill., Armagh 2831
(sometimes *Culloville*)
*On the border with Monaghan, 3km SW of Crossmaglen*
par: *Creggan* bar: *Fews Upper*
Cullaville is a shortened form of *MacCullagh's Ville*, the MacCullaghs being the landowners in the 17th century [*Cullovill* 1766].

**Cullinane** ham., Antrim 3241
*In Glencloy, 4km SW of Carnlough*
par: *Tickmacrevan* bar: *Glenarm Lower*
Ir. *Cuileannán* [**kull**enan] 'place of holly'. Cullinane is in the townland of AUGHAREAMLAGH.

**Cullion** tl, Tyrone 2440
*9km NNE of Omagh*
par: *Cappagh* bar: *Strabane Upper*
Ir. *Cuilleann* [**kull**yin] 'slope' [*Quillan* 1613].

**Cullybackey** vill., Antrim 3040
*On E bank of the Main, 5km NW of Ballymena*
par: *Craigs* bar: *Toome Lower*
Ir. *Cúil na Baice* [kool na **back**a] 'corner/angle of the river bend'. There is a bend on the river **Main** a short distance south of the village [*Ballycholnabacky* 1607].

**Cullyhanna** tls, vill., Armagh 2932
*6km N of Crossmaglen*
par: *Creggan* bar: *Fews Upper*
Ir. *Coilleach Eanach* [killagh **an**agh] 'wood of the marshes'. The village of Cullyhanna straddles the townlands of CULLYHANNA BIG, TULLYNAVALL and FREEDUFF. The CULLYHANNA RIVER divides the townlands of CULLYHANNA BIG and CULLYHANNA LITTLE while CULLYHANNA LOUGH lies on the southern boundary of CULLYHANNA LITTLE [*Collyhanagh* 1640].

**Culmore** tl, vill., Derry 2442
*7km NNE of Londonderry*
par: *Templemore*
bar: *NW Liberties of Londonderry*
Ir. *An Chúil Mhór* [an khool **wore**] 'the large corner/peninsula'. Ir. *cúil* which normally signifies 'corner/angle' in this case appears to refer to CULMORE POINT on the west bank of the river **Foyle** [(*isin*) *chúil móir* 1600].

**Culnady** tl, ham., Derry 2840
*4km NE of Maghera*
par: *Maghera* bar: *Loughinsholin*
Ir. *Cúil Chnáidí* [kool **khradg**ee] 'corner/angle of the place of burrs' [(*go*) *Cúil Cnáimhdidhe* c.1740].

**Cultra** distr., Down 3437
*Suburb on E side of Holywood, on S shore of Belfast Lough*
par: *Holywood* bar: *Castlereagh Lower*
Cultra is a shortened form of BALLYCULTRA, the name of the townland in which it is situated. BALLYCULTRA is from Ir. *Baile Chúl Trá* [bala khool **tra**] 'townland of the back of the strand' [*Ballecultra* 1627].

**Curr** tl, Tyrone 2536
*11km SE of Omagh*
par: *Clogherny* bar: *Omagh East*
Ir. *An Chorr* [an **khorr**] 'the round hill'. Curr appears to take its name from CURR MOUNTAIN (160m) which stands in the north of the townland [*Corr* 1666].

**Curran** tl, vill., Derry 2839
*8.5km N of Magherafelt*
par: *Maghera* bar: *Loughinsholin*
Ir. *Curraín* [**kurr**een] 'moor'. There is an area of moorland in the west of the townland [*Currin* 1613].

**Curran** distr., Antrim 3440
*District of Larne adjacent to the harbour*
par: *Larne* bar: *Glenarm Upper*
Ir. *An Corrán* [an **korr**an] 'the crescent'. The place-name refers to the crescent-shaped peninsula at the north entrance to **Larne Lough**, at the tip of which is CURRAN POINT. The name Curran is incorporated in CURRAN AND DRUMALISS, the name of the townland in which it is situated [*Coran* c.1659].

**Cushendall** tl, vill., Antrim 3242
*On E Antrim coast, 5km S of Cushendun*
par: *Layd* bar: *Glenarm Lower*
Ir. *Bun Abhann Dalla* [bun owen **dal**a] 'foot of the river Dall'. The modern anglicised form of the place-name is from the alternative Ir. name *Cois Abhann Dalla* [cush owen **dal**a] which also signifies 'foot of the river Dall'. The DALL, which flows into the sea here, is formed by the convergence of the GLENAAN RIVER with the BALLYEMON RIVER, 1km to the west. The name *Dall* appears to mean 'dark one' [*Bun an Dalla* c.1854].

*The curfew tower, Cushendall*

**Cushendun** tl, vill., Antrim 3243
*On E Antrim coast, 15km SE of Ballycastle*
par: *Culfeightrin* bar: *Cary*
Ir. *Bun Abhann Doinne* [bun oan **dinn**ya] 'foot of the river Dun'. The anglicised name is from Ir. *Cois Abhann Doinne*, an alternative Ir. version with the same meaning (cf. **Cushendall**). Cushendun is at the mouth of the river Dun (commonly known as the GLENDUN RIVER) which rises close to **Trostan** mountain and has also given name to **Glendun**, one of the nine glens of Antrim [*Bun-abhann Duine* 1567].

# D

**Daisy Hill** hill Derry 2642
(*see **Coolessan***)

**Dalway's Bawn** hist. mon., Antrim 3439
*3km W of Whitehead*
par: *Kilroot* bar: *Belfast Lower*
Dalway's Bawn in the townland of BALLYHILL is a fortified rectangular enclosure with towers. It was built in 1609 by John Dallowye from Scotland. Farm buildings have been erected against the walls of the *bawn*.

**Darkley** tl, vill., Armagh 2833
*3km SSE of Keady*
par: *Keady* bar: *Armagh*
Ir. *Dearclaigh* [**jark**lee] 'place of caves or hollows' [*Darkeley* 1657].

**Dawros** tl, Donegal 1639
*On W Donegal coast, 12.5km NW of Ardara*
par: *Inishkeel* bar: *Boylagh*
Ir. *Damhros* [**dau**ross] 'ox peninsula'. Dawros is named from a conspicuous promontory which is known in E. as DAWROS HEAD. It has

Bishop Gate, Derry city

given name to DAWROS ISLAND off its north coast and to DAWROS BAY which lies to the south.

**Deehommed** tl, Down 3234
(sometimes *Dechomet*)
*9km SSW of Dromara*
par: *Drumgooland*
bar: *Iveagh Upper, Lower Half*
Ir. *Deachoimheád* [**ja**khivad] 'good view'. The townland of Deehommed is named from DEEHOMMED MOUNTAIN (318m), a foothill of **Slieve Croob**, which commands a find view over the **Mourne Mountains** [*Dycovead* 1583].

**Deele** river Donegal
*Rises in Lough Deele, 10km SW of Letterkenny. Flows into the Foyle 2km N of Lifford*
Ir. *An Daoil* [an **deel**] 'the black one'.
The river Deele is sometimes known as the DALE BURN. It has given name to the townland of GLENEELY (Ir. *Gleann Daoile* 'glen of the Deele') in the parish of DONAGHMORE. There are rivers named the DEEL in Mayo and Cork/Limerick [(*tar*) *Daoíl* 1557]

**Deer's Meadow** Down 3232
(*see **Bann** river/**Slieve Muck***)

**Derg** river, Donegal/Tyrone
*Rises in Lough Derg in Co. Donegal. Combines with the Strule to form the Mourne, 10km S of Strabane*
Ir. *An Dearg* [an **jar**ig] 'the red one'. This is the meaning of the Mod. Ir. form of the placename. However, the river is named from **Lough Derg** in which it rises, the name of which appears to go back to O. Ir. *Loch Geirg, perhaps* 'lake of the grouse/quail', the modern form *Loch Dearg* 'red lake' being a later reinterpretation (*see **Lough Derg*** below) [*The Red river al. Dearg* 1596].

**Derry** city, co., dioc. 2441
(sometimes *Londonderry*)
*City straddles the river Foyle at the head of Lough Foyle*
Ir. *Doire* [**dirr**a] 'oak-wood'. The original name for Derry was *Doire Chalgaigh* [dirra **khal**agee] '*Calgach*'s oak-wood'. Later, the place was known as *Doire Cholm Cille* 'Columcille's oak-wood' from a monastery founded by St Columcille in 546AD, the site of which appears to be marked by ST COLUMB'S CATHEDRAL in Fountain Street. In 1613 Derry was renamed LONDONDERRY by the planter London Companies on account of their association with the city of London, while the former county of **Coleraine** was also renamed Londonderry. The city is partly in the barony of TIRKEERAN and partly in the barony of NORTH-WEST LIBERTIES OF LONDONDERRY [(*eaclais*) *Doire Calgaigh* 535].

**Derryadd** tl, vill., Armagh 3036
*On S shore of Lough Neagh, 5.5km NW of Lurgan*
par: *Montiaghs* bar: *Oneilland East*
Ir. *Doire Fhada* [dirra **ad**a] 'long oak-wood'. Derryadd has given named to DERRYADD BAY in **Lough Neagh** [*Derriada* 1609].

**Derryaghy** tl, vill., par., Antrim 3236
*Village is 9km SW of Belfast city centre*
bar: *Belfast Upper*
Ir. *Doire Achaidh* [dirra **agh**ee] 'oak-wood of the field'. The Church of Ireland church in the village occupies the site of an early church. A previous name for Derryaghy was *Ardaghy* (Ir. *Ard Achaidh* 'height of the field') [*Ardrachi* 1306].

**Derryall** tl, Armagh 2935
*5km NW of Portadown*
par: *Drumcree* bar: *Oneilland West*
Ir. *Doire Ál* [dirra **aal**] 'oak-wood of broods/litters'. The final element of the placename may have its origin in a legend which has now been lost [*Derrial* 1609].

**Derryanvil** tl, Armagh 3035
(sometimes *Derryanville*)
*3km N of Portadown*
par: *Drumcree* bar: *Oneilland West*

Ir. *Doire Chonamhail* [dirra **khon**awil] '*Conamhail*'s oak-wood'. The personal name *Conamhail* which signifies 'wolf-like' was fairly common in earlier times [*Derrehanavile* 1609].

**Derrybeg** tl, vill., Donegal 1842
*15km NNE of Dunglow*
par: *Tullaghobegly* bar: *Kilmacrenan*
Ir. *Doirí Beaga* [dirree **beg**a] 'little oak-woods'. There is now no trace of the woods referred to in the place-name.

**Derryboy** tl, ham., Down 3435
*6km NW of Killyleagh*
par: *Killyleagh* bar: *Dufferin*
Ir. *Doire Buí* [dirra **bwee**] 'yellow oak-wood'. Derryboy has given name to DERRYBOY LOUGH which is partly in this townland and partly in BALLYALGAN [*Dirryboy* 1624].

**Derrychrier** tl, Derry 2640
*On W bank of the Owenbeg River, 3km SW of Dungiven*
par: *Banagher* bar: *Keenaght*
Ir. *Doire an Chriathair* [dirra an **khree**hir] 'oak-wood of the quagmire'. Ir. *criathar* (*literally* 'sieve') is used in place-names to refer to boggy or swampy places [*Derkreayr* 1397].

**Derryfubble** tl, Tyrone 2835
*7km S of Dungannon*
par: *Clonfeacle* bar: *Dungannon Middle*
Ir. *Doire an Phobail* [dirra an **fub**il] 'oak-wood of the people'. The final element suggests 'place of assembly/meeting place' [*Dirripuble* 1609].

**Derrygonnelly** tl, vill., Fermanagh 2135
*14km NW of Enniskillen*
par: *Inishmacsaint* bar: *Magheraboy*
Ir. *Doire Ó gConaíle* [dirra o **gon**eela] 'oak-wood of the (O')Connollys'. The Fermanagh sept of the widespread family of *Ó Conaíle* '(O')Connolly/Connelly' originated in the barony of LURG, and CONNOLLYSTOWN east of **Pettigo** marks one of their settlements [*Dirgonilly* 1616].

**Derryharney** tl, Fermanagh 2333
*On E shore of Upper Lough Erne, 9km SE of Enniskillen*
par: *Cleenish* bar: *Magherastephana*
Ir. *Doire Charna* [dirra **kharn**a] 'oak-wood of the cairn'. There is now no trace or record of a cairn in the townland [*Derriharne* 1659].

**Derryhaw** tl, Armagh 2734
*9.5km SW of Armagh city*
par: *Tynan* bar: *Armagh*
Ir. *Doire an Chatha* [dirra an **kha**ha] 'oak-wood of the battle' [*Derricah* 1661].

**Derrykeevan** tl, ham., Armagh 2935
*6km NW of Portadown*
par: *Tartaraghan* bar: *Oneilland West*
Ir. *Doire Uí Chaomháin* [dirra ee **kheev**ine] 'O'Keevan's oak-wood'. The surname O'Keevan is now extinct in the area but is recorded in 1664 and was formerly also found in Co. Tyrone [*Derrykivyn* 1657].

**Derrykeighan** tl, vill., par., Antrim 2943
*Village is 7.5km N of Ballymoney*
bar: *Dunluce Lower*
Ir. *Doire Chaocháin* [dirra **kheegh**ine] '*Caochán*'s oak-wood'. The personal name *Caochán* signifies 'purblind/dim-sighted'. The site of the medieval parish church, and also of an early church, is marked by the ruins of a later church in the village [(*o*) *Daire Chaechain* c.800].

**Derrylee** tl, ham., Armagh 2936
*12km NW of Portadown*
par: *Tartaraghan* bar: *Oneilland West*
Ir. *Doire Lathaí* [dirra **la**hee] 'oak-wood of the muddy place/marsh' [*Derrlaghye* 1618].

**Derrylester** tl, ham., Fermanagh 2233
*9km SSW of Enniskillen*
par: *Killesher* bar: *Clanawley*
Ir. *Doire an Leastair* [dirra an **las**tir] 'oak-wood of the vessel'. The significance of the

*Oak wood*

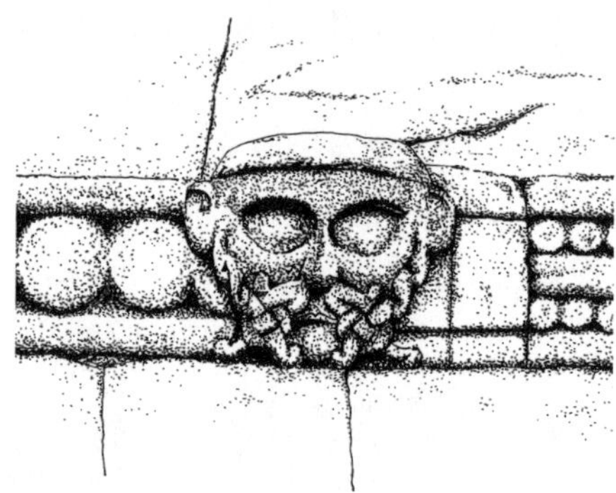

*Head carved on Devenish round tower*

element *leastar* 'vessel' is unclear. Could it possibly refer to the spa well in the townland?

**Derrylin** tl, vill., Fermanagh 2232
*18km SSE of Enniskillen*
par: *Kinawley* bar: *Knockninny*
Ir. *Doire Fhlainn* [dirra **linn**] '*Flann*'s oak-wood'. The personal name *Flann* which can be either male or female was formerly very common and is the basis of the surname *Ó Floinn/Ó Flainn* '(O')Flynn' [*Derrelin* 1609].

**Derrynoose** vill., par., Armagh 2833
*Village is 4.5km SW of Keady*
bar: *Tiranny*
Ir. *Doire Núis* [dirra **noo**ish] 'oak-wood of the beestings or new milk'. The village of Derrynoose is partly in the townland of MULLYARD and partly in CROSSNAMOYLE. The site of the medieval church is marked by the ruins of a church built c.1622 in the townland of LISTARKELT. The parish is sometimes known as **Maddan** which is the site of the present Church of Ireland church [*Derenoysse* 1427].

**Derrytrasna** tl, ham., Armagh 2936
*On S shore of Lough Neagh, 11km NW of Lurgan*
par: *Montiaghs* bar: *Oneilland East*
Ir. *Doire Trasna* [dirra **trass**na] 'transverse oak-wood'. The townland may be so-named because it stretches across from the **Upper Bann** to the shore of **Lough Neagh** [*Derrytrasney* 1661].

**Derryveagh Mountains** Donegal
*20km NW of Letterkenny*
Derryveagh Mountains is a modern geographical term, referring to the range of mountains which are in the district of DERRYVEAGH and of which **Slieve Snaght** (678m) is the highest peak. The name DERRYVEAGH is from Ir. *Doire Bheatha* [dirra **va**ha] 'wood of birch' which may be a development from an earlier form *Doire Bheathach* 'birch wood' (*see* ***Glenbeagh***).

**Dervock** tl, vill., Antrim 2943
*6.5km NNE of Ballymoney*
par: *Derrykeighan* bar: *Dunluce Lower*
Ir. *Dairbheog* [**dar**avog] 'oak plantation' [*Deroogg* c.1659].

**Desertmartin** vill., par., Derry 2839
*4.5km WNW of Magherafelt*
bar: *Loughinsholin*
Ir. *Díseart Mhártain* [jeeshart **wart**in] '(St) Martin's hermitage/retreat'. The monastic hermitage of Desertmartin was originally dedicated to St Martin of Tours. The remains of the ancient parish church are in a bend of the GRANGE WATER in the townland of KNOCKNAGIN at the east side of the village [*Dísiort Mhártain* c.1645].

**Devenish** isld, tl, par., Fermanagh 2234
*Island is in Lower Lough Erne, 3km NNW of Enniskillen*
bar: *Magheraboy*
Ir. *Daimhinis* [**dav**inish] 'ox island'. The island and townland of Devenish contains the site of a sixth-century monastery, a round tower, the ruins of the medieval parish church of St *Molaisse* and the ruins of the medieval St Mary's Abbey. Devenish has given name to the townland of TULLYDEVENISH (Ir. *Tulaigh Dhaimhinse* 'hillock of Devenish') which lies opposite it on the western shore of **Lower Lough Erne** [(*Molassi*) *Daminsi* c.830].

**Diamond, The** ham., Antrim 3137
*5km WNW of Crumlin*
par: *Killead* bar: *Massereene Lower*
In Ulster place-names the element *diamond* can apply to either a rural crossroads or to a market square in the middle of a town. In this case, the hamlet called The Diamond is named from a crossroads in the townland of BALLYMACILHOYLE.

**Diamond, The** ham., Armagh 2935
*3.5km NE of Loughgall*
par: *Newry* (*detached portion*)
bar: *Oneilland West*
The Diamond takes its name from a crossroads

in the townland of GRANGE LOWER which forms a detached portion of the parish of **Newry** a considerable distance north of the main portion. It is well known as the site of a battle which led to the foundation of the Orange Order in 1795.

**Diamond, The** ham., Tyrone 2937
*11.5km ESE of Cookstown*
par: *Arboe* bar: *Dungannon Upper*
The Diamond is named from a five-point crossroads in the townland of KILLYGONLAN.

**Divis** mtn, tl, Antrim 3237
*6km W of Belfast city centre*
par: *Shankill* bar: *Belfast Upper*
Ir. *Dubhais* [**doo**ish] 'black ridge/peak'. The townland of Divis is named from DIVIS MOUNTAIN (478m), the summit of which is on the boundary with the neighbouring townland of ALTIGARRON (*see* ***Black Mountain***).

**Doagh** tl, vill., Antrim 3238
*3km SW of Ballyclare*
par: *Grange of Doagh* bar: *Antrim Upper*
Ir. *Dumhach* [**doo**agh] 'mound'. Doagh appears to have been named from a steep mound or bank overlooking the DOAGH RIVER a short distance south of the village, on the summit of which are the remains of a fort. The site of the medieval church of GRANGE OF DOAGH is in a graveyard a short distance to the east [*Douach* 1306].

**Doagh Beg** tl, vill., Donegal 2244
(sometimes *Doaghbeg*)
*On E coast of Fanad peninsula, 19km NNE of Millford*
par: *Clondavaddog* bar: *Kilmacrenan*
Ir. *Dumhaigh Bhig* [dooee **vig**] 'little *Dumhaigh*'. Doagh Beg is named by way of contrast with DOAGH which lies a short distance to the south-west. The name DOAGH is from *Dumhaigh*, an oblique form of *Dumhach* 'mound/sand-hill'. The townland of DOAGH MORE (Ir. *Dumhaigh Mhór* 'great *Dumhaigh*') is some 10km to the west [*Dowaghbegg* c.1655].

**Dog Big/Dog Little** tls, Fermanagh 2035
*9.5km WSW of Derrygonnelly*
(sometimes *The Dogs*)
par: *Devenish* bar: *Magheraboy*
Ir. *Sliabh Dá Chon* [sleeoo daa **khon**] 'mountain of two dogs'. BIG DOG and LITTLE DOG are twin hills of 230m. They have given name to the townlands of Dog Big and Dog Little respectively. Legend has it that the dogs in question were the two hounds of Finn MacCool and that they were metamorphosed into hills by a witch who had taken on the shape of a doe [*Sliabh Da Chon* 1429].

**Dollingstown** vill., Down 3135
*Close to Armagh border, 2.5km E of Lurgan*
par: *Magheralin*
bar: *Iveagh Lower, Upper Half*
The village of Dollingstown is in the townland of TAUGHRANE on the old road from **Moira** to **Lurgan**. It is said to be named from the Rev. Boghey Dolling, rector of the parish of **Magheralin**, who resided there early in the last century.

**Donagh** tl, vill., Fermanagh 2333
*5km SE of Lisnaskea*
par: *Galloon* bar: *Clankelly*
Ir. *Domhnach* [**doan**agh] '(early) church'. There are remains of a medieval chapel in a graveyard at DONAGH CROSS ROADS and this may mark the site of an earlier church [*Donagh* 1659].

**Donaghadee** tn, par., Down 3537
*Town is 8.5km E of Bangor*
bar: *Ards Lower*
Ir. *Domhnach Daoi* [doanagh **dee**] *perhaps* '*Daoi*'s church'. The final element of the place-name may represent the name of an unattested saint, possibly of British origin. The present Church of Ireland church in the townland of TOWNPARKS OF DONAGHADEE may mark the site of both the pre-Norman and the medieval church [*Donanachti* 1204].

**Donaghanie** tl, Tyrone 2536
*6km SE of Omagh*
par: *Clogherny* bar: *Omagh East*
Ir. *Domhnach an Eich* [doanagh an **egh**] 'church of the horse'. According to a local legend, the horse belonged to St Patrick and it achieved fame by kicking and killing an amphibious creature which emerged from LOUGHPATRICK! The site of the ancient church is marked by a graveyard on a nearby hill [*Domhach an Eich* 1518].

**Donaghcloney** tl, vill., par., Down 3135
*Village is 7.5km N of Banbridge*
bar: *Iveagh Lower, Upper Half*
Ir. *Domhnach Cluana* [doanagh **kloon**a]

'church of the meadow'. The site of the medieval parish church is in the village, in a graveyard beside the river **Lagan** [*Domhnach Cluana* c.1645].

**Donaghmore** ham., par., Down 3133
*Hamlet is 6.5km N of Newry*
bar: *Iveagh Upper, Upper Half*
Ir. *Domhnach Mór* [doanagh **more**] 'great church'. In the graveyard of the present Church of Ireland church in the townland of GLEBE there is a tenth-century cross which marks the site of an early monastery. GLEBE was formerly known as *Tullynacross* (Ir. *Tulaigh na Croise* 'hillock of the cross') [(*o*) *Domnuch Mór* c.830].

**Donaghmore** tl, vill., par., Tyrone 2638
*Village is 3.5km NW of Dungannon*
bar: *Dungannon Middle*
Ir. *Domhnach Mór* [doanagh **more**] 'great church'. The site of the ancient church of Donaghmore may be marked by the graveyard behind a ninth- or tenth-century high cross which stands at the head of the village [(*C*(*h*)*olum*) *Domnaig móir* c.830].

**Donegal** tl, tn, par., co. 1937
*Town is at the head of Donegal Bay, 17.5km NNE of Ballyshannon*
bar: *Tirhugh*
Ir. *Dún na nGall* [doon na **ngal**] 'fort of the foreigners'. The 'foreigners' referred to are likely to have been the Vikings who are known to have been active in DONEGAL BAY in the ninth century. However, the town of Donegal did not grow up until after the establishment of a monastery and a castle here by one Red Hugh O'Donnell c.1474. There is now no trace of the fort which gave name to the original settlement. A portion of Donegal town is in the parish of KILLYMARD in the barony of BANAGH. The county of Donegal is sometimes known in Irish as *Tír Chonaill* '*Conall*'s land/territory', a name which originally referred to the west of the county only and derives from *Conall*, one of the sons of *Niall Naoighiallach* or Niall of the Nine Hostages who is reputed to have ruled Ireland from Tara in the fifth century [(*mainistir*) *Dúin na nGall* 1474].

**Donegore** tl, par., Antrim 3238
*Townland is 6.5km NE of Antrim town*
bar: *Antrim Upper*
Ir. *Dún Ó gCorra* [doon o **gorr**a] 'fort the Corrs or descendants of *Corra*'. The personal name *Corra* is the basis of the surname *Ó Corra* '(O')Corr' which is widespread in Ulster (see ***Clontygora***). The fort in question appears to be the prominent *motte*, locally known as DONEGORE MOTTE, which stands on DONEGORE HILL (234m) and may mark the site of an earlier, Irish, fort. The present Church of Ireland church occupies the site of the medieval parish church. The townland of Donegore is partly in the neighbouring parish of GRANGE OF NILTEEN [*Dunogcurra* 1647].

*Donegal Castle*

**Doochary** vill., Donegal 1840
*10km SE of Dunglow*
par: *Lettermacaward/Inishkeel* bar: *Boylagh*
Ir. *An Dúchoraidh* [an **doo**-khoree] 'the black weir'. The weir in question was formerly on the **Gweebarra River** just above the point where it becomes tidal. The village of Doochary straddles the river, linking the townlands of COOLVOY and DERRYNACARROW [*Doocarry Bridge* 1835].

**Dooish** mtn, Don 1942
*In Derryveagh Mountains, 20km WNW of Letterkenny*
par: *Gartan* bar: *Kilmacrenan*
Ir. *An Dubhais* [an **doo**ish] 'the black ridge/peak'. Dooish (652m) is adjoined on the south by a peak named EDENADOOISH (521m) (Ir. *Éadan na Dubhaise* 'face/brow of Dooish') and on the north by a peak named SAGARTNADOOISH (501m) (Ir. *Sagart na Dubhaise* 'priest of Dooish'). In the latter, the element 'priest' appears to be used figuratively in the sense of 'chaplain', with the significance of a smaller hill attending on a larger one.

**Dooish** mtn, tl, Tyrone 2337
*12km W of Omagh*
par: *Longfield West* bar: *Omagh West*
Ir. *Dubhais* [**doo**ish] 'black ridge/peak'. The townland of Dooish takes its name from DOOISH mountain (341m) which stands on the boundary with the neighbouring townland of COOLAVANNAGH [*Dowis* 1666].

**Dorsy** tl, Armagh 2931
*5km NE of Crossmaglen*
par: *Creggan* bar: *Fews Upper*
Ir. *Na Doirse* [na **dor**sha] 'the gateways'. The modern name is a shortened form of *Doirse Eamhna* [dorsha **auna**] 'gateways of Navan' so-called because Dorsy is the site of a series of large linear earthworks which formerly controlled the approaches from the south to **Navan Fort**, the ancient capital of Ulster. Dorsy has given name to four townlands in the neighbouring parish of **Newtownhamilton**. These are: DORSY (*Cavan O'Hanlon*) OR ROXBOROUGH, DORSY (*Hearty*), DORSY (*MacDonald*) OR CARRICKROVADDY and DORSY (*Mullaghglass*) [(*ar*) *doirsibh Emhna* 1224].

**Douglas Bridge** vill., Tyrone 2339
*8km SSE of Strabane*
par: *Ardstraw* bar: *Strabane Lower*
Ir. *Dúghlas* [**doo**-ghlass] 'black stream' + E. 'bridge'. The 'black stream' is the little river now known as DOUGLAS BURN. The bridge is over this stream which enters the river **Mourne** a short distance to the west. Douglas Bridge is partly in the townland of DRUMNAHOE and partly in SKINBOY [*Douglass-bridge* 1814].

**Down** par., co., dioc.
Ir. *An Dún* [an **doon**] 'the fort'. The fort referred to is that which gave name to the county town **Downpatrick** (*see below*).

**Downhill** tl, vill., Derry 2743
*10km NW of Coleraine*
par: *Dunboe* bar: *Coleraine*
Ir. *Dún* [doon] 'fort' + E. *hill*. The original Ir. name of the townland was *Dún Bó* [doon **bo**] 'fort of the cows'. It contains a graveyard and a ruined church and has given name to the parish of DUNBOE. Near the ruins of the church there are the remains of a fort now known as DUNGANNON FORT and this may be the feature referred to in both Downhill and *Dún Bó* [(*go*) *Dún Bó* 1182].

**Downies** tl, vill., Donegal 2043
(usually *Downings*)
*3km NW of Carrickart*
par: *Mevagh* bar: *Kilmacrenan*
Ir. *Na Dúnaibh* [na **doon**iv] 'the forts'. There are remains of a stone fort on top of a hill here and there may originally have been more than one fort. The form *Na Dúnaibh* represents a dative plural form which has come to be used as the nominative. The plural English *-s* termination reflects the plural form of the original Ir. name [(*hi ccrannóicc*) *na nDuini* 1603].

**Downpatrick** tn, Down 3434
*County town of Down, 17km NE of Newcastle*
par: *Down* bar: *Lecale Upper*
Ir. *Dún Pádraig* [doon **paad**rick] '(St) Patrick's fort'. The original Ir. name for Downpatrick was *Dún Lethglaise* [doon leh **glish**a] *perhaps* 'fort of the side of the stream'. The fort was a prehistoric ring-fort which formerly stood on CATHEDRAL HILL and within which was constructed an early monastery and the later church and abbey of St Patrick. The stream in question can only be the river **Quoile** which flows close to the bottom of CATHEDRAL HILL. *Dún da Lethglas* is also found as an ear-

lier name for the settlement at Downpatrick and while it is obviously connected with the form *Dún Lethglaise*, the exact nature of the relationship is obscure. The modern name *Dún Pádraig* is not attested prior to the 17th century. Another earlier name for Downpatrick was *Rathkeltair*, from Ir. *Ráth Cealtchair* 'fort of *Cealtchair*', the fort being, apparently, the aforementioned prehistoric ring-fort on CATHEDRAL HILL. The *Cealtchair* referred to was *Cealtchair mac Uitheachair*, a mythical warrior of the ancient Ulster Cyle of Tales. Downpatrick is in the townland of DEMESNE OF DOWN [*(expugnatio) Dúin Lethghlaisse* 496].

**Dowra** tl, vill., Cavan 1932
*On border with Leitrim, 13.5km SW of Belcoo*
par: *Killinagh* bar: *Tullyhaw*
Ir. *An Damhshraith* [an **dau**-ra] 'the river holm of the oxen'. The village of Dowra is mainly on the west bank of the river SHANNON, a short distance north of LOUGH ALLEN [*Dawrey* c.1660].

**Draperstown** vill., Derry 2739
*14km WNW of Magherafelt*
par: *Ballynascreen* bar: *Loughinsholin*
The name Draperstown was originally applied to the town of **Moneymore** which was founded by the Drapers' Company of London in the early 17th century. Draperstown was not founded until 1798 and did not take its current name until 1818. The Ir. name for the village was *Baile na Croise* [bala na **crush**a] 'townland of the cross', referring to the crossroads at which it is situated. The village was also known as *The Cross of Ballynascreen*, **Ballynascreen** being the name of the parish in which it is situated. Draperstown straddles the three townlands of MOYHEELAND, MOYKEERAN and CAHORE [*Cross* 1813].

**Dreen** tl, ham., Derry 2640
*7km SE of Claudy*
par: *Learmount* bar: *Tirkeeran*
Ir. *Draighean* [**dree**an] 'place of blackthorns'. The large townland of Dreen has subdenominations named UPPER DREEN and MIDDDLE DREEN and stretches from the village of **Park** southwards to the summit of **Sawel** (678m) on the Derry/Tyrone border [*Drien* 1613].

**Dromara** tl, vill., par., Down 3234
*Village is 8km WSW of Ballynahinch*
bar: *Iveagh Lower, Lower Half*
Ir. *Droim mBearach* [drim **mar**agh] 'ridge of heifers'. The modern Church of Ireland church marks the site of the medieval parish church [*Drumberra* 1306].

**Dromore** tn, par., dioc., Down 3235
*Town is 10.5km NE of Banbridge*
bar: *Iveagh Lower, Lower Half*
Ir. *Droim Mór* [drim **more**] 'large ridge'. The present Church of Ireland cathedral in the town marks the site of an early monastery founded by St Colman and also the site of a medieval cathedral dedicated to that saint. There is also a 10th- or 11th-century high cross and an earlier cross-inscribed stone 'pillow' associated with St Colman [*(Moc[h]olmóc) Dromma móir* c.830].

**Dromore** tl, vill., par., Tyrone 2336
*Village is 14km SW of Omagh*
bar: *Omagh East*
Ir. *An Droim Mór* [an drim **more**] 'the large ridge'. The townland of Dromore contains the site of a medieval abbey, also reputed to be the site of a nunnery founded by St Patrick, and of a cross which formerly stood on the conspicuous CROSS HILL. At the foot of the hill is ST DYMPNA'S WELL and nearby are the remains of a post-Reformation church erected c.1694 [*Drommore* 1608].

**Drones, The** ham., Antrim 3042
*10.5km ENE of Ballymoney*
par: *Loughguile* bar: *Dunluce Upper*
Ir. *Na Dronna* [na **drunn**a] 'the humps'. The hamlet named the Drones is in the townland of DRUMDALLAGH.

**Drowes** river Donegal/Leitrim
*Rises in Lough Melvin in Co. Leitrim. Flows into Donegal Bay a short distance SW of Bundoran*
Ir. *An Drobhaois* [an **drau**eesh] *perhaps* 'the muddy one/sluggish one'. The little river Drowes divides the modern counties of Donegal and Leitrim. It also marks the southern boundary of the ancient province of Ulster which at its greatest extent is described as extending 'from the Drowes on the west to the Boyne on the east'. At the mouth of the Drowse is a village named BUNDROWES (Ir. *Bun Drobhaoise* 'foot of the Drowse') [*(oc) Drobáis* c.900].

**Drum** tl, vill., Monaghan 2431
*Close to Cavan border, 5km NW of Cootehill*
par: *Currin* bar: *Dartree*
*An Droim* [an **drim**] 'the ridge'. Drum has given name to DRUM LOUGH, a short distance north of the village [*Druyme* 1591].

**Drumahoe** tl, ham., Derry 2441
*3.5km SE of Londonderry*
par: *Clondermot* bar: *Tirkeeran*
Ir. *Droim na hUamha* [drim na **hoov**a] 'ridge of the cave/souterrain'. Drumnahoe is on rising ground on the north bank of the river **Faughan**. There is now no trace or record of a cave or souterrain [*Dromhoghs* 1622].

**Drumaness** tl, vill., Down 3334
*5km SSE of Ballynahinch*
par: *Magheradrool* bar: *Kinelarty*
Ir. *Droim an Easa* [drim an **ass**a] 'ridge of the waterfall'. There is a waterfall on the stream which forms the western boundary of the townland [*Drumenessy* c.1710].

**Drumaroad** tl, vill., Down 3334
*8.5km S of Ballynahinch*
par: *Loughinisland* bar: *Kinelarty*
Ir. *Droim an Róid* [drim an **rodge**] 'ridge of the road'. The road in question may be that from **Ballynahinch** to **Castlewellan** which passes through the townland [*Ballydromerode* 1635].

**Drumbeg** tl, vill., par., Down 3336
*Village is 8.5km SSW of Belfast*
bar: *Castlereagh Upper*
Ir. *An Droim Beag* [an drim **beg**] 'the little ridge'. The Church of Ireland church, on a hill named THE DRUM, marks the site of an early church. A large portion of the parish of Drumbeg lies north of the **Lagan** in Co. Antrim [*(ecclesia de) Drum of Movilla* 1615].

**Drumbo** tl, vill., par., Down 3336
*Village is 9km SSW of Belfast*
bar: *Castlereagh Upper*
Ir. *Droim Bó* [drim **bo**] 'ridge of cows'. The site of an early monastery is marked by the stump of a round tower in the churchyard of the village Presbyterian church [*(ab) Dromma Bó* c.830]

**Drumcose** tl, Fermanagh 2135
*On W shore of Lower Lough Erne, 8km NW of Enniskillen*
par: *Devenish* bar: *Magheraboy*
Ir. *Droim Cuas* [drim **koo**as] 'ridge of caves or hollows'. The townland of Drumcose includes part of DRUMCOSE LOUGH and is bordered on the east by CASTLEHUME LOUGH. There is a hill of 299m in the north of the townland [*Drumcoose* 1609].

**Drumcree** tl, par., Armagh 2935
*Townland is 4km NNW of Portadown town centre*
bar: *Oneilland West*
Ir. *Droim Crí* [drim **kree**] 'boundary ridge'. The final element is a shortened form of *críche*, the genitive of *críoch* 'boundary'. The boundary in question may be the nearby **Upper Bann** which borders the parish on the east and at an earlier period separated the territories of *Clann Bhreasail* and *Clann Chana*. It now separates the baronies of ONEILLAND EAST and ONEILLAND WEST. The Church of Ireland church marks the site of the medieval parish church [*Drumandcryuaich* 1366].

**Drumcroon** tl, ham., Derry 2842
(sometimes *Drumcroone*)
*7km S of Coleraine*
par: *Macosquin* bar: *Coleraine*
Ir. *Droim Cruithean* [drim **kri**hin] 'ridge of the *Cruithin*'. The *Cruithin* were an early population group whose name is closely related to *Briton*. They were particularly prominent in Ulster but were also found in Leinster and Connaught. There is a townland named DUNCRUN (Ir. *Dún Cruithean* 'fort of the *Cruithin*') 16km to the north west, in the parish of MAGILLIGAN [*Drim Crum* 1813].

**Drumenny** tls, Tyrone 2937
*11km E of Cookstown*
(sometimes *Drumaney*)
par: *Arboe* bar: *Dungannon Upper*
Ir. *Droim Eanaigh* [drim **an**ee] 'ridge of the marsh'. The townland of DRUMENNY (*Stewart*) is bordered on the east by DRUMENNY (*Conyngham*) [*Dromany* 1615].

**Drumfree** vill., Donegal 2343
(sometimes *Drimfries*)
*7.5km NNE of Buncrana*
par: *Fahan Lower* bar: *Inishowen West*
Ir. *Droim Fraoigh* [drim **free**] 'ridge of heather'. Drumfree is in the large townland of SHANDRIM [*Druim freigh* 1620].

**Drumgath** tl, ham., par., Down 3331
*Hamlet is 5km SW of Rathfriland*
bar: *Iveagh Upper, Upper Half*
Ir. *Droim gCath* [drim **ga**] 'ridge of battles'. There is a graveyard in the townland which may mark the site of the medieval parish church [*Drumgaa* 1435].

**Drumintee** tl, vill., Armagh 3031
(sometimes *Drumantee*)
*2.5km NE of Forkill*
par: *Killevy* bar: *Orior Upper*
Ir. *Droim an Tí* [drum an **tee**] 'ridge of the house'. The ridge in question may be the southern end of **Slieve Gullion** which extends into the centre of the townland. The element *teach* 'house', of which *tí* is the genitive, often has monastic associations but there is no record of a monastery in the townland [*Dromenty* 1604].

**Drumlea** tl, ham., Tyrone 2538
*4km E of Gortin*
par: *Bodoney Lower* bar: *Strabane Upper*
Ir. *Droim Léith* [drim **ley**] 'grey ridge'. The townland of Drumlea lies between the rivers **Owenkillew** and **Owenreagh** [(*torcc*) *Dromma Leithi* 1391].

**Drumlee** tl, ham., Down 3233
*7.5km ENE of Rathfriland*
par: *Drumgooland*
bar: *Iveagh Upper, Lower Half*
*Droim Lao* [drim **lee**] 'ridge of the calf/calves' [*Dromlee* 1659].

**Drumlegagh** tl, ham., Tyrone 2338
*9km SW of Newtownstewart*
par: *Ardstraw* bar: *Strabane Lower*
Ir. *Droim Liagach* [drim **leeg**agh] 'ridge of stones' [*Dromlegah* 1609].

**Drummannon** tl, Armagh 2935
*6.5km W of Portadown*
par: *Tartaraghan* bar: *Oneilland West*
Ir. *Droim Meannáin* [drim **man**ine] 'ridge of the kid-goat' [*Dromenan* 1610].

**Drummully** tl, ham., par., Fermanagh 2432
*Hamlet is close to the Monaghan border, 6.5km SSE of Newtownbutler*
bar: *Coole*
Ir. *Droim Ailí* [drim **al**ee] 'rocky ridge'. There is an old graveyard in the townland which contains the remnants of the former parish church [*Druim Ailche* c.1160].

**Drumnabreeze** tl, Down 3135
*7km E of Lurgan*
par: *Magheralin*
bar: *Iveagh Lower, Upper Half*
*perhaps* Ir. *Dromainn Bhrís* [dromin **vreesh**] 'ridge of high ground'. In the centre of the townland there is a hill of 90m which commands a view over the river **Lagan** [*Drumvrishe* 1609].

**Drumnagreagh** tl, Antrim 3341
*On E Antrim coast, 11km NNW of Larne*
par: *Carncastle* bar: *Glenarm Upper*
Ir. *Droim na gCréach* [drim na **grey**agh] 'ridge of the coarse pastures' [*Dromnagreagh* 1635].

**Drumnakilly** tl, ham., Tyrone 2537
*8km E of Omagh*
par: *Termonmaguirk* bar: *StrabaneUpper*
Ir. *Droim na Coille* [drim na **kill**ya] 'ridge of the wood' [*Dromnekillye* 1613].

**Drumquin** tl, vill., Tyrone 2327
*12km W of Omagh*
par: *Longfield West* bar: *Omagh West*
Ir. *Droim Caoin* [drim **keen**] 'smooth/pleasant ridge'. A portion of the village of Drumquin is in the neighbouring townland of DRUMNAFORBE in the parish of LONGFIELD EAST [*Druimchaoin* 1212].

**Drumraighland** tl, ham., Derry 2641
*4km SW of Limavady*
par: *Tamlaght Finlagan* bar: *Keenaght*
Ir. *Droim Raithleann* [drim **rah**lin] 'ridge of (places of) bracken' [*Dromheighlin* 1613].

**Drumskinny** tl, Fermanagh 2136
*6km NNW of Ederny*
par: *Drumkeeran* bar: *Lurg*
Ir. *Droim Scine* [drim **skin**a] 'ridge of the knife/edge' [*Dromskynny* 1639].

**Drumsough** tl, Antrim 3139
*3km E of Randalstown*
par: *Drummaul* bar: *Toome Upper*
Ir. *Droim Sú* [drim **soo**] 'ridge of berries' [*Drumsoe* 1669].

**Drumsurn** tls, vill., Derry 2741
*7km NNE of Dungiven*
par: *Balteagh* bar: *Keenaght*
Ir. *Droim Soirn* [drim **sorn**] 'ridge of the furnace or kiln'. Ir. *sorn* 'furnace/kiln' could in this case apply figuratively to a cairn, the

remains of which are on DONALD'S HILL, in the townland of DRUMSURN UPPER. The village of Drumsurn is in DRUMSURN LOWER [*Drumsoren* 1613].

**Dunadry** tl, vill., Antrim 3238
*5km ESE of Antrim town*
par: *Grange of Nilteen* bar: *Antrim Upper*
Ir. *Dún Eadradh* (doon **ad**roo] 'middle fort'. The name may be a reinterpretation of an earlier name, *Dún Eadarghabhal* [drim **ad**arġoal] 'fort between forks', referring to a fort which formerly stood in the junction between the **Six Mile Water** and the RATHMORE BURN. The townland contains the site of an ancient church and graveyard [*Dunedergel* c.1251].

**Dunaff** tl, vill., Donegal 2344
*On Inishowen peninsula, 17.5km NNW of Buncrana*
par: *Clonmany* bar: *Inishowen East*
Ir. *Dún Damh* [doon **dau**] 'fort of oxen'. There are remains of a fort near the south-west boundary of the townland. Dunaff has given name to DUNAFF HEAD at the entrance to **Lough Swilly** [*Duneffe* c.1659].

**Dunbarton** vill., Down 3034
*Adjoins the village of Gilford on the NW*
par: *Tullylish* bar: *Iveagh Lower, Upper Half*
The name Dunbarton consists of the surname Dunbar + E. *town*, and is named from Mr Hugh Dunbar of Huntley, Banbridge who founded linen mills here c.1838. In 1886 Hugh Dunbar McMaster JP lived in DUNBARTON HOUSE. Dunbarton is in the townland of LOUGHANS.

**Dundela** distr., Down 3337
(*see* ***Knock***)

**Dundonald** tn, par., Down 3437
*Town forms a suburb 8km E of Belfast city centre*
bar: *Castlereagh Lower*
Ir. *Dún Dónaill* [doon **doan**il] 'Donald's fort'. There is a well-preserved Norman *motte* in the west of the town but since the personal name *Dónall* is of Ir. origin it is likely that the place was named from a pre-Norman fort, perhaps on the same site. The nearby Church of Ireland church in the townland of CHURCH QUARTER marks the site of the medieval parish church [*Dondouenald* c.1183].

**Dundrod** tl, vill., Antrim 3237
*6km E of Crumlin*
par: *Tullyrusk* bar: *Massereene Upper*
Ir. *Dún dTreodáin* [doon **droad**ine]. The modern name is a shortened form of the original *Dún Cille Treodáin* [doon killya **troad**ine] 'fort of the church of (St) *Treodán*'. The personal name *Treodán* is also the basis of the Co. Louth surname *Ó Treodáin* 'Trodden'. The townland contains the site of an ancient chapel and graveyard [*Doonkilltroddon* c.1672].

**Dundrum** tl, vill., Down 3433
*5.5km NE of Newcastle*
par: *Kilmegan* bar: *Lecale Upper*
Ir. *Dún Droma* [doon **drum**a] 'fort of the ridge'. The well-known Norman castle, the remains of which stand on the summit of a rocky hill overlooking the village, was built on the site of an early Irish fort. The wide estuary of the Irish Sea extending from **Newcastle** to **St John's Point** is known as DUNDRUM BAY, while the narrow inlet of the sea adjacent to the village of Dundrum is known as DUNDRUM INNER BAY. The latter was known in Ir. as *Loch Rúraí* [lough **roor**ee] 'estuary of *Rúraí*'. *Rúraí* (earlier *Rudhraighe*) may be originally a tribal name [*(t)ráigh Dúin droma* 1147].

**Dunfanaghy** tl, vill., Donegal 2043
*7.5km NW of Creeslough*
par: *Clondahorky* bar: *Kilmacrenan*
Ir. *Dún Fionnachaidh* [doon **fin**aghee] 'fort of the white field'. This is the normally-accepted interpretation of the place-name. However, it is possible that the original form was *Dún Fionnchaidhe* [doon **fin**aghee] 'fort of the *Fionnchaidhe* (tribe)'. There was formerly a fort a short distance west of the village [*Dunfenoghy* 1679].

**Dungannon** tn, bars, Tyrone 2736
*16km S of Cookstown*
par: *Drumglass* bar: *Dungannon Middle*
Ir. *Dún Geanainn* [doon **gan**in] '*Geanann*'s fort'. According to legend Dungannon was named from *Geanann* son of *Cathbadh* the Druid who lived here in pagan times. The site of a medieval fortress of the O'Neills is marked by ruins of an 18th-century castle which stand on CASTLE HILL just north of MARKET SQUARE. Dungannon is mainly in the townland of DRUMCOO in the barony of DUNGANNON MIDDLE which is bounded on the

north by DUNGANNON UPPER and on the south-west by DUNGANNON LOWER [(*caislén*) *Dúingenainn* 1505].

**Dungiven** tl, vill., par., Derry 2640
*Village is 19km NW of Maghera*
bar: *Keenaght*
Ir. *Dún Geimhin* [doon **gev**in] *perhaps* 'fort of the hide or skin'. The final element of the place-name may have something to do with cattle but its exact significance is obscure. The fort which gave name to Dungiven was near the ruins of the medieval Augustinian priory which occupies the site of an early monastery on the north bank of the **Roe**, a short distance south of the village. This portion of the valley of the Roe was formerly known in Ir. as *Gleann Geimhin*, anglicised *Glengiven*. The Ir. name for the village was *Baile an Mhullaigh* [bala an **wull**ee] 'town of the hilltop' [(*o*) *Dún Geimin* c.830].

**Dunglow** tl, vill., Donegal 1741
(usually *Dungloe*)
*17.5km NNW of Glenties*
par: *Templecrone* bar: *Boylagh*
Ir. *An Clochán Liath* [an kloghan **lee**a] 'the grey stepping stones'. The site of the stepping stones is marked by a bridge built in 1782 across the DUNGLOW RIVER in the middle of the village. The E. name Dunglow is from Ir. *Dún gCloiche* [doon **gloy**gha] 'fort of stone' and originally referred to a fort which stood on a rock in the sea some 8km to the north-west. A fair was held there until the middle of the 18th century and when the fair was moved to the growing village of *An Clochán Liath* the name Dunglow was transferred with it and gradually became accepted as the name of the village and also of the townland [*Doungloo* 1600].

**Dunkineely** tl, vill., Donegal 1737
*15km WSW of Donegal town*
par: *Killaghtee* bar: *Banagh*
Ir. *Dún Cionnaola* [doon kin**eel**a] 'fort of *Cionnaola*'. The personal name *Cionnaola* (earlier *Ceann Faoladh*) 'wolf-head' was very common in the early period and is also found in the place-name **Cloghaneely** (Ir. *Cloich Chionnaola* '*Cionnaola*'s stone'), the name of a district in the north of the county (*see above*). There are remains of a fort at the west end of the village which was founded in 1618 [*Duncanally* c.1659].

**Dunlewy** tls, Donegal 1941
*25km WNW of Letterkenny*
par: *Tullaghobegly* bar: *Kilmacrenan*
Ir. *Dún Lúiche* [doon **loo**-eegha] '*Lughaidh*'s fort'. *Lughaidh* is a medieval derivative of the O. Ir. personal name *Lugh* and legend has it that the *Lughaidh* in question was *Lugh Lámhfhada* '*Lugh* of the long arm' who is said to have killed his grandfather *Balar* at nearby **Poisoned Glen**. However, it is perhaps more likely that the name refers to *Lughaidh mac Séadna*, a sixth-century chieftain who gave name to *Tír Luighdheach*, a district which stretched from **Lough Swilly** to **Gweedore**. There is now no trace of a fort at Dunlewy but it is likely to have been close to an ancient church, the remains of which stand on the south-east shore of DUNLEWY LOUGH, in the townland of DUNLEWY FAR which is adjoined on the east by DUNLEWY NEAR. **Bloody Foreland** which lies some 18km to the north-west is also claimed to be the place where *Balar* was slain [*Dunluy* 1654].

**Dunloy** tl, vill., Antrim 3041
*9.5km SE of Ballymoney*
par: *Finvoy* bar: *Kilconway*
Ir. *Dún Lathaí* [doon **la**hee] 'fort of the muddy place/marsh'. There are remains of a fort in the townland of Dunloy and also the site of a stone circle, known as THE GIANT'S GRAVE [*Dunlogh* c.1672].

**Dunluce** tl, par., bars., Antrim 2944
*Townland is on N. Antrim coast, 3km WNW of Bushmills*
Ir. *Dúnlios* [**doon**liss] 'fortress/fortified residence'. The fortress in question is DUNLUCE CASTLE, the ruins of which stand on a high isolated rock above the sea. It is thought to date from c.1300 but is likely to mark the site of an earlier fortification. The site of the medieval parish church is marked by a ruin in a graveyard a short distance south of the castle. The townland of Dunluce is in the barony of DUNLUCE LOWER which is adjoined on the south by the barony of DUNLUCE UPPER [(*Caislen*) *Dhúinlis* 1513].

**Dunmore** tl, ham., Down 3334
*6km S of Ballynahinch*
par: *Magherahamlet* bar: *Kinelarty*
Ir. *Dún Mór* [doon **more**] 'great fort'.
The townland of Dunmore contains the remains of a fort within which are the foun-

dations of an ancient chapel attached to the neighbouring parish of **Dromara**, of which the parish of MAGHERAHAMLET used to form a part. A short distance to the north there are townlands named DUNBEG UPPER and DUNBEG LOWER. In the former there is a hill fort named DUNBEG FORT (from Ir. *Dún Beag* [doon **beg**] 'little fort'). Dunmore has given name to DUNMORE MOUNTAIN in the south of the townland [*Donmore al. Leytrim* 1666].

**Dunmoyle** tl, Tyrone 2636
*7km NNW of Ballygawley*
par: *Errigal Keerogue* bar: *Clogher*
Ir. *An Dún Maol* [an doon **mweel**] 'the bald or delapidated fort'. Dunmoyle is named from the fort of that name in the townland [*Dunmoyle* c.1655].

**Dunmurry** tl, vill., Antrim 3236
*7km SW of Belfast city centre*
par: *Drumbeg* bar: *Belfast Upper*
Ir. *Dún Muirígh* [doon **murr**ee] '*Muiríoch*'s fort'. There is a well-preserved *motte* and also a *rath* near the centre of the village of Dunmurry. A portion of the townland of Dunmurry is in the parish of **Shankill** [*Ballydownmory* 1604].

**Dunnamanagh** tl, vill., Tyrone 2440
(sometimes *Dunamanagh*)
*9.5km NE of Strabane*
par: *Donaghedy* bar: *Strabane Lower*
Ir. *Dún na Manach* [doon na **man**agh] 'fort of the monks'. Dunnamanagh seems to have been named by association with a nearby monastery, the site of which may be marked by the ruins of the parish church of DONAGHEDY in a graveyard in the townland of BUNOWEN. There are ruins of a castle in Dunnamanagh, perhaps on the site of the fort which gave the place its name. The modern village of Dunnamanagh was founded by Sir James Drummon in the early 17th century [*Downeamannogh* c.1655].

**Dunnamore** tl, vill., Tyrone 2638
*13km WNW of Cookstown*
par: *Kildress* bar: *Dungannon Upper*
Ir. *Domhnach Mór* [doanagh **more**] 'great

*Dunluce Castle*

(early) church'. There is now no trace or record of a church here [*Donach Mór* c.1930].

**Dunseverick *alias* Feigh** tl, Antrim 2944
*On N. Antrim coast, 5.5km NE of Bushmills*
par: *Billy* bar: *Cary*
Dunseverick derives from Ir. *Dún Sobhairce* [doon **sau**-arka] '*Sobhairce*'s fort'. The last remnants of a medieval castle of the O'Cahans (O'Kanes) mark the site of the ancient promontory fort of Dunseverick which stood on the north Antrim coast, 3.5km east of **The Giant's Causeway**. In the *Irish Triads* Dunseverick is named as one of the three major forts of Ireland and legend has it that the *Sobhairce* who gave name to it was great-great-grandson of *Míl*, the fictional ancestor of the Irish people. The *alias*-name of the townland of Dunseverick i.e. FEIGH is derived from Ir. *Faiche* [**faigh**a] 'lawn/green' and may have referred to a green attached to the ancient fortress. FEIGH has given name to the neighbouring townland of FEIGH MOUNTAIN [*Dun Sobhairce* 3501AM].

**Dyan** tl, vill., Tyrone 2734
*4km N of Caledon*
par: *Aghaloo* bar: *Dungannon Lower*
Ir. *An Daighean* [an **dy**an] 'the fortress'. The fortress in question may have stood on the prominent DYAN HILL (209m) but no trace or record now remains [*Dingan* 1613].

# E

**Eamhain Mhacha** anc. mon., Armagh 2834
(*see **Navan***)

**Eden** vill., Ant, 3438
*2.5km NE of Carrickfergus*
par/bar, *Carrickfergus*
Ir. *An tÉadan* [an **chaid**in] 'the face/brow'. The full name of the village was *Éadan Gréine* [aidin **grey**na] 'sunny face/brow'. Eden is in the townland of NORTH EAST DIVISION and faces over **Belfast Lough** (*Eden or Edengrenny* 1837).

**Edenderry** tl, vill., Down 3336
*6.5km SSW of Belfast city centre*
par: *Drumbo* bar: *Castlereagh Upper*
Ir. *Éadan Doire* [aidin **dirr**a] 'hill brow of the oak-wood'. Edenderry is on the east bank of the river **Lagan** [*Carow-Edenderry* 1623].

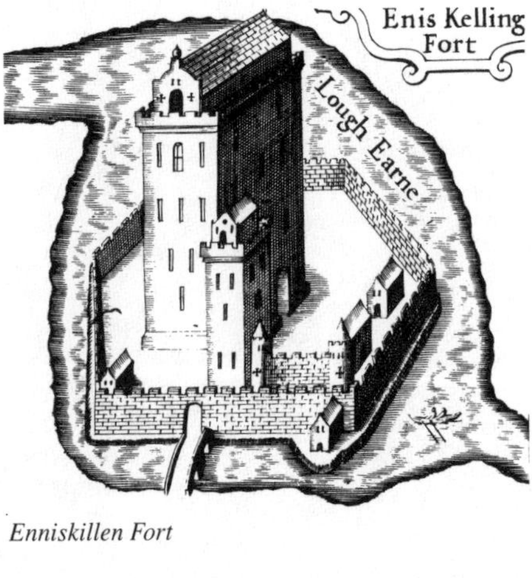

*Enniskillen Fort*

**Edendork** tl, vill., Tyrone 2836
*3km NNE of Dungannon*
par: *Tullyniskan* bar: *Dungannon Middle*
Ir. *Éadan na dTorc* [aidin na **dork**] 'hill brow of the (wild) boars' [*Adanadorg* 1609].

**Edenduff** ham., Antrim 3138
(*see **Shane's Castle***)

**Edentrillick** tl, ham., Down 3235
*4km NE of Dromore*
par: *Dromore* bar: *Iveagh Lower, Lower Half*
Ir. *Éadan Trilic* [aidin **tril**ick]
'hill brow of three (flag-)stones'. The literal meaning of *trileac* is 'three (flag-)stones'. However, the term seems to have been used to apply to *dolmens* and other megalithic remains (*see **Trillick***). There is now no trace or record of such a feature in the townland [*Balliedentrillicke* 1585].

**Ederny** tl, vill., Fermanagh 2236
(sometimes *Ederney*)
*7km NNW of Irvinestown*
par: *Magheraculmoney* bar: *Lurg*
Ir. *Eadarnaidh* [**ad**arnee] 'middle place/place between'. The reason that Ederny should have been designated 'middle place' is not readily apparent and further research is required [*Edernagh* 1610].

**Eglinton** vill., Derry 2542
*9.5km NE of Derry city*
par: *Faughanvale* bar: *Tirkeeran*
The original name of the village of Eglinton was MUFF (Ir. *An Mhagh* [an **wy**] 'the plain') from the townland in which it is situated on the east bank of the MUFF RIVER. It was changed to Eglinton in 1858 when the Earl of Eglinton was Lord Lieutenant of Ireland.

**Eglish** vill., Tyrone 2735
*6km S of Dungannon*
par: *Clonfeacle* bar: *Dungannon Middle*
Ir. *An Eaglais* [an **ug**lish] 'the church'. Eglish appears to have been named from a medieval church which occupied the site of the present St Patrick's Catholic church in the townland of ROAN. 5km to the south in Co. Armagh there is a parish named EGLISH, the name of which also derives from Ir. *An Eaglais* 'the church'.

**Eighter** tl, vill., Cavan 2528
*At W end of Lough Ramor, 5km SW of Virginia*
par: *Munterconnaught* bar: *Castlerahan*
Ir. *Íochtar* [**eegh**tar] 'lower portion'. Eighter appears to have been so-named because it was originally the lower portion of another land division, perhaps of the neighbouring townland of CARRICK.

**Eleven Lane Ends** ham., Armagh 3034
*6.5km SSW of Tanderagee*
par: *Loughgilly* bar: *Orior Lower*
Eleven Lane Ends is named from a cluster of three road junctions where eleven roads meet, in the townland of MAEVEMACULLEN [*Eleven Loanings* 1905].

**Emyvale** tn, Monaghan 2734
*11km N of Monaghan town*
par: *Donagh* bar: *Trough*
Ir. *Ioma* '(saint's) bed' + E. *vale*. The first element of the place-name is the original Ir. form of the name of the townland of EMY which lies a short distance to the east. Ir. *ioma* often refers to a place where a church was erected at the site where a saint was reputed to have lived and slept. In this case there is no trace or record of such a church. The townland in which the town is situated is EMYVALE OR SCARNAGEERAGH. The latter name derives from Ir. *Scairbh na gCaorach* [skariv na **geer**-agh] 'shallow ford of the sheep' and is also used as the Mod. Ir. name of the town. The site of the ford appears to be marked by the bridge over the MOUNTAIN WATER at the southern end of the town [*Emyvale or Skernagerragh* 1779].

**Enniskillen** tl, tn, par., Fermanagh 2234
*County town of Fermanagh, lying between Upper and Lower Lough Erne*
bar: *Tirkennedy*
Ir. *Inis Ceithleann* [inish **keh**lin] '*Ceithleann*'s island'. According to tradition *Ceithleann* (sometimes written *Ceithle*) was the wife of the legendary Fomorian giant *Balar* (*see* ***Bloody Foreland***) and she swam for refuge to the island on which Enniskillen stands after inflicting fatal wounds on the king of the *Tuatha Dé Danann* at the battle of MOYTIRRA in Sligo. The Church of Ireland cathedral in the main street of the town incorporates the tower of the original parish church, dating from c.1627. A portion of the town of Enniskillen is in the barony of MAGHERABOY [(*Caislén*) *Insi Ceithlenn* 1439].

**Erne** river Cavan, Fermanagh, Donegal
*Rises close to Cross Keys 8km SE of Cavan town and flows through a corner of Lough Gowna before flowing northwards through Lough Oughter, Upper Lough Erne and Lower Lough Erne and entering the sea at Ballyshannon*
Ir. *An Éirne* [an **ern**ya]. The use of this name to refer to the river is fairly late and is derived from *Loch Éirne* 'lake of *Érann*', the name of **Lough Erne** (*see below*). The original Ir. name of the Fermanagh/Donegal portion of the river was *Samhaoir* and this forms the final element of *Inis Samhaoir* 'island of the *Samhaoir*', a small island in the river close to **Ballyshannon**, now known as INISH SAMER OR FISH ISLAND [(*tar*) *Eirne* 1597].

**Errigal** mtn, Donegal 1942
*18km NE of Dunglow*
par: *Tullaghobegly* bar: *Kilmacrenan*

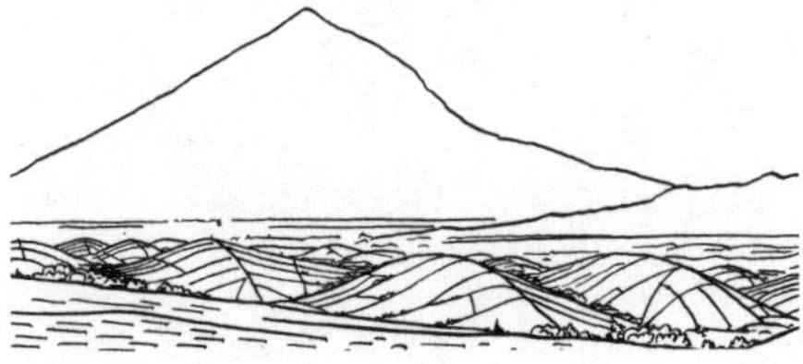

*Errigal*

Ir. *An Earagail* [an **ar**igil] 'the oratory'. Errigal (751m) is the highest mountain in Donegal. It appears to have been named from an oratory or hermitage which stood on or near the mountain at an earlier date.

**Eshnadarragh** tl, Fermanagh 2533
(sometimes *Esnadarra*)
*8km NE of Lisnaskea*
par: *Aghavea* bar: *Magherastephana*
Ir. *Ais na Darach* [ash na **dar**agh] 'ridge of the oak tree'.

**Eskragh** tl, ham., Tyrone 3535
(often *Eskra*)
*7.5km NW of Augher*
par/bar, *Clogher*
Ir. *Eiscreach* [**esk**ragh] 'place of ridges'. In 1666 the townland is recorded as two separate divisions, *Finesker* (Ir. *Fionneiscir* 'white ridge') and *Dewesker* (Ir. *Dubheiscir* 'black ridge'). Eskragh is bounded on the east by the ESKRAGH WATER.

# F

**Fahan** vill., pars, Donegal 2243
*Village is on W coast of Inishowen peninsula, 5km S of Buncrana*
bar: *Inishowen West*
Ir. *Fathain* [**fa**hin] 'burial place'. There is a graveyard here marking the site of a monastery founded in the late sixth century by St Columcille, with his disciple St *Mura* as its first abbot and patron. However, the place-name may refer to a pre-Christian burial place on the same site. The village of Fahan is in the townland of FIGARY in the parish of FAHAN UPPER which is adjoined on the north by the parish of FAHAN LOWER [*Fathunmurra* 1311].

**Fair Head** hl, Antrim 3144
(*see* ***Benmore or Fair Head***)

**Falcarragh** tl, vill., Donegal 1943
*10km SW of Dunfanaghy*
par: *Tullaghobegly/Raymunterdoney*
bar: *Kilmacrenan*
Ir. *An Fál Carrach* [an fal **kar**agh] 'the rough or rocky field/enclosure'. The original meaning of Ir. *fál* is 'hedge/fence' from which it developed the extended meaning of 'field/enclosure'. The official E. name of the village of Falcarragh is CROSS ROADS and the village is usually known in Ir. as *Na Croisbhealaí* [na **crush**valee] 'the crossroads' [*Fál Carrach* 1835].

**Fallagloon** tl, ham., Derry 2840
(sometimes *Fallaghloon*)
*4km W of Maghera*
par: *Maghera* bar: *Loughinsholin*
Ir. *Fáladh Luán* [faloo **loo**an] 'field/enclosure of the lambs'. The townland is bordered on the north by the FALLAGLOON BURN [*Fallow Lowne* 1613].

**Falls Road** Antrim 3337
*Main route in the west of Belfast*
par: *Shankill* bar: *Belfast Upper*
Falls Road is named from the Irish petty kingdom of *Tuath na bhFál* [tooa na **waal**] 'territory of the enclosures', the name of which survives in the modern name THE FALLS. The original extent of the territory was roughly equal to the civil parish of **Shankill** and it thus comprised the greater part of the Co. Antrim portion of the modern city of **Belfast** [*Tuogh of the Fall* 1605].

**Fanad** distr., Donegal
*Northern half of the peninsula which lies between Lough Swilly and Mulroy Bay*
par: *Clondavaddog* bar: *Kilmacrenan*
Ir. *Fánaid* [**faan**idge] 'sloping ground' [(*taoiseach*) *Fánat* 1186].

**Farset** river, Antrim
(*see* ***Belfast***)

**Fathom** tls, Armagh 3031
*4km S of Newry*
par: *Newry* bar: *Orior Upper*
Ir. *An Feadán* [an **fad**an] 'the water-course/stream'. The water-course in question may be the **Newry River** which forms the eastern boundary of the townlands of FATHOM UPPER and FATHOM LOWER. FATHOM MOUNTAIN (249m) is in the townland of FATHOM LOWER which has a small detached portion on the opposite side of the river [*Fedan* 1599].

**Faughan** river, Derry
*Rises near summit of Sawel in the Sperrins. Enters Lough Foyle 6km NE of Londonderry.*
Ir. *An Fhochaine* [an **ogh**inya] *perhaps* 'the noisy one'. The name of the nearby parish of FAUGHANVALE is unrelated to the name of the river, being derived from Ir. *Nuachongbháil* [nooa **khon**awile] 'new (church) habitation/establishment' [(*im*) *Ochaine* c.900].

**Favour Royal Demesne** tl, Tyrone 2535
(sometimes *Favor Royal Demesne*)
*4.5km SE of Augher*
par: *Errigal Trough* bar: *Clogher*
F. *faveur royale* 'royal favour' + E. *demesne*. Favour Royal Demesne takes its name from FAVOUR ROYAL BAWN, a large fortified mansion house, the ruins of which stand in the neighbouring townland of LISMORE, on the opposite (i.e. northern) side of the **Blackwater** and on the south bank of the BALLYGAWLEY WATER. It was built by Sir Thomas Ridgeway in 1611 and is said to be so-named because the land was granted as a royal favour from James I. The present mansion known as Favour Royal in the townland FAVOUR ROYAL DEMESNE dates from 1824. The original Ir. name of the townland was *Achadh Maoil* [aghoo **mweel**] 'field of the bald hillock' [*Favor royall* c.1655].

**Feeny** tl, vill., Derry 2640
*7km SW of Dungiven*
par: *Banagher* bar: *Tirkeeran*
Ir. *Na Fíneadha* [na **feen**yoo] 'the woods' [*Nefenne* 1613].

**Feigh** tl, Antrim 2944
(*see **Dunseverick alias Feigh***)

**Fermanagh** co.
Ir. *Fear Manach* [far **man**agh] 'the men of the *Manaigh* tribe'. The Ir. word *fear* 'man' is used here in the plural sense, 'men'. The *Manaigh* appear to be ultimately an offshoot of the Gaulish tribe the *Menapii* who in the early historical period are recorded in the west of Co. Down as well as in the neighbourhood of **Lough Erne**. As is commonly the case, the name of the tribe has been transferred to the territory where they lived [(*tigherna*) *Fermanach* 1010].

**Finaghy** vill., Antrim 3336
*5km SW of centre of Belfast of which it forms a suburb*
par: *Drumbeg* bar: *Belfast Upper*
Ir. *An Fionnachadh* [an **fin**aghoo] 'the white field'. Finaghy is situated in the townland of BALLYFINAGHY which derives from Ir. *Baile an Fhionnachaidh* [bala an **in**aghee] 'townland of the white field' [*Ballyfinnaghey* 1780].

**Finn** river Donegal/Tyrone
*Rises in Lough Finn 10km NE of Glenties in Donegal. Merges with the Mourne a short distance S of Lifford to form the Foyle*
Ir. *An Fhinn* [an **inn**] *perhaps* 'the holy one/sacred one'. As is often the case, the name of the river may be ultimately that of the goddess who was believed to inhabit it. The Finn has given name to GLENFINN to the west of **Ballybofey** and also to **Lough Finn** where the river rises (*see below*) [*Find* c.1100].

**Finnis** tl, vill., Down 3234
*2km S of Dromara*
par: *Dromara* bar: *Iveagh Upper, Lower Half*
Ir. *Fionnais* [**fin**ish] 'white ridge' [*Ballefenishe al. Grange* 1611].

**Fintona** tl, tn, Tyrone 2436
*12km S of Omagh*
par: *Donacavey* bar: *Clogher*
Ir. *Fionntamhnach* [**fin**taunagh] 'white field' [(*hi f*)*fionntamhnach* 1488].

**Fintown** tl, vill., Donegal 1940
*13km NE of Glenties*
par: *Inishkeel* bar: *Boylagh*
Ir. *Baile na Finne* [bala na **fin**ya] 'townland of the (river) Finn'. Fintown is named from its position at the eastern end of **Lough Finn**, the source of the **Finn** river [*Fintown* 1835].

**Finvoy** ham., par., Antrim 2941
*Hamlet is 6.6km S of Ballymoney*
bar: *Kilconway*
Ir. *An Fhionnbhoith* [an **inn**woy] 'the white hut/monastic cell'. The site of the monastery may be marked by FINVOY GRAVEYARD which lies 4km to the south-west, in the townland of VOW, a name which appears to represent Ir. *An Bhoith* [an **woy**], an abbreviated form of the parish name *An Fhionnbhoith* (*see **Artnagross***). There is also an old graveyard a short distance to the west of the hamlet of Finvoy in the townland of KNOCKANS [*Le Fynmaugh* 1333].

**Five Corners** ham., Antrim 3239
*2.5km NW of Ballyclare*
par: *Rashee* bar: *Antrim Upper*
Five Corners is named from a five-point crossroads in the townland of RASHEE.

**Fivemiletown** tl, tn, Tyrone 2434
*Close to Fermanagh border, 10km WSW of Clogher*
par/bar, *Clogher*
Fivemiletown is said to be named from its position five Irish miles from each of the surrounding settlements of **Clogher**, **Brookeborough** and **Tempo**. The original Ir. name of the townland of Fivemiletown was *Baile na Lorgan* [bala na **lurr**igan] 'townland of the long low ridge', a name which was anglicised as *Ballynalurgan.* Previous names for the town of Fivemiletown were *Mount Stewart,* from Sir William Stewart who founded it in 1619 and *Blessingbourn* from the name of the nearby residence of Colonel Montgomery, the proprietor of the area in the early 19th century [*Fivemiletown* 1831].

**Flag Staff** ham., Armagh 3032
(sometimes *Flagstaff*)
*6km S of Newry*
par: *Newry* bar: *Orior Upper*
It is said that a flag used to be raised on FLAGSTAFF HILL in the townland of **Fathom Upper** to inform the pilot in **Warrenpoint** or OMEATH of the approach of a ship. The Ir. name for Flag Staff was *Barr an Fheadáin* [bar an **add**ine] 'top of the water course', the final element being the feature (apparently the **Newry River**) which has given name to the townlands of **Fathom**.

**Flatfield** ham., Down 3236
*Close to Co. Antrim border, 4km E of Moira*
par: *Moira* bar: *Iveagh Lower, Upper Half*
Flatfield is in the north of the townland of BALLYKNOCK where the ground levels out towards the **Lagan**.

**Florence Court Demesne** tl, Fermanagh 2233
*11.5km SSW of Enniskillen*
par: *Killesher* bar: *Clanawley*
The first house named Florence Court was built c.1719 by Sir John Cole (1680-1726), great-grandson of Sir William Cole from Devonshire who settled at **Enniskillen** in the early 17th century. Sir John named the house after Florence Wrey of Cornwall whom he had married in 1707. His son Lord Mountflorence altered and extended the house which was further extended by Lord Mountflorence's son William Willoughby Cole who was created 1st Earl of Enniskillen in 1789. The original Ir. name of the townland of FLORENCECOURT DEMESNE was *Mullach na Seangán* [mullagh na **shan**gan] 'hilltop of the ants' [*Florence Court + Demesne* 1728].

**Flurrybridge** ham., Armagh 3031
*On the border with Louth, 8.5km S of Newry*
par: *Jonesborough* bar: *Orior Upper*
Flurrybridge in the townland of FOUGHILL ETRA is named from a bridge over the FLURRY RIVER, the name of which appears to derive from Ir. *Fliuchraigh* [**flugh**ree] 'wet one/flowing one' [*Fleury-bridge* 1804].

**Forkill** vill., par., Armagh 3031
(sometimes *Forkhill*)
*Village is 13km SW of Newry*
bar: *Orior Upper*
Ir. *Foirceal* [**fork**al] 'trough/hollow'. In 1771 twelve townlands were severed from the parish of **Loughgilly** and formed into the parish of Forkill and in 1773 another eleven townlands which previously belonged to the parish of **Killevy** were added. The village of Forkill is in the townland of SHEAN [(*i*) *nOircel* c.1350].

**Fortwilliam** distr., Antrim 3337
*Suburb, 3.5km N of Belfast city centre*
par: *Shankill* bar: *Belfast Upper*
The name Fortwilliam refers to a rectangular artillery fort, the remains of which stand beside a house called DUNLAMBERT in the townland of SKEGONEILL. It is said be named from King William III who landed at nearby **Carrickfergus** in 1690 but it is possible that it takes its name from William de Burgh, Earl of Ulster, who was murdered near here in 1333.

**Foyle** river, Donegal/Tyrone/Derry
*Formed by the convergence of the river Finn with the Mourne a little to the S of Lifford. Flows into Lough Foyle a short distance N of Derry*
Ir. *An Feabhal* [an **fyau**il]. The name of the river is derived from **Lough Foyle**, the estuary into which it flows and which at an earlier period was thought of as extending inland all

the way to **Lifford**, thus including the entire river Foyle as well. Lough Foyle is from Ir. *Loch Feabhail* which may signify 'lough/estuary of the lip' (*see* ***Lough Foyle***) [*Febal* c.1160].

**Frosses** tl, Antrim 3041
*11km NNW of Ballymena*
par: *Grange of Dundermot* bar: *Kilconway*
Ir. *Na Frosa* [na **fross**a]. *Na Frosa* is a variant of *Na Frasa* which literally means 'the showers' but in this place-name seems to have connotations such as 'watery place/marshy place'. Frosses lies on the east bank of the **Main** and contains large areas of bog. The townland contains the hamlets of BIG FROSSES and WEE FROSSES [*Frasses* c.1657].

**Frosses** vill., Donegal 1834
*7.5km W of Donegal town*
par: *Inver* bar: *Banagh*
Ir. *Na Frosa* [na **fross**a] 'the showers'. As in the case of **Frosses** in Co. Antrim the place-name appears to signify 'watery place/marshy place' (*see previous entry*). There is an area of boggy land in the vicinity. Frosses is in the townland of DRUMARD [*Frosses* 1835].

**Fury** river, Tyrone
*Rises near Essrawer, 6km S of Clogher. Enters river Blackwater 1.5km NE of Clogher*
par/bar, *Clogher*
Ir. *An Fheoraí* [an **yoar**ee] 'the stream/rivulet'.

**Fyfin** tl, Tyrone 2338
*7.5km ENE of Strabane*
par: *Ardstraw* bar: *Strabane Lower*
Ir. *Faiche Fionn* [faigha **fin**] 'bright/white lawn or green' [*Foifin* 1609].

# G

**Galbally** tl, vill., Tyrone 2736
*8.5km WNW of Dungannon*
par: *Pomeroy* bar: *Dungannon Middle*
Ir. *Gallbhuaile* [**gal**woola] 'stone *booley* or cattle-enclosure'. The Ir. element *buaile* signifies 'cattle-enclosure' and often refers to such a feature in a summer grazing pasture (*see* ***Ballyboley*** *above*) [*Galboly* 1611].

**Galgorm** tl, vill, Antrim 3040
*2.5km W of Ballymena of which it forms a suburb*
par: *Ahoghill* bar: *Toome Lower*
*perhaps* Ir. *Gall Gorm* [gal **gor**im] 'blue-black rock/castle'. The place-name may refer to a former castle of the MacQuillans which stood on the east bank of the **Main** a short distance from the present GALGORM CASTLE . An earlier name for the townland of Galgorm was *Ballystraboy* from Ir. *Baile an tSratha Bhuí* [bala an traa **wee**] 'townland of the yellow river holm' [*Galgrom al. Straboy* 1631].

**Galliagh** distr., Derry 2442
*4km NNW of centre of Londonderry*
par: *Templemore*
bar: *NW Liberties of Londonderry*
Galliagh is a shortened form of BALLYNAGALLIAGH which derives from Ir. *Baile na gCailleach* [bala na **gal**-yagh] 'townland of the nuns or hags' and is the name of the townland in which it is situated. The townland contains the hamlets of UPPER GALLIAGH and LOWER GALLIAGH. There is now no trace of the nunnery which gave name to the place [*Ballinecalleagh* 1604].

**Garrison** tl, vill., Fermanagh 1935
*On E shore of Lough Melvin, 7km S of Belleek*
par: *Devenish/Inishmacsaint*
bar: *Magheraboy*
Garrison is named from a barrack erected by William III who halted here after the battle of Aughrim in 1691. A portion of the village is in the neighbouring townland of KNOCKAREVAN [*Garrison* 1834].

**Garron Point** hl, Antrim 3342
*On E Antrim coast, 6km NNE of Carnlough*
par: *Ardclinis* bar: *Glenarm Lower*
Ir. *An Gearrán* [an **gar**an] 'the horse'. The name is used figuratively to apply to this massive basalt/limestone headland [*Point of Gerran* 1780].

**Garryduff** tl, ham., Antrim 2942
*4km SE of Ballymoney*
par: *Ballymoney* bar: *Kilconway*
Ir. *An Garraí Dubh* [an garree **doo**] 'the black garden or enclosure' [*Garrydoo* 1780].

**Gartan** tl, par., Donegal
*Townland is 12.5km WNW of Letterkenny*
bar: *Kilmacrenan*
Ir. *Gartán* [**gart**an] 'little field'. Ir. *gartán* is a diminutive of *gart*, a variant of *gort* 'field'. Gartan is famous as the birth place of St Colmcille. The site of his sixth-century monastery is marked by a holy well, the ruins of a small chapel and an ancient graveyard which overlooks LOUGH AKIBBON. The latter lies a short distance to the north of the larger GARTAN LOUGH which is sometimes known as LOUGH BEAGH SOUTH. The full title of the townland is GARTAN OR BELLVILLE [(*i*) *nGartan* c.1630].

**Garvagh** tl, vill., Derry 2841
*9km NW of Kilrea*
par: *Errigal* bar: *Coleraine*
Ir. *Garbhachadh* [**gar**ivaghoo] 'rough field'. The village was founded c.1615 by George Canning of the Ironmongers guild of London [*Garvaghy* 1634].

**Garvaghy** tl, par., Down 3234
*Townland is 8.5km ENE of Banbridge*
bar: *Iveagh Lower, Lower Half*
Ir. *Garbhachadh* [**gar**ivaghoo] 'rough field'. The present Church of Ireland church is just inside the neighbouring townland of FEDANY and may mark the site of the medieval parish church. GARVAGHY HILL (200m) commands an extensive view over the surrounding countryside [*Garwaghadh* 1428].

**Garvaghy** tl, ham.,Tyrone 2536
(sometimes *Garvaghey*)
*7km NW of Ballygawley*
par: *Errigal Keerogue* bar: *Clogher*
Ir. *Garbhachadh* [**gar**ivaghoo] 'rough field'. Garvaghy has given name to GARVAGHY BIG HILL (200m) and to GARVAGHY LOUGH which is on the western boundary of the townland [*Garaghye* 1629].

*Giant's Causeway*

**Garvary** tl, vill., Fermanagh 2235
(sometimes *Garvery*)
*3.5km NE of Enniskillen*
par: *Enniskillen* bar: *Tirkennedy*
Ir. *Garbhaire* [**gar**ivira] 'rough place' [*Garvorey* 1659].

**Gawleys Gate** ham., Antrim 3036
*8.5km N of Lurgan*
par: *Aghagallon* bar: *Massereene Upper*
Gawley's Gate is named from a 17th-century tollgate, formerly manned by an individual named Gawley. The tollhouse is now a thatched post office and public house, in the townland of MONTIAGHS. The surname Gawley is a variant of MacAuley which can be of either Irish or Scottish origin. Most of the Co. Antrim MacAuleys are descended from the Scottish MacAulay family of Dumbartonshire whose name in Ir. is *Mac Amhalaí* and a branch of whom came to the Glens of Antrim with the MacDonnells in the early 16th century [*Gawley's Gate* 1838].

**Giant's Causeway** Antrim 2944
*Famous columnar volcanic rock formation on the N Antrim coast, 4km NNE of Bushmills*
par: *Billy* bar: *Cary*
The name Giant's Causeway appears to be a loose translation of the original Ir. *Clochán na bhFomhórach* [kloghan na **wo**-woragh] 'causeway of the Fomorians', the latter being a mythical race who are depicted as demonic opponents of the divine *Tuatha Dé Danann* in the medieval *Book of Invasions*. Another Ir. name for the Giant's Causeway was *Tóchar na dTréanfhear* [togher na **drain**ar] 'causeway of the strong men/warriors'. In more recent times the Causeway was known in Ir. as *Clochán an Aifir* [kloghan an **affi**r] which appears to be a corruption of the earlier *Clochán na bhFomhórach*. A legend tells how Finn Mac Cool used the causeway to return to Ireland having vanquished his Scottish rival Benandonner. The Giant's Causeway is in the townland of AIRD [*Clochán na bhfogmharach* c.1675].

**Gilford** vill., Down 3034
*On the Upper Bann, 6km WNW of Banbridge*
par: *Tullylish* bar: *Iveagh Lower, Upper Half*
The name Gilford is a contraction of Magill's ford and is named from Captain John Magill (later Sir John Magill) who acquired lands in this area in the 17th century and who lived at GILL HALL in **Dromore**. The site of the ford is marked by the bridge which was constructed in the 18th century at the lower end of the town, linking the townlands of DRUMARAN and LOUGHANS [*Gilford* 1678].

**Glangevlin** glen, vill., Cavan 2032
(sometimes *Glengevlin*)
*Village is 12km S of Blacklion*
par: *Templeport* bar: *Tullyhaw*
Ir. *Gleann Ghaibhle* [glan **ghiv**la] 'glen of the fork'. A local tradition has it that the final element of the place-name is a variant form of *Goibhniu*, the name of the smith or armourer of the legendary *Tuatha Dé Danann*. The valley of Glangevlin is at the western foot of the **Cuilcagh Mountains** [(*i*) *nGlionn Gaibhle* 1390].

**Glarryford** ham., Antrim 3041
*10km NNW of Ballymena*
par: *Rasharkin* bar: *Kilconway*
Sc. *glarry* 'muddy' + E. 'ford'. The site of the ford is marked by GLARRYFORD BRIDGE which crosses the **Clogh River** a short distance east of its junction with the **Main** and links the townland of DUNDERMOT in the parish of GRANGE OF DUNDERMOT with the townland of KILDOWNEY in the parish of KIRKINRIOLA. The hamlet of Glarryford is west of the **Main**, in the townland of DROMORE and parish of **Rasharkin** [*Glaraford* 1835].

**Glasdrumman** tl, vill., Armagh 2931
(sometimes *Glasdrummond*)
*5km E of Crossmaglen*
par: *Creggan* bar: *Fews Upper*
*Ir. An Ghlasdromainn* [an **ghlas**drummin] 'the green ridge'. GLASSDRUMMAN LOUGH which is in the middle of the townland adjoins the village on the east [(*i gcaislén na*) *Glasdromuinne* c.1645].

**Glasdrumman** tls, ham., Down 3332
(sometimes *Glassdrummond*)
*On the coast, 2km N of Annalong*
par: *Kilkeel* bar: *Mourne*
Ir. *An Ghlasdromainn* [an **ghlas**drummin] 'the green ridge'. The townland of Glasdrumman is adjoined on the north-west by the townland of GLASDRUMMAN UPPER [*Glasedrommyn* 1540].

**Glasleck** tl, vill., Cavan 2730
(sometimes *Glassleck*)
*On S shore of Milltown Lough, 7.5km NNE of Bailieborough*
par: *Shercock* bar: *Clankee*
Ir. *Glasleic* [**glas**leck] 'green/grey stone'. The place-name may refer to stones which are found in the rampart of a fort in the townland [*Glasleck* 1629].

**Glaslough** tl, vill., Monaghan 2734
(sometimes *Glasslough*)
*7.5km NE of Monaghan town*
par: *Donagh* bar: *Trough*
*Glaslough* [**glas**lough] 'green lake'. Glaslough takes its name from the lake of that name which forms the eastern boundary of the townland [*Glaslagh* 1591].

**Glastry** tl, ham., Down 3636
*On Ards Peninsula, 1.5km SW of Ballyhalbert*
par: *Inishargy* bar: *Ards Upper*
Ir. *An Ghlasrach* [an **ghlas**ragh] 'the green grassy area' [*Balliglassarie* 1604].

**Glebe** tl, ham., Derry 2643
*7.5km NNW of Limavady*
par: *Magilligan or Tamlaghtard*
bar: *Keenaght*
Glebe is the most common townland name in Ireland. It is of E. origin and refers to land set aside for the upkeep of a clergyman in a parish. The townland of Glebe has a small detached portion named GORT, PART OF GLEBE which is entirely surrounded by the townland of TAMLAGHT, the latter containing the ruins of the former parish church of **Magilligan** [*Glebe House* 1835].

**Glen** glen, ham., Derry 2840
*Hamlet is 2.5km W of Maghera*
par: *Maghera* bar: *Loughinsholin*
Ir. *An Gleann* [an**glan**] 'the glen/valley'. The hamlet of Glen is in the townland of **Fallagloon** and takes its name from the gently sloping valley of the FALLAGLOON BURN [*Glenn chapel* 1833].

**Glen** glen, vill., Donegal 2143
*Village is 8km NW of Milford*
par: *Mevagh* bar: *Kilmacrenan*

Ir. *An Gleann* [an **glan**] 'the glen/valley'. Glen is a shortened form of GLENINEENY, the name of the townland in which the village is situated (Ir. *Gleann an Aonaigh* 'glen of the fair'). The glen referred to is the valley of the GLEN RIVER which flows into GLEN LOUGH a short distance to the south [*Glen* 1802].

**Glenaan** glen, tl, Antrim 3142
*The glen is the lower half of the valley of the Glenaan River which rises close the summit of Trostan and combines with the Ballyemon River to form the Dall 1km W of Cushendall*
par: *Layd* bar: *Glenarm Lower*
*perhaps* Ir. *Gleann Athain* [glan **aan**] 'glen of the burial chamber'. The final element may go back to O.Ir. *othain* 'burial chamber' (cf. ***Fahan***) and to refer the megalithic court grave locally known as CLOGHBRACK or OSSIAN'S GRAVE, in the neighbouring townland of LUBITAVISH. Glenaan is one of the nine glens of Antrim [*Glennaan* 1780].

**Glenanne** glen, vill., Armagh 2933
(sometimes *Glen Anne*)
*6 km S of Markethill*
par: *Loughgilly* bar: *Orior Lower*
The name Glenanne signifies simply 'Anne's glen' and was originally the name of the house of George Gray who named it after his wife Eliza Anne, daughter of Rev. James Henry of CORLOUGH in Co. Cavan whom he married in 1808. The village was founded by William Atkinson who established extensive cotton and calico mills here c.1818, in the townland of LISDRUMCHOR LOWER [Glen *Anne* 1828].

**Glenariff** glen, vill., Antrim 3242
(sometimes *Glenariffe*)
*The glen is the wide valley of the Glenariff River which rises near Parkmore to the S of Trostan and enters the sea at the village of Glenariff or Waterfoot, 2km S of Cushendall*
par: *Layd* bar: *Glenarm Lower*
Ir. *Gleann Airimh* [glan **ar**iv] 'glen of arable land'. Glenariff has given name to the townlands of GLENARIFF MOUNTAIN LOWER and GLENARIFF MOUNTAIN UPPER EAST and WEST, all of which are in the neighbouring parish of ARDCLINIS. The village of Glenariff or Waterfoot at the mouth of the GLENARIFF RIVER is in the townland of FORIFF (Ir. *Foirbh* 'pasture'). Glenariff is one of the nine glens of Antrim [*Glenarthac* 1279].

**Glenarm** glen, vill., bars, Antrim 3341
*The glen is the lower portion of the valley of the Glenarm River which flows into the sea at Glenarm, 16 km NNW of Larne*
par: *Tickmacrevan* bar: *Glenarm Lower*
Ir. *Gleann Arma* [glan **ar**ima] 'glen of the army'. The circumstances in which Glenarm was named 'glen of the army' are obscure but the name may be connected with a 13th-century Norman castle which formerly stood on the opposite side of the river from the present castle which is in the townland of GLENARM DEMESNE. The village of Glenarm is in the townland of TOWN PARKS in the barony of GLENARM LOWER which is bounded on the south by the barony of GLENARM UPPER. Glenarm is one of the nine glens of Antrim [*Glinne hArma* c.1400].

**Glenavy** tl, vill., par., Antrim 3137
*Village is 3 km S of Crumlin*
bar: *Massereene Upper*
Ir. *Lann Abhaigh* [lan **a**wee] 'church of the dwarf'. The E. word *glen* is in this case a corruption of Ir. *lann* 'church'. The place-name has its origin in a legend that St Patrick built a church here and left it in charge of his disciple Daniel who was nicknamed 'dwarf' because of his diminutive stature. The original church site at Glenavy appears to be marked by the graveyard of the present Church of Ireland church in the village [*(o) Lainn abhaich* c.1450].

**Glenballyemon** glen, Antrim 3242
*Valley of the Ballyemon River which rises to the E of Trostan and merges with the Glenaan River to form the Dall, 1km W of Cushendall*
par: *Layd* bar: *Glenarm Lower*
Ir. *Gleann Bhaile Éamainn* [glan wala **ey**min] 'glen of Ballyemon'. The glen appears to be named from a small settlement named BALLYEMON (Ir. *Baile Éamainn* 'Edmund's homestead') in the townland of TAVNAGHARRY. Glenballyemon is one of the nine glens of Antrim.

**Glenbeagh** glen, tl, Donegal 1942
(often *Glenveagh*)
*Townland is at the E foot of the Derryveagh Mountains, in Glenveagh National Park, 17.5km WNW of Letterkenny*
par: *Gartan* bar: *Kilmacrenan*
Ir. *Gleann Bheatha* [glan **va**ha] 'glen of birch'. The modern form of the place-name appears to be a development from an earlier form

*Gleann Bheathach* 'birch glen' (*see* ***Derryveagh Mountains***). The glen referred to is the valley of the OWENBEAGH RIVER which flows into the southern end of LOUGH BEAGH, the long narrow lake which forms the scenic centrepiece of GLENVEAGH NATIONAL PARK [(*ar*) *Loch Beathach* 1258].

**Glenbush** glen, distr., Antrim 3042
*The glen is a portion of the valley of the river Bush at the W foot of Slieveanorra Mountain, 14km E of Ballymoney*
par: *Loughguile* bar: *Dunluce Upper*
Ir. *Gleann na Buaise* [glan na **boo**isha] 'glen of the (river) Bush'. The E. name appears to be a translation of the original Ir. [*valley of Glenbush* 1835].

**Glencloy** glen, Antrim 3241
*Valley of the Glencloy River which flows into the sea at the S end of Carnlough*
par: *Tickmacrevan* bar: *Glenarm Lower*
Ir. *Gleann Cloiche* [glan **cloy**ha] 'glen of the stone'. The element *cloch* 'stone' may in this case refer to a megalith, perhaps to the chambered grave in the townland of DOONAN at the head of the glen. Glencloy is one of the nine glens of Antrim [*Glenclives* c.1659].

**Glencolumbkille** glen, vill., par., Donegal 1538
*Village is in SW corner of Donegal, 22.5km WSW of Ardara*
bar: *Banagh*
Ir. *Gleann Cholm Cille* [glan kholim **kill**ya] '(St) Colmcille's glen'. Glencolumbkille is named from a wide coastal valley at the head of GLEN BAY. There is a tradition that St Columcille had a contest here with demons who had evaded St Patrick on Croagh Patrick and the valley contains many Early Christian monuments associated with the saint. However, the dedication to St Columcille in the place-name appears to be a fairly late one. Glencolumbkille has given name to GLEN HEAD, a prominent headland at the northern edge of the glen [*Glend Colaim Cilli* 1532].

**Glencorp** glen, Antrim 3243
*Lies between Gruig Top and Cross Slieve, 3km SW of Cushendun*
par: *Layd* par: *Glenarm Lower*
Ir. *Gleann Corp* [glan **korp**] 'glen of bodies'. The significance of the name of the glen is obscure; possibly it could refer to the site of a battle. Glencorp is one of the nine glens of Antrim [*Gleancorp* 1703].

**Glendowan** glen, distr., Donegal 2041
*Glen is the valley of the Bullaba River which flows into the S end of Gartan Lough*
par: *Gartan* bar: *Kilmacrenan*
Ir. *Gleann Domhain* [glan **doa**in] 'deep glen'. Glendowan has given name to the GLENDOWAN MOUNTAINS which lie to the south-west. There is a townland named GLENDOWANBEG (Ir. *Gleann Domhain Beag* 'little Glendowan') on the south bank of the BULLABA RIVER.

**Glendun** glen, Antrim 3142
*The lower half of the valley of the Glendun River which rises close to Trostan, 8km SW of Cushendall and enters the sea at Cushendun*
par: *Layd/Grange of Layd*
bar: *Glenarm Lower*
Ir. *Gleann Doinne* [glan **dinn**ya] 'glen of the river Dun'. The river Dun, commonly known as the GLENDUN RIVER, divides the parishes of LAYD and GRANGE OF LAYD. Its name is from Ir. *An Donn* 'the brown (river)'. Glendun is one of the nine glens of Antrim [*Glendun* 1832].

**Gleneely** vill., Donegal 2544
*8km NW of Moville*
par: *Culdaff* bar: *Inishowen East*
Ir. *Gleann Daoile* [glan **deel**a] 'glen of the (river) *Daoil*'. *Daoil* 'black one' appears to be the now obsolete name of the GLENEELY RIVER, on which the village stands, in the townland of DRISTERNAN (cf. river **Deele** above) [(*a*) *nGleann Daoile* c.1630].

**Glenelly Valley** glen Tyrone/Derry
*Valley of the Glenelly River, which rises in the Sperrins 10km W of Draperstown and flows into the Owenkillew River 4km SW of Plumbridge*
par: *Bodoney Upper* bar: *Strabane Upper*
Ir. *Gleann Aichle* [glan **agh**la] *perhaps* 'glen of the look-out point/prospect' + E. *valley*. The 'look-out point' may be the mountain named CARNANELLY (562m) (Ir. *Carnán Aichle* '(little) cairn of the look-out point/prospect') which stands at the eastern end of the glen [(*hi n*) *Gliond Fhoichle* 854].

**Glengesh** glen, tl, Donegal 1638
*Glen is the valley of the Glengesh River which*

*flows into Bracky River 2km S of Ardara*
par: *Killybegs Lower* bar: *Banagh*
Ir. *Gleann Gheise* [glan **yesh**a] *perhaps* 'glen of the taboo or prohibition'. GLENGESH HILL (385m) stands at the north side of the glen [*Glengeish* c.1655].

**Glengormley** tl, vill., Antrim 3338
*Forms a district of Newtownabbey, 8km NNW of Belfast city centre*
par: *Carnmoney* bar: *Belfast Lower*
Ir. *Clann Ghormlaithe* [clan **ġor**imlee] 'descendants of *Gormlaith*'. *Gormlaith* which signifies 'splendid sovereignty' is normally a female name and this particular *Gormlaith* belonged to the *Dál Fiatach*, a tribe which spread northwards from what is now Co. Down in the course of the eighth century. Glengormley is an example of a name of a tribe which has been transferred to the area in which they were settled [*cland Gormlaithi* c.1200].

**Glenhead** ham., Derry 2641
*5km SW of Limavady*
par: *Tamlaght Finlagan* bar: *Keenaght*
Glenhead is in the valley of a stream in the townland of DRUMRAIGHLAND. Interestingly, a short distance to the south-west there is a place named BARANAILT (Ir. *Barr an Aillt*) of which 'Glenhead' is an exact translation.

**Glenhull** glen, ham., Tyrone 2638
*The glen is a portion of the valley of the Owenkillew River, 11.5km E of Gortin*
par: *Bodoney Lower* bar: *Strabane Upper*
Ir. *Gleann Choll* [glen **khull**] 'glen of hazels'. The hamlet of Glenhull is in the townland of TEEBANE EAST on the east bank of the river.

**Glenlark** glen, tl, Tyrone 2638
*The glen is the valley of the Glenlark River which rises in Lough Lark in the Sperrins and flows into the Owenkillew River 8km E of Gortin*
par: *Bodoney Lower* bar: *Strabane Upper*
Ir. *Gleann Láirc* [glan **lark**] 'glen of forks' [*Glenn Laarc* c.1675].

*Glenshane Pass*

**Glenoe** glen, vill., Antrim 3339
*Village is 6km S of Larne*
par: *Raloo* bar: *Belfast Lower*
Ir. *Gleann Ó* [glan **o**] 'glen of the mass or lump'. The 'mass or lump' in question may be the steep hill which rises above the village and which is the scene of a triple waterfall on the RALOO WATER. The latter becomes the GLENOE WATER and later the GLYNN RIVER before entering Larne Lough at **Glynn**. Glenoe is in the townland of CARNEAL [*Glenoe* 1833].

**Glenone** tl, Derry 2940
*Adjoins Portglenone, on W side of Lower Bann*
par: *Tamlaght O'Crilly* bar: *Loughinsholin*
Ir. *Cluain Eoghain* [klooin **oin**] 'Owen's meadow'. From the townland of Glenone is named the town of **Portglenone** across the **Lower Bann** in Co. Antrim (*see below*) [*Cloynon* 1654].

**Glenravel** glen, distr., Antrim 3141
*The glen is the valley of the Glenravel Water, 12km NNE of Ballymena*
par: *Skerry/Dunaghy*
bar: *Antrim Lower/Kilconway*
Ir. *Gleann Fhreabhail* [glan **rau**il] 'glen of the (river) Ravel'. The name of the river Ravel (commonly known as the GLENRAVEL WATER) is derived from Ir. *Freabhal* [**frau**al] (earlier *Fregabal* 'towards the fork') referring, perhaps, to the point where it unites with the SKERRY WATER at **Martinstown** to form the **Clogh River**. At an earlier period the GLENRAVEL WATER formed a boundary between the kingdoms of *Dál Riada* and *Dál Araidhe* [(*occ*) *Fregabail* 912].

**Glenshane** glen, tl, Derry 2740
*The glen is the valley of the head waters of the river Roe, 9.5km WNW of Maghera*
par: *Dungiven* bar: *Keenaght*
Ir. *Gleann Sheáin* [glen **hyine**] 'John's glen'. Glenshane has given name to GLENSHANE MOUNTAIN (470m), GLENSHANE FOREST and the well-known GLENSHANE PASS on the main road from **Belfast** to **Derry** [*Glensenny* 1654].

**Glenshesk** glen, Antrim 3143
*Lower portion of the valley of the Glenshesk River which rises near Slieveanorra 10km W of Cushendall and joins with the Carey River to form the Margy a short distance E of Ballycastle*
par: *Ramoan/Culfeightrin* bar: *Cary*
Ir. *Gleann Seisc* [glan **shesk**] 'barren glen'. This portion of the GLENSHESK RIVER forms the boundary between the parishes of RAMOAN and CULFEIGHTRIN [*(maidhm) ghlenna seisg* 1565].

**Glentaisie** glen, Antrim 3043
*At W foot of Knocklayd, 4km S of Ballycastle*
par: *Ramoan* bar: *Cary*
Ir. *Gleann Taise* [glan **tash**a] *perhaps 'Taise*'s glen'. Legend has it that *Taise* was a princess of the *Tuatha Dé Danann* who hailed from **Rathlin** and this is the commonly accepted interpretation of the place-name. However, it is also possible that the final element represents the Ir. word *taise* 'apparition, ghost, remains, relics, ruins' or *taise* 'dampness, moistness'. Another name for Glentaisie is GLENTOW, the **Tow** being the river which flows through the lower portion of the glen. The name Tow appears to be from Ir. *Tó* 'the silent one' and to be primarily a goddess-name. Glentaisie is one of the nine glens of Antrim [*(san maidhm sin) glinne taisi* 1565].

**Glenties** vill., Donegal 1839
*9km NE of Ardara*
par: *Inishkeel* bar: *Boylagh*
Ir. *Na Gleannta* [na **glan**ta] 'the glens'. Glenties appears to be named from the valleys of the rivers OWENEA and STRACASHEL which meet at the south end of the village. The plural E. form of the place-name reflects the original Ir. plural [*Na Gleanntaidh* 1835].

**Glentogher** glen, tl., Donegal 2444
*The glen is the valley of the Glentogher River which rises 8km S of Carndonagh and the lower portion of which is known as the Donagh River*
par: *Donagh* bar: *Inishowen East*
Ir. *Gleann Tóchair* [glan **togh**er] 'glen of the causeway'. Glentogher is in the parish of DONAGH, the full name of which was *Domhnach Glinne Tóchair* 'church of Glentogher' (*see* ***Carndonagh***). The full title of the very large townland of Glentogher is GLENTOGHER OR CARROWMORE [*ye causeway of Clantogher* c.1655].

**Glen Ullin** glen, distr., Derry 2841
(often *Glenullin*)
*The glen is a portion of the upper valley of the Agivey River, 4km SW of Garvagh*
par: *Errigal* bar: *Coleraine*
Ir. *Gleann Iolair* [glan **ull**ir] 'glen of the eagle'. A local tradition has it that the glen is named from *Ulleran*, son of Finn Mac Cool, who was killed here and that his grave is marked by a cairn the remains of which stand in the townland of COOLCOSCREAGHAN. The **Agivey River** is joined by the GLENULLIN WATER at LOWER BROCKAGH BRIDGE [*Glenuller* 1836].

**Glenvar** glen, vill., Donegal 2243
*The glen is the portion of the valley of the Glenvar River which lies at the southern foot of Knockalla Mountain, on the W shore of Lough Swilly*
par: *Clondavaddog* bar: *Kilmacrenan*
Ir. *Gleann Bhairr* [glan **warr**] 'glen of the top or summit'. The northern side of the glen is formed by KNOCKALLA MOUNTAIN (363m). The village of Glenvar is in the townland of TIRLAYDAN on the north side of the GLENVAR RIVER [*Glinvar* 1796].

**Glenveagh** glen, Donegal 1942
(*see* ***Glenbeagh***)

**Glenwhirry** glen, tl, par., Antrim 3239
(sometimes *Glenwherry*)
*The glen is the upper valley of the Glenwhirry River which rises 9km W of Larne and joins the Main 5.5km S of Ballymena*
bar: *Antrim Lower*
Ir. *Gleann an Choire* [glan a **khurr**a] 'glen of the cauldron/whirlpool'. The final element of the place-name refers to a deep pool beneath a waterfall near the source of the river, in the townland of SKERRYWHIRRY (Ir. *Sceir an Choire* 'rocky hill of the cauldron'). The lower portion of the GLENWHIRRY RIVER (Ir. *Abhainn an Choire* [owen a **khurr**a] 'river of the cauldron') is known as the **Kells Water**. There is no trace or record of ecclesiastical remains in the parish, though a mutilated round cairn in the townland of Glenwhirry is known as BISHOP'S CAIRN [*(Owen) Glancurry* 1605].

**Glynn** tl, vill., par., Antrim 3440
*Village is 2.5km S of Larne*
bar: *Belfast Lower*
Ir. *An Gleann* [an **glan**] 'the glen'. An earlier

*Field of oats*

name for Glynn was *Gleann Fhinneachta* [glan **inn**aghta] '*Finneacht*'s glen'. *Finneacht* is an early female personal name, possibly the name of a saint. The glen referred to is the valley of the GLYNN RIVER which flows into **Larne Lough** adjacent to the village. The site of an early church, said to have been founded by St Patrick, may be marked by the remains of the medieval parish church (known as GLYNN OLD CHURCH) on the south bank of the GLYNN RIVER. At an earlier period Glynn was regarded as marking the southern boundary of the kingdom of *Dál Riada* [*Glend-indechta* c.900].

**Gobbins, The** sea cliffs, Antrim 3439
*On Island Magee, 6km N of Whitehead*
par: *Island Magee* bar: *Belfast Lower*
Ir. *Na Gobáin* [na **gub**ine] 'the points or peaks'. The high cliffs known as The Gobbins are in the townland of BALLOO [*the Gabbon* 1683].

**Gola Island** isld, tl, Donegal 1742
*Off W Donegal coast, 4km W of Derrybeg*
par: *Tullaghobegly* bar: *Kilmacrenan*
Ir. *Gabhla* [**goal**a] 'place of the fork'. Gola has two high hills with low land between them and this appears to be the 'fork' referred to in the place-name [*Goolagh* 1614].

**Gortaclady** tl, ham., Tyrone 2737
*11.5km W of Cookstown*
par: *Kildress* bar: *Dungannon Upper*
Ir. *Gort an Chladaigh* [gort a **khlad**ee] 'field of the firm ground'. The final element of the place-name is the genitive of *cladach* which can mean 'stony shore'. In this case it seems to refer to firm, dry land on the edge of boggy land.

**Gortaclare** tl, ham., Tyrone 2536
*3.5km SW of Beragh*
par: *Clogherny* bar: *Omagh East*
Ir. *Gort an Chláir* [gort a **khlar**] 'field of the plain' [*Gortclare* 1620].

**Gortahork** tl, vill., Donegal 1943
*In NW Donegal, at the head of Ballyness Bay, 2.5km SW of Falcarragh*
par: *Tullaghobegly* bar: *Kilmacrenan*
Ir. *Gort an Choirce* [gort a **khork**a] 'field of the oats' [*Gortecorky* 1639].

**Gortavoy** tl, ham., Tyrone 2736
*4.5km E of Pomeroy*
par: *Pomeroy* bar: *Dungannon Middle*
Ir. *Gort an Bheathaigh* [gort a **va**hee] 'field of the beast/cow' [*Gortavaghy* 1666].

**Gorticashel** tls, Tyrone 2538
(sometimes *Gorticastle*)
*5km NE of Gortin*
par: *Bodoney Lower* bar: *Strabane Upper*
Ir. *Gort an Chaisil* [gort a **khash**il] 'field of the stone ring-fort'. There is no record of a stone fort here. There is, however, a standing stone and an earthen ring-fort. The GORTICASHEL BURN divides the townlands of GORTICASHEL UPPER and LOWER and there are two hamlets so named [*Gorte-Castell* 1666].

**Gortin** tl, vill., Tyrone 2438
*13km N of Omagh*
par: *Bodoney Lower* bar: *Strabane Upper*
Ir. *An Goirtín* [an **gortch**een] 'the little (cultivated) field'. The village of Gortin is partly in the neighbouring townland of BELTRIM [*Goirtín* c.1613].

**Gortnahey** tls, ham., Derry 2641
*4km NW of Dungiven*
par: *Bovevagh* bar: *Keenaght*
Ir. *Gort na hÁithe* [gort na **hai**ha] 'field of the kiln'. Ironically, the townland of GORTNAHEY BEG 'little Gortnahey' is larger than the neighbouring GORTNAHEY MORE 'big Gortnahey'! [*Gortnahey* 1814].

**Gortreagh** tl, Tyrone 2737
*7km W of Cookstown*
par: *Kildress* bar: *Dungannon Upper*
Ir. *An Gort Riabhach* [an gort **ree**wagh] 'the grey or striped field' [*Gortreagh* c.1655].

**Gosheden** tl, Derry 2441
(sometimes *Goshaden*)
*6km WNW of Claudy*
par: *Cumber Lower* bar: *Tirkeeran*
Ir. *Geosadán* [**gyoas**adan] '(place of) thistle' [*Goussidone* 1654].

**Gowna** vill., Cavan 2329
(see ***Lough Gowna***)

**Gracehill** vill., Antrim 3040
*4km W of Ballymena*
par: *Ahoghill* bar: *Toome Lower*
The village of Gracehill in the townland of BALLYKENNEDY was founded in 1756 by the Moravians, a religious sect of German origin who had settled here in 1746. The name of the village reflects the religious convictions of its founders. There is another Moravian settlement at GRACEFIELD in the townland of **Ballymaguigan** on the north-west shore of **Lough Neagh** [*Gracehill* 1835].

**Grange Corner** ham., Antrim 3039
*6km NE of Toome*
par: *Grange of Ballyscullion*
bar: *Toome Upper*
Grange Corner, in the townland of TAYLORSTOWN, is named from the parish of GRANGE OF BALLYSCULLION in which it is situated. The adjacent townland is named GRANGE PARK. The element *grange* is Norman-French, signifying 'barn/granary' and in place-names it denotes a monastic farm. The monastery referred to in this case was the Abbey of SS Peter and Paul in **Armagh** of which the Grange of Ballyscullion was formerly a possession though situated at some remove from it.

**Gransha** tl, ham., Down 3234
*5km SW of Dromara*
par: *Dromara* bar: *Iveagh Upper, Lower Half*
Ir. *An Ghráinseach* [an **ġran**shagh] 'the grange/monastic farm'. Ir. *Gráinseach* is a gaelicised form of *grange* (*see previous entry*) [*Graunge* 1609].

**Greencastle** tl, vill., Antrim 3337
*6km N of Belfast, of which it forms a suburb*
par: *Shankill* bar: *Belfast Upper*
There are now no remains of the former stone castle of Greencastle but it is marked on a map of c.1570 as *Cloughamalestie* which appears to be a corruption of Ir. *Cloch Mhic Coisteala* [clogh vick **kush**tala] 'Costello's stone castle', a name which was also used for the townland of Greencastle. *Mac Coisteala* 'Costello' is a development from an earlier form *Mac Oisdealbh(aigh)* 'son of *Oisdealbh*', *Oisdealbh* being a native personal name adopted by the Anglo-Normans [*Cloghcastella* 1620].

**Greencastle** tl, Down 3231
*5km SW of Kilkeel*
par: *Kilkeel* bar: *Mourne*
The name Greencastle refers to a Norman castle, first built about 1230 by Hugh de Lacy, the ruins of which stand at the entrance to **Carlingford Lough**. The Ir. name for Greencastle is *Caisleán na hOireanaí* [kashlan na **hurr**anee], *perhaps* 'castle of the cultivated place' [*(ad) Viride Castrum* c.1254].

**Greencastle** vill., Donegal 2644
*On E coast of Inishowen peninsula, directly opposite Magilligan Point*
par: *Moville Lower* bar: *Inishowen East*
The castle was built in 1305 by Richard de Burgo, the Red Earl of Ulster, and its remains stand a short distance east of the village. An alternative name for the castle was *Northburg*. The Ir. name of Greencastle is *An Caisleán Nua* [an kashlan **noo**a] 'the new castle'. Greencastle is in the townland of ELEVEN BALLYBOES [*Caislen Nua Insi hEocchain* 1305].

**Greencastle** vill., RC par., Tyrone 2538
*10.5km ESE of Gortin*
par: *Bodoney Lower* bar: *Strabane Upper*
There is no record of any castle here. There is a local tradition that the 'castle' was in fact the first Catholic chapel and that the element 'green' refers to grass which grew on the thatched roof. Greencastle is in the townland of SHESKINSHULE [*Greencastle* 1837].

**Greenisland** vill., Antrim 3338
*11km NE of Belfast*
par/bar, *Carrickfergus*
Greenisland, in the townland of WEST DIVISION, is named from a tiny island a short distance off the north shore of **Belfast Lough**.

**Green Lough** RC par., Derry 2940
(sometimes *Greenlough*)
*On W bank of the Lower Bann, adjacent to Portglenone*
par: *Tamlaght O'Crilly* bar: *Loughinsholin*

Green Lough takes its name from a little lake which was situated 2km north-west of the village of **Inishrush** and was drained towards the end of the 19th century. The lake is said to have been named Green Lough from the greenness of the surrounding hills. The name contrasts with nearby BLACK LOUGH, a small lake which has also been drained and was so named because of its dark peaty water. Green Lough is the site of a *crannog* or lake island which was formerly the residence of Brian Carragh O'Neill (*see* ***Inishrush***).

**Gresteel** tls, vill., Derry 2542
(often *Greysteel*)
*13km NE of Derry city*
par: *Faughanvale* bar: *Tirkeeran*
Ir. *Glas-stiall* [**glas-**styeeal] 'grey strip (of land)'. The townlands of GRESTEEL BEG 'little Gresteel' and GRESTEEL MORE 'big Gresteel' border on **Lough Foyle** [*Glasteles* 1622].

**Greyabbey** tl, vill., par., Down 3536
(sometimes *Grey Abbey*)
*10.5km SE of Newtownards*
bar: *Ards Lower*
Greyabbey is a translation of Ir. *Mainistir Liath* [manishchir **lee**a] and is named after a Cistercian abbey founded in 1193 by Affreca, wife of John de Courcy, the ruins of which stand at the east side of the village. In the earliest written reference Greyabbey is also referred to as *Whit Abbey*, with the *alias* Latin name *Jugum Dei*, i.e. 'yoke of God' [*Monasterlech* 1193].

**Greystone** ham., Tyrone 2735
*7km SW of Dungannon*
par: *Clonfeacle* bar: *Dungannon Middle*
The name Greystone most likely refers to some kind of megalith such as a standing stone or a cairn, but no trace or record now remains.

*Greyabbey*

**Groomsport** tl, vill., Down 3538
*On N Down coast, 3.5km NE of Bangor*
par: *Bangor* bar: *Ards Lower*
Ir. *Port an Ghiolla Ghruama* [port a yilla **ġrooma**] 'port of the gloomy fellow'. An earlier name for Groomsport appears to have been *Mallorytown* and Ir. *giolla gruama* 'gloomy fellow' may reflect the meaning of the Anglo-Norman surname Mallory which derives from O.F. *maloret* 'the unfortunate, the unlucky' [*Mollerytoun* 1333].

**Gulladuff** tl, vill., Derry 2839
*5km ESE of Maghera*
par: *Maghera* bar: *Loughinsholin*
Ir. *Guala Dhubh* [goola **ġoo**] 'black hill-shoulder' [*galladow* 1609].

**Gweebarra** inl., distr., Donegal 1739
*On W Donegal coast, 5km NW of Glenties*
par: *Inishkeel/Lettermacaward* bar: *Boylagh*
Ir. *Gaoth Beara* [gee **bar**a] 'estuary of the (river) *Bior*'. *Bior* 'water', was the original name of the GWEEBARRA RIVER which flows into GWEEBARRA BAY. It is now known in Ir. as either *Abhainn Bheara* [owen **var**a] 'river of *Bior*' or *Abhainn Ghaoth Bheara* 'river of Gweebarra'. The river rises in LOUGH BARRA 18km to the north-east. The Ir. word *gaoth* in the sense of 'estuary' is now obsolete.

**Gweedore** RC par., distr., Donegal 1842
*Forms the NW corner of Donegal*
par: *Tullaghobegly* bar: *Kilmacrenan*
Ir. *Gaoth Dobhair* [gee **doar**] 'estuary of the (river) *Dobhar*'. The name was originally applied to the long, narrow inlet of the sea (still known in Ir. as *An Gaoth* 'the inlet') between the district of Gweedore and the district of **The Rosses** which adjoins it on the south. The final element of the place-name, i.e. *Dobhar* 'water', is represented by the name of the townland of DORE which borders the inlet on the north. However, it originally referred to the river now known in E. as the GWEEDORE RIVER and in Ir. as *Abhainn Chroithlí* i.e. 'Crolly River' which flows into the inlet. The Catholic parish of Gweedore which forms part of the civil parish of TULLAGHOBEGLY was formerly known as *Tullaghobegly West* [*Gydower al. Lower Dower* 1657].

# H

**Hamiltonsbawn** tl, vill., Armagh 2934
(sometimes *Hamilton's Bawn*)
*7km E of Armagh city*
par: *Mullaghbrack* bar: *Fews Lower*
Hamiltonsbawn takes its name from a *bawn* or fortified mansion built in 1619 by John Hamilton of East Lothian in Scotland and destroyed in the 1641 rebellion. John Hamilton was of that family of Hamiltons who acquired extensive lands in north Down at the beginning of the 17th century and a descendant of whom founded **Newtownhamilton** c.1770 [*Hamilton's-Bawn* 1681].

**Hannahstown** tl, vill., Antrim 3337
*8km W of Belfast*
par: *Shankill* bar: *Belfast Upper*
The first element of this place-name is the Scottish surname Hanna(h) which is almost exclusive to Ulster, the majority of Hannahs being found in Cos Antrim, Down and Armagh. The Hanna(h)s originated in Galloway and most of that surname in Ulster settled here between 1640 and 1690 [*Hannahstown* 1780].

**Harryville** distr., Antrim 3140
*Forms suburb on SE side of the town of Ballymena*
par: *Ballyclug* bar: *Antrim Lower*
Harryville, in the townland of BALLYKEEL, was named after Henry O'Hara who resided at the nearby CREBILLY HOUSE in the 18th century [*the village of HarryVille* 1756].

**Helen's Bay** vill., Down 3438
*5km W of Bangor*
par: *Bangor* bar: *Castlereagh Lower*
Helen's Bay is in the townland of BALLYGROT and was named after Helen Selina Sheridan by her son Frederick Hamilton-Temple-Blackwood, 5th Lord Dufferin [1826–1902] who resided at **Clandeboy** near Bangor and who also named HELEN'S TOWER in Clandeboy estate in his mother's memory.

**Herveyhill** ham., Derry 2840
(sometimes *Harvey Hill*)
*9km NNE of Maghera*
par: *Tamlaght O'Crilly* bar: *Loughinsholin*
Ir. *Airbhigh* [**ar**avee] 'place of hedges/enclosures' + E. 'hill'. Herveyhill is in the townland of KILLYGULLIB GLEBE [*The Glebe House al. Hervey Hill* 1836].

**Hillhall** tl, vill., Down 3236
*1.5km E of Lisburn*
par: *Drumbeg* bar: *Castlereagh Upper*
The name Hillhall refers to a former house and defensive *bawn* which appears to have been built c.1637 by Peter Hill, son of Sir Moses Hill from Devonshire who was Provost Marshall of Ulster at the end of the 16th century. The remains of the house and *bawn* stand at THE COURT, a short distance west of the present HILLHALL HOUSE. The village of Hillhall is not in the townland of that name but is partly in LISNATRUNK and partly in BALLYMULLAN. The townland of Hillhall was formerly known as *Kilmuck* or *Down Kilmuck* which is possibly a corruption of *Cloncolmoc* (Ir. *Cluain Cholmóg* 'meadow of little *Colmán*') the name of a church recorded in 1306, though there is no record of ecclesiastical remains and the identification must be regarded as tentative [*Ballidunkillmuck al. Hillhall* 1831].

**Hillsborough** tl, tn, par., Down 3235
*5.5km SSW of Lisburn*
bar: *Iveagh Lower, Upper Half*
The name Hillsborough was originally applied to a fortress built c.1610 by Sir Moses Hill, Provost Marshall of Ulster, at **Malone** near Belfast, on the Co. Antrim side of the river **Lagan**. In the 1650s the same name was applied to a gatehouse built by his son Arthur on the present site of **Hillsborough**. A portion of this gatehouse is incorporated into HILLSBOROUGH FORT which stands near the Church of Ireland parish church, in the townland of LARGE PARK. The site of the original chapel of Hillsborough, which was known as *Crumlin* (Ir. *Cromghlinn* 'crooked glen'), is marked by a graveyard in the townland of SMALL PARK [*Crumlin Parish* 1661].

**Hilltown** vill., Down 3232
*4.5km S of Rathfriland*
par: *Clonduff* bar: *Iveagh Upper, Lower Part*
The village of Hilltown in the townland of CARCULLION grew up after the construction of a church here in 1766 by Wills Hill, 1st

Marquis of Downshire, a descendant of the family who gave name to **Hillsborough** and **Hillhall**. In earlier times the village was known as *The Eight Mile Bridge*, referring to a bridge over the **Upper Bann** eight Irish miles from **Newry** [*8 Mile Br.* 1743].

**Holywell** vill., Fermanagh 3034
*1km NW of Belcoo*
par: *Cleenish* bar: *Clanawley*
The name Holywell refers to a well-preserved holy well in the townland of CAVANCARRAGH. The well is dedicated to St Patrick and was known in Ir. as *Dabhach Phádraig* [dau-agh **fad**rick] '(St) Patrick's well'. It stands close to the ruins of an early church known as *Templerushin or Holywell* [*Holywell* 1835].

**Holywood** tl, tn, par., Down 3437
*Town is 7.5km NE of Belfast*
bar: *Castlereagh Lower*
The name Holywood originated with the Normans and was applied, sometimes in the Latin form *Sanctus Boscus*, to the woodland adjoining the ancient church. The wood in question appears to be that represented in the former name of the townland, i.e. *Ballyderry* (Ir. *Baile Doire* 'townland of the oak-wood'). The site of an early church is marked by the ruins of the 13th-century parish church, later a Franciscan friary, in the adjoining townland of BALLYKEEL. The Ir. name for Holywood is *Ard Mhic Nasca* [ard vick **nask**a] 'height of the son of *Nasca*', the son of *Nasca* being Saint *Laisrén* [(*o*) *Art maic Nasca* c.830].

**Horn Head** hl, Donegal 2044
*5km N of Dunfanaghy*
par: *Clondahorky* bar: *Kilmacrenan*
Ir. *Corrán Binne* [korran **bin**ya] 'crescent of the cliff'. The rendition of Ir. *Corrán* as E. *horn* is partly due to corruption but also partly to translation, 'horn' referring to the horn-shaped crescent of the outline of the cliff top here. In 1837 the mansion of Horn Head is referred to as 'a gentleman's seat, the residence of W. Stewart Esq.'.

**Hulin Rocks** Antrim 3441
(see ***Maidens, The or Hulin Rocks***)

# I

**Imeroo** tl, ham., Fermanagh 2335
*3.5km NE of Tempo*
par: *Enniskillen* bar: *Tirkennedy*
Ir. *Ime Rua* [ima **roo**a] 'red dam/weir'. The TEMPO RIVER forms the western boundary of the townland [*Imrowe* 1659].

**Inch** isld, par., Donegal 2342
*In Lough Swilly, 5km S of Buncrana*
bar: *Inishowen West*
Ir. *An Inis* [an **in**ish] 'the island'. The island of Inch, which is co-extensive with the parish, is now joined by a bridge to the eastern shore of **Lough Swilly**. The parish of Inch was formed in 1809 out of the parish of TEMPLEMORE which is now entirely in Co. Derry. Inch has given name to the townland of INCH LEVEL (INTAKE) which lies opposite it on the mainland and consists of land reclaimed from the sea. INCH TOP (200m) is the highest point on the island [*Insh* c.1659].

**Inishbeg** isld, tl, Donegal 1843
*Off NW Donegal coast, 6km N of Magheraroarty*
par: *Tullaghobegly* bar: *Kilmacrenan*
Ir. *Inis Beag* [inish **beg**] 'little island'. Inishbeg is so-named because it is the smallest in a group of three islands which lie between **Tory Island** and the mainland, the other two islands being **Inishbofin** and **Inishdooey** [*Innisbeg* 1837].

**Inishbofin** isld, tl, Donegal 1843
(sometimes *Inishbofinne*)
*Off NW Donegal coast, 2.5km N of Magheraroarty*
par: *Tullaghobegly* bar: *Kilmacrenan*
Ir. *Inis Bó Finne* [inish bo **fin**ya] 'island of the white cow'. A number of Irish islands carry this name and all the names have their origins in legends about a white cow appearing above the water as a symbol of fertility and regeneration [*Inisbofin* 1639].

**Inishdooey** isld, tl, Donegal 1843
*Off NW Donegal coast, 1km N of Inishbofin*
par: *Tullaghobegly* bar: *Kilmacrenan*
Ir. *Oileán Dúiche* [illan **doo**igha]. The modern form of the place-name appears to be a development from the original name *Inis Dubhthaigh* [inish **doo**ee] '*Dubhthach*'s island',

where *Dubhthach* is explained as the name of a local saint (*cf.* ***Aghadowey** above*).

**Inishfree Upper** isld, tl, Donegal 1741
(sometimes *Inishfraoich*)
*Off W coast of Donegal, 4.5km W of Dunglow*
par: *Templecrone* bar: *Boylagh*
Ir. *Inis Fraoigh* [inish **free**] 'island of heather' + E. *upper*. The island of INISHFREE LOWER lies 11.5km to the north-north-east, in the parish of TULLAGHOBEGLY [*isle of Inishfry* 1629].

**Inishkeen** vill., par., Monaghan 2930
(sometimes *Inniskeen*)
*Village close to Louth border, is 8.5km NE of Carrickmacross*
bar: *Farney*
Ir. *Inis Caoin* [inish **keen**] 'pleasant river meadow'. The village of Inishkeen is on the south bank of the river FANE, in the townland of INISHKEEN GLEBE. The site of an early monastery is marked by the stump of a round tower in a graveyard on the opposite side of the river. A portion of the parish is in Co. Louth [(*Daig mac Cairill*) *Insi Cáin* c.830].

**Inishkeeragh** isld, Donegal 1641
*Off W Donegal coast, 2km S of Arranmore Island*
par: *Templecrone* bar: *Boylagh*
Ir. *Inis Caorach* [inish **keer**agh] 'island of sheep'. A number of other Irish islands carry this name.

**Inishmacsaint** isld, tl, par., Fermanagh 2135
*Island is in Lower Lough Erne, 12.5km NW of Enniskillen*
bar: *Magheraboy*
Ir. *Inis Maighe Samh* [inish mwee **sau**] 'island of the sorrel plain'. The little island contains the ruins of the medieval parish church which in turn mark the site of a sixth-century monastery founded by St *Ninnidh*. The parish is extensive and includes a small portion in the barony of TIRHUGH in Co. Donegal [(*mac persúin*) *Innsi Maighe Samh* 1530].

**Inishmeane** isld, tl, Donegal 1742
*Off NW coast of Donegal, 4km NW of Derrybeg*
par: *Tullaghobegly* bar: *Kilmacrenan*
Ir. *Inis Meáin* [inish **maan**] 'middle island'. The island takes its name from its middle position between the islands of **Gola** and **Inishsirrer** [*Inismahan* 1830].

**Inishowen** pen., bars, Donegal
*Forms NE portion of Co. Donegal*
Ir. *Inis Eoghain* [inish **o**an] 'Owen's peninsula'. According to legend, the Owen who gave name to Inishowen was one of the many sons of *Niall Naoighiallach* or 'Niall of the Nine Hostages'. The latter is reputed to have ruled Ireland from Tara in the fifth century. Two of *Niall*'s other sons were *Conall*, who gave name to *Tír Chonaill*, i.e. *Tirconnell* or 'land of *Conall*', a name which originally referred to the west of Donegal but is now applied to the whole county (*see* ***Donegal***), and *Éanna* who gave name to *Tír Éanna* 'land of Enda', a now-obsolete name originally referring to south-east Donegal. The baronies of INISHOWEN EAST and INISHOWEN WEST form the northern and southern portions of the peninsula respectively [(*i*) *nInis Eoghain* 465].

**Inishowen Head** hl, Donegal 2644
(*see* ***Stroove***)

**Inishrush** tl, vill., Derry 2940
*3km W of Portglenone*
par: *Tamlaght O'Crilly* bar: *Loughinsholin*
Ir. *Inis Rois* [inish **rush**] 'island of the wood'. The island referred to was in a little lake known as **Green Lough** which was drained in the 19th century (*see above*). It is the site of a *crannog* which is reputed to have been the residence of *Brian Carrach Ó Néill* 'rough-skinned Brian O'Neill' who ruled over lands on both sides of the **Lower Bann** in the 16th century. At an earlier period Inishrush was also the name of a *ballybetagh* which included some thirty townlands stretching northwards from the **Clady** river [*Inishroisse* 1615].

*Iniskeeragh, island of sheep*

**Inishsirrer** isld, tl, Donegal 1743
*Off NW Donegal coast, 5km NW of Derrybeg*
par: *Tullaghobegly* bar: *Kilmacrenan*
Ir. *Inis Oirthir* [inish **urr**hir] 'eastern island'. The island is so-named because it is the eastern-most in a group of three islands, the other two being **Gola** and **Inishmeane**.

**Inishtrahull** isld, tl, Donegal 2446
*In Atlantic ocean, 10km NE of Malin Head*
par: *Clonca* bar: *Inishowen East*
Ir. *Inis Trá Tholl* [inish tra **hull**]. The current Ir. form of the name appears to be a development from an earlier form, perhaps *Inis Dá Thul* 'island of the two hillocks' [*Ennistrahul* 1837].

**Inver** vill., par., Donegal 1837
*Village is 10km W of Donegal town*
bar: *Banagh*
Ir. *Inbhear* [**in**ver] 'river-mouth/estuary'. Inver stands at the point where the EANY WATER enters INVER BAY, an inlet of the much larger **Donegal Bay**. The name is a shortened form of *Inbhear Náile* [inver **naal**a] 'estuary of (St) *Náile*'. The ruins of a 15th-century Franciscan monastery in the townland of INVER GLEBE mark the site of the early monastery founded by St *Náile*, while the adjoining townland is named LEGNAWLEY GLEBE (Ir. *Log Náile* '(St) *Náile*'s hollow' + E. *glebe*) (cf. ***Kinawley*** in Fermanagh) [(*Noele*) *Inbir* c.830].

**Irvinestown** tn, Fermanagh 2235
*14.5km N of Enniskillen, on the border with Tyrone*
par: *Derryvullan* bar: *Lurg*
Irvinestown, which has portions in each of the three townlands of TOWNHILL, MILLTATE and BROWNHILL, was formerly known as *Lowtherstown*, from Sir Gerard Lowther who founded it in 1618 on the Plantation estate of NEKARNE (Ir. *Na Cairn* 'the heaps'). In 1667 the estate was sold to Sir Christopher Irvine, a marriage relation of Lowther, who gave name to the nearby *Castle Irvine* (now known as NECARNE CASTLE). However, the village continued to be known as *Lowtherstown* until early in the 19th century when Henry Mervyn D'Arcy Irvine changed its name to Irvinestown [*Irvinestown or Lowtherstown* 1837].

**Island Magee** pen., par., Antrim 3440
(sometimes *Islandmagee*)
*On E Antrim coast, to the north of Whitehead*
bar: *Belfast Lower*
Ir. *Oileán Mhic Aodha* [illan vick **ee**] 'Magee's island/peninsula'. The family of *Mac Aodha* 'Magee' who gave name to Island Magee were a prominent Irish sept. An earlier Ir. name for Island Magee was *Rinn Seimhne* [rin **shev**na] 'peninsula of (the district of) *Seimhne*' where *Seimhne* seems to be originally a tribal name which has been transferred to the district. An old graveyard in the townland of BALLYPRIOR MORE appears to mark the site of the former parish church [*Rensevin* 1251].

**Isle of Muck** isld, Antrim 3440
(see ***Portmuck***)

# J

**Jerrettspass** vill., Armagh 3033
*6.5km NNW of Newry*
par: *Killevy* bar: *Orior Lower*
*Jerrett* is a variant form of the surname *Garrett* which is common in the north-east of Ireland and is derived from *Gerald*, a name introduced by the Normans. An earlier name for Jerrettspass was *Tuscan's Pass*, the origin of which is obscure. Jerrettspass is in the townland of KILMONAGHAN [*Gerrard* (*Pass*) 1835].

**Jonesborough** vill., par., Armagh 3031
*Village is 9km S of Newry*
bar: *Orior Upper*
The village of Jonesborough in the townland of FOUGHILL OTRA was founded in 1706 by Roth Jones who was landlord of the area in the early 18th century. The parish was formed in 1760 out of the more northerly parish of BALLY-MORE and six townlands from the parish of BALLYMASCANLAN in Co. Louth were added in 1861. An alias name for the village was *Four Mile House* while the Ir. name is *Baile an Chláir* [bala an **chlar**] 'town of the plain' [*4 Milehouse al. Jones Borough* 1714].

**Jordanstown** tl, vill., Antrim 3338
*Village forms a district of Newtownabbey, 10km N of Belfast city centre*
par: *Carnmoney* bar: *Belfast Lower*
The place is named from an Anglo-Norman family called Jordan who accompanied John de Courcy to **Carrickfergus** in 1182. The surname Jordan is ultimately derived from the river Jordan, the name of which was used a Christian name by returning crusaders who brought back Jordan water to baptise their children [*Bally Jurdon* 1604].

# K

**Katesbridge** vill., Down 3234
*9.5km SE of Banbridge*
par: *Drumballyroney/Newry (detached portion)* bar: *Iveagh Upper, Lower Half*
The village of Katesbridge straddles the **Upper Bann**, the bridge linking the townlands of BALLYBRICK and SHANNAGHAN. It was named after Kate McKay who is said to have owned the house where the workmen lodged when building the bridge in the 18th century [*McCay's Bridge* 1744].

**Keady** tn, par., Armagh 2833
*10km S of Armagh*
bar: *Armagh*
Ir. *An Céide* [an **kedg**a] 'the flat-topped hill'. The parish of Keady formed part of the neighbouring parish of **Derrynoose** until 1773 [*An Chéideadh* c.1854].

**Kells** tl, vill., Antrim 3139
*7km SE of Ballymena*
par: *Connor* bar: *Antrim Lower*
Ir. *Na Cealla* [na **kal**a] 'the monastic cells/churches'. Another Ir. name for Kells was *Díseart Choinnire* [jeeshart **khon**yira] 'hermitage of Connor', so called because at an early date it was a hermitage or monastic retreat for the nearby monastery of **Connor**, the twin village of Kells [(*Abbas de*) *Disert* c.1190].

**Kells Water** river, Antrim
(sometimes *Kellswater*)
*The lower portion of the Glenwhirry River, from the point where it flows past the village of Kells to the point where it joins the Main, 5.5km S of Ballymena*
par: *Connor* bar: *Antrim Lower*
The Kells Water takes its name from the village of **Kells** which stands close to the south bank of the river, 7km south-east of **Ballymena** [*Kells Water* 1833].

**Kerrykeel** tl, vill., Donegal 2243
(see ***Carrowkeel***)

**Kesh** vill., Fermanagh 2136
*7.5km ESE of Pettigoe*
par: *Magheraculmoney* bar: *Lurg*
Ir. *An Cheis* [an **khesh**] 'the wickerwork causeway'. The village of Kesh is on the south bank of the KESH RIVER, close to the point where it enters **Lower Lough Erne**. It was founded on the Plantation estate of Thomas Blenerhasset. Most of the village is in the townland of ROSSCOLBAN [*Kesh* 1834].

**Kilcar** tl, vill, par., Donegal 1637
*10km W of Killybegs*
bar: *Banagh*
Ir. *Cill Charthaigh* [kill **khar**hee] '(St) *Carthach*'s church'. Kilcar is named from the sixth-century saint and bishop *Carthach* who was a son of the king of CASHEL in Munster. The site of his monastery is marked by a holy well named *Tobar Charthaigh* '(St) *Carthach*'s well'. The village is usually known in Ir. as *Baile an Droichid* [bala an **dry**hidge] 'town of the bridge', from a bridge over the BALLAGHDOO RIVER [*Cill Carthaigh* c.1630].

**Kilclief** tl, par., Down 3534
*Townland is on the coast, 10.5km E of Downpatrick*
bar: *Lecale Lower*
Ir. *Cill Chléithe* [kill **chley**ha] 'church of wattle'. The modern Church of Ireland church appears to occupy the site of previous early and medieval churches [(*i*) *Cill Chlethi* c.1125].

**Kilcogy** tl, vill., Cavan 2328
*Close to Longford border, 7.5km NE of Granard*
par: *Drumlumman* bar: *Clanmahon*
Ir. *Cill Chóige* [kill **kho**iga] 'church of the

*Kilclief Castle*

fifth'. The term 'fifth' refers to a land division which clearly formed a fifth of some larger unit. There is now no trace or record of a church here [*Kilcoaga* 1611].

**Kilcoo** vill., par., Down 3233
*Village is 8.5km E of Rathfriland*
bar: *Iveagh Upper, Lower Half*
Ir. *Cill Chua* [kill **khoo**a] '(St) *Cua*'s church'. The ruins of the old church and the old graveyard of Kilcoo are close to the river MUDDOCK, in the townland of BALLYMONEY. The village of Kilcoo is at the intersection of the three townlands of BALLYMONEY, MOYAD and FOFANNYREAGH [*Killcow al. Ballynemony* 1609].

**Kilcronaghan** ham., par., Derry 2839
*Hamlet is 2.5km SW of Tobermore*
bar: *Loughinsholin*
Ir. *Cill Chruithneacháin* [kill **khrin**aghine] '(St) Cronaghan's church'. The Cronaghan who gave name to the parish is said to have been the priest who fostered St Colmcille. Fragments of the medieval church seem to have been incorporated in an early 19th-century church, the ruins of which are in an old graveyard in the townland of MORMEAL [(*go*) *Cill Cruineacháin* c.1645].

**Kildress** tls, par., Tyrone 2737
*Townlands are 4km W of Cookstown*
bar: *Dungannon Upper*
Ir. *Cill Dreas* [kill **drass**] 'church of (the) brambles'. The ruins of the former parish church are in an old graveyard on the south bank of the BALLINDERRY RIVER in the townland of KILDRESS UPPER which is bordered on the east by KILDRESS LOWER [*Kildressce* 1302].

**Kilfullert** tl, Down 3135
*9.5km N of Banbridge*
par: *Magheralin*
bar: *Iveagh Lower, Upper Half*
Ir. *Coill Fulachta* [kill **full**aghta] 'wood of the cooking place'. Ir. *fulacht* or *fulacht fia* is used as an archaeological term referring to an outdoor cooking pit, usually beside a stream [*Ballykillyfollyat* 1609].

**Kilkeel** tl, tn, par., Down 3331
*Town is on Co. Down coast, 13km ESE of Rostrevor*
bar: *Mourne*
Ir. *Cill Chaoil* [kill **kheel**] *perhaps* 'church of the narrow place'. The term 'narrow place' may refer to the situation of the medieval church (now in ruins) near the confluence of the AUGHRIM RIVER with the KILKEEL RIVER [*Kylkeyl* 1369].

**Kill** vill., Cavan 2530
*5km SSW of Cootehill*
par: *Kildrumsherdan* bar: *Tullygarvey*
Ir. *An Chill* [an **khill**] 'the church'. Kill is a shortened form of KILDRUMSHERDAN (Ir. *Cill Dhroim Shirideáin* 'church of *Sirideán*'s ridge'), the name of the parish in which it is situated. The personal name *Sirideán* is the basis of the surname *Ó Sirideáin* '(O')Sheridan', which originated in Longford and became prominent in the neighbouring county of Cavan. There is now no trace of the medieval parish church which stood in the townland of DRUMHURT [(*termon land of*) *the Kill* 1609].

**Killadeas** ham., Fermanagh 2235
*5km SW of Irvinestown*
par: *Trory* bar: *Lurg*
Ir. *Cill Chéile Dé* [kill khela **jey**] 'church of the *Culdee*'. A *Culdee* (literally 'servant of God') was a member of a group of monastic reformers with its origins in the eighth century. The modern Church of Ireland church in the townland of ROCKFIELD occupies the site of an early church, known as the *Yellow Church*, which belonged to the *Culdees* of nearby **Devinish** island.

**Killagan** vill., par., Antrim 3041
*Village is 3.5km NW of Clogh Mills*
bar: *Dunluce Upper/Kilconway*
*Ir. Cill Lagáin* [kill **lag**ine] 'church of the lowlying district'. In the townland of

BROUGHANORE there is an old graveyard, locally known as KILL GRAVEYARD, which marks the site of the former parish church of Killagan [(*ecclesia de*) *Killagan* 1622].

**Killaloo** tl, ham., Derry 2540
*3km NW of Claudy*
par: *Cumber Lower* bar: *Tirkeeran*
Ir. *Coill an Lao* [kill a **lee**] 'wood of the calf' [*Kille Loy* 1613].

**Killashandra** tn, par., Cavan 2330
(sometimes *Killeshandra*)
*10km W of Cavan town*
bar: *Tullyhunco*
Ir. *Cill na Seanrátha* [kill na **shan**raha] 'church of the old fort'. The original church was constructed inside a ring fort and a portion of the latter survives in the graveyard of the present Church of Ireland church [*Kylshanra* 1432].

**Killead** ham., par., Antrim 3137
*5.5km SSE of Antrim town*
bar: *Massereene Lower*
Ir. *Cill Éad* [kill **aid**]. The first element of the place-name is Ir. *cill* 'church' but the meaning of the final element is obscure. The hamlet of Killead, which contains the modern Church of Ireland church, is in the townland of SEACASH. However, the medieval parish church (of which no trace remains) was roughly 3km to the north-east in the townland of KILLEALY and close to the village named KILLEAD CORNER [*Killede* 1605].

**Killeen** tl, ham., Tyrone 2836
*4km NE of Coalisland*
par: *Clonoe* bar: *Dungannon Middle*
Ir. *An Cillín* [an **kill**een] 'the little church'. There is now no trace or record of a church in the townland [*Killeene* 1633].

**Killeeshil** tl, par., Tyrone 2635
*Townland is 6km NE of Ballygawley*
bar: *Dungannon Lower*
Ir. *Cill Íseal* [kill **eesh**il] 'low church'. The present Church of Ireland church marks the site of an early monastery. The parish of Killeeshil was created in 1732 out of the neighbouring parish of **Carnteel** [*Killissyll* 1455].

**Killen** tls, vill., Tyrone 2238
*Village is 4.5km SSW of Castlederg*
par: *Termonamongan* bar: *Omagh West*
Ir. *Cillín* [**kill**een] 'little church'. The village of Killen is in the townland of KILLEN NEAR which is adjoined on the south by KILLEN FAR. There is now no trace or record of a church in either townland [*Killen* c.1655].

**Killeter** tl, vill., Tyrone 2238
*7km SW of Castlederg*
par: *Termonamongan* bar: *Omagh West*
Ir. *Coill Íochtair* [kill **eegh**ter] 'lower wood'. The village of Killeter is mainly in the neighbouring townland of CRILLY'S HILL. KILLETER BRIDGE, a short distance to the north-east, links the townlands of MAGHERANAGEERAGH and WOODSIDE, across the river **Derg** [*Keliter* 1613].

**Killevy** ch., par., Armagh 3032
(sometimes *Killeavy*)
*Church is 6km SW of Newry*
bar: *Orior Upper*
Ir. *Cill Shléibhe* [kill **ley**va] 'church of the mountain'. The church was so-named from its position at the foot of **Slieve Gullion** (573m) in the townland of BALLINTEMPLE (Ir. *Baile an Teampaill* 'townland of the church') where the ruins can still be seen. The parish of Killevy is partly in the barony of ORIOR LOWER [(*Darercae*) *Cille sleibe Cuilinn* 517].

**Killinchy** tl, vill., par., Down 3536
*Village is 9km SSE of Comber*
bar: *Dufferin*
Ir. *Cill Dhuinsí* [kill **ġinsh**ee] '(St) *Duinseach*'s church'. *Duinseach* was a female saint of the Early Christian period who has also given name to the nearby DUNSY ISLAND in **Strangford Lough**. The modern Church of Ireland church occupies the site of the medieval parish church [(*o*) *Cill Dunsighe* c.1400].

**Killins** tls, Antrim 2941
(sometimes *Killans*)
*9km S of Ballymoney*
par: *Finvoy* bar: *Kilconway*
Ir. *Na Coillíní* [na **kill**eenee] 'the little woods'. The townland of KILLINS NORTH is bordered by KILLINS SOUTH [*Killenes* 1669].

**Killough** tl, vill., Down 3533
*On the coast, 9.5km SE of Downpatrick*
par: *Rathmullan* bar: *Lecale Upper*
Ir. *Cill Locha* [kill **logh**a] 'church of the lough'. There is now no trace of an ancient

church but the site may be marked by a mound named KNOCKAVALLEY where there was formerly an old cemetery. If this be so, the lough in question may be the inlet of the sea known as KILLOUGH HARBOUR. In the early 18th century Michael Ward, father of the 1st Lord Bangor, developed the village and renamed it *Port St Anne* in honour of his wife but the new name did not take hold [*Killogh* 1710].

**Killowen** vill., Down. 3131
*On the coast, 3km SE of Rostrevor*
par: *Kilbroney* bar: *Iveagh Upper, Upper Half*
Ir. *Cill Eoghain* [kill **o**an] 'Owen's church'. The site of the church which gave rise to the place-name is unknown. Killowen is in the townland of BALLINRAN and has given name to the nearby townland of KILLOWEN MOUNTAINS [*Kelcone* 1595].

**Killybegs** tl, tn, pars, Donegal 1737
*Town is on N shore of Donegal Bay, 22km W of Donegal town*
par: *Killybegs Upper* bar: *Banagh*
Ir. *Na Cealla Beaga* [na kala **beg**a] 'the little churches/monastic cells'. Killybegs is named from an early monastic settlement on the site of which a Franciscan friary was founded in the 15th century by MacSweeney of Banagh but no trace of either establishment now remains. The town of Killybegs is in the parish of KILLYBEGS UPPER while the parish of KILLYBEGS LOWER lies some 8km to the north-east and is partly in the barony of BOYLAGH [*(cuan) na cCeall mBicc* 1513].

**Killyclogher** tl, Tyrone 2437
*3km NE of Omagh*
par: *Cappagh* bar: *Strabane Upper*
Ir. *Coillidh Chlochair* [killy **chlogh**er] 'wood of the stony place' [*Killclogher* c.1655].

**Killycolpy** tl, ham., Tyrone 2937
*12km SE of Cookstown*
par: *Arboe* bar: *Dungannon Upper*
Ir. *Coill an Cholpa* [kill a **khol**pa] 'wood of the steeror heifer' [*Kilcolpy* 1639].

**Killycomain** tl, distr., Armagh 3035
*Forms the easternmost portion of the town of Portadown*
par: *Seagoe* bar: *Oneilland East*
Ir. *Coill Mhic Giolla Mhíchíl* [kill vick gilla **vee**heel] 'McElmeel's wood'. The surname *Mac Giolla Mhíchíl* ('son of *Giolla Mhíchíl*' or 'son of the devotee of St Michael') can also be anglicised as MacMichael and is usually associated with Fermanagh [*Killykillvehall* 1657].

**Killygarn** tl, Antrim 2939
*5km SSE of Portglenone*
par: *Portglenone* bar: *Toome Lower*
Ir. *Coill na gCarn* [kill na **garn**] 'wood of the cairns' [*Ballichilnegarne* 1606].

**Killygordon** tl, vill., Donegal 2239
*On N bank of the Finn, 5km E of Stranorlar*
par: *Donaghmore* bar: *Raphoe*
Ir. *Cúil na gCuirridín* [kool na **gurr**ideen] 'corner/angle of the horsetail ferns'. The Mod. Ir. form may be a development from the original *Coill na gCuirridín* 'wood of the horsetail ferns' [*(ó bhealach-) Choille na cCuirritín* 1523].

**Killykergan** tl, ham., Derry 2841
*3.5km N of Garvagh*
par: *Aghadowey* bar: *Coleraine*
Ir. *Coill Uí Chiaragáin* [kill ee **kheer**agine] '(O')Kerrigan's wood'. The surname *Ó Ciaragáin* '(O')Kerrigan, (O')Kergan' which is associated with Mayo was also common in Donegal and Tyrone at the end of the 16th century [*Killakerrigan* 1654].

**Killylea** tl, vill., Armagh 2934
*7.5km W of Armagh city*
par: *Tynan* bar: *Armagh*
Ir. *Coillidh Léith* [killy **ley**] 'grey wood' [*Killeleagh* 1657].

**Killyleagh** tn, par., Down 3535
*Town is on W shore of Strangford Lough, 8.5km NNE of Downpatrick*
bar: *Dufferin*
Ir. *Cill Ó Laoch* [kill o **lee**agh] 'church of the descendants of *Laoch*'. It is possible that *Laoch* is a variant spelling of *Luighdheach* [**lee**agh], a genitive form of *Lughaidh* [**loo**ee] which was a popular name in early Ireland. The ruins of the medieval parish church are 1km north of the town centre, in the large townland of CORPORATION. A small portion of the parish of Killyleagh is in the barony of CASTLEREAGH UPPER [*Cill Ó Laoch* c.1645].

**Killyman** vill., par., Tyrone 2737
*Village is 4km ESE of Dungannon*
bar: *Dungannon Middle*

Ir. *Cill na mBan* [kill na **man**] 'church of the women'. Killyman is in the townland of LAGHEY which contains the site of an ancient church and graveyard, west of the modern church of St Andrew [*Cill na mBan* c.1645].

**Killyrover** tl, Fermanagh 2333
*5km NW of Lisnaskea*
par: *Aghalurcher* bar: *Magherastephana*
Ir. *Coillidh Ramhar* [killy **rau**er] 'broad wood' [*Killyrower* 1817].

**Kilmacrenan** tl, vill., par/bar, Donegal 2142
(sometimes *Kilmacrennan*)
*Village is 8.5km NNW of Letterkenny*
Ir. *Cill Mhic Réanáin* [kill vick **ren**ine]. The modern form of the place-name is a late medieval development from the original *Cill Mhac nÉanáin* [kill wack **nen**ine] 'church of the sons of *Éanán*'. According to *Adhamhnán* (Eunan), the biographer of St Colmcille, *Éanán* was married to Colmcille's sister and his sons include a saint named *Colman Iomramha* '*Colmán* of the vogage' whose name appears to be commemorated in KILLYCOLMAN, the name of a townland near **Rathmullan** on the west shore of **Lough Swilly**. The original name of Kilmacrenan was *Doire Eithne* [dirra **en**ya] '*Eithne*'s oak-wood', *Eithne* being the mother of St Colmcille who founded a monastery here. The site of the original monastery of St Colmcille is a short distance north-east of the village and is marked by the ruins of a Franciscan friary built by the O'Donnells in the 15th century [(*i*) *cCill mic Nénain* 1129].

**Kilmore** tl, vill., par., Armagh 2935
*Village is 7km SW of Portadown*
bar: *Oneilland West*
Ir. *An Chill Mhór* [an khill **wore**] 'the great church'. The present Church of Ireland church marks the site of an early church. In 1120 Kilmore is referred to as *Cillmor Ua Niallain* 'Kilmore of *Uí Nialláin*', the final element being the territory represented by the modern barony of ONEILLAND.

**Kilmore** tl, vill., par., Down 3435
*Village is 1.5km SW of Crossgar*
bar: *Castlereagh Upper*
Ir. *An Chill Mhór* [an khill **wore**] 'the great church'. The site of the medieval parish church is marked by an old graveyard in the neighbouring townland of CARNACALLY, a short distance west of the modern Church of Ireland church [*Kilmore Moran* 1622].

**Kilnaleck** tl, vill., Cavan 2429
*13km SSE of Cavan town*
par: *Crosserlough* bar: *Castlerahan*
Ir. *Cill na Leice* [kill na **leck**a] 'church of the (flag-)stone'. The townland was formerly church land, belonging to the bishop of Kilmore. The church referred to is said to be that whose ruins stand in the townland of KILL, 2.5km to the north-west [*Killnalecky* 1609].

**Kilraghts** tl, ham., par., Antrim 3041
(sometimes *Kilraughts*)
*Hamlet is 7km E of Ballymoney*
bar: *Dunluce Upper*
Ir. *Cill Reachtais* [kill **raght**is] 'church of the legislation'. The ruins of the medieval parish church are in a graveyard south of the road from **Ballymoney** to **Armoy** [(*ecclesia de*) *Kellrethi* 1306].

**Kilrea** tl, tn, par., Derry 2941
*Town is 20km S of Coleraine*
bar: *Loughinsholin*
Ir. *Cill Ria* [kill **ree**a] *perhaps* 'church of the journey'. Kilrea may have been so named because of its position on an important route along the **Lower Bann** between **Toome** and **Coleraine**. The ruined church at the southern approach to the town dates from only the 17th century and the site of the early church may have been in the nearby townland of DRUMAGARNER. A small portion of Kilrea parish is in the barony of **Coleraine**
[(*Coeman*) *Chilli Riada* c.900].

**Kilrean** tls, vill., Donegal 1739
(sometimes *Kilraine*)
*3km SW of Glenties*
par: *Killybegs Lower* bar: *Boylagh*
Ir. *Cill Riáin* [kill **ree**ine] '*Rián*'s church'. The remains of an ancient church stand a short distance south of the village. The village of Kilrean is in the townland of KILREAN LOWER which is adjoined on the south by the townland of KILREAN UPPER [*Killrean* c.1655].

**Kilroot** tl, par., Antrim 3438
*Townland is 2.5km NE of Carrickfergus*
bar: *Belfast Lower*
Ir. *Cill Ruaidh* [kill **roo**ee] 'church of the red land'. The site of the ancient church is marked by the remains of a 17th-century house and

*bawn* known as BISHOP'S HOUSE [(*Colman*) *Cilli Ruaid* c.830].

**Kilsally** tl, ham., Tyrone 2837
*8.5km ESE of Cookstown*
par: *Ballyclog* bar: *Dungannon Upper*
Ir. *Coill Sailí* [kill **sal**ee] 'willow wood' [*Coll-sollagh* 1639].

**Kilskeery** vill., par., Tyrone 2335
*Village is close to Fermanagh border, 3.5km NE of Bellinamallard*
bar: *Omagh East*
Ir. *Cill Scíre* [kill **skeer**a] '*Scíre*'s church. The church is dedicated to the memory of a female saint named *Scíre* who is said to be a descendant of *Niall Naoighiallach* 'Niall of the Nine Hostages'. The site of the medieval parish church is marked by a graveyard in the townland of KILSKEERY GLEBE [(*orcain*) *Cille Scire* 951].

**Kilturk** tls, ham., Fermanagh 2432
*Hamlet is 4.5km E of Newtownbutler*
par: *Galloon* bar: *Clankelly*
Ir. *Coill Torc* [kill **turk**] 'wood of (wild) boars'. The hamlet of Kilturk is in the townland of KILTURK SOUTH. KILTURK NORTH lies 7km to the north-west, close to the village of **Donagh** and KILTURK WEST lies 4.5km west of **Newtownbutler**, on the shore of KILTURK LOUGH in the barony of COOLE [*Kilturke, Kilturkbeg* 1609].

**Kilwaughter** ham., par., Antrim 3340
*Hamlet is 5km SW of Larne*
bar: *Glenarm Upper*
Ir. *Cill Uachtair* [kill **oo**aghter] 'upper church'. The hamlet of Kilwaughter is in the townland of DEMESNE where there is a graveyard marking the site of the ancient church [(*ecclesia de*) *Killochre* 1306].

**Kinallen** tl, vill., Down 3235
*3.5km W of Dromara*
par: *Dromore* bar: *Iveagh Lower, Lower Half*
Ir. *An Cionn Álainn* [an kyun **al**in] 'the beautiful height'. The place-name refers to KINALLEN HILL HEAD which rises steeply above the river **Lagan** [*Ballinekenalen* 1585].

**Kinawley** tl, vill., par., Fermanagh 2233
*Village is 14km S of Enniskillen*
bar: *Clanawley*
Ir. *Cill Náile* [kill **naal**a] '(St) *Náile*'s church'. The ruins of the medieval parish church which mark the site of an early church or monastery are adjacent to the modern Catholic church and graveyard, in the townland of LISMONAGHAN. There is also a holy well, known as ST NAWLEY'S WELL. The parish of Kinawley has a portion in the barony of KNOCKNINNY and also in the barony of TULLYHAW in Co. Cavan [*Cell Naíle* c.1170].

**Kinbane or White Head** hl, Antrim 3044
*On N Antrim coast, 4km NW of Ballycastle*
par: *Ramoan* bar: Cary
The E. *alias* name is a direct translation of the original Ir. *An Cionn Bán* [an kyun **ban**] 'the white head(land)'. It refers to a prominent limestone headland in the townland of CREGGANBOY on which stand the remains of a 16th-century MacDonnell castle [*Keanbaan* 1551].

**Kincaslough** tl, ham., Donegal 1742
(sometimes *Kincasslagh*)
*On W Donegal coast, 8km NNW of Dunglow*
par: *Templecrone* bar: *Boylagh*
Ir. *Cionn Caslach* [kyun **kas**lagh] 'head of the sea-inlet'. Kincaslough is named from its position at the head of a bay opposite **Cruit** island. A stream flows out of KINCASLOUGH LAKE and into the bay here [*Cancaslough* 1835].

**Kindrum** tl, ham., Donegal 2144
*15km N of Milford*
par: *Clondavaddog* bar: *Kilmacrenan*
Ir. *Cionn Droma* [kyun **drum**a] 'hill of the ridge'. Kindrum appears to get its name from a prominent hill of 120m which stands at the head of a long inlet of **Mulroy Bay**. KINDRUM LOUGH lies a short distance to the north [*Kindrome* 1608].

**Kingscourt** tn, Cavan 2729
*Close to border with Meath and Louth, 11km E of Bailieborough*
par: *Enniskeen* bar: *Clankee*
Ir. *Dún an Rí* [doon a **ree**] 'fort of the king'. Kingscourt is a translation of the original Ir. name while DUNAREE, the name of the townland in which most of the town is situated, is an anglicisation. The remains of the fort stand a little to the west of the town [*King's Court orw. Doonaree* 1767].

**Kingsmill** vill., Tyrone 2837
(sometimes *Kingsmills*)
*6km E of Cookstown*
par: *Artrea* bar: *Dungannon Upper*

Kingsmill, in the townland of EDERNAGH, is named from a corn mill owned by a gentleman named King which formerly stood on a tributary of the BALLINDERRY RIVER [*Kings mills* 1833].

**Kingsmills** distr., Armagh 3033
*9km NW of Newry*
par: *Loughgilly* bar: *Orior Upper*
The name Kingsmills has its origin in a corn mill, the remains of which stand on the southern boundary of the townland of LISADIAN and which towards the end of the 18th century belonged to Alexander King. A loft in the mill was the original meeting place of the local Presbyterian community [*Kingsmills* 1838].

**Kinturk** tl, Tyrone 2937
*On W shore of Lough Neagh, 16km E of Cookstown*
par: *Arboe* bar: *Dungannon Upper*
Ir. *Ceann Toirc* [kyun **tirk**] 'head(land) of the (wild) boar'. The headland referred to is now known as KINTURK FLAT [*Kentirck* 1633].

**Kircubbin** tl, vill., Down 3636
*On Ards Peninsula, 5km S of Greyabbey*
par: *Inishargy* bar: *Ards Upper*
Ir. *Cill Ghobáin* [kill **ghubb**ine] *perhaps* '(St) *Gobán*'s church'. There was formerly a small ancient church a short distance east of the village but no trace of it now remains [*Ballicarcubbin* 1605].

**Kirkhill** tl, ham., Antrim 2942
(sometimes *Kirkhills*)
*5km NE of Ballymoney*
par: *Ballymoney* bar: *Dunluce Upper*
Sc. *kirk* 'church' + E. *hill*. There was an ancient graveyard a short distance north-west of the road from **Ballymoney** to **Ballycastle** and this may mark the site of the former church [*Cnockhill* 1635].

**Kirkistown** tl, vill., Down 3635
*3km SW of Portavogie*
par: *Ardkeen* bar: *Ards Upper*
The name Kirkistown was originally *Kirk's Town*, the first element being the Anglo-Norman surname *Kirk(e)* which signifies 'dweller at the church' [*Kirkston* 1631].

**Knock** tl, vill., Armagh 3035
*Close to Co. Down border, 4km SE of Portadown*
par: *Seagoe* bar: *Oneilland East*
Ir. *An Cnoc* [an **cruck**] 'the hill'. The modern name is a contraction of the original which was *Cnoc Bhaile Bhriain Bhuí* [cruck wala vreean **wee**] 'hill of the townland of yellow-haired Brian' [*Knockballebreanboy* 1583].

**Knock** tl, distr., Down 3437
*Suburb, 4km E of Belfast city centre*
par: *Knockbreda* bar: *Castlereagh Lower*
Ir. *An Cnoc* [an **kruck**] 'the hill'. The modern name is an abbreviated version of the earlier *Cnoc Cholm Cille* [cruck kholim **kill**ya] '(St) Colmcille's hill'. Knock was formerly a parish in its own right, but in 1658 it was amalgamated with the neighbouring parish of *Breda* to form the modern civil parish of **Knockbreda**. On a graveyard on a hill in the townland there are the fragmentary remains of the medieval parish church which was sometimes referred to as *the chapel of Dundela*. The name DUNDELA is now used for a district which lies a short distance to the north-west but it appears to have originally referred to a *motte* now known as SHANDON PARK MOUND which stands a short distance south-east of the ruins of the medieval church [*Knockolumkill* 1609].

**Knockaholet** tl, ham., Antrim 3042
(sometimes *Knockahollet*)
*8km ESE of Ballymoney*
par: *Loughguile* bar: *Dunluce Upper*
Ir. *Cnoc an Chollait* [cruck a **kholl**itch]. The first element of the place-name is *cnoc* 'hill' but the meaning of the final elment is obscure. Perhaps it is a form of *coll* 'hazel' [*Knockahollet* c.1657].

**Knockarevan** tl, Fermanagh 2332
(sometimes *Knockaraven*)
*6km SE of Derrylin*
par: *Kinawley* bar: *Knockninny*
Ir. *Cnoc an Riabháin* [cruck a **ree**a-wine] 'hill of the pipit or skylark'. Ir. *riabhán* appears to be a variant of *riabhóg* 'pipit, skylark' [*Knockrevan* 1629].

**Knockavoe** mtn, Tyrone 2339
*294m high, 2.5km E of Strabane*
par: *Camus* bar: *Strabane Upper*
Ir. *Cnoc an Bhadhbha* [cruck a **voa**] 'hill of the carrion crow'. *Badhbh* is also the name of a war goddess, as in **Boa Island** in Fermanagh [*Cnoc-Buidhbh* 1522].

*Knockavoe, hill of the carrion crow*

**Knockbreda** distr., par., Down 3337
*District is a suburb, 3.5km SSE of Belfast city centre*
bar: *Castlereagh Upper*
The name of the parish of Knockbreda is a combination of *Knock* and *Breda,* the names of the two parishes which were amalgamated in 1658 to make up the modern parish. Both **Knock** (Ir. *An Cnoc* 'the hill') and **Breda** (Ir. *Bréadach* 'broken land') survive as separate place-names, the former as the name of a townland and district and the latter as the name of a townland 1km to the south, in BELVOIR PARK FOREST. A portion of the parish is in the barony of CASTLEREAGH LOWER (*see **Belvoir, Knock** and **Newtownbreda***).

**Knockcloghrim** vill., Derry 2839
(often *Knockloughrim*)
*6.5km SE of Maghera*
par: *Termoneeny* bar: *Loughinsholin*
Ir. *Cnoc Clochdhroma* [cruck **clogh**roma] 'hill of the stony ridge'. Knockcloghrim is situated on a rough and rocky hill in the townland of DERGANAGH [*Knock-loghran* 1654].

**Knockfola** tl, Donegal 1843
(see ***Bloody Foreland***)

**Knocklayd** mtn, Antrim 3143
*514m high, 4.5km S of Ballycastle*
par: *Armoy/Ramoan* bar: *Cary*
Ir. *Cnoc Leithid* [cruck **ley**hidge] 'hill of the slope'. The final element is the genitive of Ir. *leithead* which literally means 'width' or 'breadth'. In this case, it reflects a Sc. G. meaning, i.e. 'slope' [*Cnoc Leaaid* 1542].

**Knockmore** tl, Antrim 3236
*Now a suburb on the W side of Lisburn*
par: *Blaris* bar: *Massereene Upper*
Ir. *An Cnoc Mór* [an cruck **more**] 'the large hill' [*Knockmore* c.1659].

**Knockmoyle** tl, ham. Tyrone 2437
*5km N of Omagh*
par: *Cappagh* bar: *Strabane Upper*
Ir. *An Cnoc Maol* [an cruck **mweel**] 'the bald or round-topped hill' [*Knockmoyle* 1834].

**Knocknacarry** tl, ham., Antrim 3243
*2km SW of Cushendun*
par: *Layd* bar: *Glenarm Lower*
Ir. *Cnoc na Cora* [cruck na **cor**a] 'hill of the weir'. There is a weir on the GLENDUN RIVER, a short distance west of the hamlet of Knocknacarry [*Knockenecarry* c.1657].

**Knocknagoney** tl., distr., Down 3337
(sometimes *Knockagoney*)
*6km NE of Belfast city centre*
par: *Holywood* bar: *Castlereagh Lower*
Ir. *Cnoc na gCoiníní* [cruck na **gun**yeenee] 'hill of the rabbits' [*Ballacknocknegonie* 1604].

**Knocknamuckly** tl, Armagh 3035
*On border with Co. Down, 4km SE of Portadown*
par: *Seagoe* bar: *Oneilland East*
Ir. *Cnoc na Muclaí* [cruck na **muck**lee] 'hill of the piggery' [*Knocknamokally* 1609].

# L

**Labby** tl, Derry 2739
*3.5km SW of Draperstown*
par: *Ballynascreen* bar: *Loughinsholin*
Ir. *An Leaba* [an **lab**a] 'the bed'. In place-names Ir. *leaba*, literally 'bed', often refers to a megalithic grave or burial chamber which was imagined to be the bed of the legendary lovers *Diarmaid* and *Gráinne*. There is now no trace or record of any such feature in the townland. However, a tradition is recorded that Labby was the location of *Leaba na Glaise* 'the bed of the grey cow' which was named after the fabulous cow, Glasgavlin, which belonged to the smith of the mythical *Tuatha Dé Danann* [*B:nellapah* 1609].

**Lack** tl, vill., Fermanagh 2236
*Close to Tyrone border, 5.5km ENE of Ederny*
par: *Magheraculmoney* bar: *Lurg*
Ir. *An Leac* [an **lack**] 'the flagstone'. The 'flagstone' might refer to a megalith which has been removed or perhaps to a flat rock forming a ford across the stream which forms the southern boundary of the townland [*Lack* 1834].

**Lagan** river Down/Antrim
*Rises at Slieve Croob 5km SE of Dromara and enters the sea at Belfast, its lower course dividing the counties of Down and Antrim*
Ir. *Abhainn an Lagáin* [owen an **lag**ine] 'river of the low-lying district'. The 'low-lying district' is the district between **Moira** and the mouth of the Lagan at **Belfast**. The original Ir. name for the river was *Lao* [lee] 'calf', referring to the bovine goddess thought to inhabit it (cf. BOYNE, Ir. *Bóinn* 'white cow') and this name is also found in the Ir. name of **Belfast Lough**, i.e. *Loch Lao* 'estuary of the *Lao* or Lagan' [*Logia* c.150].

**Lagavara** tl, Antrim 3044
*7.5km W of Ballycastle*
par: *Ballintoy* bar: *Cary*
Ir. *Lag an Bheara* [lag a **var**a] *perhaps* 'hollow of the stream'. A head water of the MOSS-SIDE WATER runs through the west of the townland [*Legevare* c.1657].

**Laghy** tl, vill., Donegal 1937
(sometimes *Laghey*)
*4.5km SSE of Donegal town*
par: *Drumhome* bar: *Tirhugh*
Ir. *An Lathaigh* [an **la**hee] 'the muddy place/marsh'. The townland of Laghy is bordered by a townland named LAGHY BARR OR ARDBANE [*Laughy* 1760].

**Lambeg** tls, vill., par., Antrim 3236
*Village is 2km N of Lisburn*
bar: *Massereene Upper*
Ir. *Lann Bheag* [lann **veg**] 'little church'. The Church of Ireland church in the townland of LAMBEG NORTH is thought to occupy the site of a Franciscan friary. A previous alternative name for Lambeg was *Tulaigh na Sagart* 'hillock of the priests'. The parish has a small portion in the barony of BELFAST UPPER but the greater portion lies east of the **Lagan** in the barony of CASTLEREAGH UPPER in Co. Down [*Landebeg* c.1450].

**Larne** tn, par., Antrim 3440
*Town is on E Antrim coast, 6km N of Carrickfergus*
bar: *Glenarm Upper/Belfast Lower*
Ir. *Latharna* [**la**harna] 'descendants of *Lathar*'. According to legend, *Lathar* was one of the twenty-five children of *Úgaine Mór*, a pre-Christian king of Ireland. In the early historical period *Latharna* was a subkingdom of Ulster and it is only in fairly recent times that the name has been used for the parish and town of Larne. The southern portion of the town is in the parish of INVER, barony of BELFAST LOWER [(*i*) *l-Latharnu* c.1160].

**Laurelvale** vill., Armagh 3034
*6km S of Portadown*
par: *Kilmore* bar: *Orior Lower*
The name Laurelvale was invented c.1830 by Mr Thomas Sinton to apply to his residence and to an extensive linen factory in the townland of TAMNAGHVELTON [*Laurel Vale* 1835].

**Lavey** RC par., distr., Derry 2839
*5km ESE of Maghera*
par: *Maghera* bar: *Loughinsholin*
Ir. *Leamhaigh* [**lau**ee] 'place of elms'. Lavey Catholic church is in the townland of **Moyagall** [*Lamny* 1837].

**Lawrencetown** vill., Down 3134
(sometimes *Laurencetown*)
*On the Upper Bann, 4km NW of Banbridge*
par: *Tullylish* bar: *Iveagh Lower, Upper Half*
In the 18th century Lawrencetown was known as *Hall's Mill*, from Francis Hall who leased the land from the Lawrence family in 1674. The name Lawrencetown goes back to Colonel Lawrence who married the widow of Captain Barrett, the original Cromwellian settler. However, the name Lawrencetown was not applied to the village until after a descendant of the Lawrence family returned to live in LAWRENCETOWN HOUSE in the late 18th century. The bridge in the village links the townlands of KNOCKNAGORE and DRUMNASCAMPH with COOSE on the south side of the **Upper Bann** [*Laurencetown formerly Hall's Mill* c.1834].

**Leannan River** Donegal
*Rises in Gartan Lough, 11km NW of Letterkenny. Flows through the S portion of Lough Fern and enters an inlet of Lough Swilly at Ramelton*

Ir. *An Leanainn* [an **lan**in] 'the liquid one/watery one' [(*ag*) *Lenainn* 1497].

**Legaghory** tl, distr., Armagh 3035
(sometimes *Legahory*)
*Forms portion of new town of Craigavon, 3km SW of Lurgan*
par: *Shankill* bar: *Oneilland East*
Ir. *Log an Choire* [lug a **khur**a] 'hollow of the cauldron'. The place-name is most likely to refer to a cauldron-like pit or hollow in the ground [*Legachorry* 1609].

**Legamaddy** tl, Down 3433
(sometimes *Leggamaddy*)
*4.5km S of Downpatrick*
par: *Bright* bar: *Lecale Upper*
Ir. *Lag an Mhadaidh* [lag a **wad**ee] 'hollow of the (wild) dog' [*Liggamaddy* 1755].

**Legananny** tl, Down 3234
*6km S of Dromara*
par: *Drumgooland*
bar: *Iveagh Upper, Lower Half*
*Liagán Áine* [leegan **any**a] 'pillar-stone of *Áine*'. The place-name clearly refers to the famous neolithic portal tomb known as LEGANANNY DOLMEN. The final element is likely to represent the goddess-name *Áine* [*Ballyleganangh* 1609].

**Leggs** tl, Fermanagh 2036
*6.5km ENE of Belleek*
par: *Belleek* bar: *Lurg*
Ir. *Na Laig* [na **lig**] 'the hollows'.

*Legananny Dolmen*

**Legland** tl, Tyrone 2337
(sometimes *Leglands*)
*7km SW of Newtownstewart*
par: *Ardstraw* bar: *Strabane Lower*
Ir. *Leithghleann* [**legh**lann] 'side of the glen'. The place-name appears to refer to the western slopes of MANUS HILL [*Legglan* 1661].

**Legoniel** tl, vill., Antrim 3237
(often *Ligoniel*)
*Now a suburb on the NW boundary of Belfast*
par: *Shankill* bar: *Belfast Upper*
Ir. *Lag an Aoil* [lag an **eel**] 'hollow of the lime'. There are several disused limestone quarries in the townland [*Ballylagaile* 1604].

**Leitrim** tl, vill., Down 3333
*4.5km NW of Castlewellan*
par: *Drumgooland*
bar: *Iveagh Upper, Lower Half*
Ir. *Liatroim* [**lee**atrim] 'grey ridge'. The LEITRIM RIVER forms the southern boundary of the townland [*Ballyletrom* 1611].

**Lenaderg** tl, ham., Down 3134
*3km NW of Banbridge*
par: *Tullylish*
bar: *Iveagh Lower, Upper Half*
Ir. *Láithreach Dhearg* [larhagh **yar**ig] 'red site'. The townland was formerly church land and therefore it is possible that the place-name could refer to a church site but none has been identified [*Laireachtdyke* 1427].

**Letter** tl, ham., Fermanagh 2036
*3km SW of Pettigoe*
par: *Templecarn* bar: *Lurg*
Ir. *An Leitir* [an **letch**er] 'the hillside' [*Letter* 1665].

**Letterbreen** tl, vill., Fermanagh 2134
*7.5km SW of Enniskillen*
par: *Cleenish* bar: *Clanawley*
Ir. *Leitir Bruíne* [letcher **vreen**] *perhaps* 'hillside of the dwelling/fairy fort'. There is a prominent *rath* a short distance west of the village [*Letterbreen* 1751].

**Letterkenny** tl, tn, Donegal 2141
*15km N of Stranorlar*
par: *Conwal* bar: *Kilmacrenan*
Ir. *Leitir Ceanainn* [letcher **kan**in] 'hillside of the white top'. Ir. *Ceanann* (sometimes *Ceannann*) is made up of *ceann* 'head' + *fionn* 'white/fair'. The latter may have connotations of 'bald/bare' [*Latterkeny* 1685].

**Letterloan** tl, ham., Derry 2842
*7km SW of Coleraine*
par: *Macosquin* bar: *Coleraine*
Ir. *Leitir Luán* [letcher **loo**in] 'hillside of lambs' [*Litter Lowan* 1613].

**Lettermacaward** ch., par., Donegal 1740
*Church is 7km NW of Glenties*
bar: *Boylagh*
Ir. *Leitir Mhic an Bhaird* [letcher vick an **wardge**] 'Ward's hillside'. The family of *Mac an Bhaird* 'son of the bard' were professional hereditary bards to the O'Donnell rulers of *Tír Chonaill* (cf. ***Ballyward*** in Co. Down). The remnants of an ancient church are adjacent to the present Church of Ireland church a short distance north-west of GWEEBARRA BRIDGE [*Lettermacaward* 1608].

**Lettershendony** tl, Derry 2541
*6.5km ESE of Derry city*
par: *Cumber Lower* bar: *Tirkeeran*
Ir. *Leitir Seandomhnaigh* [letcher **shan**doanee] 'hillside of the old church'. The 'old church' may be *Domhnach Seanlis* 'church of the old fort', which is said to have been founded by St Patrick, and the site of which was adjacent to SEINLIS FORT which formerly stood on KILLENNAN HILL. There was also an old church a short distance to the north in the townland of OGHIL from the site of which a stone cross was removed in 1898 to a Catholic graveyard in the adjoining townland of MULLABOY [*Litter Shandenoy* 1622].

**Lifford** tn, Donegal 2339
*County town of Donegal, on W bank of the river Foyle 1km W of Strabane*
par: *Clonleigh* bar: *Raphoe*
Ir. *Leifear* [**liff**ar] 'side of the water'. The Mod. Ir. form of the place-name is a combination of *Leith* 'side' + *bior* 'water/stream'. The name appears to refer to the land lying along the west bank of the river **Foyle**. Lifford has given name to the townlands of LIFFORD BOG and LIFFORD COMMON [(*caislén*) *Leithbhir* 1527].

**Limavady** tn, Derry 2642
*21km SW of Coleraine*
par: *Drumachose* bar: *Keenaght*
Ir. *Léim an Mhadaidh* [lem a **wad**ee] 'leap of the dog'. The place-name is said to have its origin in a legend about a dog belonging to a chieftain of the O'Kanes (O'Cahans) which jumped a steep gorge of the river **Roe** carrying a message of danger to the O'Cahan castle which formerly stood on the east bank of the river, 2.5km south of the modern town. The town was founded in the early 17th century by Sir Thomas Phillips under the title *Newtown Limavady* and is situated in the townland of NEWTOWN-LIMAVADY *alias* RATHBRADY BEG [(*i*) *Leim an Mhadaidh* 1542].

**Lisbane** tl, vill., Down 3436
*5km SE of Comber*
par: *Tullynakill* bar: *Castlereagh Lower*
Ir. *An Lios Bán* [an liss **ban**] 'the white fort'. There were formerly two forts in the townland [*Ba:lisbane* c.1625].

**Lisbellaw** vill., Fermanagh 2334
*6.5km ESE of Enniskillen*
par: *Cleenish* bar: *Tirkennedy*
Ir. *Lios Béal Átha* [liss bell **a**ha] 'fort at the mouth of the ford'. Lisbellaw is in the townland of MULLYBRITT where there are still traces of a ring-fort. The ford appears to have been across the stream which passes to the east of the village [*Lisbelae* 1662].

**Lisboduff** tl, ham., Cavan 2531
*9km W of Cootehill*
par: *Drung* bar: *Tullygarvey*
Ir. *Lios Bó Dubh* [liss bo **doo**] 'fort of the black cows'. There is a townland named LISBOFIN (Ir. *Lios Bó Fionn* 'fort of the white cows') near **Letterbeen** in Fermanagh and no doubt both names have mythological associations (cf. ***Inishbofin, Blackwatertown***). Lisboduff stands on the west bank of the BUNNOE RIVER and three forts are recorded in the townland [*Lisbodowe* 1610].

**Lisburn** tn, Antrim 3236
*11.5km SW of Belfast*
par: *Blaris/Derryaghy*
bar: *Massereene Upper*
The *Lis-* element in Lisburn may derive from LISNAGARVY, the name of a townland which is incorporated in the modern town and whose name goes back to Ir. *Lios na gCearrbhach* [liss na **gar**awagh] 'fort of the gamesters or gamblers'. The origin of the element *burn* in Lisburn is obscure. The oft-quoted suggestion that it refers to the burning of the town in the 1641 Rebellion must be regarded as extremely implausible. Several forts are recorded in the area, including one on PROSPECT HILL, the site of FRIENDS SCHOOL [*Lysnecarvagh* 1683].

**Liscloon** tls, ham., Tyrone 2440
*15km NE of Strabane*
par: *Donaghedy* bar: *Strabane Lower*
Ir. *Lios Claon* [liss **kleen**] 'sloping/crooked fort'. The hamlet of Liscloon is on the east bank of the ALTINAGHREE BURN which forms the western boundary of the townland of LISCLOON LOWER. The latter is adjoined on the east by LISCLOON UPPER. There is now no trace or record of a fort in either townland [*Liscle-ene* 1661].

**Liscolman** tl, ham., Antrim 2943
*5.5km SE of Bushmills*
par: *Billy* bar: *Dunluce Lower*
Ir. *Lios Cholmáin* [liss **khol**mine] '*Colmán*'s fort'. There was formerly a fort in the townland but no trace of it now remains [*Slaight-colminan* 1669].

**Lisdoart** tl, ham., Tyrone 2635
*2.5km SSW of Ballygawley*
par: *Carnteel* bar: *Dungannon Lower*
Ir. *Lios Dubhairt* [liss **doo**artch] '*Dubhart*'s fort'. Lisdoart takes it name from a prominent *rath* in the north of the townland. The otherwise-unattested personal name *Dubhart* appears to be a combination of *dubh* 'black' and *art* 'warrior' [*Lisdourt* 1614].

**Lislap** tls, ham., Tyrone 2438
*Hamlet is 3.5km SSW of Gortin*
par: *Cappagh* bar: *Strabane Upper*
Ir. *Lios Leapa* [liss **lap**a] 'fort of the bed (i.e. grave)'. The hamlet of Lislap is in the townland of LISLAP EAST, while LISLAP WEST lies 5km to the west, on the the far side of the river STRULE. In place-names Ir. *leaba* 'bed' commonly refers to a megalithic grave or burial chamber. There is no record of any such feature, nor indeed of a fort, in either townland though megalithic remains are fairly numerous in the area [*Lislapp* 1613].

**Lislea** tl, ham., Armagh 3032
*8km WSW of Newry*
par: *Killevy* bar: *Orior Upper*
Ir. *Lios Liath* [liss **lee**a] 'grey fort'. There is now no trace or record of the fort which gave name to the townland [*Lisliagh* 1609].

**Lislea** tl, ham., Armagh 2834
*5km SSW of Armagh city*
par: *Lisnadill* bar: *Armagh*
*Ir. Lios Liath* [liss **lee**a] 'grey fort'. There is a record of a fort in this townland. There is another townland of the same name in the parish, 3km to the south-east [*Ballylisliagh* 1609].

**Lislea** tl, ham., Derry 2940
*5km SSE of Kilrea*
par: *Kilrea* bar: *Loughinsholin*
Ir. *Lios Liath* [liss **lee**a] 'grey fort'. There is now no trace or record of a fort in the townland but it may have been situated at BURIAL HILL where there are remnants of former earthworks [*Lislea* 1613].

**Lisnacree** tls, Down 3231
*7km W of Kilkeel*
par: *Kilkeel* bar: *Mourne*
Ir. *Lios na Crí* [liss na **cree**] 'fort of the boundary'. There is a fort in the townland of Lisnacree, a short distance from the CASSY WATER which forms the western boundary of the barony of **Mourne**. Lisnacree is bordered on the north by the townland of LISNACREE UPPER [*Lisnechrehy* 1613].

**Lisnadill** tl, ham., par., Armagh 2834
*Hamlet is 5km S of Armagh city*
bar: *Fews Upper*
Ir. *Lios na Daille* [liss na **dill**ya] 'fort of the blindness'. The modern form of the place-name may represent a development from an earlier form *Lios an Daill* 'fort of the blind man'. There are remains of a *rath* in the townland. The parish of Lisnadill which has portions in the baronies of FEWS LOWER and ARMAGH was created in 1772 out of the neighbouring parish of **Armagh** [*Lisnedolle* 1609].

**Lisnagarvy** tl, Antrim 3236
(see *Lisburn*)

**Lisnagelvin** tl, distr., Derry 2441
*Suburb on the E side of Londonderry*
par: *Clondermot* bar: *Tirkeeran*
Ir. *Lios na nGealbhán* [liss na **nal**awan] 'fort of the sparrows'. There is now no trace or record of a fort in the townland. Lisnagelvin is close to the townland of ALTNAGELVIN (Ir. *Allt na nGealbhán* 'glen of the sparrows') [*Lisnegellwan* 1663].

**Lisnamuck** tl, ham., Derry 2839
*3.5km NW of Tobermore*
par: *Maghera* bar: *Loughinsholin*
Ir. *Lios na Muc* [liss na **muck**] 'fort or enclo-

sure of the pigs'. There is now no trace or record of a fort in the townland [*Lisnamuc* c.1834].

**Lisnarrick** vill., Fermanagh 2135
(sometimes *Lisnarick*)
*4km W of Irvinestown*
par: *Derryvullan* bar: *Lurg*
Ir. *Lios na nDaróg* [liss na **nar**og] 'fort of the (little) oaks'. The Plantation village of Lisnarrick is in the townland of DRUMSHANE where there are remains of a *rath* [*Lisnarrogue* 1659].

**Lisnaskea** tn, Fermanagh 2333
*17km SE of Enniskillen*
par: *Aghalurcher* bar: *Magherastephana*
Ir. *Lios na Scéithe* [liss na **skey**ha] 'fort of the shield'. The final element of the place-name, the genitive of *sciath* 'shield', is from *Sciath Ghabhra* [skeea **ghoar**a], the name of the inauguration site of the Maguires, now known as the MOATE FORT in the townland of CORNASHEE, 1km north of Lisnaskea. The element *sciath* (literally 'shield') in *Sciath Ghabhra* may mean 'defensive position/fortress' and *Sciath Ghabhra* may signify 'fortress of the (white) horses'. The Plantation town of Lisnaskea is mainly in the townland of LISONEILL where there are also remains of a rath and the name Lisnaskea may represent a combination of the *lios* element of LISONEILL (Ir. *Lios Uí Néill* 'O'Neill's fort) and *sciath* from *Sciath Ghabhra*. In the adjoining townland of CASTLE BALFOUR DEMESNE are the ruins of CASTLE BALFOUR, a plantation castle which was sometimes known as CASTLESKEA [(*ag*) *Scéith Ghabhra* 1589].

**Lisnastrean** tl, Down 3236
*2km SE of Lisburn*
par: *Drumbo* bar: *Castlereagh Upper*
Ir. *Lios na Srian* [liss na **sree**an] 'fort of the reins, bridles'. The exact significance of the final element of the place-name is obscure. Three forts are recorded in the townland [*Ballelisneshrean* 1623].

**Lisrodden** tl, Antrim 2940
*2km NE of Portglenone*
par: *Portglenone* bar: *Toome Lower*
Ir. *Lios Rodáin* [liss **rod**ine] '*Rodán*'s fort'. The personal name *Rodán* is the basis of the Ulster surname *Mac Rodáin* '(Mac)Crudden' and also of *Ó Rodáin* '(O')Rodden' which is found in Donegal, Monaghan and Clare. There was formerly a large fort near the southern boundary of the townland [*Ballylessraddan* 1605].

**Lissan** tl, par., Tyrone 2838
*Townland is on the border with Co. Derry, 4km NNW of Cookstown*
bar: *Dungannon Upper*
Ir. *Leasán* [**lass**an] 'little fort'. Even though the townland of Lissan is in Co. Tyrone, roughly half of the parish lies in the barony of LOUGHINSHOLIN in Co. Derry. The site of the ancient church is in the townland of CLAGAN in the Derry portion of the parish but no remains survive. Two forts are recorded in the townland of Lissan which has given name to the neighbouring townland of LISSAN DEMESNE in Co. Derry [*Leassan* 1455].

**Listooder** tl, ham., Down 3435
*3.5km WNW of Crossgar*
par: *Kilmore* bar: *Castlereagh Upper*
Ir. *Lios an tSúdaire* [liss a **tood**ara] 'fort of the leather tanner'. There is a fort with a double bank on the top of a hill west of the hamlet of Listooder [*Balle-Listowdrie* 1623].

**Little Bridge** vill., Derry 2836
(sometimes *Littlebridge*)
*6.5km E of Cookstown*
par: *Arboe* bar: *Loughinsholin*
The village of Little Bridge in the townland of DRUMMULLAN is named from a bridge over the LISSAN WATER which flows through the townland. The bridge is so named by way of contrast with the 'big bridge', i.e. ARDTREA BRIDGE which spans the BALLINDERRY RIVER a short distance to the south [*Little bridge* 1836].

**Little Dog/Big Dog** hills, Fermanagh 2035
(*see **Dog Big/Dog Little***)

**Loanends** ham., Antrim 3238
*8.5km SE of Antrim town*
par: *Killead* bar: *Massereene Lower*
Sc./N.E. *loan*(*in*) 'lane' + E. 'ends'. The term *loan-end* refers to the end of a lane where it joins the road. In this case the hamlet is named from the junction of three minor roads with the main road to Antrim (the SEVEN MILE STRAIGHT), partly in the townland of BALLYMATHER LOWER and partly in GRANGE OF CARMAVY.

**Londonderry** city, co. 2441
(*see* ***Derry***)

**Lough Altan** lake, Donegal 1942
*At NE foot of Errigal, 5km NE of Dunlewy*
par: *Tullaghobegly* bar: *Kilmacrenan*
Ir. *Loch Alltáin* [lough **alt**ine] 'lake of the little glen'. The glen referred to lies between **Errigal** and **Aghla More** mountains. The same glen has also given name to the townland of ALTAN in which the lake is situated [*Lough Altan* 1654].

**Loughanure** tl, vill., Donegal 1841
*7.5km NE of Dunglow*
par: *Templecrone* bar: *Boylagh*
Ir. *Loch an Iúir* [lough an **yure**] 'lake of the yew tree'. Loughanure takes its name from the lake named LOUGH ANURE which adjoins the village on the east.

**Loughareema (Vanishing Lake)** Antrim 3243
*5km NW of Cushendun*
par: *Culfeightrin* bar: *Cary*
Ir. *Loch an Mhadhma* [lough a **wey**ma] 'lake of the eruption/bursting out'. The E. name Vanishing Lake reflects the fact that this little lake in the townland of BALLYVENNAGHT can quickly disappear in dry weather. The Ir. name reflects the speed with which the lake can fill and overflow when the weather is wet [*Loughaveema* c.1855].

**Lough Beagh** lake, Donegal 2042
(*see* ***Glenbeagh***)

**Lough Beg** lake, Antrim/Derry 2939
*A widening of the Lower Bann, 2km N of Toome*
Ir. *Loch Beag* [lough **beg**] 'little lake'. Lough Beg was named 'little lake' by way of contrast with the nearby 'big lake', i.e. **Lough Neagh** which lies a short distance to the south [(*for*) *Loch Bec* c.1630].

**Lough Beg or Portmore Lough** lake, Antrim 3136
*1km inland from E shore of Lough Neagh*
par: *Glenavy/Ballinderry*
bar: *Massereene Upper*
As in the case of the previous entry the name *Loch Beag* 'little lake' reflects its smallness as compared with the nearby **Lough Neagh**. The *alias* name PORTMORE LOUGH is from the townland of PORTMORE in which the lake is partially located. Portmore (Ir. *An Port Mór* 'the great fort') may be named from a medieval fortress of the O'Neills on the site of which a castle was built by Lord Conway in 1664 but no trace of which now remains [*Portmore* 1625].

**Loughbrickland** vill., Down 3134
*4km SW of Banbridge*
par: *Aghaderg* bar: *Iveagh Upper, Upper Half*
The village takes its name from the small lake named LOUGH BRICKLAND which lies a short distance to the south-east. Its name derives from Ir. *Loch Bricleann* [lough **brick**lan] '*Bricle*'s (earlier *Bricriu*'s) lake'. *Bricriu* was a male character in the famous Ulster Cycle of early tales. Lough Brickland has also given name to the townland of BRICKLAND which includes the southern portion of the lake. The village of Loughbrickland is at the junction of the townlands of COOLNACRAN, BOVENNETT, GREENAN and DRUMNAHARE [(*ic*) *Loch B*[*r*]*icreann* c.830].

**Lough Derg** lake, Donegal 2037
*5km NW of Pettigoe*
par: *Templecarn* bar: *Tirhugh*
Ir. *Loch Dearg* [lough **jar**ig] 'red lake'. This is the established Mod. Ir. form of the place-name. However, it is clearly a reinterpretation of the original name, as the earliest sources refer to the lake as *Loch Geirg*, the final element being the genitive form of O.Ir. *gerg* which means 'grouse/quail' but could be used figuratively in the sense of 'king/warrior'. *Gerg* was also found as a personal name and in an early tale from the Ulster Cycle, the name of the lake is explained as '*Gerg*'s lake' and the tale relates that *Conchúr mac Nessa* king of Ulster slew *Gerg* and plundered his dwelling on the lake, taking away his cooking cauldron. Lough Derg has given name to the river **Derg** which flows out of it [(*Aed*) *Locha Geirg* c.830].

**Lough Egish** lake, Monaghan 2731
*6.5km SW of Castleblayney*
par: *Aghnamullen* bar: *Cremorne*
Ir. *Loch Éigis* [lough **egg**ish] 'lake of the sage or poet'. On the west shore of the lake there are townlands named TULLYNANEGISH (Ir. *Tulaigh an Éigis* 'hillock of the sage or poet') and COOLTRIMEGISH (Ir. *Cúil Troim Éigis* 'elder-corner of the sage or poet').

**Lough Erne Lower/Upper** lakes, Fermanagh
*The two lakes stretch from Belleek on the Donegal border to the Cavan border, near Belturbet, with the town of Enniskillen between them*
Ir. *Loch Éirne* [lough **ern**ya] '*Érann*'s lake'. *Érann* is the name of a goddess who also gave name to the *Érainn*, an ethnic grouping who were widely scattered in Ireland and to whom belonged the *Manaig* of **Fermanagh** (*see above*). Lough Erne has given name to the river **Erne** which flows through both lakes [*Loch Erne* 3751AM].

**Lough Eske** lake, Donegal 1938
*5km NE of Donegal town*
par: *Donegal/Killymard* bar: *Tirhugh/Banagh*
Ir. *Loch Iasc* [lough **ee**ask] 'lake of fish'.

**Lough Fea** lake, Derry/Tyrone 2738
*On the Derry/Tyrone border, 9km NW of Cookstown*
par: *Lissan*
bar: *Loughinsholin/Dungannon Upper*
Ir. *Loch Feá* [lough **fey**] 'lake of rushes' [*Loch Feadha* c.1200].

**Lough Finn** lake, Donegal 1940
*10km NE of Glenties*
par: *Inishkeel* bar: *Boylagh*
Ir. *Loch Finne* [lough **fin**ya] 'lake of the (river) Finn'. The lake takes its name from the river **Finn** which flows out of it and the name of which is from Ir. *An Fhinn* which may signify 'the holy one/sacred one'. A local legend suggests that the lake is named from *Finn*, a sister of one of Finn Mac Cool's followers and that she was drowned here while engaging in a vain attempt to save her brother *Fearghamhain* from a savage attack by a wild sow.

**Lough Foyle** inl., Derry/Donegal 2542
*Large sea estuary into which flows the river Foyle a short distance N of Derry city*
Ir. *Loch Feabhail* [logh **fyau**il] *perhaps* 'lough/estuary of the lip'. The element *feabhal* may be cognate with Welsh *gwefl* 'lip' and may refer to MAGILLIGAN POINT at the mouth of Lough Foyle which resembles a lip when viewed from **Greencastle** on the Donegal side of the lough. According to a legend, Lough Foyle is named from *Feabhal* son of *Lodan* who belonged to the mythical *Tuatha Dé*

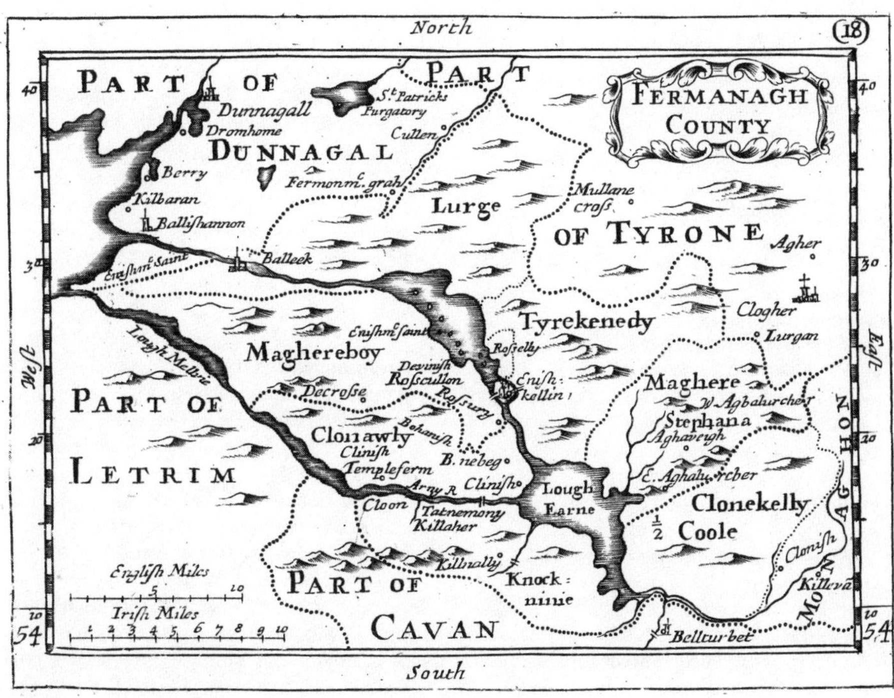

*Map of 17th century Fermanagh showing Lough Erne*

*Danann*. At an earlier period, Lough Foyle was regarded as also including the river **Foyle** (*see above*) [*Loch Feabhail* 2581AM].

**Loughgall** tl, vill., par., Armagh 2935
*Village is 7.5km NNE of Armagh city*
bar: *Oneilland West*
Ir. *Loch gCál* [lough **gal**]. Loughgall takes its name from a small lake named LOUGH GALL a short distance south of the village. The first element of the place-name is clearly Ir. *loch* 'lake'. However, the meaning of the final elment is obscure. The ruins of the medieval parish church are in a graveyard in the townland of LEVALLEGLISH (Ir. *Leathbhaile Eaglaise* 'church half-town') in the west of the village. A portion of Loughgall parish is in the barony of ARMAGH [*Loch Cal* 2859AM].

**Loughgilly** ham., par., Armagh 2933
*Hamlet is 6km SE of Markethill*
bar: *Orior Lower*
Ir. *Loch Gile* [lough **gill**ee] 'lake of brightness/bright lake'. Loughgilly is named from LOUGH GILLY, a small lake partly in the townland of DRUMMILT and partly in CREEVE. The site of an early church is marked by the modern Church of Ireland parish church in the townland of CORNAGRALLY. Loughgilly parish has portions in the baronies of ORIOR UPPER and FEWS LOWER [*Loughgilly* 1608].

**Lough Gowna** lake, vill., Cavan 2329
*Village is 17km SSW of Cavan town*
par: *Scrabby* bar: *Tullyhunco*
Ir. *Loch Gamhna* [lough **gaun**a] 'lake of the calf'. A local legend has it that a calf appeared from a well which burst forth here to form Lough Gowna and that the water of the well then pursued the calf all the way to **Ballyshannon**, thus forming the river **Erne** and the two lakes of that name. The village of Lough Gowna is on the western shore of a small lake named SWAN LAKE, a short distance east of Lough Gowna lake. The latter is partially in Co. Longford. The village was formerly known as SCRABBY (Ir. *Screabaigh* [**skrab**ee] 'rough, stony land') which is also the name of the townland and parish in which it is situated [(*co*) *Loch Gamhna* 931].

**Loughguile** vill., par., Antrim 3042
(sometimes *Loughgiel*)
*Village is 13km E of Ballymoney*
bar: *Dunluce Upper*
Ir. *Loch gCaol* [lough **geel**] 'lake of the narrows'. Loughguile takes its name from the lake named LOUGH GUILE which lies 1.5km south-west of the village, in the townland of CASTLEQUARTER. The lake appears to be named from two narrow channels which connect it with FIVE ISLANDS LOUGH a short distance to the north. The site of the medieval parish church is marked by the ruins of a 19th-century Church of Ireland church and a graveyard on the east shore of the lake. The southern portion of Loughguile parish is in the barony of KILCONWAY [*Lochkele* 1262].

**Loughinisland** vill., par., Down 3434
*Village is 7km W of Downpatrick*
bar: *Kinelarty*
Ir. *Loch an Oileáin* [lough an **ill**ine] 'lake of the island'. The island, which was the headquarters of the McCartan rulers of KINELARTY, is in LOUGHINISLAND LAKE in the townland of TIEVENADARRAGH and can be reached by a causeway. It contains the ruins of three churches, of which the middle one is the earliest, as well as an ancient graveyard [*Loghnellan* 1616].

**Lough Macnean Lower/Upper** lakes
Fermanagh
*17.5km SW of Enniskillen*
Ir. *Loch Mac nÉin* [lough mack **ney**in] 'lake of the sons of *Éan*'. There is a local tradition that the final element of the place-name (literally 'bird') refers to eagles which built nests on one of the islands in the lake. LOUGH MACNEAN LOWER which is also known as LOUGH NILLY has a small portion in Co. Cavan while LOUGH MACNEAN UPPER has portions in both Cavan and Leitrim [(*for*) *Loch Mec Nén* 1499].

**Loughmacrory** tl, Tyrone 2537
*14km ENE of Omagh*
par: *Termonmaguirk* bar: *Omagh East*
Ir. *Loch Mhic Ruairí* [lough vick **roor**ee] 'MacCrory's lake'. The townland is named from LOUGH MACRORY, a small lake which is partly in this townland and partly in the neighbouring townland of ALTDRUMMAN. An earlier name for the townland was *Avishmacrory*, from Ir. *Aibhéis Mhic Ruairí* [evish vick **roor**ee] 'MacCrory's coarse mountain pasture'. The surname *MacRuairí* 'MacCrory' is indigenous to Tyrone and Derry [*Avishmacgrory* 1633].

**Lough Melvin** lake Fermanagh/Leitrim 1935
*Lies between Garrison in Co. Fermanagh and Bundoran in Co. Donegal*
Ir. *Loch Meilbhe* [lough **mel**eva] '*Meilbhe*'s lake'. According to a legend the lake is named from *Meilbhe Molbhthach* '*Meilbhe* the praiseworthy' who was king of Ireland for 17 years in the prehistoric period [*Loch Melghe* 4659AM].

**Lough Morne** lake, ham., Monaghan 2731
(sometimes Loughmorne)
*Hamlet is 6.5km SE of Ballybay*
par: *Aghnamullen* bar: *Cremorne*
Ir. *Loch Múrn* [lough **moorn**] 'lake of the *Múrna* (tribe)'. The hamlet of Lough Morne in the townland of TOSSY is named from the little lake of that name which lies 1.5km to the south. The lake, in turn, takes its name from the tribe named *Múrna* (earlier *Mughdhorna*) who also gave name to the barony of CREMORNE (Ir. *Crích Mhúrn* 'territory of the *Múrna*') in which it is situated, and to the **Mourne Mountains**, after the migration of the tribe to Co. Down in the 12th century [*Loghmorne* c.1660].

**Lough Mourne** lake Antrim 3439
*4.5km NNE of Carrickfergus*
par/bar, *Carrickfergus*
Ir. *Loch Morna* [lough **moarn**a] 'lake of (the district of ) *Morna*'. The name *Morna* is a shortened form of *Machaire Morna* 'plain of *Morna*', now the village of **Magheramorne** a short distance to the north-east but formerly the name of the district (sometimes abbreviated to *Morna*) in which both the village and the lake are situated (*see* ***Maghermorne*** *below*) [*Loughmorne* 1603].

**Lough Nacung** lake Donegal 1942
*6km E of Bunbeg*
par: *Tullaghobegly* bar: *Kilmacrenan*
Ir. *Loch na Cuinge* [lough na **king**a] 'lake of the isthmus'. The lake takes its name from a narrow neck of land which formerly divided it into two but which disappeared when the level of the lake was raised during the construction of an electricity-generating station. The lake is adjoined on the north-west by a townland named MEENACUNG (Ir. *Mín na Cuinge* [meen na **king**a] 'mountain pasture of the isthmus') [*Loughnecong* 1654].

**Lough Neagh** lake
Antrim/Armagh/Derry/Down/Tyrone
*20km W of Belfast*
Ir. *Loch nEathach* [lough **nyagh**agh] '*Eochu*'s lake'. According to one legend, Lough Neagh is named after *Eochu* son of *Mairidh*, a Munster prince who was drowned when a well overflowed to form the lake in the first century AD. In fact, the *Eochu* who gave name to Lough Neagh appears to have been the mythical progenitor of the sept of *Uí Eachach* [ee **agh**agh] 'descendants of *Eochu*' who inhabited the area at an early date. In the late 16th- and early 17th centuries unsuccessful attempts were made to re-name the lake *Lough Sidney* and *Lough Chichester* after Lord Deputies Sir Henry Sidney and Sir Arthur Chichester respectively [(*fri*) *Loch nEchach* c.600].

**Lough Oughter** lake, Cavan 2330
*3km E of Killashandra*
par: *Kilmore/Drumlane*
bar: *Loughtee Upper, Lower/Clanmahon*
Ir. *Loch Uachtair* [lough **oo**aghter] 'upper lake'. Lough Oughter is so-named because it lies 'above', i.e., to the south of, **Upper Lough Erne**, to which it is connected by the river **Erne** [(*cloch*) *Locha hUachtair* 1369].

**Lough Ramor** lake, Cavan 2628
*Close to Meath border, immediately S of Virginia*
par: *Lurgan/Munterconnaught/Castlerahan*
bar: *Castlerahan*
Ir. *Loch Ramhar* [lough **rau**er]. The literal meaning of the place-name is 'broad lake'. However, the modern name is a shortened form of the earlier name *Loch Muinreamhair* [lough **mwin**rauer] '*Muinreamhar*'s lake', *Muinreamhar*, whose name signifies 'fat neck', being a warrior in the Ulster Cycle of tales [(*o*) *Loch Munremuir* c.830].

**Loughros Point** hl, Donegal 1639
*On W Donegal coast, 9.5km W of Ardara*
par: *Inishkeel* bar: *Banagh*
Ir. *Luacharos* [**loogh**aross] 'rushy point' + E. *point*. The E. element 'point' which means the same as Ir. *ros* has cleary been added at a later date. Loughros Point has given name to the large bay named LOUGHROS MORE BAY which lies to the north and also to the smaller bay named LOUGHROS BEG BAY which lies to the south [(*hi*) *Luachros* 1509].

*Lough Sillan, lake of willow groves*

**Lough Sheelin** lake, Cavan 2428
*7.5km NE of Granard*
par: *Drumlumman/Ballymachugh/Kilbride*
bar: *Clanmahon*
Ir. *Loch Síleann* [lough **sheel**in] *perhaps Síle*'s lake. *Síle* appears to be an early Ir. male personal name and is not to be confused with the female name which is identical in form but which is a borrowing from the Latin name *Caecilia* and is commonly anglicised as *Sheila*. There is a tradition that Lough Sheelin was one of nine Irish lakes which burst forth in prehistoric times. Lough Sheelin has portions in Cos Meath and Westmeath [*(for) Loch Silenn* 1155].

**Lough Sillan** lake, Cavan 2730
*Close to Monaghan border, W of the village of Shercock*
par: *Shercock/Knockbride* bar: *Clankee*
Ir. *Loch Saileán* [lough **sal**an] 'lake of willow groves'.

**Lough Swilly** inl, Donegal
*Long sea inlet which divides Inishowen peninsula from the rest of Donegal*
(*see* ***Swilly*** river)

**Loup, The** vill., Derry 2938
(sometimes *Loup*)
*4.5km ENE of Moneymore*
par: *Artrea* bar: *Loughinsholin*
Ir. *An Lúb* [an **loob**] 'the loop'. The E. name appears to be a translation of the original Ir., *loup* being a variant spelling of *loop*. The name appears to refer to a bend on the stream which rises close to the village. The Loup is partly in the townland of BALLYMULLIGAN and partly in BALLYNENAGH [*The Loop Lodge* 1798].

**Lowtown** ham., Down 3234
*11km NE of Rathfriland*
par: *Drumgooland*
bar: *Iveagh Upper, Lower Half*
Lowtown is in the townland of **Deehommed** and is named from its situation at the bottom of DEEHOMMED MOUNTAIN (318m).

**Lurgan** tl, tn, Armagh 3035
*8.5km ENE of Portadown*
Ir. *An Lorgain* [an **lurr**agin] 'the long low ridge/strip of land'. Ir. *lorgain* is a form of *lorga* which literally means 'shin' but in place-names is applied figuratively to 'a long low ridge', sometimes to 'a long strip of land'. Earlier names for Lurgan were *Lorgain Chlann Bhreasail* 'Lurgan of Clanbrassil', *Clanbrassil* being the name of the district in which it was situated, and *Lorgain Bhaile Mhic Cana* 'long low ridge of McCann's townland' [*Lorgenball mcCann* 1661].

**Lurigethan** mtn, Antrim 3242
*250m high, 2km SW of Cushendall*
par: *Layd* bar: *Glenarm Lower*
*perhaps* Ir. *Lorg Éadain* [lurrig **aid**in] 'ridge/shank of the face or brow'. The final element of the place-name may refer to the sheer rocky face of the mountain on the summit of which there is a promontory fort, in the townland of FORIFF [*Lorgeaden, commonly called Lurgethan* 1832].

# M

**Mackan** vill., Fermanagh 2233
(sometimes *Macken*)
*10km S of Enniskillen*
par: *Killesher* bar: *Clanawley*
Ir. *Meacan* [**mack**in]. The literal meaning of Ir. *meacan* is 'root/tuber' but it appears to be used figuratively to signify 'a swelling hill'. Mackan is situated in the townland of MACKAN GLEBE. LOUGH MACKAN lies on the eastern boundary of the townland [*Mackin* 1609].

**Macosquin** tl, vill., par., Derry 2842
*Village is 4.5km SW of Coleraine*
bar: *Coleraine*

Ir. *Maigh Choscáin* [my **khos**kine] '*Coscán*'s plain'. The modern Church of Ireland church in the village is built on the site of a medieval Cistercian abbey. 4.5km to the east, in the townland of CAMUS, there is an ancient graveyard and cross which marks the site of the early monastery of St *Comhghall*, on the bank of the **Lower Bann** [(*abb mainistre*) *Mhaighe Cosccrain* 1505].

**Maddan** tl, ham., Armagh 2833
(sometimes *Madden*)
*4.5km NW of Keady*
par: *Derrynoose* bar: *Armagh*
Ir. *Madán* [**mad**an] *perhaps* 'place of sticks'. Maddan is sometimes used as the name of the parish of **Derrynoose** since it is the site of the Church of Ireland parish church [*Maddan* 1657].

**Maghaberry** tl, vill., Antrim 3136
*3km NE of Moira*
par: *Magheramesk* bar: *Massereene Upper*
Ir. *Maigh gCabraí* [my **gab**ree] 'plain of the poor land' [*Meigabery* 1661].

**Maghera** tn, par., Derry 2840
*Town is 10.5km NW of Magherafelt*
bar: *Loughinsholin*
Ir. *Machaire Rátha* [maghera **ra**ha] 'plain of the fort'. An earlier name for the parish of Maghera was *Ráth Lúraigh* [rah **loor**ee] '*Lúrach*'s fort', *Lúrach* son of *Cuanu* being a sixth-century saint who was patron of the parish. St *Lúrach* is said to be buried in the graveyard of the medieval parish church, the ruins of which stand in the townland of LARGANTOGHER in the middle of the town [(*Fergus*) *Rátha Lúiricch* 814].

**Magheracashel** tl, Antrim 3044
(sometimes *Maghery Castle*)
*6km W of Ballycastle*
par: *Ballintoy* bar: *Cary*
Ir. *Machaire Caisil* [maghera **cash**il] 'plain of the stone ring-fort'. There was formerly a large stone ring-fort in the townland [*Magherecastle* c.1657].

**Magherafelt** tn, par., Derry 2839
*Town is 16km NE of Cookstown*
bar: *Loughinsholin*
Ir. *Machaire Fíolta* [maghera **feel**ta] '*Fíolta*'s plain'. An earlier name for the parish was

*Old courthouse, Magherafelt*

*Teach Fíolta* [chagh **feel**ta] '*Fíolta*'s (monastic) house'. The site of the medieval parish church may be marked by the ruins of a later church and graveyard at the bottom of BROAD STREET [*Teeoffigalta* 1426].

**Magheragall** tl, ham., par., Antrim 3136
*Hamlet is 5km W of Lisburn*
bar: *Massereene Upper*
Ir. *Machaire na gCeall* [maghera na **gal**] 'plain of the churches'. The site of the medieval parish church is in the townland of BALLYELLOUGH. The present Church of Ireland church in the townland of Magheragall is built on the site of an early 17th-century church [*Magheregall* 1661].

**Magheralin** vill., par., Down 3135
*Village is 3km SW of Moira*
bar: *Iveagh Lower, Upper Half*
Ir. *Machaire Lainne* [maghera **lin**ya] 'plain of the church'. An earlier name for the parish was *Lann Rónáin Fhinn* 'church of fair-haired Ronan'. There are remains of an early 15th-century church in the townland of BALLYMAKEONAN but it is uncertain if this marks the site of the early church [(*ó*) *Lainn Ronain* c.830].

**Magheramason** tl, vill., Tyrone 2441
*On Co. Derry border, 7km SSW of Derry city*
par: *Donaghedy* bar: *Strabane Lower*
Ir. *Machaire Measáin* [maghera **mas**ine] 'plain of the (place of) *mast* or forest fruits and nuts' [*Magheremason* 1661].

**Magheramorne** vill., Antrim 3439
*5.5km SE of Larne*
par: *Glynn* bar: *Belfast Lower*

Ir. *Machaire Morna* [maghera **moarn**a] 'plain of *Morna*'. *Morna* may possibly represent a tribal name but its meaning is obscure. Magheramorne was formerly the name of a *tuath* or petty Ir. kingdom and also of a rural deanery. It contained an early church which is said to have been founded by St Patrick but the site of which has not been located. The village of Magheramorne is in the townland of NEWLANDS [(*Domnach mor*) *Maigi Damóerna* c.900].

**Magheraveely** vill., Fermanagh 2432
(sometimes *Magheravelly*)
*3.5km NW of Clones*
par: *Clones* bar: *Clankelly*
Ir. *Machaire Mhílic* [maghera **veel**ik] 'plain of the marshy margin'. The village was built on the estate of CLONCARN which was granted to Robert Bogas from SUFFOLK in 1610 [*Magheravilly* 1766].

**Maghery** tl, vill., Armagh 2936
*At the point where the Blackwater enters Lough Neagh, 11.5km NW of Portadown*
par: *Tartaraghan* bar: *Oneilland West*
Ir. *An Machaire* [an **magh**era] 'the plain'. An earlier Ir.name for Maghery was *Machaire Grianáin* [maghera **grain**ine] 'plain of the gravelly place' [*Magharagreenan* 1557].

**Maghery** vill., Donegal 4017
*On W Donegal coast, 6km WSW of Ardara*
par: *Templecrone* bar: *Boylagh*
Ir. *An Machaire* [an **magh**era] 'the plain'. There is a large plain here which includes a wide sandy beach. Maghery is in the townland of MAGHERY GLEBE and has given name to MAGHERY BAY and to MAGHERY LOUGH, the latter lying a short distance to the north-east.

**Magho** tl, Fermanagh 2036
*13km E of Belleek*
par: *Inishmacsaint* bar: *Magheraboy*
*Machadh* [**magh**oo] 'milking-field, pasture'. The conspicuous CLIFFS OF MAGHO lie a short distance to the south-west.

**Magilligan** distr., par., Derry 2643
*Flat coastal district adjoining the NE shore of Lough Foyle*
bar: *Keenaght*
Ir. *Aird Mhic Giollagáin* [ardge vick **gill**agine] 'MacGilligan's point'. Magilligan is named from the low, sandy MAGILLIGAN POINT at the entrance to **Lough Foyle** in the townland of LOWER DOAGHS. The parish of Magilligan goes by the *alias* name of TAMLAGHTARD and the ruins of the medieval parish church are adjacent to the modern Catholic church of St Aidan, in the townland of TAMLAGHT. The surname *Mac Giollagáin* 'MacGilligan/Magilligan' is indigenous to Co. Derry [*Tamhloght Aird Mhic Giollagan* c.1675].

**Maguiresbridge** vill., Fermanagh 2333
(sometimes *Maguire's Bridge*)
*On Colebrooke River, 5km NNW of Lisnaskea*
par: *Aghalurcher* bar: *Magherastephana*
The modern village of Maguiresbridge appears to have grown up after 1760 when a Brian Maguire of **Tempo** was given a grant to hold a Wednesday market here. However, the early 19th-century bridge which crosses the river linking the townlands of KILLASHANBALLY and TATTINDERRY replaced a bridge built in the 17th century. The Maguires were once the chief ruling family of Co. Fermanagh and the COLEBROOKE RIVER was formerly known as *Maguire's River* (*see* ***Colebrooke Demesne*** *above*) [*Magwyre's bridge* 1639].

**Mahee Island** isld, tl, Down 3536
*Off W coast of Strangford Lough, 9km SE of Comber*
par: *Tullynakill* bar: *Castlereagh Lower*
Ir. *Inis Mochaoi* [inish mogh**ee**] '(St) *Mochaoi*'s island'. Mahee Island, which can be reached by a causeway, is named from St *Mochaoi* who is said to have founded a monastery here in the fifth century. The monastery itself was known as NENDRUM which is from Ir. *nAondroim*, an eclipsed form of *Aondroim* 'single ridge' (cf. ***Antrim*** *above*) [(*Mochae*) *nOendroma* 497].

**Maidens, The, or Hulin Rocks** Antrim 3441
*In the North Channel, 9km NE of Larne*
par: *Carncastle* bar: *Glenarm Upper*
Ir. *Na Faoilinn* [na **fweel**in]. The Maidens is a direct translation of the original Ir. name, of which the element *Hulin* in *Hulin Rocks* appears to be a corruption. The literal meaning of Ir. *Faoileann* is 'seagull' but it is used figuratively to signify 'graceful woman/maiden'. No doubt the use of the term to apply to rocks in the sea has mythological associations [*The Maydens* 1595].

**Main** river, Antrim
*Rises to the NW of Dunloy and flows into Lough Neagh at Mainwater Foot, 3.5km SSE of Randalstown*
*perhaps* Ir. *An Mhin* [an **vin**] 'the river/the water'. The name appears to ultimately go back to an Indo-European root meaning 'water'. It also seems to be related to *Mana*, the O.Ir. name for the Isle of Man which in turn is connected with *Manannán mac Lir* the name of the god of the sea [*Min (abann mor)* c.1400].

**Malin** vill., distr., Donegal 2445
*On Inishowen peninsula, 5km N of Carndonagh*
par: *Clonca* bar: *Inishowen East*
Ir. *Málainn* [**maal**in]. The name *Málainn*, the etymology of which is obscure but which seems to mean 'high ground/sloping ground', was originally applied to the hilly area between the modern village of Malin and MALIN HEAD. MALIN HEAD lies 12.5km to the north-west, in the townland of ARDMALIN and is the most northerly point in Ireland. The village of Malin is in the townland of DRUMCARBIT [*Máluinn* c.1700].

**Malin Beg** tl, vill., Donegal 1438
*In western extremity of Donegal, 21km W of Killybegs*
par: *Glencolumbkille* bar: *Banagh*
Ir. *Málainn Bheag* [maalin **veg**] 'little *Málainn*'. The element *málainn* appears to mean 'high ground/sloping ground' (*see previous entry*). The townland of Malin Beg contains LEAHAN MOUNTAIN (427m), at the foot of which is the coastal village of Malin Beg. It is adjoined on the north by the townland of MALIN MORE.

**Mallusk** vill., Antrim 3238
*10km NW of Belfast*
par: *Templepatrick* bar: *Belfast Lower*
Ir. *Maigh Bhloisce* [my **vluska**] '*Bloisce*'s plain'. The personal name *Bloisce* is a variant of *Bloscadh* which is the basis of the surname *Mac Bloscaidh* 'MacCloskey/MacCluskey'. Mallusk has given name to the townland of GRANGE OF MALLUSK in which it is situated. The graveyard at Mallusk marks the site of an ancient church [*Manyblos* 1231].

**Malone** tls, distr., Antrim 3336
*Now a suburb, 3.5km SSW of Belfast city centre*
par: *Shankill* bar: *Belfast Upper*
Ir. *Maigh Luain* [my **loo**in] '*Luan*'s plain'. The very large townland of MALONE LOWER is adjoined on the north by the townland of MALONE UPPER and between them they make up the whole of South Belfast [*Mylon* 1604].

**Manorcunningham** tl, vill., Donegal 2241
*7.5km E of Letterkenny*
par: *Raymoghy* bar: *Raphoe*
Manorcunningham is named after James Cunningham from Ayrshire in Scotland who was granted 1000 acres of land here in 1610. The same family also gave name to the townland and village of **Newtown Cunningham** which lies 7.5km to the north-east. The townland of Manorcunningham is adjoined by the townlands of MANORCUNNINGHAM CHURCHLAND and MANORCUNNINGHAM CHURCHLAND ISLE [*The Manor of Fort Cownyngham* 1629].

**Marble Arch** caves Fermanagh 2134
*15km SW of Enniskillen*
par: *Killesher* bar: *Clanawley*
The Marble Arch is a natural bridge of limestone rock at the source of the river CLADAGH. It has given name to a famous system of underground caves.

**Margymonaghan** tl, Derry 2643
*10km N of Limavady*
par: *Magilligan* bar: *Keenaght*
Ir. *Margadh Uí Mhanacháin* [maragoo ee **wan**aghine] '(O')Monaghan's market'. The Monaghans of Co. Derry are descended from a Fermanagh sept from the barony of LURG. An earlier version of the place-name appears to have been *Tamhnaigh Uí Mhanacháin* '(O')Monaghan's field' [*Townamaynan* 1657].

**Markethill** tn, Armagh 2933
*10km SE of Armagh city*
par: *Mullaghbrack/Kilclooney*
bar: *Fews Lower*
In 1610 Henry Acheson from Gosford near Edinburgh was granted 1000 acres in the north of the barony of FEWS and a year later he purchased a further 2000 acres in the south of the barony. The town of Markethill grew up near the fortified *bawn* which he constructed, the ruins of which are close to GOSFORD CASTLE, built in 1843 and standing a short distance north of the town, in the townland of GOSFORD DEMESNE. There is a steep hill on the main street of Markethill and the town still has thriving livestock markets. Markethill is mainly in

the townland of COOLMILLISH [*Marketthill* c.1640].

**Martinstown** tl, vill., Antrim 3141
*11km NNE of Ballymena*
par: *Skerry* bar: *Antrim Lower*
The surname Martin can be of Irish, Scottish or English origin. In this case it is perhaps most likely to be Scottish. The village of Martinstown which is mainly in the the townland of KNOCKANULLY has portions in the townlands of LISNAMANNY and CARROWCOWAN in the neighbouring parish of DUNAGHY, barony of KILCONWAY.

**Mayobridge** vill., Down 3132
*6.5km E of Newry*
par: *Clonallan* bar: *Iveagh Upper, Upper Half*
The village of Mayobridge is named from the townland of MAYO (Ir. *Maigh Eo* [my **o**] 'plain of yew trees') in which it is partially situated. The bridge referred to links the townlands of MAYO and BAVAN across a tributary of the **Clanrye River** [*Droichead Mhuigheó* 1901].

**Maze** tl, Down 3236
(often *The Maze*)
*4km WSW of Lisburn*
par: *Blaris* bar: *Iveagh Lower, Upper Half*
Ir. *An Mhaigh* [an **wy**] 'the plain'. The townland of Maze has given name to the village of MAZETOWN which lies in the townland of LURGANURE, across the **Lagan** in Co. Antrim [*the 5 towns of the Mew* 1585].

**McGaffin's Corner** ham., Down 3133
*8.5km W of Rathfriland*
par: *Donaghmore* bar: *Iveagh Upper, Upper Half*
McGaffin's Corner is named from the junction of three roads, partly in the townland of CARGABANE and partly in TULLYMURRY. The name McGaffin has long been associated with this area. It derives from Ir. *Mac Dhuifinn* [mack **giff**in] and can also be anglicised *MacGiffin* or *MacGuffin*.

**Meenacross** tl, Donegal 1538
*6km ENE of Glencolumbkille*
par: *Glencolumbkille* bar: *Banagh*
Ir. *Mín na Croise* [meen na **crush**a] 'mountain pasture of the cross'. The final element of the place-name may refer to an ancient cross of which there is now no trace or record.

**Meenaneary** tl, ham., Donegal 1638
*12.5km NW of Killybegs*
par: *Glencolumbkille* bar: *Banagh*
Ir. *Mín an Aoire* [meen an **eer**ee] 'mountain pasture of the shepherd' [*Mininarie* 1755].

**Meenlaragh** tl, ham., Donegal 1843
*5km W of Falcarragh*
par: *Tullaghobegly* bar: *Kilmacrenan*
Ir. *Mín Lárach* [meen **laar**agh] 'mountain pasture of the mare' [*Meenlara* 1830].

**Meigh** tl, vill., Armagh 3032
*7km SW of Newry*
par: *Killevy* bar: *Orior Upper*
Ir. *An Mhaigh* [an **wy**] 'the plain'. Meigh is a flat townland in the middle of a hilly area [*Moye* 1657].

**Melmore Head** hl, Donegal 2144
*Northernmost tip of Rosguill peninsula, 8.5km N of Carrickart*
par: *Meevagh* bar: *Kilmacrenan*
Ir. *An Meall Mór* [an mal **more**] 'the great mass/lump' + E. *head*. Melmore Head has given name to the townland of MELMORE in which it is situated.

**Middletown** tl, tn, Armagh 2733
*On Monaghan border, 14.5km SW of Armagh city*
par: *Tynan* bar: *Tiranny*
The exact significance of the element *middle* in the place-name is not apparent. The original Ir. name for the townland was *Coillidh Chanannáin* [killy **khan**anine] '*Canannán*'s wood' and this is now used as the Ir. name of the town which is partly in the neighbouring townland of TULLYBRICK (*Hamilton*) [*Killaninane* 1657].

**Milebush** vill., Antrim 3438
*2km NE of Carrickfergus*
par: *Carrickfergus* bar: *Carrickfergus*
Milebush, in the townland of MIDDLE DIVISION, appears to have been named from its position approximately one Irish mile northeast of the centre of **Carrickfergus**. There is now no trace of the bush which gave name to the hamlet.

**Milford** vill., Armagh 2834
*2.5km SW of Armagh city*
par: *Lisnadill* bar: *Armagh*
Milford is situated on the west bank of the river

**Callan**, in the townland of KENNEDIES. The first element of the place-name refers to a linen mill which formerly stood here while the final element appears to refer to a ford on the river.

**Millbrook** vill., Antrim 3340
*3km WSW of Larne*
par: *Kilwaughter* bar: *Glenarm Upper*
Millbrook, in the townland of DRUMHAHOE, is named from a cotton mill which was established c.1804. Previous to that it was a bleach mill and was named *Allenbrook* after Mr Allen, the then proprietor [*Millbrook* 1840].

**Millburn** tl, distr., Derry 2843
*Suburb on N side of Coleraine*
par: *Coleraine* bar: *NE Liberties of Coleraine*
E. *mill* + Sc./N.E. *burn* 'stream'. The stream referred to flows into the **Lower Bann** to the south of the University of Ulster and forms the northern boundary of the townland. It formerly powered both a corn mill and a flax mill in the townland of DUNDOOAN 2km to the north [*Millburn* 1814].

**Millford** tl, vill., Donegal 2142
(sometimes *Milford*)
*Close to head of Mulroy Bay, 15km N of Letterkenny*
par: *Tullyfern* bar: *Kilmacrenan*
Millford takes its name from a large corn mill the remains of which stand on MAGGY'S BURN at the bottom of the steep main street of the village. The ford was presumably over the stream. The Ir. name of Millford is *Baile na nGallóglach* [bala na **nal**oglagh] 'townland of the *gallowglasses* or heavy-armed soldiers' which was the original Ir. name of the townland, anglicised *Ballinagalaglogh* [*Ballemcgalloglagh* c.1655].

**Millisle** vill., Down 3537
*On E coast of Ards Peninsula, 10.5km SE of Bangor*
par: *Donaghadee* bar: *Ards Lower*
The village of Millisle straddles the MILL BURN which divides the townlands of BALLYMACRUISE and BALLYCOPELAND. A corn mill is recorded in the village in 1834. The final element of the place-name reflects a local usage of the word *isle* to denote a hill in boggy or swampy land [*Mill Isle* c.1834].

**Milltown** ham., Antrim 3138
*3.5km NW of Antrim town*
par: *Antrim* bar: *Toome Upper*
Milltown is on the east bank of the MILL BURN in the townland of KILBEGS and is named from a corn mill which formerly stood on the stream. The MILL BURN divides the townlands of KILBEGS and **Shane's Castle** and the village was formerly sometimes known as *Shane's Castle Milltown* [*The Milltown* 1838].

**Milltown** ham., Armagh 2934
*3.5km SE of Rich Hill*
par: *Kilmore* bar: *Oneilland West*
Milltown stands on the BALLYBAY RIVER at the point where it divides the townlands of BALLYLOUGHAN and **Aghory**. There were formerly corn- and flax mills here.

**Milltown** ham., Armagh 2936
*On SW shore of Lough Neagh, 1km SE of Maghery*
par: *Tartaraghan* bar: *Oneilland West*
Milltown in the townland of DERRYAUGH is named from a corn mill which formerly stood on the stream which forms the boundary between DERRYAUGH and the townland of DERRYLARD which borders it on the east [*Milltown* 1835].

**Milltown** ham., Armagh 2733
*3.5km ENE of Middletown*
par: *Tynan* bar: *Armagh*
There was formerly a large corn mill here, on a tributary of the river **Blackwater**. Milltown is partly in the townland of BALTEAGH and partly in DERRYHAW.

**Milltown** tl, vill., Cavan 2331
*3km SSW of Belturbet*
par: *Drumlane* bar: *Loughtee Lower*
The village of Milltown stands on a stream which flows into ARDAN LOUGH a short distance to the east and divides the townlands of MILLTOWN and DRUMLANE. There is now no record of the mill. The original Ir. name of the townland appears to have been *Béal Átha na Leice* [bell aha na **leck**a] 'ford mouth of the (flag-)stone' [*Milltown* 1837].

**Milltown** vill., Derry 2842
*10km SSE of Coleraine*
par: *Agivey* bar: *Coleraine*
Milltown in the townland of **Culcrow** is on the south bank of the MACOSQUIN RIVER and is named from a corn mill which formerly stood on the river.

**Milltown** vill., Down 3336
*5km S of Belfast city centre*
par: *Drumbo* bar: *Castlereagh Upper*
Milltown, which stands close to the north bank of PURDY'S BURN (sometimes known as the MINNOWBURN) in the townland of BALLYNAVALLY, is named from a corn mill which in the latter half of the 18th century was the property of Arthur Hill Trevor, created Viscount Dungannon in 1765.

**Milltown** tl, Down 3132
*4.5km SE of Newry*
par: *Clonallan* bar: *Iveagh Upper, Upper Half*
Ir. *Baile an Mhuilinn* [bala an **will**in] 'townland of the mill'. The E. name appears to be a translation of the original Irish. In the west of the townland, MILLTOWN BRIDGE straddles a stream which connects MILLTOWN LOUGH with DERRYLECKAGH LAKE but there is no record of any mill. There is a village named MILLTOWN 3.5km to the south, in the townland of **Burren** [*Ballinvoline* c.1655].

**Milltown** tl, Tyrone 2340
*8.5km NE of Strabane*
par: *Donaghedy* bar: *Strabane Lower*
The townland of Milltown contains the village of MILLTOWN BURNDENNET which stands on the north bank of the **Burn Dennet** river. There is no record of a mill in the townland.

**Milltown** tl, Tyrone 2340
*5km NE of Strabane*
par: *Leckpatrick* bar: *Strabane Lower*
Milltown includes the three hamlets of UPPER MILLTOWN, MIDDLE MILLTOWN and LOWER MILLTOWN, the latter standing on the south bank of the GLENMORNAN RIVER which marks the northern boundary of the townland. There is no record of a mill in the townland though there is a mill in the townland of **Artigarvan** which adjoins it on the east.

**Mill Town** tl, Derry 2743
*At the W foot of Binevenagh, 7.5km N of Limavady*
par: *Magilligan* bar: *Keenaght*
The name may be a translation of the original Ir. *Baile an Mhuilinn* [bala an **will**in] 'townland of the mill' but there is now no record of a mill in the townland [*Milltown* 1835].

**Minerstown** vill., Down 3433
*On Dundrum, 4.5km W of Killough*
par: *Rathmullan* bar: *Lecale Upper*
Minerstown in the townland of BALLYVASTON was founded in the late 18th century by miners of lead ore, a substance which was also found at the nearby village of **Killough**.

**Minterburn** ham., Tyrone 2735
(sometimes *Munterbyrne*)
*7km ESE of Aughnacloy*
par: *Aghaloo* bar: *Dungannon Lower*
Ir. *Muintir Bhirn* [muntcher **virn**] 'descendants of *Birn*'. The Ir. personal name *Birn* is derived from the Norse forename *Bjorn*. It is the basis of the Connaught surname *Ó Birn*/*Ó Beirn* '(O')Beirne' which is also found in Co. Tyrone. The hamlet of Minterburn is in the townland of LISMULLADOWN [(*toiseach*) *Muinntire Birn* 1173].

**Moira** vill., par., Down 3136
*Village is close to border with Co. Antrim, 6.5km NE of Lurgan*
bar: *Iveagh Lower, Upper Half*
Ir. *Maigh Rath* [my **ra**] *perhaps* 'plain of the wheels'. Moira was originally a district name before it came to refer to the village. The significance of the element 'wheels' in the place-name is obscure. Possibly it could refer to a meeting place of routes. The civil parish of Moira was created in 1725 out of the neighbouring parish of **Magheralin** [(*cath*) *Maighe Rath* 634].

**Monaghan** tn, par/bar, co. 2633
*Town is 22.5km SW of Armagh*
Ir. *Muineachán* [**mwin**yaghan] 'place of thickets or hills'. Near the DIAMOND in the middle of the town there formerly stood a monastery for Conventual Franciscans, founded in 1462 by Phelim Mac Mahon on the site of an earlier monastery [(*i*) *Muineachán* 1462].

**Monea** tl, vill., Fermanagh 2134
*4.5km SE of Derrygonnelly*
par: *Devenish* bar: *Magheraboy*
Ir. *Maigh Niadh* [my **nee**a] 'plain of warriors'. St Molaise's Church of Ireland church in the townland of Monea marks the site of an early monastery. The village of Monea is in the neighbouring townland of CASTLETOWN MONEA which contains the ruins of a Plantation castle [(*Monua*) *Maigi Niad* c. 830].

**Moneydig** tl, vill., Derry 2841
*5km NNW of Kilrea*
par: *Desertoghill* bar: *Coleraine*
Ir. *Muine Díge* [mwinya **jeeg**a] 'thicket or hill of the ditch/trench'. The reference of the final element of the place-name may be to some kind of earthworks. Two forts are recorded in the townland and a short distance north of the village there is a megalithic chambered cairn known as the DAFF STONE [*Monnodegg* 1654].

**Moneygashel** tl, Cavan 2033
*6km S of Blacklion*
par: *Killinagh* bar: *Tullyhaw*
Ir. *Muine na gCaiseal* [mwinya na **gash**el] 'thicket or hill of stone ring-forts'. Near the centre of the townland there are the remains of three stone ring-forts, the largest being 25m in diameter [*Monygashell* 1619].

**Moneyglass** tl, distr., Antrim 3039
*3.5km NE of Toome*
par: *Duneane* bar: *Toome Upper*
Ir. *An Muine Glas* [an mwinya **glass**] 'the green thicket or hill' [*Ballymoyneglass* 1605].

**Moneymore** tl, vill., Derry 2838
*8km NE of Cookstown*
par: *Artrea/Desertlyn* bar: *Loughinsholin*
Ir. *Muine Mór* [mwinya **more**] 'large thicket or hill' [*Minimore* 1654].

**Moneyneany** tl, vill., Derry 2739
(sometimes *Moneyneaney*)
*4km NW of Draperstown*
par: *Ballinascreen* bar: *Loughinsholin*
Ir. *Móin na nIonadh* [moyn na **neen**oo] 'bog of the wonders'. There are traditions associating this townland with fairies and enchantment, including a story of a well, the water of which would curdle new milk [*Monaneney* 1622].

**Moneynick** tl, Antrim 3039
*4km WSW of Randalstown*
par: *Duneane* bar: *Toome Upper*
Ir. *Muine Chnoic* [mwinya **khrick**] 'thicket of the hill' [*Ballivonanykie* 1605].

**Moneynoe Glebe or Chanterhill**
tl, Fermanagh 2234
*On NE outskirts of Enniskillen*
par: *Enniskillen* bar: *Tirkennedy*

*Monea Castle*

Moneynoe Glebe represents a combination of Ir. *Muine na nEo* [munya na **nyo**] 'thicket of the yew-trees' + E. *glebe* 'land set aside for the upkeep of a clergyman'. The *alias* name Chanterhill was originally the name of a glebe house which was built in 1784 for Rev. Thomas Smith, rector of **Enniskillen** and still stands on the crown of a hill. The word *chanter* signifies a chorister or the chief singer in a chapel [*Munnenoe* 1659].

**Moneyreagh** tl, vill., Down 3436
(sometimes *Moneyrea*)
*5km WSW of Comber*
Ir. *Mónaidh Riabhach* [moanee **ree**wagh] 'grey bog/moor'. There is still an area of rough moorland in the south-west of the townland [*Ballymoyne-Righ* 1606].

**Moneyscalp** tl, Down 3333
*5.5km WNW of Newcastle*
par: *Kilcoo* bar: *Iveagh Upper, Lower Half*
Ir. *Muine Scailpe* [mwinya **skalp**a] 'thicket or hill of the rocky chasm'. There are steep rocky slopes in both the east and west of the townland [*Ballymonyskalpie* 1609].

**Moneysharvan** tl, Derry 2840
*4.5km N of Maghera*
par: *Killelagh* bar: *Loughinsholin*
Ir. *Muine Searbhán* [mwinya **shar**awan] 'thicket or hill of dandelions' [*Muine Searbhán* c.1740].

**Moneyslane** tl, vill., Down 3233
*7km NE of Rathfriland*
par: *Drumgooland*
bar: *Iveagh Upper, Lower Half*
Ir. *Muine Sleánna* [mwinya **slan**a] 'thicket or hill of spears/javelins'. The place-name may indicate the site of a battle. Otherwise the final element may be understood in the sense of 'long thorns/splinters' [*Ballymonyshlany* 1611].

**Monkstown** tl, vill., Antrim 3338
*Forms a district of Newtownabbey, 12km N of Belfast city centre*
par: *Carnmoney* bar: *Belfast Upper*
Ir. *Baile na Manach* [bala na **man**agh] 'townland of the monks'. The E. name is a translation of the original Irish. The site of the monastery is marked by the ruins of a church in a graveyard at the south foot of KNOCKAGH mountain [*Ballynemanagh* 1605].

**Montiaghs** distr., par., Armagh 2936
*District is on S shore of Lough Neagh, 12km WNW of Lurgan*
bar: *Oneilland East*
Ir. *Na Móinteacha* [na **moyn**chagha] 'the bogs/moors'. The parish of Montiaghs formed part of the neighbouring parish of SEAGOE until 1765. There is a townland named MONTIAGHS (also from Ir. *Na Móinteacha* 'the bogs/moors') 10km to the east, in the parish of **Aghagallon** in Co. Antrim [*Montaes* 1662].

**Moorfields** ham., Antrim 3139
*8.5km ESE of Ballymena*
par: *Ballyclug* bar: *Antrim Lower*
The first element appears to represent the surname Moore which can be of Irish, Scottish or English origin but in this case is likely to be Scottish. Moorfields is in the townland of CROSS.

**Mossley** vill., Antrim 3338
*On northern edge of Newtownabbey, 11km N of Belfast city centre*
par: *Carnmoney* bar: *Belfast Lower*
The name Mossley has been imported from England where it is found as the name of a town south-east of Oldham in Lancashire. The name means 'clearing by mossy land', from O.E. *mos* 'peat-bog' + O.E. *leah* 'clearing'. Mossley is in the townland of BALLYHENRY [*Mossley* 1839].

**Moss-side** tl, vill., Antrim 3043
(sometimes *Mosside*)
*12km SW of Ballycastle*
par: *Grange of Drumtullagh* bar: *Cary*
*perhaps* Ir. *Maigh Saighead* [my **sey**id] 'plain of arrows'. The place-name may indicate the site of a battle but it is also possible that the name represents Sc. *moss* 'peat-bog' (from O.E. *mos*) + E. *side*. There is still an area of moorland in the south-east of the townland. A portion of the village of Moss-side lies west of MOSS-SIDE WATER, in the townland of MOYCRAIG HAMILTON, parish of BILLY [*Mosside* c.1657].

**Mountcharles** tl, vill., Donegal 1837
*Close to N shore of Donegal Bay, 5km WSW of Donegal town*
par: *Inver* bar: *Banagh*
Mountcharles is named from Charles Conyngham who was landlord here in the 17th century. The village, which grew up in the 18th century, goes by two names in Irish, *Moin Séarlas* [mun **sher**las] 'Charles's mount/hill', which is clearly a gaelicisation of the E. name of the townland, and *Tamhnach an tSalainn* [townagh a **tal**in] 'field of the salt', referring to a great salt works established in the 17th century by the Conyngham family. The townland of Mountcharles is adjoined on the south-west by the townland of SALTHILL DEMESNE. SALTHILL HOUSE, the residence of the Conyngham land agent, was built in the late 18th century [*town*(land) *of Mount Charles al. Tawnytallan* 1676].

**Mountfield** vill., Tyrone 2537
*10km NE of Omagh*
par: *Cappagh* bar: *Strabane Upper*
The village of Mountfield in the townland of AGHALANE grew up in the 18th century, on land granted in the 17th century to Sir William Stewart of Galloway in Scotland (*see* ***Newtownstewart*** *below*). It was completely rebuilt by Sir William McMahon after the construction of the present Church of Ireland church in 1827. It is named from its position at the foot of MULDERG (317m) [*Montfull* 1683].

**Mountjoy** vill., Tyrone 2437
*6km NNW of Omagh*
par: *Cappagh* bar: *Strabane Upper*
The village of Mountjoy in the townland of TATTRACONAGHTY grew up in the early 19th century as the centre of the demesne of Charles

John Gardiner, 2nd Viscount Mountjoy and Earl of Blessington, who resided at *Mountjoy Cottage* (now OLD MOUNTJOY), 4km to the south-east. The land was originally granted c.1623 to Sir William Stewart from Galloway in Scotland (*see* ***Newtownstewart*** *below*). The demesne included the large nearby townlands of MOUNTJOY FOREST EAST and MOUNJOY FOREST WEST [*Mountjoy forest* 1834].

**Mountjoy** ham., Tyrone 2936
*6.5km ENE of Coalisland*
par: *Clonoe* bar: *Dungannon Middle*
Mountjoy takes its name from the nearby MOUNTJOY CASTLE which was built as a military station by the Lord Deputy Charles Blount (Lord Mountjoy) in 1602, during his campaign against Hugh O'Neill, Earl of Tyrone (*see* ***Charlemont***). The ruins of the castle stand on the west shore of **Lough Neagh**, in the townland of MAGHERALAMFIELD. Mountjoy is referred to as a barony in documents of the Plantation of Ulster [*Mountjoy* 1837].

**Mountnorris** tl, vill., Armagh 2933
*5.5km SSE of Markethill*
par: *Loughgilly* bar: *Orior Lower*
Mountnorris is named after Sir John Norris (1547–97) from England who at the end of the 16th century built a fort here, on lands belonging to the O'Hanlons, to guard the pass between **Armagh** and **Newry**, in the course of his war with Hugh O'Neill, Earl of Tyrone. The original Ir. name of the townland was *Achadh na Cranncha* [aghoo na **kran**agha] 'field of the wooded place' and this is now used as the Ir. name of the village [*(fort of) Mountnorris orw. Aghnecranchie* 1606].

**Mount Nugent** tl, tn, Cavan 2428
*Close to E shore of Lough Sheelin, 6km SW of Ballyjamesduff*
par: *Kilbride* bar: *Clanmahon*
Mount Nugent takes its name from a branch of the Nugent family, barons of DELVIN, who were granted forfeited lands in Cavan and Longford in 1597. The surname Nugent is Norman in origin and was originally *de Nogent* 'of Nugent', *Nogent* being a common place-name in France. The first Nugents came to Ireland during the 12th-century Anglo-Norman invasion and were granted lands in Meath and Westmeath. The town stands on the south bank of the UPPER INNY and was formerly known as *Daly's Bridge* which may be a translation of the Ir. name *Droichead Uí Dhálaigh* [dryhid ee **ġaal**ee]. The bridge seems to have been built in the first half of the 17th century, on the site of a ford. According to a local tradition, it was named from a Rev. Hugh Daly who was parish priest here in the 17th century [*Mount Nugent or Dalysbridge* 1837].

**Mountpottinger** distr., Down 3337
*Suburb close to river Lagan on E side of Belfast*
par: *Knockbreda* bar: *Castlereagh Upper*
Mountpottinger is in the townland of **Ballymacarret** which in 1672 was granted to the merchant Thomas Pottinger who had been created sovereign or mayor of Belfast in 1688. The Pottinger family has also given name to POTTINGER'S ENTRY in the centre of Belfast.

**Mount Sandel** tl, Derry 2843
*1.5km S of Coleraine*
par: *Coleraine* bar: *NE Liberties of Coleraine*
The townland of Mount Sandel takes its name from MOUNTSANDEL FORT which stands on the east bank of the **Lower Bann**. The name of the fort may be a corruption of Ir. *Cill Sanctáin* 'church of *Sanctán*', a name which originally applied to an ancient church in the nearby townland of FISH LOUGHAN. It was then transferred to an adjacent castle built by John de Courcy and, in turn, came to be applied to Mount Sandel which is a Norman mound built on the site of a prehistoric settlement. *Cill Sanctáin* may have been corrupted to Mount Sandel as a result of an imagined association with the Anglo-Norman family of Sandell who appear to have settled in Co. Antrim under John de Courcy [*Killsantill alias Mount Sandall* 1605].

**Mount Stewart** tl, dmsne, Down 3536
*5km SE of Newtownwards*
par: *Greyabbey* bar: *Ards Lower*
The townland and demesne of Mount Stewart take their name from a house originally constructed by the Rt Hon. Robert Stewart, 1st Marquess of Londonderry, on land bought by his father Alexander Stewart in 1744, but greatly enlarged since then. Robert Stewart junior, son of the aforesaid Robert, was Viscount Castlereagh and British Foreign Secretary during the Napoleonic Wars. The original Ir. name of the townland was *Templecrone*,

from Ir. *Teampall Chróine* '*Cróine*'s church' [*Temple Crom now Mount Stewart* c.1834].

**Mourne** river Tyrone
*Formed by the convergence of the Strule and the Derg 4km NW of Newtownstewart. Combines with the Finn to form the Foyle a short distance S of Lifford*
Ir. *An Mhorn* [an **woarn**] *perhaps* 'the noble one/holy one'. *Morn* (earlier *Modharn*) may go back to an Indo-European root which has given the Ir. word *muadh* 'noble/illustrious'. As in the case of many river names, it may originally be the name of a goddess. The river Mourne appears to have formerly included the **Strule** which is the name now given to the portion of the river between **Omagh** and the point where it receives the river **Derg** [(*oc*) *Modhairn* 1030].

**Mourne Beg** river Donegal/Tyrone
(sometimes *Mournebeg*)
*Rises in Lough Mourne, 7.5km W of Ballybofey in Co. Donegal. Enters the river Derg 3.5km SW of Castlederg*
Ir. *An Mhorn Bheag* [an woarn **veg**] 'the little *Morn*'. The Mourne Beg seems to be named by way of contrast with the river **Mourne** which is roughly 15km to the north-east (*see previous entry*). It appears to have given name to LOUGH MOURNE in which it rises. It has also given name to the townland of MOURNE BEG which lies at the junction of the Mourne Beg with the river **Derg**, in the parish of TERMONAMONGAN.

**Mourne Mountains** Down
*In SE corner of Co. Down*
Ir. *Múrna* (tribe) + E. 'mountains'.
The name Mourne originally referred to the district (later a barony) in which the mountains are situated. The district takes its name from the tribe named *Múrna* (earlier *Mughdhorna*) who originated in modern Co. Monaghan where they gave name to the barony of CREMORNE (Ir. *Críoch Mhúrn* 'district of the *Múrna*) but migrated to Co. Down in the 12th century (*see* ***Lough Morne***). In early Irish genealogies their name is traced back to a mythological ancestor *Mughdhorn Dubh* 'black *Mughdhorn*'. However, the name may in fact represent a combination of *Mug* 'slave/servant' and *Dairine*, the name of an early population group. Thus *Múrna* may signify 'the vassal or subject people (called) *Dairine*'. The original Ir. name for the Mourne Mountains was *Beanna Boirche* [bana **bir**agha] *perhaps* 'peaks of the peak district'. There are townlands named MOURNE MOUNTAINS EAST, WEST and MIDDLE in the parish of **Kilkeel** which is coterminous with barony of Mourne [*Benna Bairche* c.800].

**Movanagher** tl, Derry 2941
*3km N of Kilrea*
par: *Kilrea* bar: *Coleraine*
Ir. *Má Bheannchair* [ma **van**agher] 'plain of the palisaded enclosure'. Movanagher is on the west bank of the **Lower Bann** and contains the remains of CONEYBURROW FORT as well as a ruin known as MOVANAGHER CASTLE BAWN [(*do*) *Mhagh Bhennchair* c.1645].

**Movilla** tl, Down 3537
*Forms a suburb on E side of Newtownards*
par: *Newtownards* bar: *Ards Lower*
Ir. *Maigh Bhile* [my **villa**] 'plain of the sacred tree'. The townland of Movilla contains the ruins of a medieval abbey which marks the site of a monastery founded by St Finian in c.540 [*Moige Bile* 580].

**Moville** vill., pars., Donegal 2643
*Village is on E shore of Lough Foyle, 27.5km NE of Derry city*
bar: *Inishowen East*
Ir. *Magh Bhile* [my **villa**] 'plain of the sacred tree'. The village of Moville is on the north bank of the BREDAGH RIVER on the southern boundary of the parish of LOWER MOVILLE while the ruins of the medieval parish church stand a short distance to the west, in the parish of MOVILLE UPPER. The village was formerly known as *Bonafobble*, from Ir. *Bun an Phobail* [bun a **fubb**il] 'foot of the parish' [(*for lár*) *Maighe Bile* 1167].

**Mowhan** vill., Armagh 2833
*3km S of Markethill*
par: *Loughgilly* bar: *Fews Lower*
Ir. *Má Bhán* [ma **wan**] 'white plain'.
Mowhan stands on the MOWHAN RIVER and links the townland of DRUMGANE with the townland of KILBRACKS in the neighbouring parish of KILCLOONEY [*Mowhan* 1838].

**Moy** tl, vill., Tyrone 2835
(often *The Moy*)
*On Co. Armagh border, 7km SE of Dungannon*
par: *Clonfeacle* bar: *Dungannon Middle*

Ir. *An Mhaigh* [an **wy**] 'the plain'. The Moy is twin village to **Charlemont** which lies across the **Blackwater** in Co. Armagh [*(san) Madh* c.1645].

**Moyagall** tl, Derry 2940
(often *Mayogall*)
*5km E of Maghera*
par: *Maghera* bar: *Loughinsholin*
Ir. *Maigh Ó gColla* [my o **goll**a] 'plain of the (O')Cullys'. The surname *Ó Colla* '(O')Cully' is found in Cos Armagh and Antrim and is also recorded in Co. Derry in the 17th century [*Moyogalla* 1609].

**Moyallan** tl, Down 3035
(sometimes *Moyallon*)
*Close to Armagh border, 2km NW of Gilford*
par: *Tullylish* bar: *Iveagh Lower, Upper Half*
Ir. *Maigh Alúine* [my **al**oona] 'plain of *alum* or yellow clay' [*Moynalvin* c.1657].

**Moyarget** tls, Antrim 3043
*4.5km SW of Ballycastle*
par: *Ramoan* bar: *Cary*
Ir. *Maigh Airgid* [my **ar**agidge] 'plain of silver'. The final element may refer to the colour silver rather than to the metal. The townland of MOYARGET UPPER is bounded on the south by MOYARGET LOWER [*Myerget* c.1657].

**Moydamlaght** tl, ham., Derry 2739
*4km NW of Draperstown*
par: *Ballynascreen* bar: *Loughinsholin*
Ir. *Maigh dTamhlachta* [my **dau**laghta] 'plain of the (pagan) burial place'. The element *tamhlacht* is traditionally interpreted as '(pagan) burial place' but is fairly common in the names of ecclesiastical sites. There are no ecclesiastical remains here but early in the last century many skulls and bones were unearthed at a fort in the townland [*Ballymadaulaght* 1613].

**Moygashel** tl, vill., Tyrone 2836
*2km S of Dungannon*
par: *Clonfeacle* bar: *Dungannon Middle*
Ir. *Maigh gCaisil* [my **gash**el] 'plain of the stone ring-fort'. There is now no trace or record of a stone ring-fort in the townland [*Moygashell* 1609].

**Moyola** river, Derry
*Rises in the Sperrins, 11km WSW of Draperstown. Flows into Lough Neagh 3km SW of Toome*
The original Ir. name of the Moyola was *Bior*, a word meaning simply 'water'. At a later period the river was known as *Abhainn na Scríne* [owen na **skreen**a] 'Ballynascreen river'. Ballynascreen (Ir. *Baile na Scríne* 'territory of the shrine') is a parish which is named from a medieval church containing a shrine of St Colmcille and the river was so-named from the fact that it flows past the ruins of the parish church, in the townland of MONEYCONEY, 7km south-west of **Draperstown**. The name Moyola originally applied to two land units which are bounded by the lowermost portion of the river and are now represented by the large townland of **The Creagh**; its application to the river is comparatively late. Moyola appears to derive from Ir. *Maigh Fhoghlach* [my **oal**agh] 'plain of plundering'.

**Moyraverty** tl, distr., Armagh 3035
*On S outskirts of Craigavon*
par: *Seagoe* bar: *Oneilland East*
Ir. *Maigh Raifeartaigh* [my **raff**artee] '*Raifeartach*'s plain'. The personal name *Raifeartach* is the basis of the surname *Ó Raifeartaigh* '(O') Rafferty' which is found in Ulster and also in Co. Louth [*Moyrevertie* 1609].

**Moys** tl, ham., Derry 2641
*4km SSW of Limavady*
par: *Carrick* bar: *Keenaght*
Ir. *Na Magha* [na **my**-ya] 'the plains'. The large townland of Moys was originally made up of *Moybeg* (Ir. *Magh Bheag* 'little Moy') and *Moymore* (Ir. *Magh Mhór* 'great Moy') [*Moybeg, Moymore* 1613].

**Muckamore** tl, vill., Antrim 3138
*2km SE of Antrim town*
par: *Grange of Muckamore* bar: *Massereene*
Ir. *Maigh Chomair* [my **khom**er] 'plain of the confluence'. The final element of the place-name appears to refer to the point where the **Six Mile Water** enters **Lough Neagh** 3km to the north-west, suggesting that the place-name formerly applied to a wider area than it does today. MUCKAMORE HOUSE on the south bank of the river marks the site of a medieval Augustinian priory, originally a sixth-century monastery founded by St Colman Ela [*Magh-Comair* 3529AM].

**Muckish** mtn, Donegal 2042
*5km SW of Creeslough*
par: *Clondahorky* bar: *Kilmacrenan*

Ir. *An Mhucais* [an **wuck**ish] 'the pig back/ridge'. Muckish (670m) is named from its resemblance to the back of a pig.

**Muckno Lake** Monaghan 2831
*Adjoins the town of Castleblayney on the E*
par: *Muckno/Clontibret/Donaghmoyne*
bar: *Cremorne/Farney*
Ir. *Loch Mucnú* [lough **muck**noo]. The meaning of the final element of the place-name is obscure. The place-name has been 'rationalised' as *Loch Mucshnámha* 'lake of the pig's swimming place or ford' and there is a local story about a pig which swam across the narrow part of the lake to CHURCH HILL, the site of the medieval church of the parish of MUCKNO in which the greater part of the lake is situated [*(ar mhachaire) Mucnamha* 1424].

**Muff** tl, vill., par., Donegal 2442
*Village is 8km N of Derry city*
bar: *Inishowen West*
Ir. *Magh* [my] 'plain'. The parish was created in 1809 when eleven townlands were severed from the neighbouring parish of **Templemore** [*Mough* 1621].

**Muldonagh** tl, Derry 2641
*9km W of Dungiven*
par: *Bovevagh* bar: *Keenaght*
Ir. *Maol Domhnaigh* [mweel **doan**ee] 'round hill of the (early) church'. The townland appears to be named from the prominent MULDONAGH HILL (291m). There is no trace or record of an ancient church but evidence of an old graveyard has been found in the neighbouring townland of BALLYMONEY [*Meldony* 1613].

**Mullagh** tl, vill., par., Cavan 2628
*Village is close to Meath border, 8km SE of Virginia*
bar: *Castlerahan*
Ir. *An Mullach* [an **mull**agh] 'the hilltop'. The old name of Mullagh was *Mullach Laoighill* [mullagh **leel**] '*Laoigheall*'s hilltop', referring to the nearby MULLAGH HILL (220m). The ruins of the medieval parish church which was known as *Teampall Cheallaigh* '*Ceallach*'s church' are at the foot of the hill, close to the shore of MULLAGH LOUGH [*(tigearna) Mullaigh Laoighill* 1488].

**Mullaghbane** tl, vill., Armagh 2931
*11km SW of Newry*
par: *Forkill* bar: *Orior Upper*
Ir. *An Mullach Bán* [an mullagh **baan**] 'the white hilltop'. The 'hilltop' referred to appears to be MULLAGHBANE MOUNTAIN (242m) which stands in the east of the townland, 1km south-west of Mullaghbane village. The village is not in the townland of that name; rather, it straddles the townlands of SHANROE, MAPHONER and GLEBE [*Mullabane* 1609].

**Mullaghcarn** mtn, Tyrone 2538
*10km NE of Omagh*
par: *Cappagh* bar: *Strabane Upper*
Ir. *Mullach Cairn* [mullagh **carn**] 'hilltop of the cairn'. There are remains of a cairn on the summit of the mountain (542m) which is in the townlands of CULLION, STRADOWAN and GLENMACOFFER [*Mullogh Cairne* c.1655].

**Mullaghglass** tl, vill., Armagh 3032
*3.5km NW of Newry*
par: *Killevy* bar: *Orior Upper*
Ir. *An Mullach Glas* [an mullagh **glas**] 'the green hilltop'. The townland of Mullaghglass consists of hilly land, overlooking the NEWRY RIVER. The village of Mullaghglass is not in the townland of that name but is shared between the neighbouring townlands of DERRYWILLIGAN and LATT [*Mullaglas* 1609].

**Mullaghslin Glebe** tl, Tyrone 2537
(sometimes *Mullaslin Glebe*)
*11km E of Omagh*
par: *Clogherny* bar: *Omagh East*
Ir. *Mullach Slinne* [mullagh **slin**ya] 'hilltop of the flat stone/flat surface' + E. *glebe* 'clergyman's land'. Mullaghslin Glebe forms a detached portion of the parish of CLOGHERNY, lying 3km north-east of the main portion of the parish [*Mullaghslimey* c.1655].

**Mullan** tl, Derry 2842
(*See* ***Blackhill.***)

**Mullartown** tl, Down 3332
*On the coast, 1km N of Annalong*
par: *Kilkeel* bar: *Mourne*
Ir. *Maol Dortáin* [mweel **dort**ine] '*Dortán*'s round hill'. *Mullartown* is an unusual corruption of the original Ir. name. The personal name *Dortán* is rare, though it does appear to occur as a saint's name in KILDARTON, the name of a church in the parish of Armagh [*Ballymoldurtan* 1540].

**Mulroy Bay** inl., Donegal
*Long sea inlet on N coast of Donegal, its N portion dividing Fanad peninsula from Rosguill peninsula*
Ir. *An Mhaoil Rua* [an weel **roo**a] *perhaps* 'the red current/stream' + E. *bay*. The first element of the place-name appears to refer to the strong tidal nature of the water in this narrow sea inlet. The element *rua* 'red' may refer to the reddish-yellow colour of the tidal sand banks in the upper portion of the inlet [*Moyroy* 1608].

**Murlough Bay** bay, Antrim 3244
*On N Antrim coast, 8km E of Ballycastle*
par: *Culfeightrim* bar: *Cary*
Ir. *Murlach* 'sea inlet' + E. *bay*. *Murlach*, the recognised Ir. form of the place-name, is a development from O.Ir. *Muirbolc* 'sea-bag', i.e. 'lagoon, inlet of the sea' [*Murbolc* c.1390].

**Myroe** ham., distr., Derry 2642
*3km NW of Limavady*
par: *Tamlaght Finlagan* bar: *Keenaght*
Ir. *Maigh Ró* [my **ro**] 'plain of the (river) Roe'. The hamlet of Myroe is in the townland of LOMOND which is bounded on the east by the river **Roe**. Myroe has given name to the townland of MYROE LEVEL which consists of land reclaimed from **Lough Foyle**, 3km to the north-west [*Moyrowe* 1613].

# N

**Naran** tl. ham., Donegal 1739
(sometimes *Narin*)
*On Gweebarra Bay, 8km NNW of Ardara*
par: *Inishkeel* bar: *Boylagh*
*perhaps* Ir. *An Fhearthainn* [an **yar**hin] 'the rain'. The significance of the place-name is obscure, unless it refer to the exposed nature of the location.

**Narrow Water** tl, Down 3131
*2km NW of Warrenpoint*
par: *Warrenpoint*
bar: *Iveagh Upper, Upper Half*
Ir. *An Caol* [an **keel**] 'the narrow (water)'. Narrow Water is at the head of **Carlingford Lough** where the lough narrows to become the **Newry River**. The E. name is a translation of the original Ir. Narrow Water is well-known as the location of NARROW WATER CASTLE which was built c.1560, apparently on the site of a Norman *motte-and-bailey*, and the ruins of which stand on the east bank of the river [*Cáol* c.1170].

**Navan** tl, ham., Armagh 2834
*2km W of Armagh city*
par: *Eglish* bar: *Armagh*
Navan takes its name from the famous NAVAN FORT which stands in the middle of the townland and which was the ancient capital of Ulster. The name of the fort is derived from Ir. *Eamhain Mhacha* [au-in **wagh**a]. Traditionally *Eamhain Mhacha* has been interpreted as '*Macha*'s brooch or fibula' the element *eamhain* going back to an original form *eomhuin*, literally 'neck-pin', and the name being explained by a legend that when the fort was being built the goddess *Macha* used the pin to draw a circle round herself to mark out its outline. Another traditional interpretation of *Eamhain Mhacha* is 'the twins of *Macha*'. Here the story relates that *Macha* gave birth to the twins after outpacing king *Conchobhar mac Neasa*'s horses in a race, whereupon she died, but not before putting a curse on the men of Ulster that in their time of greatest need they would be afflicted by a great debility. The true meaning of *Eamhain Mhacha* is obscure. In early Celtic mythology *Eamhain* is used as a name for the otherworld and perhaps the most satisfactory explanation for its use to refer to Navan Fort is that the people believed that the fortress was built by their ancestor deities on the model of an otherworld city. The element *Macha* may represent the name of the goddess who features in the stories quoted above. However, *Macha* could also be regarded as the name of the district (*see* ***Armagh*** *above*), the name of the land-goddess *Macha* (which signifies 'pasture') being used to refer to the general area. The anglicisation of the place-name as NAVAN is based on Ir. *An Eamhain*, a later form of the name which includes the definite article [(*bellum*) *Emnae Machae* 759].

**Nendrum Monastic Site** Down 3636
(see ***Mahee Island***)

**Newbliss** tl, vill., Monaghan 2532
*6km ESE of Clones*
par: *Killeevan* bar: *Dartree*

The village was founded early in the 18th century by a local landowner named Robert Kerr. The old name for the townland of Newbliss was *Mullaghnashanner*, while the Ir. name of the village is *Cúil Darach* [kool **dar**agh] 'corner/recess of the oak-tree' [*Newbliss al. Mullaghneshanner* 1730].

**Newbridge** ham., Derry 2939
*3km W of Toome*
par: *Artrea* bar: *Loughinsholin*
Newbridge is named from a now-superseded bridge which was built c.1806 across the **Moyola** river, linking the townlands of DERRYGARVE and **The Creagh** [*'new bridge'* 1836].

**New Buildings** vill., h.est. Derry 2441
*4km SSW of Derry city*
par: *Clondermot* bar: *Tirkeeran*
The original village at New Buildings grew up around an early 17th-century castle-and-*bawn* of the Goldsmiths' Company, one of the planter companies of Londoners. The present housing estate in the townland of PRIMITY is of fairly recent origin [*Nutown* 1622].

**Newcastle** tn, Down 3333
*On E coast of Co. Down, 5.5km SE of Castlewellan*
par: *Kilcoo* bar: *Iveagh Upper, Lower Half*
Ir. *An Caisleán Nua* [an kashlan **noo**a] 'the new castle'. The E. name of the town is a translation of the original Ir. Newcastle is said to be named from a castle built in 1588 by Felix Magennis in the middle of the present town and knocked down by the Earl of Annesley c.1830. However, the name must refer to an earlier castle which is mentioned in an Irish source in 1433 and the site of which is unknown [(*ag fersait*) *an chaisléin nui* 1433].

**New Ferry** distr., Antrim 2939
*On Lower Bann, 7km N of Toome*
par: *Grange of Ballyscullion*
bar: *Toome Upper*
New Ferry, in the townland of CULNAFAY, is named from a ferry which was established by the Earl of Massereene c.1765, replacing an older one across the **Lower Bann** about 200m farther south. The ferry connected the counties of Antrim and Derry [*New Ferry* 1785].

**New Inn** vill., Cavan 2529
*4.5km NE of Ballyjamesduff*
par: *Lavey* bar: *Loughtee Upper*
New Inn is named from a former stagecoach inn on the road from **Cavan** to **Virginia**. The Ir. name of New Inn is *An Dromainn* [an **drumin**] 'the ridge', which is a shortened form of *An Dromainn Bhán* 'the white ridge', the original Ir. name of the townland of DRUMMANBANE in which the village is situated. Drummanbane is bordered by the townland of DRUMMANDUFF (Ir. *An Dromainn Dhubh* 'the black ridge').

**Newmills** mill complex, Donegal 2140
*5km SSW of Letterkenny*
par: *Conwal* bar: *Raphoe*
The name Newmills refers to corn and flax mills in the townland of MILLTOWN on the south bank of the **Swilly**. The mills were operated for generations by the Gallagher family until their closure in 1982. They have now been re-opened under state care.

**Newmills** vill., Tyrone 2836
*2.5km NW of Coalisland*
par: *Tullyniskan* bar: *Dungannon Middle*
Newmills takes its name from a corn mill and kilns which formerly stood on the **Torrent** river. The village straddles the river and is partly in the townland of DRUMREAGH OTRA and partly in DORAS [*New Mills* 1837].

**Newport Trench** Tyrone 2937
(*see* ***Battery, The***)

**Newry** tn, par., Down 3032
*28km SE of Armagh city*
bar: *Lordship of Newry*
Ir. *An tIúr* [an **choor**] 'the yew tree'. An earlier name for Newry was *Iúr Cinn Trá* [yoor kin **tra**] 'yew tree at the head of the strand'. Local tradition has it that the town was named from two large yew trees which formerly grew in the grounds of the Cistercian abbey, founded by St Malachy in 1144. The site of the abbey, which was destroyed by fire in 1162 and subsequently rebuilt, is marked by the ABBEY GRAMMAR SCHOOL in the townland of BALLYNACRAIG. The element *trá* 'strand' in the place-name can only refer to the tidal mudflats of the **Newry River** at the southern end of the town. Newry has given name to the barony of LORDSHIP OF NEWRY [*Iobhar Chind Trachta* 1089].

**Newry River** Down
(see ***Clanrye River***)

**Newtownabbey** tn, Antrim 3338
*Adjoins the city of Belfast on the north*
par: *Carnmoney* bar: *Belfast Lower*
The new town of Newtownabbey was created in 1958 out of the existing villages of **Carnmoney**, **Glengormley**, **Jordanstown**, **Monkstown**, **Whitehouse**, **Whitewell** and **Whiteabbey**, the latter providing the final element of the place-name and referring to a 13th-century abbey, no trace of which now remains (*see* ***Whiteabbey*** *below*).

**Newtownards** tn, par., Down 3437
*Town is 15km E of Belfast*
bar: *Ards Lower/Castlereagh Lower*
The town of Newtownards was founded by the Anglo-Normans and was known as *New Town* or *New Town of Blathewic*, from the Ir. kingdom of *Uí Bhlathmhaic* [ee **vlath**wick] 'descendants of *Blathmhac*' in which it was situated. The personal name *Blathmhac* signifies 'famous son'. The form Newtownards is not recorded before the first quarter of the 19th century and the final element refers to the position of the town at the head of the **Ards Peninsula**. The Irish name for Newtownards was *Baile Nua* 'new town', more recently *Baile Nua na hArda* 'new town of the (Ards) peninsula'. In the centre of the town are the ruins of a Dominican priory which was founded c.1244 and refurbished as the Anglican parish church in 1632-6 [*New Town of Blathewyc* 1333].

**Newtownbreda** vill., Down 3335
*Now a surburb, 4.5km SSE of Belfast city centre*
par: *Knockbreda* bar: *Castlereagh Upper*
The name of the village is a combination of E. *New Town* and **Breda** (Ir. *Bréadach* 'broken land'), the name of the townland in which it is situated and which also forms the final element of the name of the parish of **Knockbreda** (*see above*). The village was founded in the second half of the 18th century by Arthur Hill Trevor, 1st Viscount Dungannon (*see* ***Belvoir***) [*Newtownbreda* 1832].

**Newtownbutler** vill., Fermanagh 2432
*9km SE of Lisnaskea*
par: *Galloon* bar: *Coole*
In the 17th century the Plantation village of Newtownbutler, in the townland of AGHAGAY, was known simply as *Newtown*. The name of the village was changed to Newtownbutler when Theophilus Butler was created Baron of Newtownbutler in 1715. The latter was a descendant of Sir Stephen Butler of Huntingdon who settled in Ireland in 1610 and whose family later took the title of Earls of Lanesborough (*see* ***Belturbet***, ***Butler's Bridge***) [*Newtowne* 1622].

**Newtown Crommelin** vill., par., Antrim 3141
*Village is 14km NNE of Ballymena*
bar: *Kilconway*
The village of Newtown Crommelin in the townland of SKERRY EAST was commenced in 1824 by the Hugenot Nicholas Crommelin of CARROWDORE CASTLE in Co. Down, a descendant of Louis Crommelin (1652-1727) from Picardy in France who led a colony of Hugenots to **Lisburn** c.1690. Nicholas Crommelin purchased the townlands of SKERRY EAST, SKERRY WEST and SCOTCHOMERBANE in the parish of DUNAGHY and had them erected into a parish [*Newtown Cromlin* 1833].

*Market cross, Newtownards*

**Newtown Cunningham** tl, vill., Donegal 2341
*12.5km W of Derry city*
par: *Allsaints* bar: *Raphoe*
Newtown Cunningham is named after John Cunningham from Ayrshire in Scotland who was granted 1000 acres of land here in 1610. The same family gave name to the townland and village of **Manorcunningham** which lies 7.5km to the south-west. The village is known in Ir. as *An Baile Nua* [an bala **noo**a] 'the new town' [*Newtowne Cunningham* c.1655].

**Newtownhamilton** vill., par., Armagh 2932
*Village is 10.5km SE of Keady*
bar: *Fews Upper*
The village of Newtownhamilton was established c.1770 by Alexander Hamilton, a descendant of the John Hamilton from Scotland who founded **Hamiltonsbawn** in 1619. The parish was created in 1773 out of the neighbouring parish of **Creggan**. The village of Newtownhamilton is in the townland of TULLYVALLAN which is bordered by townlands named TULLYVALLAN (HAMILTON) EAST and WEST [*Newtown Hamilton* 1792].

**Newtownstewart** tl, vill., Tyrone 2438
*On W bank of the Strule, 13km SSE of Strabane*
par: *Ardstraw* bar: *Strabane Lower*
Newtownstewart was founded as a village on the estate of Sir Robert Newcomen who was granted the land during the plantation of Ulster. It is named from Sir William Stewart from Galloway in Scotland who was granted extensive lands in Tyrone and Donegal and married Sir Robert Newcomen's daughter c.1628. The remains of a castle built by Sir Robert still stand on CASTLE BRAE at the foot of the main street of the village. However, the Ir. name for Newtownstewart, i.e. *An Baile Nua* 'the new town/settlement', originally referred to an earlier settlement at a castle of *Toirealach Luineach Ó Néill* at PIGEON HILL on the opposite bank of the **Strule** [*An Baile Nua* 1600].

**Nutt's Corner** road junction, Antrim 3137
*4.5km ENE of Crumlin*
par: *Killead* bar: *Massereene Lower*
Nutt's Corner is the name of a major traffic intersection where three routes meet. The first element is the E. surname Nutt which is fairly common in Cos Antrim, Derry and Down.

# O

**Omagh** tl, tn, bars., Tyrone 2437
*County town of Tyrone, 35km WSW of Cookstown*
par: *Drumragh/Cappagh* bar: *Omagh East*
Ir. *An Ómaigh* [an **oa**mee] 'the virgin plain'.

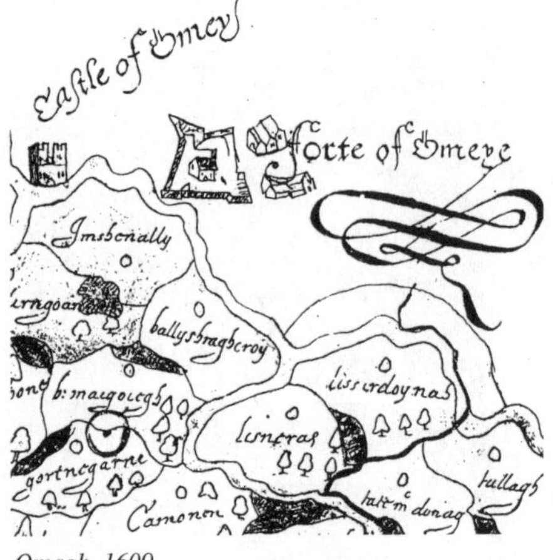


*Omagh, 1609*

The place-name may have originally referred to a plain which was not yet broken in for agriculture. The town of Omagh is partly in the barony of OMAGH EAST and partly in STRABANE UPPER, the river **Strule** marking the boundary [(*caislen*) *na hOghmaighe* 1470].

**Oritor** tl, ham., Tyrone 2737
(sometimes *Orritor*)
*4km WNW of Cookstown*
par: *Kildress* bar: *Dungannon Upper*
The name Oritor originally referred to the wider district in which the townland is situated. It goes back to the Ir. form (*F*)*arachtra* the meaning of which is obscure but the root of which may be *oireacht* (var. *aireacht*) 'assembly, district, territory'. The current Ir. name of Oritor is *Na Corracha Beaga* [na koragha **beg**a], originally simply *Na Corracha* 'the round hills'. The element *beaga* 'little' has been added to distinguish it from *Na Corracha Móra* 'the round hills (large)' which is

the Ir. name of **Sixmilecross** 20km to the south-west [*B:negorrah* 1609].

**Orra Beg** mtn, Antrim 3142
(see ***Slieveanorra or Orra More***)

**Ossian's Grave** anc. mon., Antrim 3242
(see ***Glenaan***)

**Owenkillew River** Tyrone
*Rises near Broughderg 16km NW of Cookstown, where it is known as the Broughderg River. Flows into the Strule 1km E of Newtownstewart*
Ir. *Abhainn Choilleadh* [owen **khill**yew] 'river of the wood'.

**Owenreagh River** Tyrone
*Rises in the Black Lough, 5km NW of Pomeroy. Enters the Owenkillew River 3.5km ENE of Gortin*
Ir. *An Abhainn Riabhach* [an owen **ree**wagh] 'the grey/speckled river'.

**Owey Island** isld, tl, Donegal 1742
*Off NW Donegal coast, 12km NW of Dunglow*
par: *Templecrone* bar: *Boylagh*
Ir. *Uaigh* [**oo**ee]. The modern form of the place-name, which literally means 'grave', appears to be a shortened form of *Uamhaigh* 'place of caves/coves' [*The Island of Inishowy* 1613].

**Oxford Island** pen., Armagh 3036
*On S shore of Lough Neagh, 4.5km NW of Lurgan*
par: *Seagoe* bar: *Oneilland East*
The name Oxford Island is a corruption of *Hawksworth's Island*. A Captain Robert Hawksworth is recorded as a tenant of the Brownlow estate here in 1666. Oxford Island is in the townland of ANNALOIST and is now attached to the mainland due to the lowering of the level of **Lough Neagh** [*Oxford's Island* 1835].

# P

**Park** vill., Derry 2540
*On S bank of the river Faughan, 7km SE of Claudy*
par: *Learmount* bar: *Tirkeeran*
Ir. *An Pháirc* [an **fark**] 'the field'. The village of Park is in the townland of TIREIGHTER. Previously the village was also known as LEARMOUNT which is the name of the parish in which it is situated [*Learmont or Park* 1837].

**Parkgate** vill., Antrim 3238
*7.5km E of Antrim town*
par: *Grange of Nilteen/Donegore*
bar: *Antrim Upper*
Parkgate in the townland of MOYADAM is so-named because it was one of the entrances to a great park laid out in the early 17th century by Sir Arthur Chichester, Lord Deputy of Ireland (1563-1625). The park stretched as far east as the western outskirts of **Ballyclare** [*Parkgate* 1780].

**Parkmore or Aganlane** tl, Antrim 3142
*At the head of Glenariff Glen, 7km SW of Cushendall*
par: *Layd* bar: *Glenarm Lower*
Parkmore is from Ir. *An Pháirc Mhór* [an fark **wore**] 'the large field' while AGANLANE represents Ir. *Aigeán Leathan* [agan **la**hin] 'broad hollow' or 'broad hill'.

**Pettigoe** tl, tn, Donegal/Fermanagh 2136
(sometimes *Pettigo*)
*On Donegal/Fermanagh border, close to N shore of Lower Lough Erne*
par: *Templecarn/Drumkeeran*
bar: *Tirhugh/Lurg*
Ir. *Paiteagó* [**patch**ego]. The modern Ir. name may be a development from an earlier form such as *Pait Tighe Gabha* 'plot of ground of the smith's house' or, possibly, *Pait Tighe Gabha* 'hump/hill of the smith's house'. The townland of Pettigoe is entirely in Co. Donegal while the Fermanagh portion of the town is in the townland of TULLYHOMMON (Ir. *Tulaigh Uí Thiomáin* [tullee ee **him**ine] 'Timmons's hillock'). The surname *Ó Tiomáin*, which can also be anglicised *Tummons*, was formerly common in Fermanagh [*Paitagooa* 1596].

**Pharis** tl, Antrim 3042
*10.5km E of Ballymoney*
par: *Loughguile* bar: *Dunluce Upper*
Ir. *Fáras* [**far**as] 'residence/dwelling'. The place-name may be used figuratively to apply

*Pomeroy, 'apple orchard'*

to the prominent PHARIS HILL (157m) [*Faras* 1780].

**Plumbridge** vill., Tyrone 2439
*At W end of Glenelly Valley, 15km SE of Strabane*
par: *Bodoney Upper* bar: *Strabane Upper*
*perhaps* Sc. *plum* 'a deep pool in a river or stream' + E. *bridge*. The bridge is in a deep valley of the GLENELLY RIVER, linking the townlands of GLENCOPPOGAGH and LISNACREAGHT [*Plumb Bridge* 1837].

**Poisoned Glen** glen, Donegal 1941
*Valley of the Cronaniv Burn which rises in the Derrryveagh Mountains and flows into the Devlin River a little to the E of Dunlewy Lake*
par: *Tullaghobegly* bar: *Kilmacrenan*
The E. name is a translation of the Ir. *Cró Nimhe* [cro **nyiv**a], *literally* 'hollow/glen of poison'. CRONANIV BURN, the name of the stream which flows through the valley, represents Ir. *Cró na Nimhe* 'hollow/glen of the poison' + Sc./N.E. *burn* 'stream'. There is a tradition that *Lugh Lámhfhada* or '*Lugh* of the long arm' killed his grandfather *Balar* here by piercing his 'evil eye' and that the blood from the eye flowed down the glen and poisoned it (*see* ***Dunlewy, Bloody Foreland***). It is also said that since that event no bird has ever sung in the glen.

**Pomeroy** tl, vill., par., Tyrone 2637
*Village is 13km NW of Dungannon*
bar: *Dungannon Middle*
POMEROY HOUSE was built c.1780 by James Lowry. No trace of the house remains but the site is marked by POMEROY FORESTRY SCHOOL a short distance east of the village. The origin of the name is uncertain. It may derive from F. *pommeraie* 'apple orchard'. It has also been suggested that Pomeroy may derive from F. *Pomme de Roi* (literally 'apple of the king') and have its origin in a grant of the district from James I to Sir William Parsons, Deputy Surveyor General of Ireland in 1619. Another tradition suggests that Pomeroy derives its name from the gift of apples by a local woman to William III in 1690, hence *pommes au roi* 'apples for the king'. Pomeroy is also recorded as an English surname of Norman origin but is not attested in this part of Ireland. The village of Pomeroy is in the townland of CAVANAKEERAN while the townland of Pomeroy, most of which is in the neighbouring parish of DESERTCREAT, lies a short distance to the east. The parish of Pomeroy was formed out of the neighbouring parish of **Donaghmore** in 1775 [*Pomeroy Demesne* c.1834].

**Portadown** tn, Armagh 3035
*15km NE of Armagh city*
par: *Drumcree/Seagoe*
bar: *Oneilland East/West*
Ir. *Port an Dúnáin* [port a **doon**ine] 'landing-place of the little fort'. The 'landing-place' may have been for the ferry which crossed the **Upper Bann** here, before the construction of a bridge in the early 18th century. The location of the 'little fort' is uncertain. There was formerly a fort at DUNEGLISH a short distance to the north-east [*Port a' Dúnáin* 1646].

**Portaferry** vill., Down 3535
*At lower end of Ards Peninsula, 12km NE of Downpatrick*
par: *Ballyphilip* bar: *Ards Upper*
Ir. *Port an Pheire* [port a **fair**ee] 'landing-place of the ferry'. Portaferry, in the townland and parish of BALLYPHILIP, is named from a ferry link dating back to Anglo-Norman times at the entrance to STRANGFORD LOUGH between Portaferry and **Strangford** [*Port na Peireadh* c.1617].

**Portavogie** tl, vill., Down 3635
*On E coast of Ards Peninsula, 11km NE of Portaferry*
par: *St Andrews al. Ballyhalbert*
bar: *Ards Upper*
Ir. *Port an Bhogaigh* [port a **wugg**ee] 'harbour of the bog'. Portavogie is an important fishing port. There was formerly an extensive peat bog in the townland [(*the bog of*) *Portaboggagh* 1605].

**Portballintrae** vill., Antrim 2944
(sometimes *Port Ballintrae*)
*On N Antrim coast, 7.5km ENE of Portrush*
par: *Dunluce* bar: *Dunluce Lower*
Ir. *Port Bhaile an Trá* [port wala an **traa**] 'harbour/landing place of Ballintrae'. The village of Portballintrae is named from a little harbour in the townland of BALLINTRAE in which it is situated. The name of the townland is from Ir. *Baile an Trá* 'townland of the strand' [*Portballentra* 1605].

**Portbraddan** ham., Antrim 3044
*On N Antrim coast, 11.5km WNW of Ballycastle*
par: *Ballintoy* bar: *Cary*
Ir. *Port Bradán* [port **brad**an] 'port/harbour of salmon'. Portbraddan which is in the townland of TEMPLEASTRAGH overlooking **White Park Bay** was one of three salmon fisheries in the parish of **Ballintoy** in 1830 [*Port Braden* 1830].

**Portglenone** tn, par., Antrim 2940
*Town is on E bank of the Lower Bann, 12km W of Ballymena*
bar: *Toome Lower*
Ir. *Port Chluain Eoghain* [port khlooin **ow**en] 'landing place of **Glenone**'. Portglenone in the townland of GARVAGHY takes its name from the townland of **Glenone** (Ir. *Cluain Eoghain* 'Owen's meadow') which adjoins it on the western side of the **Lower Bann** in Co. Derry. Before the construction of a bridge c.1680 there was a ferry across the Bann here. The parish of Portglenone was created out of the neighbouring parish of **Ahoghill** in 1840 [*Portecloneonone* 1593].

**Portmore Lough** Antrim 3136
(see ***Lough Beg or Portmore Lough***)

**Portmuck** tl, ham., Antrim 3440
*On Island Magee, 5km E of Larne*
par: *Islandmagee* bar: *Belfast Lower*
Ir. *Port Muc* [port **muck**] 'port/harbour of pigs'. Portmuck has given name to the little island called the ISLE OF MUCK which lies just off the coast [*Portmok* 1320].

**Portnablahy** vill., Donegal 2043
(often *Portnablagh*)
*On N Donegal coast, 2.5km E of Dunfanaghy*
par: *Clondahorky* bar: *Kilmacrenan*
Ir. *Port na Bláiche* [port na **blaigh**a] 'port/harbour of the buttermilk'. At Portnablahy in the townland of ROCKHILL there is a little cove and harbour which was clearly associated with dairying at an earlier period.

**Portnoo** vill., Donegal 1739
*7.5km NNW of Ardara*
par: *Inishkeel* bar: *Boylagh*
Ir. *Port Nua* [port **noo**a] 'new port/harbour'. Portnoo in the townland of LACKAGH is named from a little harbour which was built in the early 19th century for access to the island of INISHKEEL which lies just off the shore [*Port Noo* 1849].

**Portora** tl, Fermanagh 2234
*On NW outskirts of Enniskillen*
par: *Rossorry* bar: *Magheraboy*
Ir. *Port Abhla* [port **au**la] 'port of the orchard'. The name is a shortened form of *Port Abhla Faoláin* [port aula **fweel**ine] 'port of *Faolán*'s orchard' [(*co*) *Port Abla Faoláin* 1439].

**Portrush** tl, tn, Antrim 2844
*On N Antrim coast, 8km NNE of Coleraine*
par: *Ballywillin* bar: *Dunluce Lower*
Ir. *Port Rois* [port **rush**] 'port of the promontory'. There is a harbour and a conspicuous promontory here, the tip of which is known as RAMORE HEAD [*Portros* 1262].

**Portsalon** distr., Donegal 2244
*On Fanad peninsula, 15km NNE of Millford*
par: *Clondavaddog* bar: *Kilmacrenan*
Ir. *Port an tSalainn* [port a **tal**in] 'port of the salt'. Portsalon is named from a little fishing pier which stands at the northern end of BALLYMASTOCKER BAY in the townland of CROAGHROSS. The final element of the place-name refers to salt-panning in **Lough Swilly** (cf. SALTHILL DEMESNE at **Mountcharles**).

**Portstewart** tn, Derry 2843
*On N coast of Co. Derry, 6km NNW of Coleraine*
par: *Ballyaghran*
bar: *NE Liberties of Coleraine*
Portstewart is named from a Lieutenant Stewart of the nearby townland of BALLYLEESE who in 1734 obtained a lease of the land from the Earl of Antrim. The modern town was established in 1794 by John Cromie, a local wine merchant, whose father Stephen Cromie had purchased the land from the Stewarts. The ancestors of the Stewarts of Ballyleese hailed

from BUTE in Scotland. There is a harbour in the townland of MULLAGHACALL NORTH [*Portstewart* 1780].

**Poyntz Pass** vill., Armagh 3033
(sometimes *Poyntzpass*)
*On border with Co. Down, 7km SSE of Tandragee*
par: *Ballymore* bar: *Orior Lower*
The pass which gave name to the village is on a major route southwards and was named after Lieutenant Charles Poyntz from Gloucestershire who defended it against Hugh O'Neill Earl of Tyrone in 1598. In 1600 Poyntz was granted land here which was created the Manor of **Acton** in 1618 (*see above*). However, the modern village of Poyntz Pass was not founded until 1796. Poyntz Pass straddles the townlands of BRANNOCK, TULLYNACROSS and FEDERNAGH in Co. Armagh, with a small portion in the townland of LOUGHADIAN in Co. Down [*Poyns pass* c.1655].

**Purdysburn** ham., Down 3336
*6.5km S of Belfast*
par: *Drumbo* bar: *Castlereagh Upper*
Purdysburn in the townland of BALLYCOWAN stands on the south bank of the stream known as PURDYS BURN which rises 1.5km north of **Carryduff** and, under the name MINNOWBURN, flows into the **Lagan** a short distance south of SHAW'S BRIDGE. The first element of the place-name is the surname *Purdy*, the modern version of the O.E. name *Purta* or *Purda* which is found in Scotland and has been fairly common in north-east Ulster since the 17th century. The final element is Sc./N.E. *burn* 'stream'. PURDYSBURN HOUSE, now a psychiatric hospital, was at one time the residence of the Bishop of Down and in the last century it was the centre of the splendid PURDYSBURN DEMESNE [*Purdysburn* 1744].

# Q

**Quarrytown** ham., Antrim 3140
*5.5km NNE of Ballymena*
par: *Skerry* bar: *Antrim Lower*
Quarrytown is in the townland of BALLYCLOGHAN. In 1833 we find a reference to the quarrying of 'hard, white claystone and porphyry' (i.e. igneous rock) in this townland.

**Quigley's Point** hl, Donegal 2543
*On W shore of Lough Foyle, 18km NE of Derry city*
par: *Moville Upper* bar: *Inishowen East*
A sept of the family of *Ó Coigligh* '(O')Quigley' is indigenous to Inishowen, though the name is found throughout Ireland and is also common in Co. Derry. Quigley's Point is in the townland of CABRY [*Quigley's Point* 1721].

**Quoile** river, Down
*Rises in Lough Aghery in the parish of Dromore and enters Strangford Lough 5km NE of Downpatrick. Known successively as the Ballynahinch River, the Annacloy River and the Quoile*
Ir. *An Caol* [an **keel**] 'the narrow (water)'. The river has given name to the townland of QUOILE which lies on its east bank, 2km north of **Downpatrick**. An obsolete name for the river is *Narrow Water* which is a direct translation of the original Ir. [*Coyle* 1618].

# R

**Raholp** tl, ham., Down 3534
*5.5km NE of Downpatrick*
par: *Ballyculter* bar: *Lecale Lower*
Ir. *Ráth Cholpa* [ra **khull**pa] 'fort of the steer or heifer'. There are two conjoined *raths* in the townland and another a short distance to the north-east [*Raith Colptha* c.1170].

**Ramelton** tl, vill., Donegal 2242
(see ***Rathmelton***)

**Ramore Head** hl, Antrim 2844
(see ***Portrush***)

**Ram's Island** isld, Antrim 3037
*Off E shore of Lough Neagh, 5km W of Glenavy*
par: *Glenavy* bar: *Massereene Upper*
Ir. *Inis Dairgreann* [inish **dar**igran]. The Mod. Ir. form is a development from the earlier form *Inis Darcairgreann*. The meaning of the final

element is obscure. The name has been rendered 'Ram's Island' in E. from a (mistaken) perceived resemblance between Ir. *reithe* 'ram' and the final element of *Inis Draicrenn*, a later version of the place-name [*(primanmcara) Innsi Daircairgrenn* 1056].

**Randalstown** tl, tn, Antrim 3039
*On the river Main, 7.5km NW of Antrim town*
par: *Drummaul* bar: *Toome Upper*
The town of Randalstown is named after Randal MacDonnell (1609-82), 2nd Earl and 1st Marquis of Antrim, who c.1650 married his second wife Rose O'Neill, daughter of Sir Henry O'Neill who died in 1637. Rose O'Neill inherited her father's extensive estates in this area and resided at nearby **Shane's Castle**. Previous names for the town were *Iron-Works* referring to iron-smelting furnaces here and *Mainewater* referring to its situation on the river **Main**. Most of the town is west of the Main in the townland of RANDALSTOWN which was formerly known as *Dunmore*, from Ir. *An Dún Mór* [an doon **more**] 'the big fort', referring to a *motte-and-bailey*, the remains of which stand on the west bank of the **Main**, a short distance south of the town. The small portion of the town which is east of the Main is in the townland of BALLYGROOBY [*the Iron-Works* 1637].

**Rannafast** pen., tl, Donegal 1742
(see ***Rinnafarset***)

**Raphoe** tn, par/bar, dioc., Donegal 2240
*Town is 12km SE of Letterkenny*
Ir. *Ráth Bhoth* [raa **voh**] 'fort of the huts or monastic cells'. The place-name refers to an early monastery founded by St Columcille, the site of which is marked by the present Church of Ireland cathedral of St Eunan which was built in the town in 1702. The 'fort' referred to in the first element of the name was most likely the earthen enclosure which would have surrounded the early monastic buildings. The town of Raphoe is partly in the townland of RAPHOE DEMESNE and partly in RAPHOE TOWN PARKS [*(epscop) Ratha Bhoth* 813].

**Rasharkin** vill., par., Antrim 2941
*Village is 15km NW of Ballymena*
bar: *Kilconway*
Ir. *Ros Earcáin* [ross **ark**ine] '*Earcán*'s wooded height'. The personal name *Earcán* is the basis of the surname *Ó hEarcáin* '(O')Harkin'. The site of the ancient parish church is marked by the ruins of a 17th-century church a short distance south of the present Church of Ireland church, in the townland of GLEBE [*Ros Earcáin* c.1400].

**Rathcoole** h.est., Antrim 3338
*Forms a district of Newtownabbey, 7.5km N of Belfast city centre*
par: *Carnmoney* bar: *Belfast Lower*
Ir. *Ráth Cúile* [ra **kool**a] 'fort of *Coole*'. *Coole* (Ir. *Cúil* 'corner/recess') was the ancient name of the parish of **Carnmoney**. Rathcoole is in the townland of **White House** and there are *raths* in the neighbouring townland of DUNANNEY [*Coule* 1306].

**Rathfriland** tn, Down 3233
*13km NE of Newry*
par: *Drumgath/Drumballyroney*
bar: *Iveagh Upper, Upper Half/Lower Half*
Ir. *Ráth Fraoileann* [ra **freel**an] '*Fraoile*'s fort'. There was formerly a Magennis castle here, most likely on the site of the original ring-fort. The town of Rathfriland is at the intersection of the townlands of LISSIZE, KILTARRIFF, CROSS and ROSSCONOR [*Raphrylan* 1583].

**Rathkenny** tl, ham., Antrim 3141
*7.5km NNE of Ballymena*
par: *Skerry* bar: *Antrim Lower*
Ir. *Ráth Chainnigh* [ra **khan**yee] '*Cainneach*'s fort'. The personal name *Cainneach* (var. *Coinneach*) which can be anglicised *Canice* or *Kenny* is the basis of the surname *Mac Coinnigh* 'MacKinney'. There was formerly a ring-fort in the townland [*Ralphkenny* 1669].

**Rathlin Island** isld, par., Antrim 3145
*Off N Antrim coast, 6.5km N of Ballycastle*
bar: *Cary*
Ir. *Reachlainn* [**ragh**lin] *meaning uncertain*. A number of Irish islands are named *Reachlainn* (with variant *Reachrainn*) but the derivation of the name is obscure. Perhaps the most plausible suggestion to date is that it contains a Celtic root represented by W. *rhygnu* 'to rub/scrape', and that the name signifies something like 'indented island/rugged island'. Along with the mainland parish of **Ballintoy**, Rathlin was annexed to the parish of BILLY in medieval times but it was reconstituted a parish in its own right in 1722. There was an early church on Rathlin, the location

of which is uncertain [(*ecclaise*) *Rechrainne* 630].

**Rathmelton** tl, vill., Donegal 2242
(usually *Ramelton*)
*11km NNE of Letterkenny*
par: *Aughnish* bar: *Kilmacrenan*
Ir. *Ráth Mealtain* [ra **mal**tin] '*Mealtan*'s fort'. *Mealtan* is a rare early Irish personal name. A medieval castle of the O'Donnells formerly stood in the village and this may mark the site of the original fort of Rathmelton [*Ramalton* 1601].

**Rathmullan** tl, vill., Donegal 2242
(sometimes *Rathmullen*)
*On W shore of Lough Swilly, 10km E of Millford*
par: *Killygarvan* bar: *Kilmacrenan*
Ir. *Ráth Maoláin* [ra **mweel**ine] '*Maolán*'s fort'. The personal name *Maolán* was formerly common in Ireland and is the basis of the surnames *MacMaoláin* 'MacMullan' and *Ó Maoláin* '(O')Mullan'. The ruins of a medieval castle of the MacSweeneys of **Fanad** which stands in the village appear to mark the site of the original fort [*Ráith Maoláin* 1516].

**Rathmullan** tls, ham., par., Down 3435
*Hamlet is 7km SSW of Downpatrick*
bar: *Lecale Upper*
Ir. *Ráth Mhaoláin* [ra **weel**ine] '*Maolán*'s fort'. The derivation of this place-name is the same as that of **Rathmullan** in Donegal (*see previous entry*). The Church of Ireland church in the townland of RATHMULLAN UPPER appears to mark the site of the medieval parish church. There is a prominent *motte-and-bailey* in RATHMULLAN LOWER [*Rathmoyln* 1306].

**Ravernet** tl, vill., Down 3236
(sometimes *Ravarnett*)
*3km S of Lisburn*
par: *Blaris* bar: *Iveagh Lower, Upper Half*
Ir. *Ráth Bhearnáin* [ra **varn**ine] 'fort of the little gap'. There is now no trace or record of a fort in the townland [*Balliravarnan* 1585].

**Ray** tl, Donegal 2242
*On W shore of Lough Swilly, 5km NNE of Rathmelton*
par: *Aughnish* bar: *Kilmacrenan*
Ir. *An Ráith* [an **ra**] 'the fort'. There is a fort near the western boundary of the townland. Ray has given name to RAY BRIDGE which crosses the GLENALLA RIVER here, linking the townlands of RAY and DRUMHERRIVE [*Raghe* 1622].

**Reclain** tl, ham., Tyrone 2736
*10km ENE of Dungannon*
par: *Donaghmore* bar: *Dungannon Middle*
Ir. *Ráth Claon* [ra **cleen**] 'crooked/sloping fort'. There is now no trace or record of a fort in the townland [*Rathcline* 1609].

**Red Bay** tl, bay Antrim 3242
*2km S of Cushendall*
par: *Layd* bar: *Glenarm Lower*
The element *red* in the place-name derives from the Ir. name *Uaimh Dhearg* [ooiv **yar**ig] 'red cave', the name of a 16th-century castle of the MacDonnells, the remnants of which stand on the cliff top above the RED ARCH, 2km south of **Cushendall**. The castle is built on the site of a *motte-and-bailey* and took its name from a cave in the red sandstone cliff underneath it [*Owderick* 1565]

**Redcastle** ham., Donegal 2543
*On W shore of Lough Foyle, 20km NE of Derry city*
par: *Moville Upper* bar: *Inishowen East*
Redcastle is named from a castle which was formerly a stronghold of the MacQuillans and later of the MacLaughlins. The latter were *erenaghs* of the church lands of the parish of **Moville**. Redcastle is in the townland of CARRICKMAQUIGLEY (Ir. *Carraig Mhic Uidhilín* [carrick vick **eel**een] 'MacQuillan's rock') and this is the Mod. Ir. name for the hamlet. The element *carraig* 'rock' in the name of the townland no doubt refers to the original MacQuillan castle. The element *red* of Redcastle contrasts with the *green* of **Greencastle** which lies 10km to the north-east [*Red Castle* 1613].

**Redhills** vill., Cavan 2431
(sometimes *Redhill*)
*8km E of Belturbet*
par: *Annagh* bar: *Tullygarvey*
Redhills is in the townland of REDHILL DEMESNE which includes the remains of a large strongly-fortified house, built in the late 18th century and inhabited in 1837 by a Mr White. The demesne appears to have been named from the reddish soil of the hills in the vicinity [*Redhills* 1837].

**Revallagh** tls, Antrim 2943
*4km SW of Bushmills*
par: *Ballyrashane* bar: *Dunluce Lower*
Ir. *Ráth Mhallacht* [ra **wal**aght] 'fort of the curses'. In the townland of REVALLAGH NORTH there are remnants of a *motte-and-bailey*, on the site of which a stone castle was later constructed. The circumstances in which the name was bestowed are unknown [*Revallagh North* 1835].

**Rich Hill** tl, vill., Armagh 2934
(sometimes *Richhill*)
*7km ENE of Armagh city*
par: *Kilmore* bar: *Oneilland West*
Rich Hill takes its name from Edward Richardson, MP for Co. Armagh from 1655 to 1696, who constructed RICHHILL CASTLE, a Dutch-gabled manor house. The official name of the townland of Rich Hill is RICH HILL OR LEGACORRY, the latter name deriving from Ir. *Log an Choire* [lugg a **khurr**a] 'hollow of the cauldron', referring to a cauldron-like hollow in the ground (cf. ***Legaghory***) [*Leggacorry* 1609].

**Ringboy Point** hl, Down 3635
*On E coast of Ards Peninsula, 2.5km SSW of Portavogie*
par: *Ardkeen* bar: *Ards Upper*
Ir. *Rinn Bhuí* [rinn **wee**] 'yellow point' + E. *point*. The E. element *point*, which means the same as Ir. *rinn*, has obviously been added at a later stage. Ringboy Point is in the townland of KIRKISTOWN. There is a hamlet named RINGBOY a short distance inland.

**Ringsend** ham., Derry 2842
*12.5km E of Limavady*
par: *Aghadowey* bar: *Coleraine*
There are a number of other places named RINGSEND and all appear to be named after Ringsend in Co. Dublin. The name of the latter represents Ir. *An Rinn* 'the promontory' + E. *end*, so that it signifies 'the place at the end of the promontory'. Ringsend is mainly in the townland of CRAIGMORE [*Ringsend* 1836].

**Rinnafarset** pen., tl, Donegal 1742
(usually *Rannafast*)
*10km N of Dunglow*
par: *Templecrone* bar: *Boylagh*
Ir. *Rinn na Feirste* [rinn na **ferst**ya] 'peninsula of the sand-bank ford'. The final element of the place-name refers to a ford where at low tide one can walk across the estuary of the **Gweedore River** (*see* ***Gweedore***). The name contrasts with RINNAMONA (Ir. *Rinn na Mónadh* 'peninsula of the bog/moor'), the name of a narrow peninsula a short distance to the south, in the neighbouring townland of ANNAGARY [*Ranafearst* 1634].

**Rock, The** vill., Tyrone 2737
*7.5km SW of Cookstown*
par: *Desertcreat* bar: *Dungannon Upper*
The Rock is mainly in the townland of OUGHTERARD which is bounded on the south by the ROCK RIVER. A rocky outcrop adjoins the village on the east [*The Rock* c.1835].

**Rockcorry** vill., Monaghan 2631
*Close to Cavan border, 5.5km NE of Cootehill*
par: *Ematris* bar: *Dartree*
The element *rock* in Rockcorry refers to the stony nature of the soil. The element *–corry* represents the surname of the village's founder Thomas Charles Stewart Corry, High Sheriff of Monaghan, who established it in the second half of the 18th century on land originally belonging to the MacMahons but granted to his ancestors in the Cromwellian period. The Ir. name of Rockcorry is *Buíochar* [**bweegh**er] 'yellow land' which is the original Ir. name of the townland of BOYHER in which the village is situated [*Rockorry* 1778].

**Roe** river Derry
*Formed by the convergence of a number of small streams in Glenshane Forest, 8.5km WNW of Maghera. Enters Lough Foyle 6.5km NW of Limavady*
Ir. *An Ró* [an **ro**] *perhaps* 'the roaring one'. It is said that the Scottish Munro family take their name from the place of origin of their ancestors at the foot of the Roe in the parish of **Magilligan** (Ir. *Bun Ró*, Sc.G. *Bun Rotha* 'foot of the Roe') [*an Roa* 1532].

**Roguery Brae** hill Antrim 3039
*5.5km NE of Toome*
par: *Grange of Ballyscullion*
bar: *Toome Upper*
Ir. *Ruadhoire* [**roo**a-ġirra] 'red oak-wood' + Sc./N.E. *brae* 'hill'. Roguery Brae is a steep hill in the south-east corner of the townland of TAYLORSTOWN. A local story attributes the origin of the name to the 'roguery' of a man who built a house here against the wishes of his elderly and unsuspecting mother! [*Roguery* c.1858].

**Roscavey** tl, ham., Tyrone 2536
*3km S of Beragh*
par: *Clogherny* bar: *Omagh East*
Ir. *Ros Cabha* [ross **kau**a] 'height of the slope or hollow' [*Rasscowye* 1640].

**Rose's Lane Ends** ham., Antrim 3137
*3km SW of Glenavy*
par: *Ballinderry* bar: *Massereene Upper*
The term 'lane end' refers to the end of a lane where it joins the road (*see* **Loanends**). In this case, the hamlet is named from a crossroads formed by the intersection of a minor road with the main road from **Glenavy** to **Lurgan**, in the townland of BALLYMACREVAN.

**Rosguill** pen., Donegal
*On N Donegal coast, 2.5km NW of Carrickart*
par: *Meevagh* bar: *Kilmacrenan*
Ir. *Ros Goill* '*Goll*'s peninsula'. Rosguill is said to have got its name from *Goll mac Morna*, a character in the *Fiannaíocht* cycle of literature, who was a rival of Finn Mac Cool and is reputed to have been killed here. The name *Goll* signifies 'one-eyed'. The peninsula lies between **Sheephaven** and the lower portion of **Mulroy Bay** [(*in*) *Ros Guill* 1603].

**Rossbeg** tl, Donegal 1639
(sometimes *Rosbeg*)
*At head of Dawros Bay, 9.5km NW of Ardara*
par: *Inishkeel* bar: *Boylagh*
Ir. *Ros Beag* [ross **beg**] 'little promontory'. Rossbeg is named from a headland which projects into DAWROS BAY in the west of the townland.

**Rosscor** tl, Fermanagh 1935
(sometimes *Roscor*)
*At W end of Lower Lough Erne, 5km E of Belleek*
par: *Inismacsaint* bar: *Magheraboy*
Ir. *Ros Corr* [ross **korr**] 'rough/uneven headland'. Rosscor is bounded on the north by the river **Erne** which flows out of **Lower Lough Erne** here. A short distance to the north-east there are townlands named ROSSBEG and ROSSMORE, signifying 'little headland' and 'great headland' respectively. ROSSCOR ISLAND lies a short distance offshore [*Roscorr* 1751].

**Rosses, The** distr., Donegal 1741
*In W Donegal, between Gweebarra in the S and Gweedore in the N*
par: *Lettermacaward/Templecrone*
bar: *Boylagh*
Ir. *Na Rosa* [na **rossa**] 'the promontories/headlands'. The place-name refers to the many headlands which are characteristic of the coastline of the area [(*do na*) *Rosaibh* 1603].

**Rosslea** tl, vill., Fermanagh 2533
(sometimes *Roslea*)
*7.5km NNE of Clones*
par: *Clones* bar: *Clankelly*
Ir. *Ros Liath* [ross **lee**a] 'grey wood or wooded height' [*Roslea* 1618].

**Rossnowlagh** tls, vill., Donegal 1836
*On Donegal Bay, 7km N of Ballyshannon*
par: *Drumhome* bar: *Tirhugh*
Ir. *Ros Neamhlach* [ross **nau**lagh]. The Mod. Ir. form of the name may be a development from an earlier form *Ros nAbhlach* 'headland of the apple trees'. The village of Rossnowlagh is in the townland of ROSSNOWLAGH UPPER, the full title of which is ROSSNOWLAGH UPPER OR CROCKAHANY. The latter is bordered on the north by the townland of ROSSNOWLAGH LOWER in which there is a conspicuous headland [*Rusnowla* c.1655].

**Rostrevor** tls, vill., Down 3131
(sometimes *Rosstrevor*)
*3km E of Warrenpoint*
par: *Kilbroney* bar: *Iveagh Upper, Upper Half*
Ir. *Ros Treabhair* [ross **trau**ir] 'Trevor's wood'. *Treabhar* is a gaelicised form of the surname of Edward Trevor, a Welshman who commanded the English garrison at **Newry** at the end of the Nine Years War (1594-1603) and who later acquired lands in this area. An earlier Ir. name for Rostrevor was *Caisleán Ruairí* [kashlan **roo**ree] 'Rory's castle', referring to a castle built by Rory Magennis Lord of Iveagh, of which no trace now remains. The townland of Rostrevor is bordered on the east by ROSSTREVOR UPPER which in turn is bordered by the townland of ROSSTREVOR MOUNTAINS [*Rose Trevor* 1613].

**Roughan** tl, Tyrone 2836
*6km NNE of Dungannon*
par: *Donaghenry* bar: *Dungannon Middle*
Ir. *Ruachán* [**roo**aghan] 'reddish place'. Roughan has given name to the adjoining ROUGHAN LOUGH which is the site of a *crannog*, said to be the place of capture of Sir Phelim O'Neill c.1653 [*Ruehan* 1664].

**Rousky** tl, ham., Tyrone 2538
*6km E of Gortin*
par: *Bodoney Lower* bar: *Strabane Upper*
Ir. *Rúscaigh* [**roos**kee] 'place of moors' [*Rouskie* 1629].

**Rowallane Gardens** Down 3435
*1km S of Saintfield*
par: *Saintfield* bar: *Castlereagh Upper*
Rowallane Gardens covering 50 acres are attached to ROWALLANE HOUSE and were established over a century ago by the Rev. John Moore. The latter named both house and gardens after the native place of his ancestor, one of the *Mures* of ROWALLAN in Ayrshire, a colonel in the army of William III who had obtained land in Ulster and settled here. The name Rowallan derives from Sc.G. *Rudha Álainn* 'beautiful promontory', referring to the site of the original castle of Rowallan on the bank of the river Carmel near KILMARNOCK. Rowallane Gardens are partly in the townland of CREEVYLOUGHGARE and partly in LEGGYGOWAN.

**Rubane** ham., Down 3636
*On Ards Peninsula, 2km SE of Kirkubbin*
par: *St Andrews alias Ballyhalbert*
bar: *Ards Upper*
Ir. *Rubha Bán* [rooa **ban**] 'white clearing or thicket'. The former townland of Rubane is now known as ECHLINVILLE and appears to be named after James Echlin, a descendant of Robert Echlin who was bishop of Down and Connor in the early 17th century. James Echlin built RUEBANE HOUSE early in the 18th century. The Echlin family derive their name from a territory of that name in Linlithgow in Scotland. Echlinville is bordered by the townland of ROWREAGH (Ir. *Rubha Riabhach* 'grey clearing or thicket') in the parish of INISHARGY [*Rowbane* c.1615].

**Rue Point** hl, Antrim 3144
*The S tip of Rathlin Island*
par: *Rathlin Island* bar: *Cary*
Ir. *Rubha* [**roo**] 'headland' + E. *point*.
As well as signifying 'clearing or thicket' (*see previous entry*) Ir. *rubha* can mean 'headland/promontory'. The E. element *point* has a similar meaning and has clearly been added later. *Rubha* 'promontory' is common in Scottish place-names where it is spelt *rudha* (*see **Rowallane***).

**Rutland Island or Inishmacadurn**
isld, tl, Donegal 1741
*Off W coast of Donegal, 7.5km NW of Dungloe*
par: *Templecrone* bar: *Boylagh*
The original Ir. name of Rutland Island was *Inis Mhic an Doirn* [inish vick a **dirn**] which may go back to an earlier form *Inis Mhic Dhoirn* 'island of the son of *Dorn*'. The same individual named *Dorn* (literally 'fist') may have given name to *Dún Doirn*, i.e. '*Dorn*'s fort', the name of a place on the island. The island was renamed Rutland Island in 1785 by William Burton Conyngham, in honour of Charles Manners, 4th Duke of Rutland, who became Lord Lieutenant of Ireland in 1784. Conyngham built a fishing village on Rutland, no trace of which remains, and also a fishing port at **Burtonport** on the mainland [*Rutland* 1837].

**Ryefield** tl, Cavan 2628
*Close to Meath border, 5km S of Virginia*
par: *Munterconnaught* bar: *Castlerahan*
Ir. *Achadh an tSeagail* [aghoo an **chag**il] 'field of the rye'. The E. name is a translation of the original Ir. There is a townland named AGHATEGGAL OR RYEFORT some 15km to the north-west [*Aghenteggell* 1664].

# S

**Saintfield** tn, par., Down 3435
*16km NW of Downpatrick*
bar: *Castlereagh Upper*
Ir. *Tamhnach Naomh* [taunagh **nee**oo] 'field of saints'. The E. name represents a rough translation of the original Ir. form of the name of the former townland of *Tonaghneeve* in which the town is situated (now SAINTFIELD PARKS). The exact circumstances in which the name was bestowed are unknown. The nearby townland of TONAGHMORE (Ir. *Tamhnach Mhór* 'great field') appears to be named by way of contrast with *Tonaghneeve*. The present Church of Ireland church may mark the site of the ancient church of Saintfield [*Tawnaghnym* 1605].

**Saint John's Point** hl, Donegal 1736
*Long narrow headland extending into Donegal Bay, 7.5km S of Killybegs*
par: *Killaghtee* bar: *Banagh*
The Ir. name for Saint John's Point is *Pointe Charraig an Rois* [pwintcha kharrick a **rush**] 'point of the rock of the headland', the original Ir. name of the townland of POINT which makes up the southern portion of the headland. The origin of the dedication to St John is obscure: perhaps it is connected with the friary, the ruins of which are in the neighbouring townland of BALLYSAGGART [*St. John's Point* 1837].

**Saint John's Point** hl, tl, Down 3533
*3km SW of Ardglass*
par: *Rathmullan* bar: *Lecale Upper*
Ir. *Rinn Eoin* [rinn **ow**en] '(St) John's point'. The E. name appears to be a translation of the original Ir. The place gets its name from a former chapel of St John, the ruins of which may date back to the eighth century and which, along with ST JOHN'S WELL, stand in the south of the townland. The Ir. name of the chapel was *Tigh Eoin* '(St) John's (monastic) house' and the townland appears to have carried the *alias* name *Baile Eoin* '(St) John's townland', sometimes anglicised *St Johnstown* [*Ballihione al. Rinchione* 1549].

**Saint Johnstown** tl, vill., Donegal 2340
(sometimes *Saint Johnston*)
*On W bank of Foyle, 10km SW of Londonderry*
par: *Taughboyne* bar: *Raphoe*
Saint Johnstown is named after Saint Johnstone in Scotland, the old name of the town of PERTH. It was founded c.1618 on lands granted to Ludovic Stewart 2nd Duke of Lennox and Duke of Richmond (1574–1624). St Johnstown is adjoined on the north by a townland named DUNDEE [*St Johnston* c.1655].

**Salmon Leap** rapids, Derry 2843
*On Lower Bann, 2km S of Coleraine*
par: *Macosquin* bar: *Coleraine*
Here there are lock-gates and formerly an important salmon fishery. The Ir. name for the Salmon Leap is *Eas Craoibhe* [ass **cree**va] 'waterfall of *Craobh*', *Craobh* 'branch/(sacred) tree' being the old name of the adjoining district to the west of the Bann. The element *eas* 'waterfall, rapids' forms the final element of the name of the townland of BALLYNESS (Ir. *Baile an Easa* 'townland of the waterfall') which lies on the west side of the river. The Salmon Leap goes by the *alias* name of THE CUTTS, a Sc. term which refers to the narrow channels at the fishery through which the waters of the river were directed [*(co) hEsscraibhe* 1197].

**Sandholes** vill., Tyrone 2737
*5km SSW of Cookstown*
par: *Desertcreat* bar: *Dungannon Upper*
Sandholes in the townland of CROSS GLEBE is named from coarse sand or gravel pits in the vicinity of the village [*Sandholes* 1834].

**Sandy Knowes** distr., Antrim 3338
*On W edge of Newtownabbey, 9.5km NW of Belfast city centre*
par: *Shankill* bar: *Belfast Lower*
E. *sandy* + Sc./N.E. *knowes* 'hillocks'.
The district of Sandy Knowes is in the townland of BALLYWONARD and takes its name from nearby sandhills. It has given name to the well-known SANDYKNOWES ROUNDABOUT, a major route intersection which stands on the boundary of the parish of **Templepatrick**.

**Saul** tl, vill., par., Down 3534
*Village is 3km NE of Downpatrick*
bar: *Lecale Lower*
Ir. *Sabhall* [**sau**el] 'a barn'. According to tradition, Saul is named from a barn which stood on land presented to St Patrick in 432AD by the local chieftain *Dichu* as a site for his first church. At a later stage Saul came to be known as *Sabhall Pádraig* 'the barn of (St) Patrick'. The site of the original church is marked by the ruins of a 12th-century Augustinian friary which stands a short distance west of the village. The townland of SAUL QUARTER lies 3km to the south [*Sabul Patricii* c.670].

**Sawel** mtn, Derry/Tyrone 2639
*On the Derry/Tyrone border, 16.5km WNW of Draperstown*
par: *Learmount/Bodoney Upper*
bar: *Tirkeeran/Strabane Upper*
Ir. *Samhail* [**sau**il] 'likeness or resemblance'. The full name of the mountain is *Samhail Phite Méabha* [sau-il fitcha **mey**va] 'likeness to Maeve's vulva' and it is said to be used metaphorically to refer to a hollow on the side of the mountain. *Méabh* (earlier *Medb*), whose name signifies 'she who intoxicates', was the goddess of sovereignty and features in a later

literary reincarnation as queen of Connaught in the great Irish epic *Táin Bó Cuailnge* or *The Cattle Raid of Cooley*. In local folklore *Méabh* appears as a wily enchantress (*see* ***Benbradagh***). At 678m, Sawel is the highest peak in the **Sperrin Mountains** [*Samhail Phite Meadhbea* c.1680].

**Scaddy** ham., Down 3435
*5km N of Downpatrick*
par: *Inch* bar: *Lecale Lower*
Ir. *Sceadaigh* [**skad**ee] 'bare place/patchy place'. Skaddy is in the townland of BALLYGALLY [*Scaddy* 1886].

**Scarva** tl, vill., Down 3034
*On the border with Co. Armagh, 6km SW of Banbridge*
par: *Aghaderg* bar: *Iveagh Upper, Upper Half*
Ir. *Scarbhach* [**skar**awagh] 'place of the shallow ford'. Scarva now stands on the NEWRY CANAL so that the name must refer to a shallow in a previous, natural, water feature. The portion of the village of Scarva which is west of the Newry Canal is in the townland of AUGHLISH in the parish of BALLYMORE in Co. Armagh [*the Skarvagh* 1618].

**Scotch Street** vill., Armagh 2935
*3.5km W of Portadown*
par: *Drumcree* bar: *Oneilland West*
The village of Scotch Street is in the townland of TIMAKEEL. It has a single street and is so-named because it was founded by Scottish settlers [*Scotch Street* 1835].

**Scotshouse** vill., Monaghan 2431
*6km S of Clones*
par: *Currin* bar: *Dartree*
The village of Scotshouse takes its name from William Scott who was granted the townland of AGHNAHOLA after the Cromwellian land settlement. In local folklore, people used to go to Mr Scott's house to buy resin and for that reason the village was named SCOTSHOUSE. The modern village was founded at the beginning of the 19th century and is mainly in the townland of DUNSCRIM [*Scotshouse* 1835].

**Scotstown** vill., Monaghan 2633
*On the river Blackwater, 7.5km NW of Monaghan town*
par: *Tedavnet* bar: *Monaghan*
A Henry Owen Scott built a bridge across the **Blackwater** here in 1791 but since the placename is recorded in 1735, the village probably took its name from an earlier member of the Scott family. Scotstown straddles the townlands of BOUGH, TERAVERTY and CARROWHATTA [*Scotstown* 1735].

*Scotstown*

**Scrabo** tl, Down 3437
*2km SW of Newtownards*
par: *Newtownards* bar: *Castlereagh Lower*
Ir. *Screabach* [**skrab**agh] 'rough, stony land'. Scrabo has given name to the conspicuous SCRABO HILL (161m) on the summit of which stands SCRABO TOWER dedicated to the memory of Charles William Stewart, 3rd Marquis of Londonderry (1778-1854) (*see* ***Mount Stewart***) [*Scraboc* c.1275].

**Scribbagh** tl, ham., Fermanagh 1934
*6km SE of Garrison*
par: *Devenish* bar: *Magheraboy*
Ir. *Scriobach* [**skrib**agh] 'rough, stony land'. There is a hill named SCRIBBAGH in the north of the townland.

**Scriggan** tl, Derry 2641
*2km N of Dungiven*
par: *Dungiven* bar: *Keenaght*
Ir. *An Screagán* [an **skrag**an] 'the rocky place' [*Scriggin* c.1659].

**Seaforde** vill., Down 3434
*8.5km WSW of Downpatrick*
par: *Loughinisland* bar: *Kinelarty*
Ir. *Suí* [see] 'seat' + (surname) *Forde*.
Seaforde grew up in the 18th century and takes its name from the Fordes, a Wexford family whose earlier ancestry goes back to Wales. SEAFORDE HOUSE which stands a short distance north of the village in the townland of SEAFORDE DEMESNE was the seat of Colonel M. Forde and was destroyed by fire in 1816 and rebuilt in 1819. The village of Seaforde is in the townland of NAGHAN [*Seaforde* 1837].

**Seapatrick** vill., par., Down 3134
*Village is 1.5km NW of Banbridge*
bar: *Iveagh Upper, Upper Half*
Ir. *Suí Phádraig* [see **fad**ric] '(St) Patrick's seat'. St Patrick was patron of the ancient parish church, the site of which is marked by a remnant of a church constructed in 1698 in the townland of KILPIKE. Part of Seapatrick parish is in the baronies of IVEAGH LOWER, UPPER/LOWER HALF [*Soyge-Patrick* 1546].

**Seskinore** tl, vill., Tyrone 2436
(sometimes *Seskanore*)
*9.5km SE of Omagh*
par: *Clogherny* bar: *Omagh East*
Ir. *Seisceann Odhar* [sheskin **oar**] 'brownish bog' [*Shaskannoure* 1613].

**Sess Kilgreen** tl, ham., Tyrone 2635
(sometimes *Seskilgreen*)
*3km NW of Ballygawley*
par: *Errigal Keerogue* bar: *Clogher*
Ir. *Seisíoch Chill Ghrianna* [sheshyagh khill **gree**ana] '*Sessiagh* of *Grianna*'s church'. Ir. *seisíoch* (anglicised *sessiagh*) literally means 'sixth part' and was used to signify a sixth of a larger land unit. There is now no trace or record of ecclesiastical remains in the townland [*Killgreen* 1666].

**Seymour Hill** distr., Antrim 3236
*1km SSE of Dunmurry*
par: *Derryaghy* bar: *Belfast Upper*
The name Seymour Hill has its origin in SEYMOUR HILL HOUSE, a mansion constructed by Robert Johnson Esq. at the end of the 18th century on a hill overlooking the DERRYAGHY RIVER. Seymour Hill is in the townland of KILMAKEE [*Seymourhill* 1835].

**Shane's Castle** tl, Antrim 3138
*3km SE of Randalstown*
par: *Antrim* bar: *Toome Upper*
Shane's Castle is named after Shane mac Brian mac Phelim O'Neill, ruler of LOWER CLANDEBOY from 1595 to 1617. The original Ir. name of the castle, and from it the townland, was *Éadan Dúcharraige* [aidan **doo**khariga] 'brow of black rock', and a portion of this name is preserved as EDENDUFF, the name of a row of houses in the south of the townland. The ruins of the castle stand on the north shore of **Lough Neagh**, in the large neighbouring townland of SHANE'S CASTLE PARK, parish of DRUMMAUL [*Castel Edaindaubchairrgi* 1490].

**Shankbridge** bridge, Antrim 3139
*5km SE of Ballymena*
par: *Connor* bar: *Antrim Lower*
The bridge is said to have been so named because it connects the townland of CARNACHTS on the north bank of the **Kells Water** with a narrow 'shank' or 'leg' of the townland of KILDRUM, on the south bank of the river, formed by a sharp bend in the river [*Shankbridge* c.1858].

**Shankill** distr., par., Antrim 3337
*District forms a suburb, 1.5km NW of centre of Belfast*
bar: *Belfast Upper*
Ir. *Seanchill* [**shan**khill] 'old church'. The site of the medieval parish church is marked by the present Church of Ireland church of St Matthew on the UPPER SHANKILL ROAD (townland of EDENDERRY). The parish of Shankill, a small portion of which is in the barony of BELFAST LOWER, includes almost all of the city of Belfast which is west of the **Lagan** in Co. Antrim [*The White-church* 1306].

**Shantallow** tl, distr., Derry 2442
*On N edge of Derry city*
par: *Templemore*
bar: *NW Liberties of Londonderry*
Ir. *Seantalamh* [**shan**taloo] 'old land'. The adjective 'old' may have connotations of 'long cultivated' [*Shantallow* 1654].

**Sheddings, The** ham., Antrim 3240
(see ***Carnalbanagh***)

**Sheep Haven** bay, Donegal 2043
*In N Donegal, between Rosguill peninsula and Horn Head peninsula*

par: *Clondahorky/Mevagh* bar: *Kilmacrenan*
Ir. *Cuan na gCaorach* [kooin na **geer**agh] 'bay of the sheep'. The E. name appears to be a translation of the original Ir. It is, however, possible that the element *sheep* is a corruption of E. *ship*, in which case the origin of the place-name is E. *Ship Haven* and the Ir. version *Cuan na gCaorach* was a mistranslation. Nowadays the bay is known in Ir. as *Báighe na nDúnaibh* 'Downings Bay', from the village of **Downings** on its eastern shore [*Cownagh gerragh al. Sheap haven* 1608].

**Shercock** vill., par., Cavan 2730
*Village is close to Monaghan border, 10km NNE of Bailieborough*
bar: *Clankee*
Ir. *Searcóg* [**shark**og]. The meaning of this place-name is obscure. It appears to be a diminutive of Ir. *searc* 'love/affection' and one could tentatively argue for an interpretation such as 'dear place/beloved place'. The parish of Shercock was created in 1778 out of the former medieval parish of *Killan* which also included the parish of **Bailieborough** [*Skarkeoge al. Sharcocke* 1629].

**Sheskinshule** tl, Tyrone 2538
*11km ESE of Gortin*
par: *Bodoney Lower* bar: *Strabane Upper*
Ir. *Seisceann Siúil* [sheskin **shoo**il] 'moving bog'. The Ir. name literally means 'bog of walking' and refers to a bog which under certain conditions can flow or 'walk' [*Seasgan Siúil* 1930].

**Shimna** river Down
*Rises between Ott Mountain and Slieve Loughshannagh in the Mournes. Enters the Irish Sea at Newcastle*
Ir. *Abhainn na Simhne* [owen na **shiv**na] 'river of the (bul)rush(es)'. The final element of the place-name is singular, i.e. '(bul)rush' but is used with a collective meaning [*Shimna River* c.1830].

**Shrigley** vill., Down 3535
*1km NW of Killyleagh*
par: *Killyleagh* bar: *Dufferin*
The name of the village of Shrigley appears to have its origin in a mansion of that name which in 1837 was the seat of J. Martin jun., Esq. The name may be a corruption of *Sruighligh* which is sometimes used as the Sc. G. name of the town of STIRLING in Scotland.

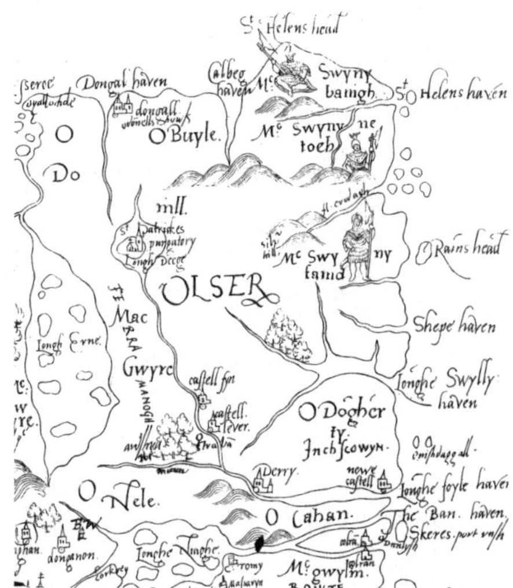

*16th century map of County Donegal showing Sheep Haven Bay. Note the gallowglasses (See Milford p. 107).*

Shrigley is in the townland of TULLYVEERY [*Shrigley* 1837].

**Silent Valley, The** Down 3332
*At W foot of Slieve Binnian, 7.5km N of Kilkeel*
par: *Kilkeel* bar: *Mourne*
The Silent Valley was named by the Belfast Water Commissioners on the construction of a reservoir by damming the KILKEEL RIVER here in 1932. Hitherto the valley had been known as *The Happy Valley*. The SILENT VALLEY RESERVOIR and BEN CROM RESERVOIR, which lies a short distance to the north, between them supply most of the water needs of Belfast.

**Sillees River** Fermanagh
*Rises in Lough Navar Forest Park, 10.5km SE of Belleek. Flows through Carrick Lough, Bunnahone Lough and Ross Lough and enters Upper Lough Erne at Rossorry a short distance S of Enniskillen*
Ir. *An tSailchis* [an **tal**-khish] 'the willow *kesh* or wickerwork causeway' + E. *river*. The causeway appears to have been across the Sillees at the foot of the village of **Derrygonnelly** where there was formerly a place named *Aghnasillis* (Ir. *Áth na Sailchise* 'ford of the willow *kesh*') [*Soilchis* c.1350].

**Silver Bridge** vill., Armagh 2931
(sometimes *Silverbridge*)
*6km NE of Crossmaglen*
par: *Creggan/Forkill*
bar: *Fews Upper/Orior Upper*
Ir. *Béal Átha an Airgid* [bell aha an **ar**agidge] 'ford-mouth of the silver'. The site of the ford is marked by a bridge across the CULLY WATER linking the townland of LEGMOYLIN in the parish of **Creggan** with the townland of CARRIGANS in the parish of **Forkhill** but the significance of the element *airgead* 'silver' is obscure [*(go) bél atha in airgit* c.1607].

**Sion Mills** vill., Tyrone 2339
*4.5km S of Strabane*
par: *Urney* bar: *Strabane Lower*
Ir. *Sián* [**shee**an] 'fairy mound' + E. *mills*. The first element of the place-name represents the name of the neighbouring townland of SEEIN. The final element refers to the extensive linen mills which were established in 1835 and stand on the west bank of the river **Mourne**. The village of Sion Mills is partly in the townland of BALLYFATTEN and partly in LIGGARTOWN [*the 'Sion Mills'* 1843].

**Sixmilecross** tl, vill., Tyrone 2536
*12km ESE of Omagh*
par: *Termonmaguirk* bar: *Omagh East*
Sixmilecross is named from a staggered crossroads in the middle of the village which was reckoned to be six Irish miles from **Omagh**. The Ir. name for Sixmilecross is *Na Corracha Móra* [na koragha **mor**a], originally *Na Corracha* 'the round hills', the plural adjective *móra* 'big', having been added to distinguish it from the other place named *Na Corracha*, i.e. **Oritor** which lies 20km to north-east and to which the element *beaga* 'small' has now been added [*(go haonach) na gCorrach* 1930].

**Six Mile Water** river, Antrim
*Rises at Shane's Hill, 8km SW of Larne. Flows into Lough Neagh a short distance W of Antrim town*
The river is said to be named from a crossing point six Irish miles from Antrim, on the road to Carrickfergus. The Ir. name for the river is *Abhainn na bhFiodh* [owen na **vyoo**] 'river of the woods'. An earlier Ir. name was *Ollarbha* [**ull**arwa], the meaning of which is obscure [*Owen ne view or Six Mile Water* 1605].

**Six Road Ends** vill., Down 3537
*4km SE of Bangor*
par: *Bangor* bar: *Ards Lower*
The village takes its name from its situation at a triple road junction [*Six Road Ends* 1927].

**Six Towns, The** distr., Der 2739
(sometimes *Sixtowns*)
*Close to the Tyrone border, 7km SW of Draperstown*
par: *Ballynascreen* bar: *Loughinsholin*
The name refers to the six townlands which were formerly the property of the church of Ballynascreen, namely CAVANREAGH, GLENVIGGAN, MONEYCONEY, MOYARD, OWENREAGH and TULLYBRICK.

**Skegoneill** tl, distr., Antrim 3337
*Suburb, 3km N of Belfast city centre*
par: *Shankill* bar: *Belfast Upper*
*Sceitheog an Iarla* [skehog an **eer**la] 'the earl's (little)thorn-bush'. The earl in question is likely to have been one of the Anglo-Norman earls of Ulster but no local tradition concerning the origin of the place-name survives [*Balliskeighog-Inerla* 1605].

**Skerries, The** islds, Antrim 2844
*In the Atlantic, 2km NE of Portrush*
par: *Ballywillin* bar: *Dunluce Lower*
Ir. *Na Sceirí* [na **sker**ee] 'the low, rocky islands'. Ir. *sceir* is a borrowing from O.N. *scer* 'reef' [*The Skerries* 1837].

**Sketrick Island** Down 3536
*Off W shore of Strangford Lough, 9km SE of Comber*
par: *Ardkeen* bar: *Ards Upper*
Ir. *Scathdeirg* [**ska**jerrig]. The meaning of the place-name is obscure. The Ir. name may be a gaelicised form of an earlier, non-Gaelic name, perhaps O.N. *Skothryggr* 'humpback ridge' [*(caislén) Sgath Deircce* 1470].

**Slaghtmanus** tl, Derry 2541
(sometimes *Slaughtmanus*)
*13km WNW of Dungiven*
par: *Cumber Lower* bar: *Tirkeeran*
Ir. *Sleacht Mhánasa* [slaght **wan**asa] 'Manus's grave-mound/memorial cairn'. There was a very large *cromlech* or megalithic portal tomb in this townland but it was destroyed in the last century [*Laghtmanus* 1613].

**Slaghtneill** tl, ham., Derry 2840
*5.5km NNW of Maghera*
par: *Killelagh* bar: *Loughinsholin*
Ir. *Sleacht Néill* [slaght **nyey**-il] 'Niall's grave-mound/memorial cairn'. There is a cairn in the north-east of the townland and local tradition has it that a Niall McLaughlin was killed here in a battle with the son of a prince of the O'Neills and that he is buried on a hill in the nearby townland of KNOCKONEILL (Ir. *Cnoc Néill* 'Niall's hill') [*Slachtneale* 1609].

**Slemish** mtn, Antrim 3240
*11.5km ENE of Ballymena*
par: *Racavan* bar: *Antrim Lower*
Ir. *Sliabh Mis* [sleeoo **mish**] '*Mis*'s mountain'. Slemish (437m), in the townland of CARNSTROAN, has the same derivation as SLIEVE MISH, a range of mountains which lie south-west of Tralee in Co. Kerry. According to medieval place-name lore, the *Mis* who gave name to the latter was a sister of *Eochu* (var. *Eochaidh) mac Maireadha*, the Munster king who gave name to **Lough Neagh** [*(i) Slébh Mis* 771].

**Slieveanorra or Orra More** mtn, Antrim 3142
*508m high, 10km W of Cushendall*
par: *Loughguile* bar: *Dunluce Upper*
Ir. *Sliabh an Earra* [sleeoo an **ara**] 'mountain of the tail/ridge'. The alternative name ORRA MORE is from Ir. *Earra Mór* 'great ridge' and contrasts with ORRA BEG (Ir. *Earra Beag* 'small ridge'), a peak of 383m a short distance to the north-east [*Slievenorry* 1780].

**Slieve Ban** mtn, Down 3131
*2.5km SE of Rostrevor*
par: *Kilbroney* bar: *Iveagh Upper, Upper Half*
Ir. *Sliabh Bán* [sleeoo **ban**] 'white mountain'. Slieve Ban (470m) is sometimes known as ROSTREVOR MOUNTAIN [*Slieve Bane* 1755].

**Slieve Beagh** mtn, Tyrone/Fermanagh 2534
*380m high, 8.5km SE of Fivemiletown*
par: *Clogher/Aghalurcher* bar: *Clogher*
Ir. *Sliabh Beatha* [sleeoo **ba**ha] *perhaps* 'mountain of birch'. A legend explains the element *beatha* as the genitive of *Bioth*, the name of one of the very first settlers in Ireland who is claimed to be buried here. However, it is more likely to represent a genitive form of *beith* 'birch' (*see also* ***Derryveagh Mountains*, Glenbeagh**). The name *Sliabh Beatha* is used for both the mountain itself and for its mountain range, which extends into Co. Monaghan as well as Tyrone and Fermanagh [*(ar) Sliabh Betha* 1501].

*Tors on Slieve Bernagh*

**Slieve Bernagh** mtn, Down 3332
*Peak of 739m in the Mournes, 7km SW of Newcastle*
par: *Kilkeel* bar: *Mourne*
Ir. *Sliabh Bearnach* [sleeoo **barn**agh] 'gapped mountain'. The name refers to the mountain's gapped or jagged appearance [*Sliabh Béarnach* c.1834].

**Slieve Binnian** mtn, Down 3332
*Peak of 747m in the Mournes, 9km N of Kilkeel*
par: *Kilkeel* bar: *Mourne*
Ir. *Sliabh Binneáin* [sleeoo **bin**yine] 'mountain of the little peak'. There is a peak named WEE BINNIAN (460m) a short distance to the south-west, the Ir. name of which is *Broinn Bhinneáin* [brin **vin**yine] 'breast of *Binneán*'. Slieve Binnian is in the townland of BRACKENAGH EAST UPPER [*Great Bennyng* c.1568].

**Slieve Commedagh** mtn, Down 3332
*Peak in the Mournes, 3.5km SW of Newcastle*
par: *Kilcoo* bar: *Iveagh Upper, Lower Half*
Ir. *Sliabh Coimhéideach* [sleeoo **kiv**edg-agh] 'watching/guarding mountain'. Slieve Commedagh (767m) which stands on the boundary between the townlands of BALLAGHBEG and TULLYBRANIGAN is the second highest peak in the Mournes [*Slieve Kimedia* c.1830].

**Slieve Croob** mtn, Down 3334
*8.5km SW of Ballynahinch*
bar: *Iveagh Upper, Lower Half*
Ir. *Sliabh Crúibe* [sleeoo **kroob**a] 'mountain of the hoof'. Slieve Croob (534m) stands at the point where the parishes of **Dromara**, MAGHERAHAMLET, KILMEGAN and DRUMGOOLAND all meet and is well known as the source of the river **Lagan**. The name suggests

an association with cattle and no doubt has mythological connotations [*Crooby Mountaine* c.1657].

**Slieve Donard** mtn, Down 3332
*At 850m, Ulster's highest mountain, in the Mournes, 3.5km SW of Newcastle*
par: *Kilcoo/Kilkeel*
bar: *Iveagh Upper, Lower Half/Mourne*
Ir. *Sliabh Dónairt* [sleeoo **doan**irtch] '(St) *Dónart*'s mountain'. St *Dónart* (earlier *Domangart*) was a contemporary of St Patrick and is said to have founded two churches in the locality. Slieve Donard (850m) is Ulster's highest mountain [*Sliabh-Domha*[*n*]*gaird* 1645].

**Slieve Gallion** mtn, Derry 2838
*528m high, 8km W of Magherafelt*
par: *Desertmartin/Lissan* bar: *Loughinsholin*
Ir. *Sliabh gCallann* [sleeoo **gal**an] *perhaps* 'mountain of the heights'. Traditionally Slieve Gallion is explained as '*Callann*'s mountain' and legend has it that a giant named *Callann Mór* is buried at CARNANBANE on the west side of the mountain. However, it is more likely that the final element is a variant of Ir. *collann perhaps* 'height/high ground' (*see* **Collin**) [*Collund Patricii* c.670].

**Slieve Gullion** tl, mtn, Armagh 3031
*8.5km SW of Newry*
par: *Forkill* bar: *Orior Upper*
Ir. *Sliabh gCuillinn* [sleeoo **gull**yin] 'mountain of the (steep) slope'. The townland of Slieve Gullion takes its name from the mountain, the summit of which stands on the boundary with the parish of **Killevy** and which at 573m is the highest mountain in Co. Armagh [(*moninni*) *Sleibi Culinn* c.830].

**Slievekirk** mtn, Tyrone 2440
*On the border with Co Derry, 9km W of Claudy*
par: *Donaghedy* bar: *Strabane Lower*
Ir. *Sliabh Circe* [sleeoo **kirk**a] 'mountain of the hen'. The element 'hen' is likely to refer to a grouse or a moorhen. Slievekirk (370m) is in the townland of TABOE GLEBE [*Slievkirk* 1836].

**Slievelamagan** mtn, Down 3332
*Peak of 704m in Mournes, 6.5km SW of Newcastle*
par: *Kilkeel* bar: *Mourne*
Ir. *Sliabh Lámhagáin* [sleeoo **laa**waggine] 'mountain of creeping/crawling'. An older name for Slievelamagan was *Slieve Snavan or Creeping Mountain*. The mountain is said to be so-named because it has to be climbed in a crawling position. *Slieve Snavan* derives from Ir. *Sliabh Snámháin* which has the same meaning as *Sliabh Lámhagáin* [*Slieve-Snavan or the creeping Mountain* 1744].

**Slieve League** mtn, Donegal 1537
*In SW corner of Donegal, 16km W of Killybegs*
par: *Glencolumbkille* bar: *Banagh*
Ir. *Sliabh Liag* [sleeoo **lee**ag] 'mountain of the pillar-stone(s)'. There are stone remains at the site of an early oratory of St *Aodh mac Bric* near the summit of the mountain but the place-name is more likely to refer to earlier, pre-Christian remains which may have been on the same site. Slieve League (595m) rises sharply out of the Atlantic and is one of the highest sea cliffs in western Europe [(*i*) *Sleibh Liacc* c.830].

**Slievemore** mtn, Tyrone 2536
*5.5km NW of Ballygawley*
par: *Errigal Keerogue* bar: *Clogher*
Ir. *An Sliabh Mór* [an sleeoo **more**] 'the big mountain'. Slievemore (315m) is in the highest point in the parish of ERRIGAL KEEROGUE. Its summit is in the townland of SHANTAVNY IRISH and the mountain is sometimes known as SHANTAVNY MOUNTAIN [*Shantavny mountain* 1834].

**Slieve Muck** mtn, Down 3232
*Peak in the Mournes, 10.5km NNW of Kilkeel*
Ir. *Sliabh Muc* [sleeoo **muck**] 'mountain of the pigs'. Slieve Muck (672m) stands on the boundary between the parishes of **Kilkeel** and CLONDUFF and also between the baronies of MOURNE and IVEAGH UPPER, LOWER HALF. The **Deer's Meadow**, which is the source of the river **Bann**, is at the west foot of the mountain [*Slieve Muck* 1755].

**Slievenahanaghan** mtn, Antrim 3142
*16km ESE of Ballymoney*
par: *Loughguile* bar: *Kilconway*
Ir. *Sliabh na hAnachaine* [sleeoo na **han**aghina] 'mountain of the mischance/disaster'. The circumstances in which the name was bestowed are unknown. Slievenahanaghan (405m) is in the townland of DRUMRANKIN [*Slieve-na-Hanagan* 1833].

**Slieve Snaght** mtn, Donegal 1941
*22.5km W of Letterkenny*
par: *Tullaghobegly* bar: *Kilmacrenan*
Ir. *Sliabh Sneachta* [sleeoo **snaght**a] 'mountain of snow'. Slieve Snaght (678m) is the highest peak in the **Derryveagh Mountains**. LOUGH SLIEVESNAGHT, the source of the SCARDANGAL BURN, lies at the eastern foot of the mountain.

**Slieve Snaght** mtn., Donegal 2443
*10km NE of Buncrana*
par: *Donagh* bar: *Inishowen East*
Ir. *Sliabh Sneachta* [sleeoo **snaght**a] 'mountain of snow'. Slieve Snaght (615m) is the highest peak on the **Inishowen** peninsula. The adjoining peak to the north is named SLIEVE SNAGHTBEG (505m) (Ir. *Sliabh Sneachta Beag* 'little Slieve Snaght') [*(Brian) Sléibhe Sneachta* 1260].

**Slievetooey** mtn, Donegal 1639
*On Atlantic coast, 12.5km W of Ardara*
par: *Glencolumbkille* bar: *Banagh*
Ir. *Sliabh Tuaidh* [sleeoo **too**ee] 'northern mountain'. Slievetooey (472m) appears to be so-named because it is the northernmost of a number of mountains which lie to the south of LOUGHROS BEG BAY [*Slieve-a-tory* 1835].

**Smithborough** vill., Monaghan 2533
(sometimes *Smithsborough*)
*8km WSW of Monaghan town*
par: *Clones* bar: *Monaghan*
Smithborough is named after a man named Smith who established monthly cattle fairs here in the latter part of the 18th century. The village straddles the townlands of MULLADUFF and MULLABRACK, hence its Ir. name, *Na Mullaí* [na **mull**ee] 'the hilltops' [*Smithsborough* 1778].

**Soldierstown** vill., Antrim 3136
*On the border with Co. Down, 2km N of Moira*
par: *Aghalee* bar: *Massereene Upper*
Soldierstown in the townland of BALLYNANAGHTEN is named from a former military station which is said to have been garrisoned there by two companies of soldiers during the rebellion of 1641 [*Soldierstown* 1780].

**Spa, The** vill., Down 3334
(sometimes *Spa*)
*2.5km S of Ballynahinch*
par: *Magheradrool* bar: *Kinelarty*
The Spa straddles the townlands of BALLYMAGLAVE SOUTH and BALLYMACARN SOUTH and takes its name from a sulphur and iron spa well on the south-west edge of the village.

**Spamount** tl, vill., Tyrone 2236
*On S bank of the river Derg, 2.5km E of Castlederg*
par: *Ardstraw* bar: *Omagh West*
Spamount was originally a house name, being the name of the residence of Edward Sproule who founded linen mills here in the early 19th century. The house was named from a spring well in the vicinity [*Spawmount* 1814].

**Spelga** mtn, Down 3232
*Peak of 479m in Mournes, 11km WSW of Newcastle*
par: *Clonduff* bar: *Iveagh Upper, Lower Half*
Ir. *Speilgeach* [**spell**igagh] 'place of pointed rocks'. Spelga has given name to SPELGA PASS and SPELGA DAM RESERVOIR which is on the headwaters of the **Bann**, close to the **Deer's Meadow** [*Spelga* 1810].

**Sperrin Mountains** Derry/Tyrone
*On the Derry/Tyrone borders*
Ir. *Sliabh Speirín* [sleeoo **sper**een] 'mountain (range) of *Speirín*'. Ir. *sliabh* which usually refers to a single mountain can sometimes apply to a mountain range or upland area. The element *speirín* (literally 'little spur of rock') in this case refers to an area abounding in such features. There is a hamlet named SPERRIN OR MOUNT HAMILTON in **Glenelly Valley**, 15km east of PLUMBRIDGE [*(aig) an Speirín* 1930].

**Staffordstown** tl, ham., Antrim 3038
*Close to N shore of Lough Neagh, 5km SW of Randalstown*
par: *Duneane* bar: *Toome Upper*
Staffordstown is named after Martha Stafford, daughter of Sir Francis Stafford, Governor of Ulster in Elizabethan times, who early in the 17th century married Sir Henry O'Neill, son of Shane mac Brian O'Neill of nearby **Shane's Castle**. The headquarters of the Staffords were at MOUNT STAFFORD near **Portglenone** but after the aforementioned marriage they were granted Staffordstown and nine other townlands in this area which were formerly the property of the O'Neills. The original Ir. name of the townland of Staffordstown was

*Baile Mhic an Bheatha* 'MacVeigh's townland' [*Mounstafford* 1669].

**Stewartstown** vill., Tyrone 2837
*10km SE of Cookstown*
par: *Donaghenry* bar: *Dungannon Middle*
In 1608 Sir Andrew Stewart (Lord Ochiltree) from Ayrshire in Scotland was granted land in this area on which he built a castle known as CASTLE STEWART in the townland of CASTLE FARM. It was around this castle (of which little trace now remains) that the village of Stewartstown grew up. The Ir. name for Stewartstown is *An Chraobh* [an **khree**oo] 'the branch/tree', a name which can figuratively apply to a fort or mansion. The name is preserved in CREW HILL, a hill short distance north of the village, in the townland of TAMNYLENNAN [*Stewartoune* c.1655].

**Stonyford** vill., Antrim 2514
(sometimes *Stoneyford*)
*8km NW of Lisburn*
par: *Derryaghy* bar: *Massereene Upper*
Stonyford, in the townland of ISLAND KELLY, is named from a ford which was replaced c.1730 by a bridge across STONYFORD RIVER a short distance west of the village [*Stoneyford* 1780].

**Stormont** distr., Down 3437
*6km E of Belfast city centre*
par: *Dundonald* bar: *Castlereagh Lower*
The name Stormont appears to be a shortened form of E. *Storm Mount*. It was first used c.1830 as the name of the house and estate of Rev. John Cleland, replacing the original estate name, *Mount Pleasant*. In 1859 the house was replaced by STORMONT CASTLE. Adjacent to this, the construction of PARLIAMENT BUILDINGS, seat of the former parliament of Northern Ireland, was commenced in 1924. Stormont is also the name of a district of Perthshire in Scotland which raises the possibility that it was borrowed by John Cleland as the name of his house. The name Stormont in Scotland is from Sc.G. *Stoirmhonadh* 'stepping-stones moor'. Stormont is in the townland of BALLYMISCAW [*Storm Mount* 1834].

**Strabane** tn, bars., Tyrone 2339
*Town is on the border with Donegal, 21.5km SSW of Derry city*
par: *Camus/Leckpatrick/Urney*
Ir. *An Srath Bán* [an sra **ban**] 'the white river-holm'. The town of Strabane is on the river **Mourne** and in the barony of STRABANE LOWER which is bordered on the east by the barony of STRABANE UPPER [*Sraith Bán* c.1616].

**Stradone** vill., Cavan 2530
*7.5km E of Cavan town*
par: *Larah* bar: *Loughtee Upper*
Ir. *Sraith an Domhain* [sra an **doain**] *perhaps* 'river-holm of the valley floor'. The first element of the place-name refers to the position of the village close to the STRADONE RIVER. The final element is the genitive form of *domhan* which normally means 'world/earth' but in this case case may represent a variant form of *domhain* 'depth' and signify something like 'valley bottom/valley floor' (cf. ***Stranorlar***). Stradone is in the townland of DRUMLAUNAGHT [*Shraghadoone* 1629].

**Stragolan** tl, Fermanagh 2136
*4km E of Pettigoe*
par: *Drumkeeran* bar: *Lurg*
Ir. *Srath Gabhláin* [sra **goal**ine] 'river-holm of the fork'. There is a fork on the stream which bounds the townland on the east [*Stragolan* 1751].

**Straid** tl, vill., Antrim 3339
*5km E of Ballyclare*
par: *Ballynure* bar: *Belfast Lower*
Ir. *An tSráid* [an **tradge**] 'the street/village'. Ir. *sráid* 'street' or *sráidbhaile*, literally 'street-town', is quite common in place-names in the sense of a village with one street. At an earlier date Straid was known as *Straidballythomas* (Ir. *Sráidbhaile Thomais* 'Thomas's village') or *Thomastown*. STRAID HILL (220m) stands in the south of the townland while STRAID DAM lies to the north, in the townland of BRYANTANG. The townland of Straid was formerly known as *Straidland*. It was extensive and also included the neighbouring townlands of CALHAME, DAIRYLAND, IRISH HILL and LISGLASS. There is still a farm named STRAIDLAND in CALHAME [*The Stread* 1669].

**Straid** ham., Antrim 3044
*10.5km W of Ballycastle*
par: *Ballintoy* bar: *Cary*
Ir. *An tSráid* [an **tradge**] 'the street/village'. Straid is in the townland of CROAGHMORE which also contains the hamlet of STRAID-

KILLEN (Ir. *Sráid Chillín* 'village of the small burial-ground') [*Straid* 1803].

**Straidarran** ham., Derry 2540
*10.5km SW of Dungiven*
par: *Learmount* bar: *Tirkeeran*
Ir. *Sráidbhaile Uí Áráin* [sradge-wala ee **aar**ine] '(O')Haran's village'. The (O')Harans are an *erenagh* family of Fermanagh origin. Straidarran is in the townland of STRAID which appears to be a shortened version of the name. STRAID HILL (303m) stands on the southern boundary of the townland [*Baile Uí Hárán* c.1680].

**Stralongford** tl, ham., Tyrone 2235
*4.5km NE of Irvinestown*
par: *Kilskeery* bar: *Omagh East*
Ir. *Srath Longfoirt* [sra **lung**furtch] 'riverholm of the fortress'. A stream forms the south and west boundaries of the townland. There is no trace or record of a fort in this townland but there is a large fort to the north, in the townland of LISDOO, and also to the south-east, at LISNAGORE in the townland of FEGLISH [*Shralonghert* 1609].

**Stranagalwilly** tl, Tyrone 2540
*On border with Co Derry, 5km S of Claudy*
par: *Cumber Upper* bar: *Strabane Lower*
*Ir. Srath na Gallbhuaile* [sra na **gal**woola] 'river-holm of the stone *booley* or cattle enclosure'. Stranagalwilly is partially bounded by the GLENRANDAL RIVER on the east [*Shraghnagallnilly* 1661].

**Strandtown** tl, distr., Down 3337
*Suburb, 3km E of Belfast city centre*
par: *Holywood* bar: *Castlereagh Lower*
The townland of Strandtown which straddles the HOLYWOOD ROAD originally bordered on **Belfast Lough** but now lies a short distance inland due to land reclamation schemes [*Strandtowne* 1672].

**Strangford** tl, vill., Down 3534
*At S entrance to Strangford Lough, 11km NE of Downpatrick*
par: *Ballyculter* bar: *Lecale Lower*
O.N. *Strangrfjörthr* 'strong sea-inlet'. The townland and village take their name from STRANGFORD LOUGH, a long sea-inlet which sparates the ARDS PENINSULA from the mainland. The element *strangr* 'strong' in the place-name refers to the strength of the currents in the narrow entrance to the lough, between Strangford and **Portaferry**. The Ir. name for Strangford Lough is *Loch Cuan* [lough **koo**an] 'sea-inlet of bays/havens' and the village of Strangford is known as *Baile Loch Cuan* 'town on Strangford Lough' [*Strangfiord* 1205].

**Stranmillis** distr., Antrim 3337
*Suburb, 2.5km S of Belfast city centre*
par: *Shankill* bar: *Belfast Upper*
Ir. *An Sruthán Milis* [an sroohan **mill**ish] 'the sweet stream'. The place-name appears to refer to the point where the river **Lagan** ceases to be tidal and beyond which the water therefore becomes 'sweet' [*(bun) a' tSrutháin Mhilis* 1644].

**Stranocum** tl, vill., Antrim 3043
*7km NE of Ballymoney*
par: *Ballymoney* bar: *Dunluce Upper*
The first element of the place-name is Ir. *Srath* [sra] 'river-holm', referring to level land along the river **Bush** which bounds the townland on the north and east. The origin of the final element is obscure [*Stronokum* c.1659].

**Stranorlar** tl, tn, par., Donegal 2139
*Town is 16.5km S of Letterkenny*
bar: *Raphoe*
Ir. *Srath an Urláir* [sra an **urr**lar] 'river-holm of the valley floor'. The valley is that of the river **Finn** which forms the southern boundary of the townland. Stranorlar is twin town to **Ballybofey** which lies on the opposite side of the river. The parish of Stranorlar was created in 1835, having at an earlier period formed a part of the deanery of **Raphoe** [*Stranhurland* 1590].

**Straughroy** tl, Tyrone 2437
(sometimes *Strathroy*)
*2km NNW of Omagh*
par: *Cappagh* bar: *Strabane Upper*
Ir. *An Srath Crua* [an sra **kroo**a] 'the hard river-holm'. Straughroy is bounded on the west by the river **Strule** [*Ballyshraghcroy* 1629].

**Stroove** tl, vill., Donegal 2644
(sometimes *Shrove*)
*NE tip of Inishowen peninsula, 3.5km NE of Greencastle*
par: *Moville Lower* bar: *Inishowen East*
Ir. *An tSrúibh* [an **troo**ive] 'the beak/ point'.

*An tSrúibh* is a shortened form of *Srúibh Bhrain* [sroo **vran**] 'raven's beak', the Ir. name of INISHOWEN HEAD in the north-east of the townland. Ir. *Bran* 'raven' is also used as a personal name and according to the eighth-century vogage tale *Immram Brain* 'the voyage of *Bran*' the final element of the place-name refers to the tale's hero *Bran mac Feabhail Bran,* son of *Feabhal* and *Srúibh Brain* '*Bran*'s point' was the place to which he and his men returned after their journey to the otherworld [*(hi tóib) Srúbe Brain* c.1075].

**Struell** tl, Down 3534
*2km E of Downpatrick*
par: *Down* bar: *Lecale Upper*
*An tSruthail* [an **troo**hil] 'the stream'. The stream is partially underground and supplies water to two holy wells associated with St Patrick and also to bath-houses [*(Capella de) Strohull* 1306].

**Strule** river, Tyrone
*Formed by the convergence of the Camowen River with the Drumragh River at Omagh. Merges with the Derg to form the Mourne 4km NW of Newtownstewart*
Ir. *An tSruthail* [an **troo**hil] 'the stream'. The name seems to be a fairly late one and it appears that at an earlier period the river **Mourne** also comprised the portion of the river which is now known as the Strule (*see* ***Mourne*** *above*) [*Strule* 1831].

**Suffolk** vill., Antrim 3237
*Now a suburb on the SW outskirts of Belfast*
par: *Shankill* bar: *Belfast Upper*
The name appears to have its origin in SUFFOLK HOUSE, the residence of John McCance in 1830. Suffolk is an imported name, originally referring to the English county, and deriving from O.E. *suð folc* 'south folk' [*Suffolk house* 1830].

**Swanlinbar** tn, Cavan 2132
*Close to Fermanagh border, 17.5km S of Enniskillen*
par: *Kinawley* bar: *Tullyhaw*
The name Swanlinbar is made up of the first syllable of each of the surnames of the three proprietors of the iron-works which formerly stood here, i.e. Swansea, Lindsay and Barry. Swanlinbar is partly in the townland of HAWKSWOOD and partly in FURNACELAND. The Ir. name of the town is *An Muileann Iarainn* [an mwillan **eer**in] 'the iron mill'. Swanlinbar stands on the CLADAGH OR SWANLINBAR RIVER [*Swanlinbar* 1837].

**Swatragh** tl, vill., Derry 2840
*7km N of Maghera*
par: *Killelagh* bar: *Loughinsholin*
Ir. *An Suaitreach* [an **soo**itch-ragh] 'the (billeted) soldier'. The name is an abbreviated form of *Baile an tSuaitrigh* [bala an **too**itch-ree] 'townland of the (billeted) soldier'. The circumstances in which the name was coined are unknown [*Ballitotry* 1613].

**Swilly** river, Donegal
*Rises at Altinierin, 15km WSW of Letterkenny. Flows into Lough Swilly 4km E of Letterkenny*
Ir. *An tSúileach* [an **too**il-agh] 'the one with eyes'. As in the case of so many river names, the name is likely to have supernatural connotations, perhaps suggesting something like 'the seeing one/the bright one'. The Swilly has given name to the large sea inlet known as LOUGH SWILLY into which it flows (Ir. *Loch tSúilí* 'inlet of the Swilly') and to GLENSWILLY (Ir. *Gleann Súilí* 'glen of the Swilly'), the name of its river valley. There is also a hill named BINSWILLY (337m) (Ir. *Binn tSúilí* 'hill of the Swilly') a short distance north of the source of the river [*Suileach* 1258].

**Sydenham** distr., Down 3337
*Suburb, 3km NE of Belfast city centre*
par: *Holywood* bar: *Castlereagh Lower*
Sydenham is an imported name, originally referring to a district of Lewisham in Greater London. The name derives from the O.E. personal name *Cippa* + O.E. *ham* 'homestead', thus '*Cippa*'s homestead'. Sydenham is built on land reclaimed from **Belfast Lough**.

# T

**Taghnevan** tl, Armagh 3035
*Suburb on SW side of Lurgan*
par: *Shankill* bar: *Oneilland East*
Ir. *Teach Neamhain* [chagh **nyau-**in] '*Neamhan*'s house'. The element *teach* often refers to a monastic house but there is no trace or record of any such in the townland [*Toghnevan* 1609].

**Tamlaght** vill., Derry 2940
*6.5km NW of Portglenone*
par: *Tamlaght O'Crilly* bar: *Loughinsholin*
Ir. *Tamhlacht* [**tau**laght] 'sanctuary/land set apart'. The name is an abbreviated form of TAMLAGHT O'CRILLY (Ir. *Tamhlacht Uí Chroiligh* [taulaght ee **khrill**ee] '(O')Crilly's sanctuary'), the name of the parish in which it is situated. The O'Crillys were *erenaghs* or hereditary lay custodians of the church lands. Tamlaght is partly in the townland of DRUMNACANON where a ruined church and graveyard are thought to occupy the site of the medieval parish church. The original meaning of Ir. *tamhlacht* appears to be '(pagan) burial ground' but it is fairly common in names of early ecclesiastic sites where it means something like 'sanctuary/land set apart' [*Tawlat Ichrilly* c.1657].

**Tamlaght** tl, ham., Fermanagh 2234
*4.5km SE of Enniskillen*
par: *Derryvullan* bar: *Tirkennedy*
Ir. *Tamhlacht* [**tau**laght] 'sanctuary/land set apart'. The ruins of an 18th-century church mark the site of an early church in the neighbouring townland of DERRYVULLAN [*Tamlagh* 1834].

**Tamnamore** ham., Tyrone 2836
*7km E of Dungannon*
par: *Killyman* bar: *Dungannon Middle*
Ir. *An Tamhnach Mhór* [an taunagh **wore**] 'the large field'. Tamnamore is in the townland of TAMLAGHTMORE [*Tamunaghmore* c.1655].

**Tandragee** vill., Armagh 3034
*7.5km SSE of Portadown*
par: *Ballymore* bar: *Orior Lower*
Ir. *Tóin re Gaoith* [tone ri **gee**] 'backside to the wind'. There are hills so-named throughout Ireland, no doubt on account of their exposed situations. Tandragee is mainly in the townland of BALLYMORE [(*go*) *Tóin re Gaoith* 1642].

**Tardree** tl, Antrim 3139
*8.5km NNE of Antrim town*
par: *Connor* bar: *Antrim Lower*
Ir. *An tArd Fhraoigh* [an tard **ree**] 'the height of heather'. Tardree is named from TARDREE MOUNTAIN (240m) which stands in the middle of the townland [*Ardry* c.1657].

**Tassagh** tl, ham., Armagh 2833
*9km S of Armagh city*
par: *Keady* bar: *Armagh*
Ir. *An Tasach* [an **tass**agh] 'the dwelling'. Ir. *tasach* appears to be a variant of *fas/fosadh* 'abode, dwelling'. The name may refer to a former ecclesiastical settlement. There is an old graveyard in the north of the townland which lies on the west bank of the river **Callan** [*Tassaagh* 1539].

**Tattyreagh Glebe** tl, Tyrone 2436
*8.5km S of Omagh*
par: *Drumragh* bar: *Omagh East*
Ir. *An Taite Riabhach* [an tatcha **ree**wagh] 'the grey/striped *tate*' + E. *glebe*. A *tate* is a now-obsolete land measure found mainly in Tyrone and Fermanagh and used as the equivalent of a townland, though in theory only half the size [*Tattereagh* c.1655].

**Tawny** tl, vill., Donegal 2143
(sometimes *Tamney*)
*On Fanad peninsula, 12.5km N of Millford*
par: *Clondavaddog* bar: *Kilmacrenan*
Ir. *An Tamhnaigh* [an **taun**ee] 'the field'. Tawney has given name to TAWNEY LOUGH which borders the townland on the west [*Tamenagh* c.1655].

**Tedavnet** tl, vill., par., Monaghan 2633
(sometimes *Tydavnet*)
*Village is 6km NW of Monaghan town*
bar: *Monaghan*
Ir. *Tigh Damhnata* [tee **dau**nata] '(St) *Damhnat*'s (monastic) house'. St *Damhnat* (sometimes anglicised *Dympna*) was a virgin saint who founded a monastery here in the sixth century. The site of the monastery is marked by a graveyard in the village. St *Damhnat*'s memory is also preserved in CALDAVNET (Ir. *Ceall Damhnata* 'Damhnat's cell/church'),

the name of a townland which lies 5km to the north-west, on the lower slopes of **Slieve Beagh** [*Thechdamnad* 1306].

**Tedd** tl, Fermanagh 2236
*On the border with Tyrone, 4km NE of Irvinestown*
par: *Derryvullan* bar: *Lurg*
Ir. *An tSéad* [an **ched**] 'the path or track'. There is a hamlet named TEDD CROSS ROADS in the middle of the townland [*Tead* 1655].

**Teebane** tl, Tyrone 2637
*14km W of Cookstown*
par: *Kildress* bar: *Dungannon Upper*
Ir. *Taobh Bán* [teeoo **ban**] 'white hill-side' [*Teebawn* c.1835].

**Teelin** vill., distr., Donegal 1537
*On SW Donegal coast, 2km S of Carrick*
par: *Glencolumbkille* bar: *Banagh*
Ir. *Teileann* [**chell**in] 'dish'. The word 'dish' is used metaphorically to refer to the little rounded bay at one end of which is TEELIN PIER and which forms part of the larger TEELIN BAY. The village of Teelin is in the townland of LERGADAGHTAN while TEELIN POINT which adjoins the pier is in the townland of RINNAKILL [(*go*) *Cuan Teilionn* 1600].

**Teemore** tl, ham., Fermanagh 2332
*5.5km SE of Derrylin*
par: *Kinawley* bar: *Knockninny*
Ir. *An Tigh Mór* [an tee **more**] 'the large house'. The element *tigh* in place-names often refers to a monastic house but there is no trace or record of any such in the townland. The hamlet of Teemore is not in the townland of that name but in the neighbouring townland of KINOUGHTRAGH [*Teemore* 1747].

**Temple, The** vill., Down 3336
*4.5km ENE of Saintfield*
par: *Killaney* bar: *Castlereagh Upper*
The name The Temple was first applied to a public house in the townland of CARRICKNAVEAGH. It was called The Temple because it was the meeting place for a freemasons' lodge [*The Temple* 1858].

**Templepatrick** tl, vill., par., Antrim 3238
*Village is 16km NW of Belfast*
bar: *Belfast Upper*
Ir. *Teampall Phádraig* [champal **fad**rick] '(St) Patrick's church'. The church was attached to a medieval priory which was the principal house in the diocese of **Connor** of the Order of St John of Jerusalem, now called the Knights of Malta. The site is marked by **Castle Upton**, an early 17th-century castle which stands a short distance north of the village. The dedication of the church to St Patrick appears to be a comparatively late one [*Templeton or Templepatricke* 1605].

**Tempo** vill., Fermanagh 2334
*11.5km NE of Enniskillen*
par: *Enniskillen* bar: *Tirkennedy*
Ir. *An tIompú Deiseal* [an chumpoo **jesh**el] 'the right-hand turn'. The TEMPO RIVER forms the eastern boundary of the townland of EDENMORE in which the village of Tempo is situated and the place-name may refer to a bend on the river a short distance south of the village. There is a local legend that St Patrick left a manuscript here on his way to **Enniskillen** and that he instructed his servant to 'turn right' to go back and retrieve it [*Tempodessell* 1622].

**Termon** vill., Donegal 2142
*11km NNW of Letterkenny*
par/bar: *Kilmacrenan*
Ir. *An Tearmann* [an **char**aman] 'the sanctuary'. The word *tearmann* originally referred to the lands of a church or monastery within which the rights of sanctuary prevailed. In place-names it is often used in a looser sense to signify simply 'church lands'. In this case the church lands belonged to the early monastery of **Kilmacrenan**, 3km to the south-east. Termon is in the townland of CURRIN [*Termon* 1838].

**Thompson's Bridge** vill., Fermanagh 2134
*5.5km W of Enniskillen*
par: *Rossorry* bar: *Magheraboy*
Thompson's Bridge takes it name from a bridge over the **Sillees River**, linking the townland of CROAGHRIM with the townland of KILLYCAT. The surname Thompson ('son of Thomas') is a common one in Fermanagh and many Thompsons are descendants of settlers who arrived in Plantation times from the border regions of Scotland.

**Three Mile Water** stream, Antrim 3338
*Rises in the townland of Kingsbog, 4km SE of Ballyclare. Enters Belfast Lough at Whiteabbey, 9km N of Belfast city centre*
Three Mile Water is said to be so-named

because it enters Belfast Lough three Irish miles south-west of **Carrickfergus**. At an earlier period the stream was also known as *Ballylinny River* because for part of its course it borders the parish of BALLYLINNY on the south. There is also a stream named BALLYLINNY BURN a short distance to the north [*Three Mile Water* 1839].

**Tirkane** tl, Derry 2840
*4km NW of Maghera*
par: *Killelagh* bar: *Loughinsholin*
Ir. *Tír Chiana* [cheer **kheeana**] *perhaps* '*Cian*'s land/territory'. *Cian* is an early Irish personal name [*Tír Chiana* c.1740].

**Tirmacoy** tl, ham., Derry 2642
*7.5km SW of Limavady*
par: *Faughanvale* bar: *Tirkeeran*
Ir. *Tír Mhic Eochaidh* [cheer vick **augh**ee] 'MacCaughey's land/territory'. The surname *Mac Eochaidh* is a variant of *Mac Eachaidh* which is widespread in the north of Ireland and can be anglicised *Caughey, MacCaughey* and *MacGahey* [*Tirennekoghy* 1613].

**Tobermore** tl, vill., Derry 2839
*5km NE of Draperstown*
par: *Kilcronaghan* bar: *Loughinsholin*
Ir. *Tobar Mór* [tubbar **more**] 'large well'. The well, which was at the eastern end of the main street, had already dried up by the 19th century [*Tobarmore* 1613].

**Tollymore** tl, Down 3333
*In NW outskirts of Newcastle*
par: *Maghera* bar: *Iveagh Upper, Lower Half*
Ir. *An Tulaigh Mhór* 'the big hillock'. The townland of Tollymore is bordered on the west by the townland of TOLLYMORE PARK in the parish of **Kilcoo**. The latter townland includes TOLLYMORE FOREST PARK and a portion of the river **Shimna** which flows through the forest is also known as the TOLLYMORE RIVER [*Balletollemore* 1610].

**Tonyduff** tl, vill., Cavan 2630
(sometimes *Tunnyduff*)
*7.5km NW of Bailieborough*
par: *Knockbride* bar: *Clankee*
Ir. *An Tonnaigh Dhubh* [an tunny **ġoo**] 'the black marsh'. There is a small area of boggy land around TONYDUFF LOUGH [*Tonduffe* 1639].

**Toome** tl, vill., bars, Antrim 2939
*Village is at NW corner of Lough Neagh, 9km W of Randalstown*
par: *Duneane* bar: *Toome Upper*
Ir. *Tuaim* [**too**im] 'pagan burial place'. The site of the burial place has not been identified. An earlier name for Toome was *Fearsaid Thuama* 'sand-bank ford of Toome', referring to a former ford across the **Lower Bann** where it flows out of **Lough Neagh** here. The village of Toome is sometimes known as TOOMEBRIDGE, referring to the bridge which was built to replace the ford in 1785. The village is in the barony of TOOME UPPER which is adjoined on the north by TOOME LOWER [*(for) Fertais Tuamma* c.900].

**Torrent** river Tyrone
*Rises at Black Hill 10km NW of Dungannon. Merges with the Blackwater 4km W of Lough Neagh*
*perhaps* Ir. *Torann* [**tor**an] 'thundering one/noisy one'. The Torrent is one of the three legendary 'black rivers of Ireland' which are said to have burst forth in prehistoric times [*Torann* 3656AM].

**Torr Head** hl, Antrim 3244
*On N Antrim coast, 11km E of Ballycastle*
par: *Culfeightrin* bar: *Cary*
Ir. *Tor* [tor] 'steep rocky height' + E. *head*. Torr Head straddles the townlands of EAST TORR and WEST TORR [*(go) Torbhuirg* c.1633].

**Tory Island** isld, tl, Donegal 1844
*Off N coast of Donegal, 12km N of Bloody Foreland*
par: *Tullaghobegly* bar: *Kilmacrenan*
Ir. *Toraigh* [**tor**ee] 'place of steep rocky heights' + E. *island*. The island is named from the great rocky cliffs around its coast [*(fasughadh) Toraighe* 611].

**Tow** river, Antrim
(*see **Glentaisie***)

**Traad Point** hl, Derry 2938
*On W shore of Lough Neagh, 4.5km S of Toome*
par: *Artrea* bar: *Loughinsholin*
Ir. *Trá Fhada* [tra **adda**] 'long strand' + E. *point*. There is a sandy beach here, in the townland of DRUMENAGH.

**Trasna Island** isld, tl, Fermanagh 2332
*In Upper Lough Erne, 4km E of Derrylin*
par: *Kinawley* bar: *Knockninny*

*Tullycoe, 'hillock of the cuckoos'*

Ir. *Trasna* 'transverse (island)' + E. *island*. The island is now connected to the mainland by two road bridges [*Trassna* 1610].

**Trillick** vill., Tyrone 2335
*7.5km SSW of Dromore*
par: *Kilskeery* bar: *Omagh East*
Ir. *Trileac* [**trill**ack] 'three (flag-)stones'. This is the literal meaning of the place-name. However, the word *trileac* seems to have been used for *dolmens* and other megalithic remains (*see* ***Edentrillick***). Trillick is in the townland of CAVANAMARA and there are remains of a stone circle near the ruins of TRILLICK CASTLE a short distance to the north, in the townland of CASTLEMERVYN DEMESNE [(*airchindeach*) *Trelecc* 814].

**Trostan** mtn, Antrim 3142
*550m high, 6.5km SW of Cushendall*
par: *Layd* bar: *Glenarm Lower*
Ir. *Trostán* [**trust**an]. *Trostán* 'pole/staff' is found elsewhere in hill names and is generally explained by a perceived resemblance of the hill to a pilgrim's staff. However, it appears to be a borrowing from L. *transtrum* 'cross-beam' and in place-names it may signify something like 'cross hill/transverse hill' [*Trostan* 1780].

**Tullaghoge** tl, vill., Tyrone 2837
(sometimes *Tullyhogue*)
*3.5km SSE of Cookstown*
par: *Desertcreat* bar: *Dungannon Upper*
Ir. *Tulach Óg* [tulagh **oag**] 'hillock of the youths or warriors'. On the summit of a hillock in the neighbouring townland of BALLYMULLY GLEBE there is a ring-fort named TULLAGHOGE FORT which was the inauguration site of the O'Neills of Ulster from the 11th to the 16th century [(*oc*) *Telach Occ* 913].

**Tullintrain** tl, ham., Derry 2540
*2.5km SSE of Claudy*
par: *Cumber Upper* bar: *Tirkeeran*
Ir. *Tulaigh an Tréin* [tullee an **train**] 'hillock of the strong man/warrior' [*Tulletraine* 1654].

**Tullycarnet** tl, distr., Down 3337
*Suburb, 4.5km E of Belfast city centre*
par: *Knockbreda* bar: *Castlereagh Lower*
Ir. *Tulaigh Charnáin* [tullee **kharn**ine] 'hillock of the little cairn'. There is now no trace or record of a cairn in the townland [*Tullecarnan* 1623].

**Tullycoe** tl, Cavan 2530
*10km ENE of Cavan town*
par: *Larah* bar: *Tullygarvey*
Ir. *Tulaigh Chuach* [tullee **khoo**agh] 'hillock of cuckoos'. The remains of TULLYCOE FORT stand on the summit of of a hill in this townland [*Tollocoe* 1586].

**Tullydonnell** tls, ham., Armagh 3031
*Close to the Louth border, 8.5km E of Crossmaglen*
par: *Creggan* bar: *Fews Upper*
Ir. *Tulaigh Uí Dhónaill* [tullee ee **ġoan**il] 'O'Donnell's hillock'. The surname *Ó Dónaill* 'O'Donnell' is of Donegal origin but it is attested in this area in the early 17th century. The hamlet of Tullydonnell is in the townland of TULLYDONNELL (O'CALLAGHAN) which is bordered on the south by TULLYDONNELL (GAGE) [*Tulligonell* 1609].

**Tullyroan** tl, Armagh 2935
(sometimes *Tullyrone*)
*11km W of Portadown*
par: *Clonfeacle* bar: *Oneilland West*
Ir. *Tulaigh Uí Ruáin* [tullee ee **roo**ine] '(O)'Rowan's hillock'. The surname *Ó Ruáin* which can be anglicised *Ruane, Roane* or *Rowan* is generally associated with the west of Ireland but is also found in Ulster. The hamlet of TULLYROAN CORNER is in the middle of the townland [*Tulliroan* 1611].

**Tullyvin** tl, vill., Cavan 2531
*5km SW of Cootehill*
par: *Kildrumsherdan* bar: *Tullygarvey*
Ir. *Tulaigh Bhinn* [tullee **vin**]. The first element of the place-name means 'hillock', and appears to refer to a steep hill at the junction of the ANNALEE RIVER with the DROMORE RIVER. The normal meaning of the final

element *binn* is 'sweet/melodious' but its significance in this place-name is obscure [*Tullyvin* 1835].

**Tulnacross** tl, Tyrone 2738
*9.5km WNW of Cookstown*
par: *Kildress* bar: *Dungannon Upper*
Ir. *Tulach na Croise* [tulagh na **crush**a] 'hillock of the cross'. The Ir. element *cros* (literally 'cross') appears to sometimes refer to a cairn or to megalithic remains. There are remains of a stone circle in the south of the townland, on the north bank of the BALLINDERRY RIVER [*Tullanecrosse* 1619].

**Tureagh** tl, Antrim 3143
(sometimes *Turreagh*)
*3.5km E of Armoy*
par: *Armoy* bar: *Cary*
*An Tor Riabhach* [an torr **ree**wagh] 'the grey/striped crag or hill'. On the summit of a hill in the townland there is a rocky feature known as MAEVE'S POT [*Torreagh*1659].

**Twinbrook** h.est. Antrim 3236
*11km SW of Belfast city centre*
par: *Derryaghy* bar: *Belfast Upper*
Twinbrook in the townland of KILLEATON appears to be named from TWINBROOK DAIRY FARM in the south of the neighbouring townland of POLEGLASS. The farm takes its name from two streams, one of which is the COLLIN BURN. The current Ir. name of Twinbrook is *Cill Uaighe* [kill **oo**-eeya] 'church of the grave', a name represented by E. KILWEE and referring to an ancient church which formerly stood in the neighbouring townland of **Dunmurry**.

**Tynan** tl, vill., par., Armagh 2734
*Village is 11km WSW of Armagh city*
bar: *Tiranny*
Ir. *Tuíneán* [**tee**nan] *perhaps* 'place of the (man-made) watercourse'. The place-name may represent a form of *taoidhin* '(man-made) watercourse, mill pond' plus the suffix *-eán* 'place of'. The place-name may provide evidence of an early water mill. The site of the medieval parish church is marked by the graveyard of the Church of Ireland church in the village. There is a townland named COR TYNAN a short distance to the west [*(airchindeach) Tuidnidha* 1072].

*Cross at Tynan*

**Tyrella** tls, ham., par., Down 3433
*Hamlet is on the coast, 9km SW of Downpatrick*
bar: *Lecale Upper*
Ir. *Tigh Riala* [tee **ree**ala] '(St) *Riail*'s (monastic) house'. The feast day of St *Riail* of Tyrella was 17 September. The modern Church of Ireland church in the townland of TYRELLA SOUTH marks the site of the medieval parish church and also of an Early Christian church [*(o) Thigh Riaghla* c.1630].

**Tyrone** co.
Ir. *Tír Eoghain* [cheer **o**an] 'Owen's and territory'. Tyrone is named from *Eoghan* (anglicised *Owen*), one of the many sons of *Niall Naoighiallach* 'Niall of the Nine Hostages', a fifth-century king who is reputed to have ruled Ireland from TARA. Originally *Eoghan*'s territory was confined to **Inishowen** in Donegal (*see above*) but gradually his descendants, the *Cineál Eoghain* i.e. 'race of Owen', extended their power over the modern county of Tyrone and part of Co. Derry as well. The present boundaries of the county were established in the early 17th century [*(tighernuis) Thíre hEoghain* c.1500].

# U

**Ulster** province
Ir. *Ulaidh* 'Ulstermen' + O.N. possessive *s* + Ir. *tír* 'land'. The present E. form of the name has its origins in the Norse period though first recorded in Norman times. The original Ir. name of Ulster was *Ulaidh* 'Ulstermen' or *Cúige Uladh* 'province of the Ulstermen'. The *Ulaidh* 'Ulstermen' were the dominant population group in the north of Ireland in the pre-Christian period, the traditional description of the extent of their territory being *Ó Drobaís go Bóinn*, i.e. from the river **Drowes** in Donegal to the BOYNE in Co. Louth. However, later centuries saw a progressive reduction in their territory until by the sixth century the name *Ulaidh* applied only to the modern counties of Antrim and Down, along with north-east Derry and Co. Louth as far south as the Boyne. Still later, the Anglo-Norman Earldom of Ulster was confined mainly to counties Antrim and Down. The extent of the present nine-county province of Ulster was laid down in the early 17th century. The meaning of the tribal name *Ulaidh* is obscure [*Ouolountioi* c.150AD].

**Unshinagh** tl, Antrim 3042
*6km SE of Ballymoney*
par: *Finvoy* bar: *Kilconway*
Ir. *Uinseannach* [**unsh**anagh] 'place of ash-trees' [*Unsanagh* 1669].

**Upperland** tl, vill., Derry 2840
(often *Upperlands*)
*Village is 4km NNE of Maghera*
par: *Maghera* bar: *Loughinsholin*
The name is a peculiar anglicisation of Ir. *Áth an Phoirt Leathain* [aha furt **lah**in] 'ford of the broad (river) bank'. The ford in question was probably over the KNOCKONEILL RIVER which forms the southern boundary of the townland. The village is partly in the neighbouring townland of TIRGARVIL [*Aghfortlany* 1613].

**Urney** tl, par., Tyrone 2339
*Townland is 5km SW of Strabane*
bar: *Strabane Lower*
Ir. *An Urnaí* [an **urn**ee] 'the oratory/prayer house'. In the neighbouring townland of URNEY GLEBE there is a ruined church and graveyard which marks the site of the medieval parish church and also of an early church. A portion of the parish lies in Co. Donegal and another portion which includes the town of **Castlederg** is sometimes known as the SKIRTS OF URNEY [(*aircinnigh*) *na hErnaidhe* 1178].

*An Ulster cottage*

# V

**Victoria Bridge** vill., Tyrone 2339
*7km S of Strabane*
par: *Ardstraw* bar: *Strabane Lower*
The village of Victoria Bridge is on the west bank of the river **Mourne** in the townland of BREEN and takes its name from a bridge which links that townland with the townland of LISKY. The bridge was built in 1842 and named after Queen Victoria.

**Virginia** tl, tn, Cavan 2628
*On N shore of Lough Ramor, 10km SW of Bailieborough*
par: *Lurgan* bar: *Castlerahan*
The town of Virginia was originally named *Lough Ramor* and was founded on lands previously owned by Brian mac Phelim O'Reilly and granted to Captain John Ridgeway in 1611. It was re-named Virginia from the newly-established colony of Virginia in America which in turn took its name from Queen Elizabeth I, the 'Virgin Queen'. The Ir. name of the town is *Achadh an Iúir* [aghoo an **yure**] 'field of the yew-tree'. The original Ir. name of the townland of Virginia was *Achadh Ladhair* [aghoo **lair**] 'field of the fork', apparently referring to the position of the townland between the river BLACKWATER and **Lough Ramor**. A small portion of the town is west of the river, in the townland of RAHARDRUM [*Virginia* 1611].

**Vow** tl, ham., Antrim 2941
(sometimes *The Vow*)
(*see **Finvoy***)

**Waringsford** vill., Down 3234
*10km ENE of Banbridge*
par: *Garvaghy* bar: *Iveagh Lower, Lower Half*
Waringsford in the townland of TULLINISKY takes its name from a former house and demesne which is recorded as 'the seat of Henry Waring Esq.' in 1744. Henry Waring was a descendant of William Warren or Waring who gave name to the village of **Waringstown**, 14km to the north-west (*see next entry*) [*Waringsford* 1743].

**Waringstown** vill., Down 3135
*4km SE of Lurgan*
par: *Donaghcloney*
bar: *Iveagh Lower, Upper Half*
Waringstown is named from William Warren or Waring, a Cromwellian general who built WARINGSTOWN HOUSE in 1666, the weaving village of Waringstown growing up under the same family at a later date. Waringstown is partly in the townland of MAGHERANA and partly in TULLYHERRON [*Warings-towne* 1667].

**Warrenpoint** tn, par., Down 3131
(sometimes *Warrenspoint*)
*Town is close to head of Carlingford Lough, 10km SE of Newry*
bar: *Iveagh Upper, Upper Half*
Warrenpoint is a comparatively recent name, the town having grown up only in the late 18th and early 19th centuries. The initial element *Warren* is undoubtedly a surname but there is no evidence to suggest that the founder was connected with the family of Waring or Warren who gave name to **Waringstown**. Warrenpoint town is mainly in the townland of RINGMACKILROY which derives from Ir. *Rinn Mhic Giolla Rua* [rinn vick gilla **roo**a] 'MacElroy's point or peninsula'. The parish of Warrenpoint consists of only three townlands and was part of the neighbouring parish of CLONALLAN until 1825 [*Warings's Point* 1744].

**Washing Bay**, Tyrone 2936
*In SW corner of Lough Neagh, 6km E of Coalisland*
par: *Clonoe* bar: *Dungannon Middle*
Washing Bay in the townland of AUGHAMULLAN is so-named because the water of a stream which flows into **Lough Neagh** here was supposed to have healing powers. The stream was formerly known as *The Holy River*. A short distance to the north is DUCKINGSTOOL POINT where the sick were ducked in the water. Early in the 19th century, Dr E. Sill of **Stewartstown** bequeathed his estate to build a hospital here

but the project was never carried out [*Washing bay* 1837].

**Waterfoot or Glenariff** vill., Antrim 3242
(see ***Glenariff***)

**Waterside** distr., Derry 2441
*Suburb on the E side of Londonderry*
par: *Clondermot* bar: *Tirkeeran*
Waterside in the townland of CLOONEY is named from its position on the east bank of the river **Foyle** [*Waterside* 1837].

**Wattle Bridge** ham., Fermanagh 2432
(sometimes *Wattlebridge*)
*Close to Cavan border, 5.5km S of Newtownbutler*
par: *Drummully* bar: *Coole*
Wattle Bridge is named from a bridge, formerly made of wattle, which connects the townlands of EDERGOOL and ANNAGHMORE GLEBE across the river FINN, close to the point where it flows into **Upper Lough Erne** [*Wattle Bridge* 1835].

**Wee Collin** mtn, Antrim 3239
*13km WSW of Larne*
par: *Rashee* bar: *Antrim Upper*
Sc. *wee* 'small' + Ir. *collann* [**kol**an] *perhaps* 'height/high ground'. Wee Collin (306m) in the townland of BALLYNASHEE stands 4.5km north-east of **Big Collin** (353m) [*Little Collin* 1780].

**Wheathill** tl, Fermanagh 2133
*14km SW of Enniskillen*
par: *Killesher* bar: *Clanawley*
Ir. *Gort na Cruithneachta* [gort na **crin**haghta] 'field of wheat'. The E. name is an inaccurate translation of the original Ir. name. There is a townland named WHEATHILL GLEBE 3km north-east of **Derrygonnelly** [*Wheathill* 1835].

**Whiteabbey** tl, vill., Antrim 3338
(sometimes *White Abbey*)
*Forms a district of Newtownabbey, 9km N of Belfast city centre*
par: *Carnmoney* bar: *Belfast Lower*
Whiteabbey takes its name from a 13th-century abbey of the Premonstratention Order (popularly known as the 'White Canons'), the ruins of which were in the south of the townland close to the present Whiteabbey Hospital but were removed in 1926. The E. name may be a translation of the Ir. name *Mainistir Fhionn* [manishcher **inn**] 'white monastery'. An earlier name for the abbey was *Druim La Croix*, a hybrid of Ir. and French, signifying 'ridge (of) the cross'. Whiteabbey was one of the seven villages which went to make up the new town of **Newtownabbey** in 1958 and has provided the final element of the name of the town [*White-Abbey, in Irish Mainistir Fhionn* c.1700].

**Whitecross** vill., Armagh 2933
*20km SE of Armagh city*
par: *Ballymyre* bar: *Fews Upper*
The village of Whitecross is named from a crossroads at which there were formerly whitewashed houses. The Ir. name of Whitecross is *Corr Leacht* [korr **laght**] 'round hill of the memorial cairns' which is the original Ir. form of CORLAT, the townland in which the village is situated [*Whitecross* c.1835].

**Whitehead** tl, tn, Antrim 3439
*On E Antrim coast, 7km NE of Carrickfergus*
par: *Templecorran* bar: *Belfast Lower*
The place takes its name from a prominent limestone headland known as WHITE HEAD, a name which contrasts with **Black Head**, a promontory a short distance to the north-east. The original settlement appears to have grown up around CASTLE CHICHESTER, a small tower-house built by Sir Moses Hill c.1604 the remains of which stand in the neighbouring townland of CASTLETOWN, parish of **Islandmagee** [*the White-Head* 1683].

**White Head** Antrim 3044
(see ***Kinbane or White Head***)

**Whitehill** tls, vill., Fermanagh 2235
*3km W of Bellinamallard*
par: *Derryvullan* bar: *Lurg*
The village of Whitehill is in the townland of WHITEHILL SOUTH in which there is a hill of 80m. The townland of WHITEHILL NORTH lies 6km to the north-west. The Ir. name for Whitehill is *Tír Uí Bhranáin* '(O')Brennan/Brannain's land/territory', the family of *Ó Branáin* being an *erenagh* family of Fermanagh origin [*Whitehill* 1837].

**Whitehouse** tl, vill., Antrim 3338
(sometimes *White House*)
*Forms a district of Newtownabbey, 6.5km N of Belfast city centre*
par: *Carnmoney* bar: *Belfast Lower*

Whitehouse, on the shore of **Belfast Lough**, is named from a fortified house built c.1574 by an English adventurer named Brunker the remains of which are still standing. In 1958 Whitehouse was one of seven villages which went to make up the new town of **Newtownabbey**. The townland of Whitehouse was previously known as *Ballyrintollard* [*white house* c.1657].

**White Lady or Cloghastucan** rock, Antrim 3242

(*see* ***Cloghastucan***)

**White Mountain** mtn, tl, Antrim 3236
*14.5km SW of Belfast*
par: *Derryaghy* bar: *Massereene Upper*
The townland takes its name from White Mountain (250m) on which there are extensive limestone quarries [*White Mountain* 1780].

**White Park Bay** bay, Antrim 3044
*On N Antrim coast, 9.5km NW of Ballycastle*
par: *Ballintoy* bar: *Cary*
White Park Bay takes its name from the townland of WHITE PARK which borders it and appears to have been named from the whiteness of the sand on the well-known crescent-shaped strand, or perhaps from the chalky nature of the terrain [*White Park Bay* 1780].

**Whiterock** distr., Antrim 3337
*Suburb, 4km W of Belfast city centre*
par: *Shankill* bar: *Belfast Upper*
Whiterock in the townland of BALLYMURPHY gets its name from a limestone quarry on the lower slopes of **Black Mountain**. It has given name to the WHITEROCK ROAD [*White Rock* c.1830].

**Whitesides Corner** ham., Antrim 3039
*6km NNW of Randalstown*
par: *Drummaul* bar: *Toome Upper*
The 'corner' is formed by the intersection of the road from **Toome** to **Ballymena** with the road from **Randalstown** to **Ahoghill**, in the townland of PROCKLIS. A gentleman named Whiteside was the proprietor of a public house here in the last century.

**White Water** river Down
*Rises on W side of Slieve Muck in the Mournes, close to the source of the Bann. Enters Carlingford Lough 5km SW of Kilkeel*

*The White Lady rock formation on the Antrim Coast*

The name White Water contrasts with YELLOW WATER, the name of a river which rises on the east side of **Slieve Muck** and flows into White Water near the village of **Attical**. There is also a YELLOW WATER RIVER which rises 4km to the north-west [*White Water* 1743].

**Whitewell** vill., Antrim 3338
*Forms a district of Newtownabbey, 6km N of Belfast city centre*
par: *Carnmoney* bar: *Belfast Lower*
Whitewell is named from a spring which formerly issued from the base of a limestone rock in the north of the townland of COLLINWARD [*Whitewell* 1858].

**Windy Hall** tl, ham., Derry 2843
*2.5km SE of Coleraine*
par: *Coleraine* bar: *NE Liberties of Coleraine*
The element *hall* is common in place-names, meaning a great house or mansion. There is a house named WINDY HALL in the east of the

townland and also a house named WINDY HALL HOUSE in the south-west [*Winny Hawe* 1780].

**Woodburn** ham., Antrim 3338
*2.5km NW of Carrickfergus*
par: *Carrickfergus* bar: *Belfast Upper*
E. *wood* + Sc./N.E. *burn* 'stream'. Woodburn was originally the name of an early 14th-century abbey of the Premonstratentian or White Canons. The abbey, no trace of which now remains, was named from the WOODBURN RIVER, on the west bank of which it stood, in the townland of WEST DIVISION. The place-name was sometimes corrupted to *Goodburn*, the change from *wood* to *good* possibly reflecting its monastic associations [*Woddeborne* 1326].

# INDEX OF PLACE-NAME ELEMENTS

**bior** Ir. water, stream 80, 93, 95, 113
**blách** Ir. buttermilk 26, 121
**bladh** Ir. portion 26
**bléin** Ir. groin; inlet, creek, bay 26
**bó** Ir. cow 5, 11, 18, 25, 59, 61, 82, 93, 95
**boc** Ir. stag; male goat 30
**bog** Ir. soft 1
**bogach** Ir. bog, boggy ground 11, 120
**boireann** Ir. rocky district; rock (*var.* ***boirinn***) 31
**boirinn** Ir. *see* ***boireann***
**boith** Ir. *see* ***both***
**borb** Ir. bold, prominent 23
**bottle** H.E./Sc. bundle of straw 27
**both** Ir. hut, monastic cell (*var.* ***boith***) 27, 69
**bradach** Ir. treacherous, dangerous 23
**bradán** Ir. salmon 121
**bráid** Ir. neck, gorge, valley 16, 28
**brae** Sc./N.E. hill 118, 125
**bran** Ir. raven 138
**breac** Ir. speckled, variegated 29
**breachtach** Ir. speckled, variegated 29
**bréad** Ir. fragment, remnant 28, 95, 117
**bréan** Ir. foul-smelling, odorous 28
**brí** Ir. hill 28
**bríos** Ir. high ground(?) 62
**broclais** Ir. den, hovel, hollow, hole in the ground 30
**broinn** Ir. *see* ***broinne***
**broinne** Ir. breast, bosom; brink, verge (*var.* ***broinn***) 28, 133
**bruach** Ir. bank, brink, edge, margin 29
**brugh** Ir. dwelling, mansion 29
**bruíon** Ir. dwelling; fairy fort 94
**buaile** Ir. (summer) cattle-enclosure 11, 71, 137 (*see Glossary*, p. xiii)
**buí** Ir. yellow, yellow-haired 18, 20, 29, 35, 41, 55, 71, 91, 125
**bun** Ir. bottom, foot (of river); bottom-land 23, 24, 27, 30, 53, 60, 112
**burn** Sc./N.E. stream 3, 4, 10, 24, 30, 31, 33, 45, 46, 49, 54, 59, 63, 68, 73, 78, 96, 107, 108, 120, 122, 135, 141, 143, 148

**cabha** Ir. hollow, slope 126
**cabhán** Ir. hollow; round hill 39
**cabrach** Ir. poor land; copse 32, 103
**cacamar** Ir. slob-land, mud flat 13
**cadach** Ir. land held by treaty(?) 32
**cailceach** Ir. chalky (*var.* ***cuilceach***) 51
**caill** Ir. *see* ***coill***
**cailleach** Ir. nun, hag 71
**caiseal** Ir. stone ring-fort 37, 78, 103, 109, 113
**caisleán** Ir. castle 11, 17, 38, 79, 116, 126
**caistéal** Ir. castle 33, 34
**cáithleach** Ir. chaff, husks 32
**cal** Sc. *see* ***cald***
**cald** Sc. cold (*var.* ***cal***) 32, 136
**call** Ir. *see* ***coll***
**callán** Ir. noise 32
**cam** Ir. crooked 32
**camán** Ir. little bend; hurley stick 1
**camas** Ir. river-bend, river-bay 33
**camsán** Ir. succession of river bends 32, 33
**caoin** Ir. pleasant, fair, smooth 6, 62, 83
**caol** Ir. narrow; a narrow 14, 86, 100, 115, 122
**caolán** Ir. marshy stream 13
**caora** Ir. sheep 46, 67, 83, 131
**caoth** Ir. swamp 39
**carbad** Ir. jaw, boulder 47
**carn** Ir. memorial pile of rocks, cairn, heap 33, 34, 35, 55, 84, 114
**carnán** Ir. little cairn (*diminutive of* ***carn***) 34, 75, 142
**carr** Ir. rock, rocky patch 33
**carrach** Ir. rocky, rough 68
**carraig** Ir. rock, rocky hill 16, 33, 35, 36, 48, 51, 124, 128
**casla** Ir. sea-inlet, creek 90
**cat** Ir. (wild-) cat 37, 44
**cath** Ir. battle 55, 62
**ceann** Ir. head, headland; hill (*var.* ***cionn***) 32, 36, 90, 91, 94, 116
**ceap** Ir. tree stump; tillage plot 33
**ceapach** Ir. tillage plot 33
**cearc** Ir. hen, moorhen, grouse 134
**cearrbhach** Ir. gamester, gambler 95
**ceathrú** Ir. quarter (land-measure) 35, 36, 37, 40
**céide** Ir. (flat-topped) hill 27, 85
**céile Dé** Ir. *Culdee* or servant of God 86
**ceis** Ir. wickerwork causeway (*var.* ***cis***) 85, 131
**ciabh** Ir. long grass 51
**cill** Ir. church, monastic cell 14, 48, 63, 85, 86, 87, 88, 89, 90, 91, 103, 111, 130, 137, 139, 143
**cineál** Ir. race, family, kindred 143
**cionn** Ir. *see* ***ceann***
**cis** Ir. *see* ***ceis***
**clab** Ir. mouth, opening 41
**cladach** Ir. stony shore; firm ground(?) 78
**cláidigh** Ir. the one who washes (*stream name*) (*var.* ***clóidigh***) 41, 42
**clann** Ir. family, descendants, kindred 41, 61, 76, 102
**claon** Ir. sloping, inclined, crooked 96, 124
**clár** Ir. plank, plank-bridge; plain 11, 29, 42, 78
**cléireach** Ir. cleric 10
**cliabh** Ir. basket, wickerwork frame; chest, breast, bosom 8
**cliath** Ir. wattle, hurdle 8, 85
**cloch** Ir. stone, stone castle (*var.* ***cloich***) 4, 8, 42, 43, 44, 64, 79, 92

**léim** Ir. leap 95
**leith** Ir. *see* ***leath***
**léith** Ir. *see* ***liath***
**leithead** Ir. breadth, width; slope 92
**leitir** Ir. hillside 94, 95
**lia** Ir. *see* ***liag***
**liag** Ir. stone, pillar-stone, head stone (*var.* ***lia***) 62, 134
**liagán** Ir. stone, pillar-stone, headstone 94
**liath** Ir. grey (*var.* ***léith***) 27, 62, 64, 80, 88, 94, 96, 126
**lifín** Ir. halfpenny (= ***leathphingin***) 14
**linn** Ir. pool 14
**lios** Ir. ring-fort 25, 26, 64, 95, 96, 97
**loan** Sc. *see* ***loanin***
**loanin** Sc. lane (*var.* ***loan***) 97
**loch** Ir. lake; estuary 21, 32, 33, 37, 50, 54, 63, 67, 71, 75, 93, 98, 99, 100, 101, 102, 114, 137, 138
**log** Ir. hollow (*var.* ***lag***) 93, 94
**logán** Ir. low-lying district; little hollow (*var.* ***lagán***) 86, 93
**lon** Ir. blackbird 29
**long** Ir. ship 5
**longfort** Ir. stronghold/fortress 14, 137
**lorg** Ir. *see* ***lorgain***
**lorga** Ir. *see* ***lorgain***
**lorgain** Ir. long low ridge, shank; strip of land (*var.* ***lorg***, ***lorga***) 37, 41, 70, 102
**luachair** Ir. rushes, rushy place 6, 101
**luan** Ir. loin, haunch, haunch-like hill 4, 32
**luán** Ir. lamb 68, 95
**lúb** Ir. loop, twist, bend 102

**má** Ir. plain (*var.* ***magh***, ***maigh***) 7, 67, 83, 103, 105, 106, 108, 110, 112, 113, 115, 118
**macha** Ir. milking-field, pasture (also the name of the goddess of sovereignty) (*var.* ***machadh***) 7, 104, 115
**machadh** Ir. *see* ***macha***
**machaire** Ir. plain 36, 44, 46, 101, 103, 104
**mada** Ir. (wild-) dog (*var.* ***madadh***) 48, 94, 95
**madadh** Ir. *see* ***mada***
**magh** Ir. *see* ***má***
**maide** Ir. stick 103
**maidhm** Ir. eruption, bursting out 98
**maigh** Ir. *see* ***má***
**mainstir** Ir. monastery 80, 146
**málainn** Ir. high ground, sloping ground(?) 105
**mallacht** Ir. curse 16, 22, 125
**manach** Ir. monk 65, 110
**maol** Ir. bald, round-topped; dilapidated; bald, round-topped hillock 65, 69, 92, 114
**maoil** Ir. current, stream(?) 115
**marg** Ir. boundary 27
**margadh** Ir. market 22
**meacan** Ir. root, tuber; swelling hill(?) 102
**meall** Ir. knoll, mass, lump 106
**meán** Ir. middle 83
**meánach** Ir. middle, central 15
**meannán** Ir. kid-goat 62
**meas** Ir. *mast*, i.e. fallen forest fruits and nuts 103
**míleac** Ir. marshy margin 104
**milis** Ir. sweet 137
**millín** Ir. little knoll (*diminutive of* ***meall***) 6
**mín** Ir. smooth, level 20
**mín** Ir. mountain pasture 40, 101, 106
**moin** Ir. mount, hill 110
**móin** Ir. bog, moor (*var.* ***mónaidh***) 109, 110, 125
**mómhar** Ir. pleasant, gentle 4
**monadh** Sc.G./Ir. moor, hill, hilly land 16, 35, 136
**mónaidh** Ir. *see* ***móin***
**mont** F. hill, mountain 23
**mór** Ir. great, big 2, 4, 7, 19, 22, 24, 25, 26, 27, 36, 41, 52, 57, 58, 60, 64, 65, 89, 92, 98, 106, 109, 113, 118, 119, 123, 127, 132, 133, 134, 139, 140, 141
**mos** O.E. peat-bog 110
**moss** Sc. peat-bog (*from* O.E. ***mos***) 110
**muc** Ir. pig 96, 114, 121, 134
**muclach** Ir. piggery 40, 92
**muileann** Ir. mill 2, 108, 138
**muinchille** Ir. sleeve; ridge(?) 47
**muine** Ir. thicket, hill 108, 109, 110
**muintir** Ir. kindred, family, people 108
**mullach** Ir. hilltop 37, 64, 70, 114, 135
**mullán** Ir. hillock 25
**murlach** Ir. sea-inlet, estuary 115
**múscán** Ir. spongy ground 3

**naomh** Ir. saint 127
**niadh** Ir. warrior 108
**nimh** Ir. poison 120
**nua** Ir. new 69, 79, 116, 117, 118, 121
**nús** Ir. new milk, 'beestings' 56

**ó** Ir. mass, lump 76
**odhar** Ir. brownish, dun 130
**óg** Ir. youth, warrior 142
**ó(gh)-** Ir. virgin, intact (*prefix*) 118
**oileán** Ir. island, peninsula 47, 82, 84, 100
**oircéal** Ir. trough, hollow (*var.* ***foirceal***) 70
**oireacht** Ir. assembly, district, territory (*var.* ***aireacht***) 118
**oireanach** Ir. *see* ***aireanach***
**oirear** Ir. coast; border, boundary 2
**oirthear** Ir. east, eastern part 7, 84
**othain** O.Ir. burial chamber (Mod. Ir. ***fathain***, (?)**athan**) 68, 74

# FURTHER READING

Although there is no previous substantial work on the place-names of Ulster, Jonathan Barton's *Investigating place names in Ulster* (Belfast, 1991) provides a good starting point for the general reader. There are also a number of regional place-name studies, including two (not very reliable!) county volumes, Alfred Moore Munn's *Notes on the place-names of the parishes and townlands of the county of Londonderry* (Cookstown, 1925, reprinted Draperstown, 1985), and P. McAleer's *Townland names of Co. Tyrone* (c.1936, republished Draperstown, 1988). Two noteworthy regional studies are B.J. Mooney's *The place-names of Rostrevor* (Newry, 1950) and *The parish of Seagoe, its place-names and history* (Newry, 1954). More recently, the Northern Ireland Place-Name Project has published very detailed studies of seven areas in the *Place-Names of Northern Ireland* series (see list of publications on p. ii).

Otherwise, valuable articles on Ulster place-names can be found in dedicated place-name periodicals such as *Dinnseanchas* (Dublin, 1964–75), *The Bulletin of the Ulster Place-Name Society* ser.1 (Belfast, 1952–7), ser.2 (Belfast, 1978–82) and its successor *Ainm* (Belfast, 1986–), as well as in a wide range of local journals and periodicals such as *Seanchas Ard Mhacha: Journal of Armagh Diocesan Historical Society* (Armagh, 1954–), *Clogher Record* (Monaghan, 1953–) *Dúiche Néill: Journal of the O'Neill Country Historical Society* (Benburb, 1986–), *Ulster Folklife* (Belfast, 1955–), and *Ulster Local Studies* (Belfast, 1975–).

For the reader who has a general interest in Irish place-names P.W. Joyce's *The origin and history of Irish names of places* (3 vols, Dublin, 1869–1913) is still the most comprehensive work and, although now rather dated, it contains plenty of northern material. A more recent publication in the same vein is Deirdre and Laurence Flanagan's *Irish place names* (Dublin, 1994). Both works focus mainly on place-names which have their origin in the Irish language. The most authoritative list of the original Irish language versions of the place-names of Ireland is contained in *Gasaitéar na hÉireann/Gazetteer of Ireland* (Dublin, 1989) which was prepared by the Placenames Branch of the Ordnance Survey of Ireland and includes the names of all settlements which have a post-office as well as the names of the main physical features. However, it must be borne in mind that the function of the book is to provide an Irish-language version of each place-name and no interpretations are offered. For a work which provides interpretations of the place-names of Ireland irrespective of their linguistic origin one must turn to Adrian Room's *A dictionary of Irish place-names* (Belfast, 1986). There are a number of other popular dictionaries which unfortunately tend to be unreliable. The best of the bunch (though now somewhat dated!) is the *Pocket guide to Irish place names* (Belfast, 1984), a reprint of P.W. Joyce's *Irish local names explained* (Dublin, 1870).

# SELECT BIBLIOGRAPHY


Atkinson, E.D., *Dromore, an Ulster diocese* (Dundalk, 1925).

Automobile Association, *AA illustrated road book of Ireland* (Dublin, 1970).

Bell, Robert, *The book of Ulster surnames* (Belfast, 1988).

Benn, George, *A history of the town of Belfast from the earliest times* (London, 1877).

Black, G. F., *The surnames of Scotland* (New York, 1946).

Brindley, Anna L.(ed.) *Archaeological inventory of Co. Monaghan* (Dublin, 1986).

*Census of Ireland 1851, general alphabetical index to the townlands and towns, parishes and baronies of Ireland...*(Dublin, 1861, reprint, Baltimore, 1984).

Canavan, T. (ed.) *Every stoney acre has a name: a celebration of the townland in Ulster* (Belfast, 1991).

Chart, D.A., *Preliminary survey of the ancient monuments of Northern Ireland* (Belfast, 1940).

Crawford, W.H. and Foy, R.H., *Townlands in Ulster: local history studies* (Belfast, 1998).

Cunningham, John B. (ed.) *The letters of John O'Donovan from Fermanagh, 1834* (Belleek, 1993).

Day, Angelique and McWilliams, Patrick (eds), *Ordnance Survey Memoirs of Ireland*, 1830–8, 40 vols (Belfast, 1990–8).

Dinneen, Patrick S., *Foclóir Gaedhilge agus Béarla: An Irish-English dictionary* (Dublin, 1927).

Dwelly, Edward, *The illustrated Gaelic-English dictionary* (Glasgow, 1977).

*Éire thuaidh / Ireland north, a cultural map and gazetteer of Irish place-names* (Belfast, 1988).

Fenton, James, *The hamely tongue* (Newtownards, 1995).

Field, John, *Place-names of Great Britain and Ireland* (Newton Abbot, 1980).

Harris, Walter, *The ancient and present state of the county of Down* (Dublin, 1744).

Hill, George, *An historical account of the MacDonnells of Antrim* (Belfast, 1873).

HMSO, *Census of population 1961, topographical index* (1962).

—, *An archaeological survey of Co. Down* (Belfast, 1966).

—, *Historic monuments of Northern Ireland, an introduction and guide* (Belfast, 1987).

Hogan, E. I., *Onomasticon Goedelicum, an index, with identifications, to the Gaelic names of places and tribes* (Dublin, 1910).

Irvine, Barry Macartan, *Place-names of the parish of Aghalurcher, Co. Fermanagh*, unpublished PhD thesis (The Queen's University of Belfast, 1994).

Killanin, Lord and Duignan, Michael, *Shell guide to Ireland* (London, 1962).

Knox, Alexander, *A history of the county of Down* (Dublin, 1875).

Lacy, Brian (ed.), *Archaeological survey of County Donegal* (Donegal, 1983).

Leslie, J.B., *Armagh clergy and parishes* (Dundalk, 1911).

Laoide, Seosamh (ed.) *Post-Sheanchas*, 2 vols (Dublin, 1905).

Lewis, Samuel, *A topographical dictionary of Ireland*, 2 vols (London, 1837).

Livingstone, Peter, *The Fermanagh story* (Enniskillen, 1969).

—, *The Monaghan story* (Enniskillen, 1980).

MacAfee, D.I. (ed.) *A concise Ulster dictionary* (Oxford, 1996).

MacAirt, Séan and Mac Niocaill, Gearóid, *The annals of Ulster*, vol. i to AD1131 (Dublin, 1983).

McCann, Hugh Patrick, *The townland names of the parish of Desertcreat, County Tyrone*, unpublished MA dissertation (The Queen's University of Belfast, 1982).

Mac Donnchadha, Tadhg (ed.) *Cín Lae Ó Mealláin* (O'Mallon's Diary, 1641–7) in *Analecta Hibernica* no.3 (Dublin, 1931).

MacLysaght, Edward, *The surnames of Ireland* (Dublin, 1991).

McMahon, Sean, *The Poolbeg book of Irish placenames* (Swords, 1990).

Mallory, J.P. and McNeill, T.E., *The archaeology of Ulster* (Belfast, 1991).

Mason, William Shaw, *A statistical account or parochial survey of Ireland,* 3 vols (Dublin, Edinburgh, 1814–19).
Mawhinney, Graham (ed.) *John O'Donovan's letters from County Londonderry, 1834* (Ballinascreen, 1992).
Newmann, Kate, *Dictionary of Ulster biography* (Belfast, 1993).
Nicolaisen, W.F.H., *Scottish place-names* (London, 1976).
Nolan, W. (ed.) *Donegal, history and society* (Dublin, 1995).
*Northern Ireland sites and monuments record: stage 1* (Archaeological Survey of Northern Ireland, published privately 1979).
O'Brien, M.A., *Corpus Genealogiarum Hiberniae* vol.i (Dublin, 1976).
Ó Ceallaigh, Séamus *Gleanings from Ulster history* (1951, reprint Ballinascreen, 1994).
Ó Corráin, Donnchadh and Maguire, Fidelma, *Gaelic personal names* (Dublin, 1981).
O'Daly, Bernard, 'Parish of Kilskeery: the place-names explained', *Clogher Record* vol.ii no.1 (Monaghan, 1957).
Ó Dónaill, Niall (ed.) *Foclóir Gaeilge-Béarla* (Dublin, 1977).
O'Donovan, John (ed.) *Annála Rioghachta Éireann: annals of the kingdom of Ireland by the Four Masters*, 7 vols (Dublin, 1848–51).
O'Donovan, Patrick F. (ed.) *Archaeological inventory of Co. Cavan* (Dublin, 1995).
Ó Gallachair, P., *Shrines of the Sillies Valley* (Ballyshannon, 1984).
Ó hÓgáin, Dáithí, *Myth, legend and romance, an encyclopaedia of the Irish folk tradition* (New York, 1991).
O'Kane, James *Placenames of Inniskeel and Kilteevoge* in *Zeitschrift fur Celtische Philologie,* Band 31 (1970).
O'Laverty, James, *An historical account of the diocese of Down and Connor*, 5 vols (Dublin, 1878–95).
O'Neill, John, *The placenames of Glencolumbkille parish, Co. Donegal*, unpublished Ph.D thesis (The Queen's University of Belfast, 1973).
O'Rahilly, T.F., *Early Irish history and mythology* (Dublin, 1946).
Ó Riain, Pádraig, *Corpus Genealogiarum Sanctorum Hiberniae* (Dublin, 1985).
*Ordnance Survey name books*, compiled 1827–35. Microfilm copies in The Queen's University of Belfast library.
Reaney, P.H., *A dictionary of British surnames* (London, 1958).
Reeves, William (ed.) *Ecclesiastical antiquities of Down, Connor and Dromore* (Dublin, 1847).
—, *Acts of Archbishop Reeves in his metropolitan visitation of the diocese of Derry, AD1397* (Dublin, 1850).
Robinson, Philip, *The plantation of Ulster* (Belfast, 1994).
Room, Adrian, *A concise dictionary of modern place-names in Great Britain and Ireland* (Oxford, 1983).
—, *A dictionary of place-names in the British Isles* (London, 1988).
Royal Irish Academy, *Dictionary of the Irish language* (compact edition) (Dublin, 1983).
Rowan, Alistair, *The buildings of Ireland: north-west Ulster* (Middlesex, 1979).
Sandford, Ernest, *Discover Northern Ireland* (Belfast, 1977).
Stockman, Gerard and Wagner, Heinrich, 'Contributions to a study of Tyrone Irish' in *Norsk Tidschrift fur Sprogvidenskap* supp. binding 8 (1965).
Stokes, Whitley (ed.) *The tripartite life of Saint Patrick*, 2 vols. (London, 1887).
—, *Félire Óengusso Céli Dé: the martyrology of Oengus the Culdee* (London, 1905, reprint 1984).
tSuirbhéireacht Ordanáis, An [The Ordnance Survey] *Liostaí Logainmneacha: Contae Mhuineacháin/County Monaghan* (Dublin, 1996).
*The Glynns/Journal of the Glens of Antrim Historical Society* (Belfast, 1973–).
Todd, James H. and Reeves, William (ed.) *The martyrology of Donegal* (Dublin, 1864).
Townend, Peter (ed.) *Burke's genealogical and heraldic history of the peerage, baronetage and knightage*, 105th ed, 2 vols (London, 1953).
Watson, W.J., *The history of the Celtic place-names of Scotland* (Edinburgh and London, 1926).
Woulfe, Patrick, *Sloinnte Gaedheal is Gall, Irish names and surnames* (Dublin, 1923).